The First Time Around

BOOKS BY JOSEPH WECHSBERG

LOOKING FOR A BLUEBIRD

HOMECOMING

SWEET AND SOUR

THE CONTINENTAL TOUCH

BLUE TROUT AND BLACK TRUFFLES

THE SELF-BETRAYED

AVALANCHE!

RED PLUSH AND BLACK VELVET

DINING AT THE PAVILLON

JOURNEY THROUGH THE LAND OF ELOQUENT SILENCE

THE BEST THINGS IN LIFE

THE MERCHANT BANKERS

THE FIRST TIME AROUND

The First Time Around
Some Irreverent Recollections
by JOSEPH WECHSBERG

(1907 –

Little, Brown and Company

Boston • Toronto

Published simultaneously in Canada
by Little, Brown & Company (Canada) Limited

PRINTED IN THE UNITED STATES OF AMERICA

TO BILL SHAWN

Foreword

THIS BOOK is not an autobiography. It began with some disconnected reminiscences that I wrote, mainly for myself, when the memories of the past seemed to get stronger, almost alive; perhaps a symptom of getting older. Some friends in the business encouraged me to go on, though they hadn't seen the manuscript. I was touched by their faith — and slightly disturbed by their suggestion that it might be time to write this book.

To write my autobiography would frighten me as much as to drive my automobile, which I no longer do. An autobiography obliges generals, statesmen, and stuffed shirts of distinction to set down the record for posterity. It is a definite, serious undertaking. I've never taken myself seriously, and it would be foolish to start now. I've had an interesting life, as the saying goes — as a fiddler, soldier, croupier, *claqueur*, lawyer, writer, and amused observer of human idiocies, including my own. My book is as confused and confusing as life itself, going forth and back, with no rhyme nor reason. It doesn't begin with my early childhood fixations and doesn't end with my late sexual confessions. It doesn't pretend to be a contribution to anything. It doesn't pretend, period.

My celebrated colleague Goethe, who disliked hard facts and fast libel suits, called his reminiscences *Dichtung und Wahrheit*, putting the truth *after* the fiction. I stick to the truth, though sometimes not to the explicit truth, and leave the fiction to my readers, who are invited to jump to conclusions. I am uninterested in exact dates and full names. In fact, I am less concerned about the people I mention than those I don't. *They* will be mad.

At certain moments, while I wrote this book, I found myself in amused agreement with myself. It was almost fun doing it, so far as writing can ever be fun. Anyway, that's the spirit in which it is presented and should be accepted. As Harold Ross would say, God bless you.

Contents

The First Time Around

The View from the Office

ON A FINE DAY in October, 1943, I rode up to the nineteenth floor of 25 West Forty-third Street, in New York City. I wore the GI uniform of an army private. I was on a three-day pass from Camp Ritchie, Maryland, and had come to meet the editors of *The New Yorker* who had published my first stories earlier that year.

I still go there today as soon as I arrive in town from Europe. Twenty-seven years is a long time to stay with the same woman, or with the same magazine. In a marriage there is a silver wedding after the twenty-fifth year. In my liaison with *The New Yorker*, the jubilee was tactfully ignored. At *The New Yorker*, sentimental anniversaries don't count. When the magazine, after much soul-searching and discussion, gave itself a party at its twenty-fifth birthday in 1950, many people had been strongly against it. They said it "wasn't done."

Getting up there these days in the electronically steered elevator, after an absence of several months abroad, I always experience a sense of wonder that *The New Yorker*, and I, and we together, have lasted so long. The affair has had its ups and downs, but today I know that the downs have been blotted out by the ups. As a conservative (though only in my private life), I am pleased that it is still the same building I go to, the same floor, the same editor-friend. Not many people in New York, or elsewhere, can make that claim after twenty-seven years. The walls and partitions there were frequently changed, new cubicles and strange recesses were created, as in a surrealist film, recently the formerly battleship-gray walls turned yellow, and after my return from Europe I often get lost there. I look for the scheduling room and wind up at the lady with the annuity plan. The college girl at the reception desk doesn't know me — and why should she?, she isn't even twenty-seven — and misspells my name on messages. But though a great many things have changed there, the important ones haven't. We still think of *The New Yorker* as a sort of Sacred Institution rather than a commercial enterprise.

The New Yorker reminds me of the Vienna State Opera, with which I've carried on a love affair since my teen-age days. (I seem to be a man of long affairs.) The Vienna Opera isn't just an opera — and *The New Yorker* isn't just a magazine. The Viennese aficionados will tell you, emphatically though irrationally, that their Staatsoper is a house-with-a-soul. An aficionado may not have heard a performance for years, but *die Oper* remains close to his heart. *Die Oper* is a woman, capricious, often disappointing as women are, but there are sudden moments of happiness when one would least expect them. I remember her cool scent as I enter the marbled entrance, and I relive the youthful excitement I felt as I would run up the low stairs to the fourth gallery, taking three and four steps at a time, to arrive among the first standees and get one of the best spots in the center, from where one could see the whole stage. The lights in the auditorium would still be dim, and the boxes were empty, but the air was filled with excitement, the inaudible echo of wonderful melodies, the glorious operatic climaxes of the past, with ringing high C's. The soft, sensuous sound is still in my inner ear. Maybe tonight's performance will be mediocre — but after forty years, the woman you love should be permitted to have an occasional dull evening.

Something similar happens to me every time I come back from Europe and walk into the unoperatic lobby of 25 West Forty-third Street. It's always a little like coming home. I've lost "home" so many times in my life that I'm now resigned to living in a homeless world. The lobby gives me more of a home feeling than the rented apartment in Vienna, Austria, where I now write these lines. Physically I am in Europe, but spiritually I've never really left America. I am a refugee in reverse. Being away so long from America, I remain deeply conscious of it — more, in fact, than if I lived in America. Unlike native Americans, I don't take it for granted. Exile is not a matter of geography but a state of mind.

The lobby is lined with some imitation marble that didn't come from the noble quarries of Carrara. There is a peculiar scent that I would recognize anywhere with closed eyes: the cool smell of the stone linings, the sweetish perfume from the barbershop, a bit of outside air with the unmistakable fragrance of New York, and a whiff of toilet soap and cigarette smoke. Soft music comes from the record store and a whirring sound from the RCA office with several clocks on the wall. It's eleven A.M. in New York, and five P.M. in Vienna. In another hour, it will be time for a drink in both Vienna and New York. Alcoholics of the World, Unite! There is a new tailor's workshop in the lobby. A man has a fitting, standing in front of the mirror, and I'm reminded of Mr. Šilhavý, my Moravian tailor in Vienna, who knows my anatomy better than my surgeon.

The world is getting small. All the lobby needs is a sidewalk café and a few boulevardiers promenading, as in Milan's Galleria Vittorio Emanuele, near the Duomo. Whistling, shirt-sleeved boys carry large manila envelopes (manuscripts?), and well-made-up girls, whose hair always surprises me after seeing the unkempt women in Europe, take up coffee in plastic containers. Some people know no one, and others say "Hi!" to the elevator supervisor. This is New York, where everybody is trying hard to be an unperson between nine A.M. and five P.M.

I liked the old elevators better. They were run by members of the human race in good standing. Only the freight elevator has survived the age of automation. It is operated by John, an old Puerto Rican with a face of crumpled parchment who always recognizes me, even after ten months, making my homecoming warm and official. "Glad see you again," he says, patting me fondly on the back, and he goes on to complain about the unseasonal heat or cold or humidity. The walls of the freight elevator are lined with canvas. I enjoy going up with John in the padded cell, leaving all the lunatics outside.

When John isn't on duty, I have to take one of the whimsical electronic elevators. I keep wondering what floor it will take me to, if any. I glance furtively (one doesn't want to behave like a damn foreigner) at my fellow riders as though we were in an airplane. Will our names appear in the paper as the "list of victims"?

Sometimes a man in a cashmere coat rides up with me, exuding affluence and security-first. I wouldn't be surprised if he gets out on the seventeenth floor, *The New Yorker*'s business department. Perhaps a supersalesman of full-page, four-color ads: Cadillacs, liveried chauffeurs carrying cases of vintage champagne; slim, frigid-looking women bathing daily in Joy, the World's Costliest Perfume. My friends in Europe who look at the ads in my back copies of *The New Yorker* wistfully think, "This is America." They ask me about the *other* America — slums, race riots, crime in the streets, police beating students — that they know from their TV sets. I cannot explain it. There are so many things in America today that are inexplicable. I'm beginning to wonder whether to keep the back copies of the magazine.

Yes, the man in the cashmere coat gets out on the seventeenth floor. No one getting out on the nineteenth, the editorial floor, exudes so much confidence and prosperity. Writers and editors are insecurity-first people.

Harold Ross, who invented and started *The New Yorker*, allegedly didn't encourage seventeenth-floor types to appear two floors higher up, at the editorial Olympus. He felt there should be a *cordon sanitaire* between our creative heaven and the business department's commercial hell. William Shawn, who succeeded Ross, continues the belief that "editorial people shouldn't get involved in the business side of the magazine."

I went to the seventeenth floor once, and not as a stockholder. (I own fifty shares of *New Yorker* stock. I wanted to buy more, but R. Hawley Truax, the chief liaison officer between the two floors, said sternly that fifty shares were "more than enough" for a writer.) I'd been asked to come down by Raoul Fleischmann, the publisher, who originally financed Harold Ross. Fleischmann, a white-haired, soft-spoken banker type, looked more like a boulevardier vacationing on the Riviera than the publisher of *The New Yorker*. But at *The New Yorker* many people don't look as they are expected to, and that goes for *all* floors.

Fleischmann told me how much he'd liked my recent profile on Hermann Gmeiner, the Austrian who founded the SOS Children's Villages that have since spread all over the world, all the way to Korea and South Vietnam. Fleischmann had been so impressed by Gmeiner's vision that he'd sent him a check for five thousand dollars. He seemed slightly embarrassed, explaining to me that he'd been born in Bad Ischl, in Austria's Salzkammergut, as though that explained his generosity. No one on the *Kurpromenade* in Bad Ischl who met Fleischmann would imagine him to be the publisher of *The New Yorker*. Ischl became famous during the *Götterdämmerung* days of the Habsburg monarchy, when Emperor Franz Joseph I spent his summers there. He always went back to Vienna after his birthday, August 18, and that's why in the Republic of Austria, which celebrated its fiftieth anniversary a couple of years ago, some of the elderly people, who consider themselves the "right" people, also return from their vacations at that time.

The Emperor was surrounded by his family, and by the high aristocracy, but he rarely talked to them. Also present were the aristocrats among Austria's operetta composers — Franz Lehár, Leo Fall, Oscar Straus — who were inspired by the presence of the elegant archdukes and distinguished countesses to create silly operettas in which aristocrats fell in love with commoners but never married them. Such operettas have become Austria's best-known export commodity, along with apple strudel and psychoanalysis. After the end of World War Two, Bad Ischl became headquarters of the nonaristocratic CIC, the American Counter-Intelligence Corps. Its operatives investigated the often mysterious activities of former Nazi leaders who had submerged in the Salzkammergut, "the final redoubt." The CIC men are gone, but the ex-Nazis are still there, more mysterious than ever.

Fleischmann and I talked about Gmeiner and Ischl and *The New Yorker*, and then I said good-bye to the publisher, and left the seventeenth floor, and I've never been there since. Later, Gmeiner told me in Vienna that Herr Fleischmann had sent him another big check. It was an expensive profile.

When people ask me how it is "up there," I am evasive. The secret of a successful affair is not to divulge its secrets. *The New Yorker* is more exclusive than most exclusive clubs. When I first came there, I was unobtrusively scrutinized, as if I were a candidate for a supersecret society. Whether I eventually made it, I still don't know, after all these years, but I don't think I was blackballed. I got that impression a few years ago when I saw a manuscript on an editor's table with the penciled remark "Seems to me like watered-down Wechsberg." Still, one can never be sure. The rules are strict and the rituals so cryptic that even the sacramentalists in the innermost sancta won't admit them to themselves, least of all to others.

Not long ago, Shawn said to me, "These young people read their manuscripts to each other before I see them." The editor was referring to the young generation of writers; he sounded mildly disconcerted that this could happen at *The New Yorker*. The young people are neither on the nineteenth, the main editorial floor, nor on the twentieth, its extension, with short stairways in between, but down on the eighteenth floor, recently acquired territory, the magazine's Alaska, where the future wealth lies.

A few members of the oldest generation are still around, as I write this. They worked for Ross in the earliest days of the Sacred Institution, then at 25 West Forty-fifth Street. E. B. and Katherine White, Janet Flanner, Mollie Panter-Downes, Joseph Mitchell. R. Hawley Truax, who lived with Ross when the great venture began and was with him when Ross died. Since then, several new generations have appeared. Looking through the 1969 editorial personnel list, 234 names, I found twenty-one people whom I'd met at one time or another. There are less than nine whom I really know. Of course, I've been away much of the time, and the place has become big and crowded. *The New Yorker* has remained relatively immune to many ills that now infect America's communications media, but it is losing the fight against bigness in business, perhaps the inevitable consequence of success. I knew the New Era had begun when they asked me, years ago, not to type my manuscripts anymore on yellow paper, which is soothing to the eyes and mind, but on hostile white paper. They had a new copying machine installed that demanded white paper. I still use yellow paper for my early drafts. *The New Yorker* people have to order the paper especially for me from a Middle Western province. They airmail it to me in Vienna, which creates enormous corporative difficulties and considerable expense. The New Era destroys the last remnants of romance, in writing and editing. Shawn once called me a "romantic" writer. I was pleased, but some of the young people on the eighteenth floor wouldn't consider it a compliment.

I've always sought the romance in writing. Unfortunately, it's also a cold-blooded business, if one wants to survive economically as a writer. I'm trying to keep away from the business side — deadlines and rewrites, agents and accountants, appointments and luncheons. Being three thousand miles away from the office has its advantages. I never owned a file cabinet or a tape recorder. I never had a full-time secretary, never hired anybody to do my research. Once I thought of buying an electric typewriter but dropped the idea after Paul Gallico told me that it is like "typing on steak." Who wants to type on sirloin, medium-rare? I often wish that my phone were out of order, or would ring only with good news.

One knows few people at *The New Yorker*. What Thurber called "one of the chill traditions of *The New Yorker*" still persists. "Almost nobody was ever introduced to anybody else." I never had a permanent office there, one of those small rooms with a desk, a typewriter, a malicious swivel chair eager to throw me off on the floor, a shelf with reference books, recent rough copies of the magazine, and a container with beautifully sharpened pencils. Who sharpens them? Do they have an invisible gnome up there sharpening all pencils? Maybe. At one time, Ross considered hiring a staff psychiatrist.

Nowadays, when I am in New York, they let me use the office of a writer who happens to be away. Writers are restless, and there is always a vacant office. Once I arrived in New York just after the publication of my three-part profile on Vienna, which some people up there liked, and they let me briefly use Mrs. White's rather sumptuous (by *New Yorker* standards) corner office, but that may have been a coincidence. Anyway, after a few days I was shifted to a much smaller place. I may not know the permanent occupant of the room, but his, or her, identity remains no secret. The writer's books are on the shelf, unsold remainder editions that no author likes to see. The smell of stale smoke is in the air, or a trace of garlic or Réplique, equally obnoxious. In the desk drawer there is a letter beginning, and ending, "Dear Debby," that was thrown away emotionally though not physically. On the rack hangs a faded trenchcoat. The writer is all over the place. I couldn't write a sentence of my own in this room.

The view is beautiful, though. I just sit there, looking out. I feel like a tourist who sees for the first time the Acropolis in Athens, or the Grand Canyon in Arizona. Rockefeller Center, the towers of the Plaza, Central Park in the rear. Magnificent new structures, dark and forbidding. Late in the afternoon their windows reflect the cloud patterns, and then comes the blue hour. I am usually there in October, the best time of the year, when New York can be beautiful, almost a poem. The lights go on in the tall, dark glass palaces. For a short while the city becomes peaceful. Alas, it doesn't last; nothing does. After a few days, I get used to the view and no longer look out. One gets quickly used to the beautiful things but never to the noise, the dirt, the dust, the pressure, the restlessness, the humidity, all the other big and little problems of the terrifying marginal city that is always on the verge of a breakdown.

Once they put me into an office where I was disturbed by the constant *prestissimo* staccato hammering next door. Somebody was writing with astonishing speed on a battered typewriter, turning out word after word, sentence after sentence. Now and then there would be a soft chuckle, and the creative drumfire would be resumed. I expected a pause somewhere; one has to reread a page, revise a sentence, think it over. But there was never a pause. No page was ever torn up in anger.

Later, I met my neighbor, A. J. Liebling. He was one of the few writers I've known who gave the impression of enjoying the torture of writing. He seemed to have as much fun writing his pieces as many people had reading them. I kept wishing they would give me an office next to a silent poet, but I don't really know whether *The New Yorker*'s poetry writers have offices there. Even in a quiet office, I couldn't write. There are too many distractions. People drop in, or you stop at somebody's office. When writers are together, they always look for an excuse for not writing.

But there are compensations. When I'm stuck with a writing problem in Vienna, I've got to wrestle with it myself; there is no one to talk to. At the office, meaning at the *New Yorker* office, it may happen that the door opens and Shawn comes to see me. I didn't call him, but he *knows*. Maybe I dropped a hint somewhere, or it's part of the editorial-floor osmosis. The editor doesn't summon you by his secretary but comes to see you. It is a unique publication.

As a young man, I worked for another unique publication. I spent my journalistic *Sturm und Drang* nights at the editorial offices of the *Prager Tagblatt* in Prague. It was *die Redaktion*, "the editorial office," not "the office," as at *The New Yorker*. Offices were for businessmen, not for poets, writers, journalists. In daytime I was working as *Konzipient*, a sort of junior junior partner, at the law offices of Adler and Pick, a distinguished law firm except for its junior junior partner.

The incompatible combination of law and journalism was a peculiar Prague phenomenon, especially in bourgeois Jewish circles. I studied law mainly to please my mother, who wished her older son to have an academic degree. Medicine was out, since I couldn't stand the sight of blood, and I didn't see myself as a student of theology or philosophy. The easiest way of getting a degree was to study law. The curriculum at Prague's Charles University enabled me to spend much time elsewhere as long as I came back and passed the prescribed examinations. For a small fee, the proctor's man entered the professors' official stamps into my student's book — proof that I had faithfully attended their lectures. I was the only member of our venerable alma mater who attended de jure the lectures in Roman law, canon law, criminal code, while de facto playing the fiddle in Montmartre clip joints and on French boats all over the world.

In Ostrava, my Moravian hometown, writing was considered a hobby, like playing soccer or gambling; it could never become a profession. Writing wasn't *serious*. In our country a young man was expected to study, become a Herr Doktor, and do something serious. Herr Doktor Franz Kafka wasted his fragile health in an insurance institute. Herr Doktor Max Brod worked for years as a minor civil servant, until he gave up bureaucratic security to begin an insecure life as the *Tagblatt*'s drama and music critic. And there were other Herren Doktoren at the editorial office.

I, too, graduated and became a Herr Doktor, but I dislike being addressed by my academic title. In Vienna, where people bestow upon one another nonexistent titles, Herr Doktor ranks low; coffeehouse waiters call every man Doktor who has a receding hairline and wears glasses. At the State Opera, the older ushers address me as Herr Professor, a mark of respect, since famous conductors are also called Herr Professor. I gained the title through stamina and seniority, after many performances of *Die Walküre*, with its boring second act, and Pfitzner's *Palestrina*, with its boring three acts.

In Prague, titles were more elusive. Emil Orlik was a world-famous artist but locally he was *not* known as "*the* great Orlik." That was his brother, a successful tailor. To atone for his undeserved fame, Orlik the tailor made fine suits, at cut rates, for impoverished poets and artists.

I was perhaps the worst lawyer in Prague, and possibly in all Czechoslovakia. My bosses used to complain that I wrote fiction instead of facts into my briefs, and used facts instead of fiction when I defended a client in court. I convinced neither the jury nor the judge of my client's innocence because I myself didn't believe in it. Unfortunately, my clients were never innocent. I finally quit, after causing much damage to the legal profession in general, and to the law firm of Adler and Pick in particular. Herr Doktor Adler and Herr Doktor Pick were angry when I took up journalism as a sideline and my name began to appear in the *Prager Tagblatt*, to which they subscribed. They claimed I wrote "on their time." I argued that I wrote only at night. They said it wasn't ethical for a member of the legal profession to be a "journalist," pronouncing the word with disdain. I argued the case, pointing out there was nothing about journalists in the criminal code, and one word led to another. Come to think of it, I was fired before I could quit. My mother was unhappy, and my family felt dishonored. They said what could you expect from a boy who had played the fiddle in brothels in Montmartre? No wonder he had become a writer.

The *Prager Tagblatt* was read by the German-speaking Jewish minority in Czechoslovakia. The Czech-speaking Jews read *Lidové Noviny*, the country's best newspaper, which expressed the views of President Thomas G. Masaryk, of the brothers Karel and Josef Čapek, and their Friday-evening circle. President Masaryk, statesman and philosopher, often spent Friday evening at Karel Čapek's villa among writers, artists, philosophers. My relatives were displeased when I began to write, in Czech, for *Lidové Noviny*. Some people said I ought to be ashamed to write for "those Czechs." Prague was completely segregated, with nationalities and minorities boycotting each other. Many Germans in Prague boycotted the *Tagblatt*, calling it a "Jewish" paper (not unlike some Americans calling the *New York Times* a "Jewish" paper). The liberal Germans would read *Bohemia*, which also employed some Jews. The Sudeten Germans — this was shortly before Hitler came to power in Germany — read some early Nazi papers in the provinces.

Prague was a complex city, historically, politically, journalistically. There were at one time seventeen political parties in the Czechoslovak Parliament, and over twenty newspapers in the capital. In this city of Czechs, Germans, Jews, of Catholics, Protestants, Hussites, Greek Orthodox, atheists, one wasn't always certain who was who. Appearances were deceptive. Prague was a city of mysticism and avant garde, the former capital of the kings of Bohemia and now the capital of a truly democratic republic, a soft and a violent city, the city of Hašek's good soldier Schweik and of Kafka's Josef K.

The *Prager Tagblatt*, a newspaper with a mystique, could exist only in Prague, the mystical city. It had little political influence but dominated the literary, economic, intellectual, and emotional landscape between Prague, Vienna, Berlin. The *Berliner Tageblatt* and the *Neue Freie Presse* in Vienna had larger circulations, but they were just newspapers. No mystique whatsoever.

The *Prager Tagblatt* was the triumph of heated dilettantism over cold professionalism, of imaginative frivolity over pompous solemnity. No one could explain exactly how the paper was written, edited, and put together day after day — a process based on the mysteries of madness and the mechanics of confusion. By eight o'clock in the evening it was never certain that there would be *any* paper at all, but somehow — yes, but how? — the first wet copies were off the presses at nine-thirty P.M. They were guaranteed to amuse, irritate, delight, entertain, infuriate the readers, but they would never bore them. Some local doctors told their patients who suffered from high blood pressure that they must not read the *Tagblatt*.

The paper didn't claim to print even half the news that was fit to print, but it was twice as interesting as a certain paper making that claim. It was frankly prejudiced, but it didn't conceal its prejudices editorially. It offended subscribers and advertisers with maddening regularity. The editors carried on in its very pages their *Weltanschauung* feuds and intramural squabbles. On the same day, the *Tagblatt* might be against higher taxes editorially, and in favor of them on the economics page. A literary trend might be praised by one contributor and damned by an editor, on the same page. The readers were expected to reach their own conclusions. The paper occasionally reminded its subscribers of President Masaryk's motto, Democracy is Discussion. Everybody agreed that the paper was well written. The German-speaking minority in Prague was known in all German-speaking countries of Europe for its excellent *Hochdeutsch*. Living on a small linguistic island surrounded by the Czech and Slovak seas, we were quite conscious of grammar, taste, and style.

The *Tagblatt*'s editorial offices were the stage version of a *dramma giocoso* that takes place in a lunatic asylum. The play had had such a long run that the borderline between fantasy and reality had become blurred. Innocent visitors and subscribers who walked up the old-fashioned stairway with the wrought-iron railing in a rear building in Herrengasse, or Panská ("Gentlemen's Street"), just one block from the old Nostitz Theatre where Mozart's *Don Giovanni*, the greatest *dramma giocoso*, had had its world premiere one night in 1787, would open the entrance door and find themselves in a room with eight walls. This *"Oktogon"* (not an octagon) would have made a fine set for a surrealistic play. Anyone might come out of its many doors, and nearly anyone did.

The first door to the left opened into the library where a white-haired, white-bearded patriarch, Hofrat (Court Councilor) Wien, was looking up some trivial detail in the old bound volumes. Hofrat Wien looked a little like Johannes Brahms, but he was said to hate music; furthermore, he was deaf. Whether he was a *Hofrat* (a title not officially permitted in the Czechoslovak Republic) and his name was Wien, no one could say, but it was agreed that if there existed a Hofrat Wien in Prague, he *would* look up the bound volumes in the *Tagblatt*'s editorial library.

The next door led into the stenographers' room. There was no city room, as in an American newspaper office. The stenographers wore long black coats, looking like clerks in some old-fashioned textile store. One stenographer was a noted astrophysicist who had failed to get a job at the local observatory. Another was Rezek, a famous mathematician who corresponded with Albert Einstein. One of them wore a white pharmacist's coat; he was one of the country's best chess players, often playing simultaneously against half a dozen editors and writers. In between he would take notes on the phone, and rewrite the story of the murder of a beautiful prostitute "in a baroque side street" in Malá Strana. Editorially, the *Tagblatt* considered all prostitutes beautiful and alluring, and was always defending them. They were deemed morally superior to their "seducers," and veritable angels compared to "their disgusting clients, the dirty old men." Such stories were often followed by an avalanche of irate letters from frustrated spinsters and philistine citizens. Everybody at the *Redaktion* would be delighted. We'd done it again.

The first door on the right side led to the office of Professor Ludwig Steiner, the chief editorial writer. He had once taught classical languages at a nearby *Gymnasium*, but then he abandoned Homer and Ovid for journalism. He conversed in Latin, and even the messengers had to learn a few Latin phrases. Casual visitors at his office thought they were attending a secret meeting of some slightly demented members of the Vatican's Curia. Professor Steiner's Latin observations were often as ambiguous as his editorials; he was a master of the on-the-one-hand, on-the-other-hand school of editorial writing. One day he met me at the *"Oktogon"* and shouted, *"Non olet!"* — Vespasian's comment

"Money doesn't smell." I wondered about it for days, until I realized he'd wanted to console me for getting money for a feature that had remained unused.

The door facing the entrance led to the office of the editor-in-chief. Dr. Blau, true to his name (*blau* means blue), always wore a blue blazer. The deputy editor wore a red blazer, though his name was not Rot (red), but Thomas; a nonsequitur typical of the *Tagblatt*. Dr. Blau was a small, balding man with a round, clean-shaven face and smiling eyes. A scent of cologne hovered above him, a fragrant halo. He had a brilliant mind and endless patience. He was always brimming over with ideas and would send out "shrapnels" — small oblong slips of white paper with queries, ideas, orders, assignments. The shrapnels were written in shorthand. The editor expected everybody to read and write shorthand. A shrapnel might deal with a cosmic event, order a reporter to cover an improbable disaster, such as the theft of a jewel-studded dress of Jezulátko, the small statue of the Jesus Child at Saint Savior's Church in Karmelitská Street, or ask a man to write an essay on Savonarola. Dr. Blau's intellectual curiosity was inexhaustible, and his tastes were catholic. His personal messenger, old Bečvář, would take two-dozen shrapnels and deliver them everywhere with somnambulistic certainty.

Old Bečvář had only one eye, after getting involved in a mysterious brawl in a "baroque side street" (viz., prostitutes) in Malá Strana. When his only remaining eye became infected, he began to deliver Dr. Blau's shrapnels to the wrong people. Once the music critic received an order to cover a bank robbery, and the sports editor's shrapnel told him to review the local premiere of *Lohengrin*. The result was unexpectedly successful; the sports editor wrote a thrilling blow-by-blow report about the first-act fight between Lohengrin and Telramund, and left the theater, assuming it was all over. The music critic meanwhile was inspired by the robbery, which he treated like the preposterous libretto of a Verdi opera. Dr. Blau was so pleased with old Bečvář's quid pro quo (I'm quoting Professor Steiner) that he gave him enough money for five glasses of Pilsen beer. Old Bečvář's son, young Bečvář, was much admired for carrying up to seventeen glasses of Pilsen beer in his hands, with several *párky* (hot dogs) and rolls sticking out of his pockets.

Late in the afternoon, the editorial offices became erotically perfumed when ambitious young actresses from stage and screen paid dutiful visits to influential editors in hopes of furthering their artistic careers. Nearly every member of the editorial staff had his private office, and nearly every private office had its own couch, on the theory that "editors get easily tired." It was always advisable to knock and wait awhile until you were told to come in. Even then it might not be advisable.

By seven o'clock, with the various deadlines getting close, there would be mounting bedlam. Absurd local events might be invented because the makeup man needed six more lines. Or a lawyer called up unexpectedly, delivering an ultimatum, and ten lines had to be taken out in a hurry; or there might be a libel suit. On some evenings there was so much confusion that people would say, "Let old Bečvář do it." But when the first copies of the paper were brought up from the press room, everybody was pleasantly surprised that there really was another issue once more, and the following morning the subscribers would be amused or irritated — but they would not be bored.

The last issue was made up after midnight by Eisner, the night editor, locally a much admired philosopher. Eisner was said to know everybody in Prague, especially in the lower social strata. He was always surrounded by some of his cronies while he edited the late news, or wrote fantastic headlines. Among the cronies was Michál Mareš, a close friend of the late Jaroslav Hašek's; another was a sinister man who looked like a paroled murderer, and was exactly that. His job was to prepare countless cups of poisonous black coffee.

The *Prager Tagblatt* was a great newspaper with a glorious life that ended ingloriously when its owners, after the Munich tragedy, fired Dr. Blau, an upright, decent Masaryk Democrat, and tried to come to an understanding with the Sudeten Germans who were beginning to switch from underground activities to open threats. The attempt at *detente* did not save the paper but literally broke Dr. Blau's heart. He died soon after he'd been forced out.

On March 15, 1939, the Nazis marched into Prague. For the *Prager Tagblatt*, and for many other good things, the end had come. Some members of the editorial staff escaped, and some were arrested. Max Brod left the country by entering a subterranean coal mine in the border region that began in Czechoslovakia, near my hometown, and ended in Poland. Some sold out and enthusiastically worked for the Nazis. Rudi Thomas, the debonair, charming deputy editor, went home, had a bottle of champagne with his wife, and into the last glass he put the poison.

Where It's Always Sunday

IN THE PAST TWENTY YEARS I've done much of my writing in Merano, a town in the Italian South Tyrol. When I first came there, at the age of six, it was known as Meran, a famous *Kurort* (spa) in the Austrian South Tyrol. I fell in love with the place at first sight, though I was too young to realize it. I've gone back many times. I still go there when I am restless and depressed. Meran-Merano has been a wonderful tranquilizer where I can be at peace with myself. I am lucky to have such a place.

Shortly after being enrolled in Ostrava in grammar school, in September, 1913, I almost died of double pneumonia and pleurisy, according to later, possibly melodramatic accounts of my dear mother. Today I know that I was an early psychosomatic case; I became sick in order to avoid going to school. Even at the *Volksschule* I disliked the sound of the bell, fixed hours, teachers, discipline, and sitting in a room with thirty other school-haters.

I haven't changed my mind about schools, though I was often near the top of my class, and graduated cum laude from Prague's Charles

University. I worked hard, not out of scholastic ambition but in order to get it over with as quickly as possible. I often dream that I have to go back to school again to pass yet another examination, and I wake up in a cold sweat. This won't surprise millions of young people all over the world who revolt against their educational system.

School was never fun in Europe. Perhaps American schools have too much freedom for play; ours had too much discipline. We were afraid of our teachers, or disliked them. Sometimes we respected them. But we were never fond of them, though in retrospect I know now that we were wrong. Our school system was antiquated and rigorous, forcing us to think in strictly defined channels. Even at the university, the professor would never sit down among his students; he was always speaking ex cathedra, literally towering above us. The only valuable part of my education was the humanistic *Gymnasium* in Ostrava, where I learned Latin and Greek. Years ago, when I worked on a *New Yorker* profile of Sir Siegmund Warburg, whom the London *Sunday Times* called "the postwar wonder of merchant banking," I wasn't surprised when he told me that he considered a working knowledge of Latin and Greek better preparation for the elusive calling of a merchant banker than a study of modern finance, management technique, and economics. "Classical education . . . helps you to develop logical thinking and to perceive quickly and accurately what you read." Warburg opposed the widespread belief that to think deeply means to think in a complicated way.

Our *Gymnasium* class was a cross section of the nationalities and religions that inhabited Ostrava, traditionally a border town. There were boys from Czech, Slovak, Jewish, Sudeten German, German, Polish, Hungarian, and Austrian families. Yet we got along well with one another. There were few cliques along national or religious lines. In emergencies we covered up for each other, and in our extracurricular, slightly illegal activities, we were all together. Two classmates were able to forge all parents' signatures — a useful skill when a bad report card was to be signed by father or mother. Others were experienced burglars who would break into the conference room on the eve of the mathematics tests. Unfortunately, they were so bad in mathematics that they stole the wrong questions, and the next day there was disaster in class. Burglars should always know exactly what they want to steal. The honor system was unknown, and successful cheats were admired as smart fellows.

We didn't fight about race, religion, politics. Our only fights took place on the soccer field, when members of our class team attacked one another instead of the opposite team because we couldn't agree on the fine points of offensive tactics. Soccer was the most popular game. I was a member of the first-string soccer team, usually playing center forward. Some people now find this hard to believe; I no longer run if I can walk. There was some gossip, I remember, that I was on the first team because I happened to own the ball. Anyone familiar with soccer knows though that no team can afford a bad center forward.

The ugly facts of political life caught up with me at Vienna's Hochschule für Welthandel (College for World Trade) in 1926. I didn't care for world trade, economics, and the secrets of double-ledger bookkeeping, but I had to have a pretext for spending a year in Vienna, because I loved music and opera. The college was my alibi, and it wasn't pleasant. Quite a few of my fellow students knew a lot about one A. Hitler who had been in Vienna not long before, a confused, third-rate painter and first-rate demagogue. At the college we Jewish students were a tiny minority. We were often attacked by militant members of the Aryan student body for no other reason than being a tiny minority. The Vienna police looked on benevolently while we were beaten up by our *Kommilitonen*. They were forbidden from entering academic territory, but they were equally benevolent when the beatings took place in a nearby, unacademic street.

The situation improved somewhat at Charles University, in Prague. I ignored fraternities and their silly squabbles. Several years ago, when I happened to be in Göttingen, the old university town in Germany, I saw the drinking, shouting, singing students' "corporations," and I heard of dueling fraternities, and blood spilled at dawn. On Sunday morning, they sat in front of the city hall, drinking beer, displaying their colored caps, and singing nationalistic songs. Alumni recognize each other by their scars on the cheeks and exchange sympathetic glances, members of a powerful secret society; in certain German circles, the scar on the cheek is a membership symbol. Mankind may sometime conquer cancer but never idiocy.

When I recovered from my puerile crisis of double pneumonia, my parents bundled me off from Ostrava to nearby Vienna, where they wanted to consult a professor. For once, the judgment of our house physician, Dr. Himmelblau, was not considered valid enough. My mother had unbounded belief in Vienna's medical school, which was famous prior to the First World War.

The celebrated professor looked as Sigmund Freud does in his late pictures, and he also wore a beard and butterfly tie. Today one sees group photographs of these old, bearded professors in the waiting rooms of elderly doctors in Vienna. The celebrated professors are sitting stiffly around oval tables, looking as uncomfortable as if they were their own patients. I remember standing in front of the great professor with my naked torso, shivering in the cool dark room with a high wooden ceiling. The professor tickled me with his stethoscope; later he produced hollow sounds by knocking all over my ribs. At the Mayo Clinic they would now take a dim view of such a checkup, but elderly practitioners in Vienna still claim they would rather rely on what they call "instinct" than computers. Who knows, they may be right.

The professor looked at me thoughtfully. He seemed to X-ray me with his eyes. He suggested a long convalescence in Meran, one of the sunniest places in the Austro-Hungarian monarchy. I asked whether I would have to go to school there. He shook his head. I began to share my mother's belief in Vienna's medical school.

After an overnight trip in a glamorous wagon-lit compartment — a
needless expense, since I was too excited to sleep — my mother and I
arrived at the small, vine-covered railroad station with the sign MERAN.
This was the end of the main line; only a small branch line, rarely used,
led to Mals, near the Reschenpass. In Vienna it had been freezing, but
now the sky was deep blue, the sort of blue I'd never seen except on
cheap postcards. The sunshine too had a new kind of hard brilliance,
not at all like the sunshine in my hometown, where a cloud of coal dust
and smoke was always interfering between the sun and the people.

We rode in an open carriage drawn by two pearl-gray horses, past
palm trees, cypresses, and other subtropical plants that I knew only
from books. The mountains around us were snow-covered, but the air
was soft and velvety, and I inhaled the scent of apples. They were said
to be stored in the cellars of many houses. This was my first excursion
into the sunny south, and I was enchanted. *Der Drang nach Süden* has
been strong among the people in Europe's northern landscape long before Goethe discovered the "land where the lemons blossom." Meran
seemed an oasis of vineyards and orchards and gardens, with a few
houses here and there.

The coachman turned around and said that apples were a famous
local specialty, particularly a variety from a nearby orchard known as
Calville. "If you'll stay until spring," he said, "you'll see the *Blüte*
[blossom time]. Then the whole valley smells like a perfume factory. A
Sunday smell. In Meran it's always Sunday."

His description has remained accurate. To me, it's always Sunday
in Merano (I use both names, depending on whether the town is mentioned before or after 1919, when South Tyrol was ceded by Austria to
Italy). People work, the shops are open, the dentists and lawyers and
petty bureaucrats are as active as elsewhere, people get drunk and fight,
but everything is done in a nonchalant way, almost in a holiday mood.
Even in the middle of a working day, people always have time to sit
in the sun and look at the flowers or at the girls. Spiritually and emotionally, it's always Sunday.

We stayed at the pension (boardinghouse) of the Lambergs, in the garden suburb of Obermais, later called Maia Alta. The four-story villa was painted in *"Schönbrunn* yellow," a color dear to the hearts of all Austrian monarchists. (The Habsburg flag was black-yellow.) The Lambergs were kind, elderly people. "Uncle" Lamberg was head cashier in a local bank. His wife had always loved children but had none of her own; she'd turned two floors of the villa into a rest home for spoiled brats like me who came there after a sickness, or for kids whose parents tried to get rid of them for a while. During the weeks that followed, I spent many hours lying on the sunny open-air terrace overlooking the garden, wrapped up to my chin in blankets, wearing dark glasses. The garden was old and dark and mysterious. Firs, cypresses, oak trees, and, deep inside, a dark pool with flowers; I saw the garden in my dreams, populated with dwarflike little men and dancing angels. The garden is still there, darker and more mysterious than ever. Sometimes I walk past the house, on a nostalgic pilgrimage.

The Lambergs died in the 1920's, and the house was sold. In the past fifty years, it was painted many times, in the haphazard way things are done in Merano, and the faded inscription Villa Lamberg always emerges from under several coats of paint, indelible as my memories are. In such moments I am back in the Meran of my childhood. At that time Franz Kafka lived here for a while; he may have been here when I was lying on the terrace of the Villa Lamberg. Of course, I'd never heard his name. He was recovering from a bad cold and a disastrous love affair with Fräulein F. B., and he was ill and unhappy. He found no more peace in Meran than elsewhere. He stayed in a two-story house overlooking the Winter Promenade and the Passer, a small river that flows through town. I now see the house from the balcony of the room in my hotel, which is a converted sixteenth-century convent with thick walls, surrounded by an old park with a mammoth tree, a redwood tree, a Judas tree.

The "Kafka house" (only I call it that) has a sign, VILLA FANNY. One summer night last year, somebody, after too much of the inexpensive local Küchelberger rosé, scribbled the word "hill" after it: VILLA FANNY HILL. But it isn't that sort of place at all, and the anonymous wit betrayed his abysmal ignorance. The house once belonged to Fanny Elssler, the celebrated Viennese ballerina, whose father was Joseph Haydn's copyist. Fanny was admired in Europe and a sensation when she came to America, in 1840. In Washington, so many congressmen went to see her dance that Congress had to adjourn for lack of a quorum. (We could use such a prima ballerina once in a while in Washington, today, to make Congress adjourn and save us oratory and expense.) Kafka died a few years later. A German poet, Christian Morgenstern, died in Meran. It's a good place to live in, and a good place to die.

The Villa Lamberg has been divided into small apartments. There are half a dozen buttons with name shields next to the entrance door. The last time I walked by, *à la recherche de la jeunesse*, a young Italian couple came out. The woman's high heels made cheerful staccato sounds on the pavement. The proud young papa pushed a baby carriage, looking at the baby, never at the mother. The bambino made healthy noises that didn't sound like *bel canto*, but who can tell in the land of Monteverdi and Verdi? The other night we had cannelloni at a small Italian restaurant patronized by soldiers, members of the local garrison. Four young soldiers, in a homesick mood, sang beautiful folk songs, a cappella. They were two tenors and two baritones, and though they were untrained, they had their nation's feeling for rhythm and harmony and melody. We applauded, and two of them, a tenor and a baritone, sang as an encore Don Carlo's and Posa's beautiful duet from the first act of Verdi's *Don Carlo*.

Being Meran as well as Merano has created political problems for the Sunday place. The pro-Austrian South Tyroleans dislike the Italians who have settled here in the past fifty years; they say that the "new" Merano is not as *ordentlich* (orderly) as the "old" Meran was under the Habsburg regime. Maybe not, but it's a lot more cheerful. The

Italians have moved in with their genius for de-complicating life. They brought along laughter and spaghetti and *cassata* ice cream, their street songs and the harmonious sounds of the world's most musical language. They stand around all day long at the espresso café, talking about girls and *totocalcio*, the soccer pool. Their smiling faces contrast with the hard, grim faces of the native Tyroleans. The Sunday place has its troubles, but so did paradise.

After a few months at the Villa Lamberg, the local doctor said I was all right. My mother came to fetch me, and we went home. For a while I had a tutor, to catch up with the children who had been in school while I'd been lying in the sun. A few months later, in the summer of 1914, the First World War broke out. I was on vacation with my parents on the Semmering, near Vienna. When Emperor Franz Joseph ordered general mobilization, my father, a reserve officer in the Austrian army, said we would leave the same night, by slow train, so he could report to his unit in the morning. My mother cried. She said we might take the fast train in the morning, but my father shook his head in his gentle, firm manner. No, he said, we were going right away, it was his duty. . . .

A few months later, on a dark November day in 1914, I came home from school. My mother was lying on the sofa, crying quietly. She would often mix tears and laughter in emotional moments, for instance when she listened to the fourth act of Puccini's *La Bohème*, that starts in merriment and ends in sorrow. I'd learned the meaning of her tearful moods, though I was only seven years old, and I knew that something terrible had happened. My mother was in shock. She didn't even notice me.

She had received an official message from the War Ministry in

Vienna. My father had fallen *"auf dem Felde der Ehre,"* ("on the field of honor"). Today the message would be less ambiguous: killed in action.

Ever since, I've disliked wars, armies, and the military life. I've been forced to spend several years in uniform — first in the Czechoslovak army in the 1930's, later in the army of the United States, during the Second World War. The experience hasn't changed my early aversion to military establishments everywhere. Unlike the late, unlamented Benito Mussolini, I've never felt that in order to get the full enjoyment of life, one must live dangerously.

The "field of honor" was a clearing in the deep, black fir woods of western Poland, near the town of Bochnia. On the tenth anniversary of my father's death in 1924, we went to visit his grave. We took a slow train to Cracow, and an even slower one to Bochnia. There my mother hired a Polish peasant who was to take us with his horse-drawn haycart to the forest, two hours away. It was a nightmarish journey. My mother had wanted to be there on the day my father had died, the twenty-second of November. To me it was always a dreadful day. President John F. Kennedy was killed on another dreadful November twenty-second, in 1963.

November is a terrible month all over Europe, dark and rainy, and it was particularly depressing in the Polish countryside. Everything was gray: the fields below, the clouds above, and the steady, slow rain in between. The dirt roads had deep cracks and were covered with mud. The haycart's canvas top had holes, and the rain seemed to flow directly into the collar of my coat. We were alternately hurled against the top, or thrown against the wooden boards on the floor. The floor was covered with wet straw that had the foul smell of the dirty stable. The horse waded through mud and tripped over stones, as resigned to the weather as the peasant, who never complained. There was something frightening in his impassiveness. Perhaps it was the heritage of generations of silently suffering Polish peasants living a sad life under foreign rulers in the muddy countryside. My father had often said, half jokingly,

"In Polen ist nichts zu holen" ("There's nothing to be found in Poland."). Nothing but death. He had died there, "on the field of honor."
Thirty years later, my mother died, not far away, in Auschwitz, which
no one has called a field of honor. Poland will always remain a cemetery
to me.

It took the peasant a long time to find the grave in the dark woods.
He spat out and cursed a lot, *"psia krew cholera"* ("dog's-blood-and-
cholera"). At last he found it — a mass grave. I'd never seen one. The
peasant said my father's whole company had been killed there, and the
men had been buried together where they had died together. A large
excavation had been made, and the dead were put in and covered with
earth, and then a crude wooden cross had been set up with all the
names. My father's name was on top. The peasant knelt, crossed himself,
and said the Lord's Prayer. He was angry because I didn't kneel down.
I said a silent Hebrew prayer. How could I explain to him that a Jewish
boy doesn't cross himself?

My father's name was in Latin letters, as though he were buried in
a Catholic cemetery. I'm sure he didn't mind. He'd often told me that
religion, language, wealth, poverty, didn't really matter, that nothing
mattered but good or bad. It was the sort of ethics a seven-year-old boy
could easily understand. I thought that my father would be glad to be
buried with his men. There was a great stillness in the woods, and the
rain fell down almost inaudibly from the roof of what seemed to me a
forest cathedral. It was very peaceful. I said to my mother that it was
really a beautiful grave, but she didn't listen. She was crying.

Later, the peasant told us how the Austrian soldiers had died. I
gathered that their death had already become a heroic legend in Bochnia.
The company had been ordered "to take the clearing" where the Russians had dug in with heavy machine guns. The Austrians had no artil-
lery support. Their two light machine guns couldn't match the firepower
of the Russians. Yet the clearing had to be taken "at all cost." A high-
ranking staff officer who was sitting with his maps somewhere in the
rear, had issued the order. It was authorized mass murder.

The peasant said the men had refused to get out of their trenches when the order *"Sturm!"* ("Attack!") was given. "Don't blame them, dog's-blood-and-cholera. Then the *Herr Hauptmann* drew his saber and jumped out of the trench. All by himself. Order is order." (The peasant said it in his Polish-accentuated German: *"BE-fehl is BE-fehl."*) "Then the men followed the *Herr Hauptmann*. The Russian dogs waited until the Austrians were within easy range of the heavy machine guns, and then they cut them down at the edge of the clearing."

The peasant spat out and made a gesture of mowing, with his outstretched right hand, palm down. There were no survivors.

My mother was still crying. I thought of my father, the gentlest man I'd known. He had never raised his voice. He had been tall and quiet and elegant, often a little aloof, but I'd sensed his warmth and devotion. One of his friends later said to my mother, "He was an aristocrat at heart." And he died, with his saber in his hand, as in a silly *kitsch* painting, for no good reason at all, in the dark Polish woods.

The peasant said that later — he meant after the massacre — the Austrians had brought up field guns and shelled the enemy position. "They should have done it before," he said, and spat. "The Russians retreated, and the Austrians moved up and buried their dead."

On the way back to Bochnia, the rain got worse. My mother was still crying. I didn't look out; I couldn't stand the sight of the country. My mother said, "Your father was always such a good man, and now he doesn't even have a grave of his own."

Several months later, a colonel from the War Ministry in Vienna paid a visit to my mother and presented her with a decoration, a cross studded with small jewels, that had been posthumously awarded to my father. My mother hardly looked at the colonel. After he'd left, she put the velvet-lined case into a drawer. She said she didn't want to see it. I don't know what happened to it. It disappeared with the rest of my mother's belongings when the Gestapo came for her. It made no difference to the Gestapo that my mother was the widow of a war hero.

After the First World War, we often went to Merano on short vacations, staying at an inexpensive pension. Most of our family fortune had been patriotically but unwisely invested in Austrian war bonds that became worthless. What was left was swept away by the astronomical inflation of the early 1920's. It was a tragedy for my mother but a good thing for me. Now we were poor, like almost everybody else I knew, and I had to learn a few useful things. My Uncle Alfred — he was my father's favorite brother, also a banker — had managed to remain rich; my mother said bitterly that he was getting richer by the day. She had to take in boarders in our home while Uncle Alfred built himself a large modern villa in Vienna. The villa consisted mostly of surrealistic staircases, leading nowhere. My uncle and his socially ambitious wife arranged for their daughter, Edith, to marry an Austrian aristocrat whom she didn't like. Edith later committed suicide. And her brother Raoul, my rich cousin, killed himself one day in the late 1930's, when he heard of his father's death. "Raoul," my mother said, "never learned to cope with life." She said it regretfully; she was no longer bitter.

While I studied in Prague, Vienna, Paris, and at the same time played the violin on ships all over the world, I always found time to go back to Merano. My cousin Martha, who was my mother's age, had bought the Praderhof in Maia Alta. *Hof* means farm, but the Praderhof was a mansion with a park in the rear, and a garden, a vineyard, and an orchard on the other sides. Architecturally, it was a jumble of nonstyles, not unlike the Ringstrasse in Vienna; its façade, with an unmotivated round tower and atrocious turrets, must have been contrived by a frustrated *Jugendstil* architect in a moment of depression. But inside it was spacious and comfortable, with high, wood-paneled rooms, beams along the ceiling, and a wonderful feeling of warmth. From a vine-covered terrace in front, one could see the long valley that stretched all the way to Bolzano (Bozen), twenty miles away. In spring it became a sea of blossoms, as the old coachman had said, with the chimneys of some houses sticking out like the conning towers of submarines.

In the vineyard one walked through arcades of vines with the sun falling through, creating bizarre patterns on the bunches of red and white grapes hanging down. The Merano grapes were more spectacular than the celebrated grapes of Château Cheval Blanc, near Bordeaux, that produce my favorite great wine. The Merano grapes make my favorite small wine — a sort of light rosé with a slight taste of *terroir* that goes down like water, better even, and has ruined a considerable part of the local population who like it too much. Local doctors prescribe eating several pounds of grapes during harvest time. The Merano grape cure is as charming and inconsequential as everything else there, said to be good for body and soul.

Looking down from the Praderhof terrace at the sea of blossoms, I regretted that I was green-red color-blind. Renoir might have caught the subtle shades of the blossoms, from white (Gravensteiner apples) to rose-colored (Kalterer) to shades of pink (pears and peaches). The time I liked best was late afternoon, when we would sit on the pergola, drinking the mild wine from Castle Rametz, on a sunny slope just behind the Praderhof. The mountains would be screened by a soft, silvery haze, and the air was oscillating, as on a hot summer day above the car's radiator. Dusk would come, making me think of the lovely melody of "Traum durch die Dämmering," perhaps Richard Strauss's most beautiful song, and the contours of the mountains became sharply drawn against the darkening sky. All the mountains had definite personalities, almost faces. There was the jagged peak and glacier of the sinister Iffinger. I once went there with my cousin Dora, and almost fell off a cliff. The softly rounded Josephsberg (Monte Giuseppe), which, I thought for a long time, was named for me. The Mendel (Mendola), with the well-shaped form of a beautiful woman's bosom, a feminine mountain in a feminine landscape.

The mountains that surround the town from all sides keep out the cold storms of winter and world politics. Located at the far end of a not-a-through-valley, Merano miraculously escaped the action at the nearby fronts in the First World War and remained unharmed while Allied

bombers, during the Second World War, attacked the important railroad junction of Bolzano. Bolzano was badly hit, but Merano wasn't
touched. The large hotels were turned into hospitals by the Germans;
large red crosses were painted on the roofs. Today the people of Merano
are convinced their luck will hold out; why should anyone bother to
drop a bomb there? Merano is inaccessible, a sort of Shangri-la. The
nearest airports are Milan or Munich. In wintertime, when blizzards
block the Brenner Pass, fifty miles away, one walks without a topcoat in
Merano at noontime. Winter is never cold and damp, and summer may
be hot but never humid. No wonder the Romans loved the region, and
Charlemagne, and many after him. Three of the four medieval gates
are still there, creating terrible traffic jams during the season.

Yes, season. Unfortunately, bright travel agents and tourists have
discovered the paradise at the end of nowhere, and their arrival, by cars
and buses, has not improved the Sunday climate. Even the Tappeinerweg
(Tappeiner's Path), is crowded then. Dr. Franz Tappeiner was a famous
local physician who made a lot of money toward the end of the past
century and had a lovely promenade built, at his own expense, which
he gave to the town. He had a theory (that would be good now for
harassed executives) that many imagined and real ills can be cured by
a leisurely walk through a lovely landscape. The Tappeinerweg ascends
imperceptibly through subtropical gardens, leads past the vineyards
along the Küchelberg slope with its Roman and Romanesque ruins, and
slowly descends back into town. It's a wonderful forty-minute walk, and
I often go there before breakfast, returning hungry and all set for a few
hours' work.

Martha, my elderly cousin, and her husband came to Merano one
day between the two world wars. They saw the Praderhof, which was
for sale, fell in love with it, and bought it. Franzl was a former operetta
conductor from Vienna who looked like his idol, the great Johann
Strauss. He had silvery hair, wore a velvet jacket, spoke in three-quarters

time, and loved the wines of nearby Castle Rametz, which he bought
in large, fifty-liter containers. His motto was the theme song from Die
Fledermaus: "Happy Is He Who Forgets What Cannot Be Changed."
Franzl let others do his worrying. Everybody told them that the house,
with more than twenty bedrooms, was much too large for a childless
couple. Martha's family was spread all over Europe. At last, she said,
they would have a place to gather. They were a remarkable family, very
close to each other, always visiting. The family enterprise, Wach- und
Schliessgesellschaft (Guarding and Locking Company), was a private
outfit guaranteeing its clients — shopkeepers, factory owners, office
managers, proprietors of houses and enterprises — that their premises
would be guarded at night, patrolled, and their doors locked. The employees, mostly retired policemen, were carefully watched on their appointed rounds. The firm prospered and had branch offices all over
Europe.

Martha was a lifelong optimist. When the real estate agent in Merano told her she would need at least four people to run the Praderhof,
she hired six. Three years after she took possession, Hitler came to
power in neighboring Germany, and then terror spread all over the
Continent. Some of Martha's brothers and sisters had to get away.
Many branch offices of the firm were "Aryanized" — expropriated —
and Martha's income was sharply cut down. She decided to take a few
"paying guests." For a while, wealthy people from America, Germany,
Scandinavia, enjoyed the privacy and comfort of the beautiful Praderhof.
But gradually the paying guests stayed away from fascist Italy. Instead,
displaced relatives arrived from Rumania, Czechoslovakia, Austria. Martha dismissed the servants, one by one; even Frau Käthe, the excellent
cook, couldn't be kept. The kitchen was in the basement, with a dumb-
waiter going up to the large dining room. One of Martha's elderly
sisters did the cooking, aided by a couple of young girls, and upstairs
a former manager and a philosophy professor were in charge of the
dining room. Spaghetti and wine were still cheap; sunshine and the mild

air were gratis. Everybody said the "situation" would never be as bad as in nearby Germany and Austria.

Martha coped with endless crises. A sister needed money, a brother-in-law had to have a visa. Franzl, an Austrian monarchist, got into a fight with Mussolini's *carabinieri*. Martha had met the colonel commanding the local Italian garrison, and she invited him for coffee and *Guglhupf*. The colonel, a small, energetic man, liked Martha so well that he straightened out her husband's seditious statements. He began to consult Martha about his own staff problems. For a while Martha, a rather plain woman with warm eyes, knew more military secrets than the late Mata Hari. When the colonel had a row with the mayor of Merano, Martha invited them both for coffee, and settled their dispute. Then the mayor too became a friend of the house, and consulted her on community problems.

When my wife and I went to America, late in 1938, we lost touch with Martha in Merano, but when we came back to Europe after the war, we went there at once. Martha and Franzl were waiting for us at the small railroad station. They looked tired; so did the station. They couldn't take us to the Praderhof because they couldn't afford to operate the central-heating system, and heated only a couple of rooms with a small iron stove. Coal was expensive, and it was very cold. We stayed at the hotel but spent much time with them. There was so much to talk about.

After the Germans invaded Italy, an SS *Führer* had appeared at the Praderhof. He gave Martha and Franzl six hours to get out, staring hard at Martha. She was Jewish, and she looked Jewish. Franzl was, and looked like, an "Aryan." The SS *Führer* didn't like it at all. Franzl had often angered me by making anti-Jewish remarks in Viennese, I-didn't-really-mean-it fashion, but when the SS *Führer* told him to get rid of "that Jewess," Franzl told him to go to hell, and was arrested. Franzl had shown *Zivilcourage*, and I forgave him for all his earlier remarks. After his release from prison, he and Martha went to a small village in the mountains above Lake Garda, where they knew the abbot of a monastery. Martha was hidden by the monks; Franzl lived in the nearby house of an Italian peasant. The Germans came, but the peasants and the monks didn't betray the refugees. At the end of the war, Martha and Franzl returned to Merano. The Praderhof looked unchanged. Italian friends had prevented the Germans from looting the place before they moved out.

After the Second World War, the Praderhof became a refuge for the few members of the once large family that had survived the apocalypse. Three of Martha's sisters and their in-laws came to live there. The family lived on the ground floor. The second floor was rented to an insurance-company executive, and the third to an Italian professor, but since the house had different entrances, the arrangement bothered no one. The house was still too big. The vineyard and the orchard were leased to a neighbor. The vegetable garden was taken over by my cousin Dora, who had survived the Terezín-Theresienstadt concentration camp because she was a trained gardener and the camp commander had liked fresh strawberries for breakfast. The survivors had incredible stories to tell, but we rarely talked about the survivors, and more often about those who had not survived. Dora had been with my mother in Theresienstadt until my mother's name had been put on the transport list, the one-way transport to Auschwitz.

Relatives arrived at the Praderhof from all over the world, from Israel and America and South Africa. Distance had lost its meaning. A big atlas was lying on a table in the hall, and people consulted the maps of faraway countries as casually as the railroad schedule to Bolzano, before they took off again.

I saw Martha for the last time late in 1949, when I came to see her because I didn't know where else to go. It was a bad moment in my life; instinctively, I went to Merano. Martha was waiting for me at the station, and I felt better right away. She was alone; she sensed that I needed her and wouldn't be in the mood for Franzl's Viennese jokes. Martha had the deep understanding of many women who always wanted children and never had them, and was always willing to listen to other people's troubles; she was completely unselfish. Her first marriage had been unhappy, and later she'd met Franzl, whose outfit had been stationed near Ostrava during the First World War. He didn't look soldierly, wore his cap at an artistic angle, and walked across the Rynek (the market square) whistling a waltz melody. Martha had opened a needlework store on the ground floor of our family house, teaching local matrons the art of petit point and embroidery. Franzl was sitting on the counter, letting his legs dangle down, telling the ladies Viennese jokes and being charming.

When they got married, the family was shocked. They said it wouldn't last — Martha, unglamorous, quiet, and serious-minded, and the easygoing ex-*Kapellmeister* from Vienna. But it did last, and they were happy. Franzl drank the good wine from Castle Rametz, drove the car, often into a ditch, and played the harmonium and the fiddle. I didn't think much of him as a violinist. He had a dark old fiddle the color of his velvet coat, and instead of putting it into its case, he would hang it up on the wall, which I considered a barbarian habit. He also had a guitar, a lute, and a trumpet hanging there. Occasionally he irritated me, when he said he was sick and tired of all his goddam Jewish relatives. I got mad until I found out that he was even more sick and tired of his goddam non-Jewish relatives. It must have been a strain to be surrounded all the time by relatives. There were always problems, but Martha would ask you to come for a walk through the vineyard, listening to you, never saying much, and after a while the problem would dissolve into the bluish haze of Merano.

She was wise and patient and understanding with me that night in 1949. Once she spoke up. "It's better to love and suffer and be desperate than to miss both the happiness and the suffering. People with no capac-

ity for suffering haven't really lived." I said that Schnitzler and Hofmannsthal had said that somewhere, and she smiled. "Yes, but more
poetically." It was quiet in the vineyard, and there was a full moon, and
I saw the familiar contours of the mountains all around us. Martha was
always fond of me, and she told me the reason shortly before she died.
As a girl she'd gone through a very bad time, and Uncle Siegfried (it
was strange to hear her refer to my father as "Uncle Siegfried") had
been the only one who understood and helped her. She said I looked
very much like my father.

Martha knew the strange, twisted details of our family chronicle, and
she urged me to write the story, with its passions, suicides, incestuous
goings-on, triumphs and failures. She loved Dostoevski and thought the
family story could be very Dostoevskian, but I was afraid of being a
third-rate Dostoevski and never wrote the book. Martha's favorite character was my paternal grandfather, Albert Wechsberg, who began as a
poor boy and wound up as "our local Rothschild" in my hometown. He
was both incredibly stingy and incredibly generous, saving the backs of
used envelopes for writing, and paying the debts of his favorite son Max,
the family's black sheep. Grandfather Wechsberg liked to compare himself to his contemporary, Emperor Franz Joseph I. The Emperor's
brother, Archduke Maximilian, was executed in Mexico; his son, Crown
Prince Rudolf, killed Marie Vetsera and himself in Mayerling; and his
wife, the Empress Elizabeth, was stabbed to death by an Italian anarchist
in Geneva. Grandfather Wechsberg too had his share of tragedies. Uncle
Max, the beloved black sheep, a famous gynecologist in Vienna, a bach-
elor-about-town and musician, died of an overdose of morphine.

"It was quite a family," Martha said. "But so is everybody's family if
one searches deeply enough."

I stayed a few weeks at the Praderhof, and when I left, all was well,
or almost. Operations performed on the soul leave scars too, and when
the weather changes, you feel the scar. A few months later I had a letter
from Franzl; Martha had died of cancer. She'd known it all along, but
while she listened to everybody's problems, she'd never told her prob-

lems to anybody, not even to her husband. We came to Merano early in 1950, and Franzl took us to the Jewish cemetery, across from the railroad station, where Martha was buried. He cried and kissed the white gravel that covered her grave, and asked her to help him and come for him. Martha helped him; six months later he was dead, and was buried in the Catholic cemetery. Neither the Jews nor the Catholics would permit the couple to be buried together, but that's no problem in Merano. The two cemeteries are located wall to wall; it's a short walk between the two graves. The Catholic cemetery is always open, but the Jewish cemetery is often locked. I go to Signor Jacob, the gravestone sculptor, who keeps the large iron key on a string, and I open the cemetery gate and walk in. It is a beautiful, peaceful cemetery, under old trees, surrounded on all sides by the mountains. Sometimes a train arrives at the nearby railroad station, or departs. To depart from Merano is always to die a little. When I get on the train, I can see the cemetery. My mother always wished she would be buried there, but her wish remained unfulfilled.

I walk out and lock the gate, and take the key back to Jacob. It's like having one's private cemetery.

Poppy, our daughter, was born in Merano, in September, 1950, and we stayed at the Praderhof for several months. (Her name is really Josephine, but we weren't thinking about Napoleon's Empress. I am not sure whether Poppy was named after the poppy, the state flower of California, for which my wife was homesick, or because all small girls are called "Poppy" or "Popperl" in Merano.) On Christmas Eve, a water pipe burst on the top floor, and we spent the rest of the evening running back and forth with buckets. Later, the central-heating system that hadn't been fixed for a long time, broke down. Nothing had been done in the house for the past fifteen years, and now it became impossible to keep up with all the repairs. And there were debts and mortgage payments. One day, after seeing their lawyer, Martha's sisters decided to put the Praderhof up for sale. They kept the small gatehouse at the lower end of the vineyard, and they planned to go to America. Several relatives were already there. They wrote, what was the sense of staying in Merano? Merano was the past, and hadn't we all learned that one must not cling to the past? Come to America, America is the future.

Shortly before we moved out of the Praderhof, Janet Flanner ("Genêt"), my *New Yorker* colleague, came to visit us there. She stayed two days and still remembers the place. She sometimes talks about a for-lorn-looking little Jewish boy there who later went to Israel, lived in a kibbutz, fought in the army, and is no longer forlorn-looking, but strong and optimistic about the future. Janet tells me I should have tried to keep the Praderhof, though she admitted that it was too big a place for a writer and it would take years to put it back into shape. Janet recently asked me what happened to the many relatives she met there. The older generation is dead, and the younger people are everywhere — in New York, California, Jerusalem, London, South Africa, Brazil. . . . We don't need the big atlas that was lying in the hall; we carry the map of the world in our heads.

I've never been inside the Praderhof since, but I walk by once in a while. The present owner put in many "improvements," even a heavy metal fence with barbed wire on top. Such precautions are not unusual in Merano, where all sorts of people gathered during and after the Sec-ond World War. Castle Labers, not far from the Praderhof, was a hide-out and operations center for a group of Nazi master forgers printing millions of counterfeit English pound notes. The wife of Martin Bor-mann, Hitler's deputy and the top Nazi leader not yet accounted for, is buried in Merano. Mysterious stories are told of other people who after the war sought anonymity in the Sunday paradise. Several years ago I worked with Simon Wiesenthal on his book *The Murderers Among Us*. Wiesenthal had discovered the trail leading to the hiding place of Adolf Eichmann in Buenos Aires, that enabled the Israelis to arrest Eich-mann. Wiesenthal found out that a Nazi escape organization, called ODESSA, which channeled many war criminals to South America and elsewhere, had an important way station in Merano because no one would expect it in the place where it's always Sunday.

The Praderhof's old wrought-iron door that was always left open when Martha and Franzl lived there is now locked. Two German-shepherd dogs are lying behind the gate. The last time I walked by, they barked at me furiously.

Strange, but Merano has always attracted strange people. The Sunday place is a haven for eccentrics. I remember an old White Russian *émigré* who had read in an old Czarist guidebook that there had once been a steamship communication between Meran and Venice, and had come to find the secret waterway. I knew a man who collected stuffed dogs because he'd heard that people used to hide money and gold coins in stuffed dogs. Another collected chamber pots. There was an old Austrian aristocrat who had become old and forgetful. One day he hired a coachman for a ride, met Franzl, walked around with him, and forgot all about the coachman, who appeared in the evening, presenting a large bill. At one time many Nazi sympathizers in Merano received letters from an Austrian actor living in Brussels. The actor claimed to have evidence that Hitler was alive. He was writing the Führer's future speeches and asked for contributions, and, most surprisingly, got some.

My favorite eccentric was Fritz Herzmanovsky-Orlando, the Austrian novelist, dramatist, and artist who lived high up in the tower of Castle Rametz, and often came down to the Praderhof for a visit. A small, benign-looking man with white hair and twinkling eyes, he always carried his movable assets on his person: a handful of gold coins jingling in his trouser pocket. Previous experience had taught him not to trust banks. The gold coins — English sovereigns, Swiss vrenelis, American eagles — gave him a reassuring sense of independence. He is now post-humously famous in the German-speaking countries where his books are widely read. His name symbolizes the preposterous Austrian trinity of German, Slav, and Italian components. He wrote bizarre chronicles of the Austrian monarchy with an inimitable juxtaposition of wisdom and madness, brilliantly exposing the roots of the intellectual and moral decadence that caused the end of the Habsburg empire. His masterpiece, *Der Gaulschreck (The Nag Fright)*, is about a venerable court official who plans to celebrate the twenty-fifth anniversary of the reign of Emperor Franz I by presenting His Majesty with a tableau containing twenty-five milk teeth. The book describes the court official's improbable efforts to secure the missing twenty-fifth tooth.

Dante Alighieri was once a visitor in nearby eleventh-century Castle Tyrol, which gave the region its name. A marble slab with an inscription on a Romanesque tower reminds one of the event. (At the Brunnenburg, a great admirer of Dante, Ezra Pound, lived after 1958 with his daughter for several years.) Two great minnesingers, Oswald von Wolkenstein and Walter von der Vogelweide, also had their castles in the vicinity. Merano is a fine place for poets but not for painters, whose vision is limited by the high mountains. The exception was Titian, whose vision was unlimited; he came from the Dolomites.

There are cheerful espresso bars where the Italians gather for coffee, laughter, and *conversazione*, and Viennese coffeehouses where retired "Old Austrian" civil servants with permanently worried faces read the hometown papers from Innsbruck and Vienna. The clients of the various establishments never mix. A few "Old Austrian" aristocrats live in genteel poverty in run-down houses, next door to the modern, California-style bungalows that nouveaux-riches Germans built themselves lately. The natives ignore both the latecomers from Italy and the latest comers from Germany. Tyroleans and Italians have not only their separate language and culture, but also separate delicatessens, bookstores, ice-cream parlors, hairdressers, dry cleaners, cinemas, restaurants. But young men cross the street to follow a pretty girl, and there are many mixed marriages: *omnia vincit amor.*

Years ago, when the old-timers complained that "their" Meran was ruined since "these" people had come from southern Italy, I once rode in the ramshackle streetcar. The streetcars had no schedule and ran whimsically, like everything in the Sunday place, according to the mood of the Italian conductors. There was an old motorman who carried his friends back and forth, free of charge, because he was lonely. Sometimes they brought a bottle of wine along, and everybody, including the motorman, had a good time. Some grouchy people said this couldn't have happened in the former (Austrian) Meran, where the streetcars had run on schedule, not on wine. True enough, but it also couldn't happen that the conductors stopped anyplace to let an old lady or a child get on, even if there was no station.

Once the motorman, talking to some friends and laughing, forgot to wait for the oncoming car in the shunting spot. Suddenly another car came toward ours, and both seemed headed for a collision. But Italians react quickly. The brakes were applied, and both cars stopped just in time, as in a Keystone Cop picture. Then our car backed up, amidst laughter and clinging of bells, to let the other car pass, and everybody shouted *"Ciao!"* Only an old Tyrolean looked mad and said he would report the conductor. Unfortunately, the streetcars have now been replaced by modern buses. Even in the Sunday place, progress marches on.

From the balcony of my room I look at Josephsberg. The scent of apples or grapes or flowers — according to the season — goes up all the way to the fourth floor. It's a simple room in a small hotel, but there are special attractions that Mr. Hilton and Mr. Intercontinental cannot offer in their computerized palaces. The walls are very thick and protect us against neighborly noises. In summertime when the windows are open, there are the pleasant, tranquilizing sounds of the waters of the Passer, its steady flow giving us a sense of permanence. The hotel has neither a doorman nor a bellboy; one never sees an outstretched palm. In the morning, Matteo and Marili come to make up the rooms while we have breakfast on the sunny terrace overlooking the old park. The redwood tree makes me a little homesick for California, where I would soon get homesick for Merano. Matteo came to Meran (as it was then called), prior to World War One from a little village that was once in Austrian Croatia and is now in Yugoslavia. He speaks Italian and German with a hard accent, and has the quiet dignity and the quiet humor of his people. He is seventy-six, wears a dark blue apron, takes care of everything and everybody. He and the girls working there eat at the family table with the owners. Matteo takes my suits to the tailor, my shoes to the shoe-maker, and gets anything from aspirin to mineral water, and a copy of the Paris edition of the *Herald Tribune*, my shaky link with the United States. Marili and two other girls clean and iron my shirts in the "wash-ing kitchen" upstairs. Even at some of the world's great hotels my shirts were never so beautifully done. Of course, Mr. Ritz — Charles, the son of the great César — cannot bother about his guests' shirts. He has more important problems of financing, expanding, modernizing, at the Paris Ritz.

Our hotel in Merano is run by Franzl, the son of the family owning the place. At twenty-eight, Franzl has thoroughly learned his business. He protects me against unwanted visitors and discourages persistent callers. As a special surprise, he and Matteo ripped the phone out of the wall in my room and placed it in a drawer. Now I have a room-with-disconnected-phone. We have more privacy than in any Palace or Grand, yet three minutes away there are two simple, good restaurants (home-made *tagliatelle*, and veal *scaloppine* done with sage in the Italian man-ner), some good stores, a few cinemas, and the CIT, the Italian travel bureau, if you have to leave in a hurry. We have a doctor we trust, and we know many of the taxi drivers. They charge six hundred lire, one dollar, for any ride within the city limits, which no one knows anyway. This saves the expense of installing a meter.

There are disadvantages. Foreign papers and magazines have to be ordered from Milan. The postal workers are often on strike, or the garbage men, or somebody else. It's hard to listen to foreign radio sta-tions in daytime, though this is perhaps an advantage. The local paper gives equal space to world news and local events; race riots in America are balanced by mysterious diseases of the local grapes. Both the Austrian and Swiss borders can be reached in one hour or so, by car. In two hours one reaches the Stelvio (Stilfserjoch) Pass, over Europe's highest mountain road, after managing forty-eight hairpin curves that were built in the early nineteenth century, not for modern American cars. In Merano it was warm enough for a morning swim; up there it is snowing and you may ski even in July.

My room has a simple wooden table with a square top, just enough space for my typewriter, the sheets of yellow paper, pencils and eraser. Admittedly, it would be nice to work in a cork-lined study or in an old library smelling of parchment, leather, and dust. But one really needs very little to write, though one also needs very much: the dearly familiar contours of my mountains, the sounds of the stream, a sense of peace, and above all, the knowledge that one is not alone even during the writer's lonely hours. If you can guess what I mean.

No Gynecologist in Our Quartet

Long before I became a writer, I wanted to be a famous violin virtuoso or a conductor. Music was my youthful passion. Years ago, Herbert von Karajan, who was then in charge of the Vienna State Opera, told me how much he'd liked an essay I'd written about the opera house. He looked into space, wistfully, and said if there was anything he would rather do than conducting, it would be to write. I said that I'd often wished I could conduct Verdi's *Otello* or Wagner's *Parsifal* as he did, and on that wistful note of mutual admiration we parted. Conducting attracts me because it is a mysterious art. George Szell, the greatest interpreter of classical music today, once told me that "there are matters in conducting that cannot and should not be explained." He said if he wore a mask and stepped for the first time in front of an orchestra that he had never conducted, the players would at once recognize that he knew his business. Some call it the conductor's "magic." Perhaps it is the unanalyzable phenomenon of personality.

My early dreams of glory shouldn't convey the impression that I was an unusual boy. I went through the normal phases of wanting to be a soccer player, a mountain climber — the elation of reaching the stillness of an Alpine summit is not unlike the elation one feels in blessed moments of performing beautiful music. Among my boyhood heroes were Giacomo Casanova, not for his alleged sexual successes but because he once jumped from a second-floor bedroom window into a Venetian lagoon when the irate husband showed up; and Bronislaw Huberman, the Polish-Jewish violinist, because he was the only great master of the violin who performed in my hometown. Today some bloodless esoterics might claim that Huberman "overplayed"; he was an emotional artist who "lived" music. I've since learned that all great artists "live" music, even though they have accepted the necessity of near-perfect performing.

As a youthful violinist, I looked down upon pianists as playing a "mechanical" instrument with no soul. The violin contains a "soul." The French call it *l'âme* — the slender cylindrical rod made of pinewood, that is forced into the violin's body between back and belly, underneath the right foot of the bridge. This sound post transmits the soft belly's vibration to the hard, maple-wood back. A violin without a sound post would have a hollow tone that wouldn't carry far. I thought it fascinating that a little piece of wood, about one quarter of an inch thick, determined the tone and timbre of the instrument, its brilliance and power. If it were shifted less than a millimeter, the violin's character would be completely changed. Of the many secrets of the mysterious violin, the "soul" is perhaps the most enigmatic. I know as little about my violin as about the people who are closest to me.

My father and mother liked music in a casual way; they didn't play an instrument. At home we had an early gramophone with a gleaming brass horn, exactly like the one shown on RCA Victor records, with the little dog listening to his master's voice. Marie, our elderly cook, disliked the gramophone because she had to polish the brass horn once a

week. I spent thrilling hours sitting on the floor in front of the brass
horn, like the little dog. I remember the voice of Caruso. I didn't know
who he was, but his voice did something to me, though these were bad
acoustical recordings. Caruso's voice projected through all musical and
mechanical shortcomings. He sounded glorious even when he seemed to
take liberties in "Una furtive lagrima." I was fascinated by his *legato*
and *mezza voce*, and forgot to change needles when I played his records,
and ruined them.

Our record collection reflected my mother's catholic tastes. She liked
the recordings of people whom she knew personally. Caruso was the
exception; he was everybody's exception. Thus she collected the records
of Leo Slezak, from the nearby capital of Brno (Brünn), who, so to
speak, belonged to the family; and of Selma Kurz from nearby Bielitz,
the celebrated coloratura diva of the Vienna Opera and the Zerbinetta
in the world premiere of Richard Strauss's *Ariadne auf Naxos*. My
mother called her Selma, reminding me that the diva had "almost" married Uncle Bernhard, who later married my mother's sister, Aunt Mella.
It wasn't clear to me who had turned down whom. Selma seemed to
have recovered from the shock, for she later married Professor Halban,
a famous gynecologist in Vienna. I looked up "gynecologist" in my
German encylopedia, but the explanation was too technical, or I was
too young to understand it. My mother also loved Johann Strauss's
"Frühlingsstimmen Walzer," performed by the great Alfred Grünfeld,
whom she'd once met in Aunt Bertha's salon in Vienna, which, I gathered, was different from our salon at home. Again, the encyclopedia was
no help.

The record I liked best was *Der Traum des Reservisten* (*The Reservist's Dream*), a medley of sound effects, trumpet soli, and melodies
describing a day in the life of an Austrian army reservist during the
autumn maneuvers. My father bought it in the gay epoch prior to 1914,
when playing soldier had been fun. The record was mercifully forgotten
after 1918, when it was no longer fun, but was recently reissued by a

Viennese firm and is again popular with many people who forgot much and learned nothing since 1918.

A year after my father's death — I was eight — I had my first violin lesson. My mother said my father would have liked it, he wanted me to learn something he had missed. I became everybody's ordeal at home; a practicing fiddler is worse than a dripping faucet. My mother bravely encouraged me to practice "another five minutes." Marie, the cook, escaped into the Old Church, where it was quiet and peaceful. Fräulein Gertrud, our governess, quickly dressed up my younger brother, and they went for a walk.

My musical mentor was Uncle Bruno, my mother's youngest brother. He'd wanted to become a musician, but life turned him into a paper salesman. Uncle Bruno was a first-rate musician and fourth-rate salesman. He became my mother's partner when they opened their stationery store in the early 1920's, on the advice of Uncle Heinrich in Olmütz, who had a successful stationery store there. It was a bewildering experience for my poor mother. Once she'd been the wife of a rich man, with servants at home, a dressmaker in Vienna, traveling with my father to Biarritz and Monte Carlo when few people could afford to go there. Now she had to sell pencils, erasers, and office supplies. She never complained; she didn't want to depend on her relatives' charity. She let Fräulein Gertrud go, rented out half our apartment, economized radically, and somehow she managed to send my brother and me to good schools.

The stationery store was no success. Uncle Bruno was not interested in onionskin, and Uncle Hugo, who later joined them, had just gone through his third bankruptcy. (My mother had twelve brothers and sisters, and my father had ten; there was an abundance of aunts and uncles.) Like all bankrupts, Uncle Hugo was a perennial optimist, and began to "reorganize" the store, changing the price system, and ruining the store a couple of years later. My mother cried and made me promise that I would never go into business with relatives. She also told me never to lend money to relatives and friends. "Either give it to them outright and forget about it, or refuse," she said. Sound advice, though my father, a banker, might not have agreed.

Uncle Bruno should have become a musician; he would have had fun and made more money than selling paper. He played the violin, the viola, and the cello (well), the piano (fairly well), the clarinet and the French horn (poorly), and was popular among the local amateur musicians and much in demand. His bachelor apartment, across the street from ours, had little furniture but enough instruments to furnish a small chamber orchestra, piles of music, and a dozen chairs and music stands. He and his friends were making music almost every night. Uncle Bruno selected the three-quarter-size violin on which I produced my early, ugly efforts. Later he gave me a cheap viola with a fake Stradivari label inside, and a half-broken cello that we fixed up together. Even Marie didn't mind my practicing the cello; she said it had a nice, human sound.

My first violin teacher was Herr Böhm, but Uncle Bruno soon fired him and hired Herr Ascher, who said that everything that Herr Böhm had taught me was wrong: my posture, my fingering, my bowing. After he was fired, my third teacher, whose name I don't remember, condemned the methods of my first two teachers and taught me his own, which were declared void and useless by my fourth teacher. I wonder how many young musicians have been ruined by the conflicting methods of their teachers. Fortunately, Uncle Bruno taught me that the beauty of good music transcends the incompetence of bad teachers. He also taught me the essentials: taste, style, self-discipline. Uncle Bruno, a dilettante, loved music more than many professional musicians.

He introduced me into the wonderful world of chamber music when I was eleven. The second violinist of his steady string quartet was a women's doctor (I still couldn't pronounce the word "gynecologist") who was sometimes suddenly called away in the middle of a quartet because of an emergency. I wouldn't have a gynecologist in my own quartet now, no matter how well he plays.

One evening, around nine o'clock, Uncle Bruno came to our apartment. He was breathless from running up the stairs.

"Take your violin and come along," he said. "The gentlemen are waiting."

Today I understand the catastrophe befalling three men who have looked forward all day long to an evening of string-quartet playing, one of the most civilized and enjoyable pursuits of Western culture, and then the fourth man doesn't show up or, worse, is called away in the third movement of a beautiful Beethoven. In modern society, no man is said to be irreplaceable. The president is assassinated, but the government continues to function. Management goes on though the chairman of the board has a heart attack or runs away with his secretary. But a string quartet is sunk without one of its regular members.

Twenty-five years later, when I went to Hollywood, where I was lonely for string-quartet music and knew no players, I bought a couple of quartet study recordings with the first-violin part left out. While the record was playing, I was supposed to perform the first-violin part from the attached music with my audible but invisible fellow players. It didn't work out. Quartet playing is a subtle give-and-take among four people brought together by their common love of music. I had to follow the recording, but my three anonymous fellow players wouldn't follow me. In a moment of elation, when I sang out a melody and made an imperceptible *rubato*, I was brutally called back to reality by my fellow players, who performed with the merciless beat of a metronome. I gave up; better no music at all than antimusic.

Eventually, I found chamber-music players in the hills and canyons of Hollywood. They are the same everywhere, no matter where they come from or what language they speak: lovable lunatics conversing in the universal language of Haydn, Mozart, Beethoven, Schubert. That four people who may not know each other by their first names are able to establish a psychological rapport, as they sit down to make heavenly music, is one of the few miracles left in this era of cold rationalism.

After half a century, the memory of my first chamber-music evening is still very strong. Normally a soft-spoken, kindhearted man, Uncle Bruno became a tyrant and madman when he sat down to play a string quartet. I can see him putting the Breitkopf and Härtel parts on the stands: opus 18 no. 4, one of the early Beethoven quartets.

It was a terrifying experience. Uncle Bruno cursed like a top sergeant, stamped the floor, used his fiddle bow as a conductor's baton and riding whip. He didn't mind my playing a few false notes; he knew this was my first effort at sight reading. He was also lenient with the viola player, a prominent lawyer who couldn't keep up with the *alla breve* passages of the final movement. But he got furious when the cellist showed a lack of zeal in the Minuetto, and threatened to throw him out the window. I'd just learned in school about the Prague defenestrations and the trouble they'd caused, and I got frightened. So did the cellist, a powerful industrialist who was feared by a legion of underlings.

In the Scherzo the two violins play a ticklish *spiccato* passage together, while the viola and the cello rest. I adjusted to Uncle Bruno's light bowing and didn't lose a single semiquaver. At the end of the movement, I was commended by the lawyer and the industrialist. Uncle Bruno stared at me hard through his thick eyeglasses, and then he smiled and lightly touched my right shoulder with the tip of his bow. It was a great moment in my youthful life. At the age of eleven, I had been knighted, chamber-musically.

I've played chamber music ever since, except when wars, travel, sickness, and assorted disasters created an unavoidable interval. There is almost nothing that would now keep me from an evening of chamber music. It's more than a hobby; it is a love affair that never ends. In this kind of music I've at last achieved the switch from passive listener to active participant. I agree with Henry Peacham, the seventeenth-century British essayist, who wrote of chamber music, "I dare affirm, there is no science in the world, that so affecteth the free and generous spirit, with a more delightful and inoffensive recreation, or better disposeth the mind to what is commendable and vertuous."

The playing of chamber music — "the music of friends," as it is called — engenders an atmosphere of warmth that is unknown to most virtuosos or prima donnas. For them, music is a competitive business, a race that goes to the fastest and loudest. Not so with chamber music. It is based on the proposition that all players are born equal. It is a garden of musical fellowship from which the law of the jungle has been banished, and in which egotism cannot thrive.

But if chamber music is noncompetitive, it is far from being lukewarm. Nothing could be more wrongheaded than the view that chamber-music players are austere and bloodless esoterics, as anyone can attest who has watched a string quartet in action, soaring to the heights of happiness when a movement comes off, and plummeting to the depths of despair when (as happens more often) it doesn't. Like Uncle Bruno, I tolerate imperfection but not the slightest lack of enthusiasm on the part of my fellow players.

Chamber music was written for the enjoyment of amateurs rather than for the display purposes of professionals. Some composers had a high opinion of good amateur players. Beethoven wrote some very difficult quartets to be played in the houses of his aristocratic patrons. They had to hire professionals to play these quartets as they should be played. But even the cold-blooded professionals were conquered by this music and became "friends."

String-quartet music is the pure essence of beautiful music. Composers of far more ambitious works have turned to it from time to time as a means of distilling the sort of divine beauty that big orchestra compositions, with their brasses, woodwinds, and percussion instruments, cannot duplicate. From the player's point of view, chamber music is uniquely rewarding and wonderfully satisfying. Personally, I went through a long evolution until I reached the present, final stage, when I play this music for the sake of music, not trying to prove something to myself or others. We play in congenial surroundings, and we are alone; no one's ego is injured if something goes wrong, as it does, inevitably. Technical mistakes are forgiven but not mistakes against the musicality. In certain blessed moments, when all goes well, I sense the exaltation that, I imagine, mountain climbers experience on silent peaks above the clouds, or perhaps skiers on a downhill ride through powder snow and March sun.

In earlier years, when I hadn't quite got to that stage, we often performed for relatives and friends. We might have played as many as five or six quartets, into the early morning hours, eating and drinking and playing yet another quartet, until the irate neighbors called the police. I hereby apologize to them, though where they are now they can no longer collect the lost hours of sleep. In those days I would sit down to play with people I'd just met and might never meet again. I wouldn't do it anymore; it's the wrong way of making "the music of friends." In Hollywood, I played with professional musicians who were highly respected members of studio orchestras and made more money than the members of celebrated symphony orchestras in Europe. They were superb technicians, but chamber-musically many of them had "gone Hollywood," talking more about their expensive instruments than about the music. Many owned Stradivaris and other rare old Italian instruments, and they listened to the gorgeous sounds of their precious fiddles instead of listening to their fellow players. In chamber music, one must play and listen at the same time.

Sometimes a world-famous soloist joined us for the evening. He played his part with bravura, as though it were a concerto accompanied by three other instruments. We admired the great virtuoso, but we weren't playing chamber music, which is an expression of musical democracy, an exercise in compromise, a display of human fellowship.

The virtuoso played a solo performance, the antithesis of chamber music.

A happy amateur string quartet is a greater miracle even than a happy marriage, since twice as many people are involved and each member has to get along with his three fellow players. A string quartet is a blend of different temperaments. If the four players are not on the same wavelength, musically or psychologically, the spell is broken. I remember a very able player who irritated us because he always pushed a little bit, driven by impatience, unable to discipline himself. There was the woman player who talked too much between the movements when we three were still "in the music." There was the second fiddler who would collapse in the fast movements. There was also the woman player, a very good musician, who brought along her husband; he read the newspaper, turning the pages during the *pianissimo* passages, smoked a cigar and afterwards told us what we'd done wrong. The violinist who always came with his wife, though she hated chamber music and fell asleep during the slow movements. And there were others who had to be dropped for one reason or another.

Now, at long last, the four of us lead a happy chamber-musical life in Vienna, where I spend several months of the year. My fellow players and I are all of the same age. Our backgrounds are different, but we have all grown up in the musical landscape of Viennese classicism. We always return to the great masterpieces of Haydn, Mozart, and Beethoven that form the gold reserve of string-quartet music. We are on the same level technically; no one outshines the others, and no one stays behind. We argue vehemently, but we always reach agreement, since we have the same musical tastes. We respect traditions and classical style and try to read the composer's intentions. Musical annotation is, at best, hopeful expectation. A Brahms adagio is different from a Beethoven adagio or from a Dvořák adagio. We listen to one another — while playing *and* afterwards. Everybody is asked to criticize.

We played together for years before we knew each others' first names. We called each other Herr So-and-So, in the polite Viennese manner. I knew the telephone numbers of my fellow players but not their wives and professions. At supper, after the music, we would talk about missed rests or the exaggerated tempi of a famous professional quartet that had performed the final movement "for effect," twice as fast as the composer prescribed it. The violist collects string-quartet recordings and tells us how the various celebrated quartets played the Beethoven we've just played. The cellist is an amateur musicologist. The second violinist knows Haydn's and Mozart's letters and always has some interesting quotes.

Chamber music comes naturally to the Viennese. The modern string quartet originated in Vienna, in 1755, when Joseph Haydn, then twenty-three, was invited to spend some time at the country house of Karl von Fürnberg in nearby Weinzierl, where he composed his opus 1 no. 1, now generally regarded as the world's first string quartet. He wrote eighty-four quartets altogether, in which he brought this noble art form from birth to maturity. Mozart wrote twenty-five and Beethoven seventeen. When Beethoven died in 1827, the classical period of chamber music died with him.

The Irish singer Michael Kelly, who performed in Vienna in the 1780's, mentions in his *Reminiscences* a quartet evening at which "the players were tolerable." The players were Joseph Haydn, first violin; the composer Karl Ditters von Dittersdorf, second violin; Wolfgang Amadeus Mozart, viola; and the Viennese musician Jan Baptist Wanhal, cello. Not surprisingly, quartet playing has always been a way of life in Vienna. Prior to the Hitler invasion (or "liberation," as some Austrians then called it), there were perhaps two hundred steady amateur quartets in this city. A great many chamber-music players who belonged to the Catholic and Jewish intelligentsia perished in the war and in the concentration camps. When I came to Vienna after the war, it was almost impossible to find an amateur quartet. Only in the past few years has chamber music made a slow comeback in the city where it originated. String-quartet playing emigrated, with many other things, to England and America.

After playing together every two weeks or so for the past ten years, I've learned a little about my fellow players. The second fiddler is a retired executive of the Vienna Streetcar Company, much envied because he has a pass entitling him to free rides on all municipal cars and buses. His first name is Felix, as in "Tu, felix Austria, nube," and he is a man of a felicitous disposition, a cheerful philosopher who takes long, solitary walks in the Wienerwald. The viola player is a retired civil servant, and at one time played with the Vienna Symphoniker, an excellent orchestra permanently frustrated by the overwhelming presence of the more famous Vienna Philharmoniker. The cellist is a dentist, handling the sturdy pegs of his instrument with the physical force he applies to the recalcitrant molars of his patients. He spends long vacations skiing in the mountains. When he isn't skiing, the viola player takes a cure against rheumatism, and when they are both in Vienna, I may be in America. Sometimes it is as hard to get the four of us together as if we were Messrs. Heifetz, Oistrakh, Primrose, and Piatigorsky.

All this makes our music evenings important private events. Every hour counts. Every time may be the last time. We don't make small talk. There are no listeners in the music room, though occasionally somebody may be in the next room. All lights are turned off except the lamp with the soft silk shade between our four stands. This is chamber-music playing as it should be — no distraction, no pretense, only the music and us. Years ago we played four quartets, but now we sometimes play only two, though with great dedication and deep intensity. In chamber music and lovemaking, depth of feeling eventually replaces physical exuberance. One of the two quartets is often a late Beethoven. Ernst Heimeran, a noted German publisher and chamber musician, called playing these quartets "a veritable devotional act of music." To be able to play these quartets, perhaps the greatest music ever written, and play them so that the music behind and between the notes emerges, is the supreme aim of all amateur players. My fellow players are uninterested in my income and the sale of my books, but they watch me carefully while I play the difficult first-violin runs in the opening movement of Beethoven's late opus 132. Late and very great.

Several years ago we noticed that we made no progress just playing through one quartet after another. Now we often use the first hour for study. It's hard work but pays rich dividends. We begin to hear hidden detail, and the structure of a work becomes transparently clear. After practicing the more difficult passages of a quartet, the whole piece sounds quite different afterwards. When we are exhausted, which happens often nowadays, we end on a cheerful note with Haydn or Mozart. They leave us with a sense of exhilaration. Haydn's and Mozart's music is God's gift to our age of anxiety. On Saint Anne's Day in 1799, an Italian musician walked into Saint Michael's Church in Vienna to listen to one of Haydn's masses. "I perspired during the Credo and was terribly sick but then my headache went away, and I felt cured mentally and physically," he wrote.

Haydn's and Mozart's therapeutic powers remain as strong as ever. I often feel low and depressed at the beginning of the evening. My work didn't go well, or it's the dreaded *Föhn* — the wind from the southwest that lowers the blood pressure and has a depressing effect on people. In Vienna the *Föhn* is used as an excuse for everything, from driving through a red light to beating one's wife.

The viola player, who has had a couple of heart attacks, announces that he won't be able to do more than the Beethoven tonight. Even the second violinist and the cellist, who represent outdoor life and the health cult, are under the weather, and I've had it. At that point I suggest "a little Mozart." (An unprecise manner of speaking; there is nothing little about Mozart.) After the first bars we feel rejuvenated, and our headaches go away at the end of the opening movement. I leave the explanation to the medical experts, but for me there is no doubt that "the music of friends" is healthy music, a remedy for body and spirit. By the time we sit down for supper, we are tired but happy.

Forty years after I played Beethoven's opus 18 no. 4 with Uncle Bruno's group for the first time in my life, I heard the dearly familiar music played by another group, and any similarity stopped after the first notes. They were the Budapest String Quartet, at that time perhaps the greatest of all professional quartets and certainly one of the greatest I ever heard. They were rehearsing at the Coolidge Auditorium of the Library of Congress in Washington, D.C., and I sat in the fourth row, an audience of one, making notes for a *New Yorker* profile.

Joseph Roisman, the first violinist, kept his jacket and tie on, sat down on the left side of the small stage and immediately began to practice scales. Across from him, Boris Kroyt, the violist, hung his coat over the back of his chair, loosened his tie, and began to tune his viola, drawing long tones from the lower strings, enjoying the deep, mellow sound. At the Library of Congress, the Budapest players were privileged to perform on the instruments given to the Library by Mrs. Gertrude Clarke Whittall, who also established a million-dollar foundation for their preservation and use: three violins, a viola, and a cello, all made by Antonio Stradivari, and five bows made by François Tourte of Paris, the Stradivari of the bowmakers. The Strads must never leave the Library. That afternoon Roisman played on the Ward Stradivari, made in 1700, and Alexander Schneider, the second violinist, chose the famous Betts, made in 1704. Kroyt played on the Cassavetti viola, and the cellist, Mischa Schneider, on the Castelbarco cello.

Mischa Schneider, wearing an open-neck shirt, carefully adjusted the pegs of his beautiful instrument. Alexander, his brother, better known as Sascha, in a white shirt, suspenders, and tie, wandered all over the stage, with the violin under his chin, playing the beginning of Bach's E-major Partita and then switching abruptly to a gypsy air.

"You are going to have the treat of your life," he announced to me from the stage. "There are two outfits in this country that never let you down. The Budapest and American Tel and Tel." He played a number of brilliant *arpeggio* passages. "Listen to that fiddle! Aren't the overtones terrific?"

"All right, gentlemen," Roisman, always the gentleman, said mildly. "Let's get on with the Beethoven." A few seconds later he began with the upbeat, an open-string quarter-note G, and I was back again in Uncle Bruno's music room.

Most amateurs need a while "to play themselves in," but the Budapest was completely integrated from the very beginning, and the qualities were all there that have made it famous — the warm tone and incisive bowing, the rhythm and dynamics, the temperament and spontaneity, the balanced sound and the crystalline clarity. They were enjoying the music and they conveyed their enjoyment to me. It occurred to me that writing for *The New Yorker* was a kingly profession: how many kings or ex-kings could afford to have the Budapest play for them alone their favorite string quartet?

Technically, it was a brilliant performance that left me stunned and frustrated. When they played a sudden *forte piano*, all four men reduced their bow pressure at the same instant. After Roisman had brought off a magnificent semiquaver passage, Mischa Schneider looked up at him approvingly, and Alexander shouted, "Bravo, Joe!" Kroyt tapped his right foot (he made me think of our violist who does it too), and cocked his ear toward the viola. After the letter L, where the second violin carries the theme (a famous trap for inattentive second fiddlers), Alexander Schneider jumped up from his chair, held his violin high in the air, and played the passage with exaggerated schmaltz, like a street fiddler in Naples. Kroyt, the perfect partner, stopped playing and started singing a Russian song, sounding a little, but only a little, like the late Feodor Chaliapin. Mischa Schneider performed a number of stupendous triads on his cello that would have much impressed coffeehouse audiences in his native Vilna. Only Roisman went on quietly, untouched by the sudden pandemonium around him. I wondered what Uncle Bruno would have done to us if we had dared to create such bedlam. Alexander Schneider laughed so hard that I began to fear he might drop the Betts.

"Joe, you're killing me," he said.

"Are we rehearsing or aren't we?" Roisman inquired in a sad voice.

"All right," said Mischa Schneider. "Once more, nine bars before M."

They started again.

"You are not together, gentlemen," Mischa told the violins. "Nine bars before M."

For a while, things went smoothly, until the middle of the second movement, when Mischa Schneider called, "More lightly, please, just touch it." They were able to play a difficult passage, carry on a running conversation, and point out a musical accent in the score simultaneously. Toward the end of the movement, Alexander Schneider, winking at me, abruptly slid into "O Sole Mio." Kroyt at once chimed in with the second Kreutzer etude (the theme made famous by Jack Benny on the radio), and Mischa Schneider plucked the strings of his cello. At that point, even Roisman broke down and began playing his fiddle between his knees, like a cello. Walter Trampler, the noted violist, who would later play Mozart's G-minor quintet with them, had slipped into the seat next to me.

"You know, they are really smart," he said. "They've learned that monotony is the worst enemy of a quartet rehearsal. Anything to beat monotony. They have fun and they argue about musical matters, but they are beyond bitter, personal fights. They have learned to compromise. There is never that awful strain that has broken up so many groups. I know no other group whose personalities merge so completely and happily."

They had resumed playing. Trampler sighed deeply. "They are incredible," he said. "You would think they all exhale in the same rhythm." He nodded and said, as to himself, "Yes, that's it. They do exhale their phrases together."

On the stage, a violent argument, in Russian and German, had broken out between Kroyt and Mischa Schneider over an esoteric musical question in the last movement. They shouted, while Alexander Schneider called out, *"Messieurs, faites vos jeux,"* and after a while Roisman said, in his gentle voice, "Gentlemen, *please!"* and almost immediately the argument faded away and they played the last movement as I'd never heard it before.

"Haydn would have liked them," Trampler said.

"Yes," I said. "And Mozart would have liked them. And Beethoven, and you know how gloomy *he* could be." Even Uncle Bruno would have liked them.

Gray and Other Eminences

IN MY YOUTHFUL MUSICAL DAYS in Ostrava, when I wasn't invited to play in Uncle Bruno's quartet, I played sonatas for violin and piano with Sigi Geminder. He'd wanted to be a pianist but ended up as a dentist. Ostrava was full of would-be musicians who did something else.

Everybody knew the Geminder boys. Sigi, the younger one, was blond, tall and friendly, with horn-rimmed glasses; everybody liked him. Fritz, called "Cip," was dark, stooped, an introvert. His uncombed hair always fell onto his forehead, which gave him the air of a profound thinker. Even in subzero weather he would walk bareheaded through the streets, his body slightly hunched forward, hands in his pockets, a book under his elbow. He rarely bothered to acknowledge other people's greetings. We were not sure whether he was a bore or an interesting eccentric. He had a supercilious air that made us feel he knew more than the rest of us, and he probably did. He was a soccer player. This has perhaps colored my relationship to the Geminder brothers. I used to play music *with* Sigi, but on the field I would often play soccer *against* Fritz.

At least twice a week I would gather my fiddle and a folding stand, and walk over to the Geminder apartment near Nádražní Třída. The boys' mother had died some years back, and their home lacked a warm touch. There were Persian rugs, ornate curtains, embroidered table-cloths. On the mahogany buffet stood china figures, typical parapher-nalia of local middle-class elegance; but there were no flowers in the vases, and there were always dust covers on the armchairs. You weren't supposed to sit in these chairs.

I would put up my folding stand next to the Bechstein piano. Sigi and I were alone. Father Geminder, a kindly, bald-headed man who owned a wholesale grocery business, preferred to spend his evenings at the Café Royal playing *Tarock* with other prosperous businessmen. For a couple of hours we were happily immersed in the music of Mozart, Beethoven, Brahms. Around ten o'clock, Fritz would come in and slump down, still in his topcoat, and immediately the happy atmosphere was gone. There was a chill in the room. Once we tried to impress Fritz with the last movement of Beethoven's *Kreutzer* Sonata, our pièce de résistance, but he got up in the middle and went into his room. Sigi looked crestfallen. He admired his older brother. He said Fritz was always reading: Dostoevski, Kafka, Rilke, Freud, Marx.

"He not only reads these books, he understands them," Sigi said. "He understands *everything*." Many of my schoolmates agreed with him. Sometimes Fritz started an argument in school and would debate his point with brilliant dialectics that delighted us and confused our pompous, unpopular teachers. On such occasions, I admired him and almost came to like him.

During the next few years, I saw Fritz occasionally in Ostrava and in Prague. He was often surrounded by groups of younger boys, quite a few of them coming from wealthy bourgeois families, with unkempt hair and revolutionary leanings. He was said to study Russian, which was highly unorthodox then, so he could read the writings of Lenin in the original. He had become a member of the Czechoslovak Communist party back in 1921, read the party paper *Rudé Pravo*, and despised the bourgeois *Prager Tagblatt* for which I wrote and to which his father subscribed. It was useless to get into political arguments with him. He was already trained to win every argument — by sophistry, distortion, and dialectics. Once, in exasperation, I asked him why he, a nonproletarian, was such an ardent Communist.

"Because I believe in the Communist philosophy," he said.

In 1933, he went to Moscow. There were rumors in Prague that he'd been selected to study at the Lenin School, where outstanding members of the Communist International (Comintern) were being trained. When I went back to Ostrava to visit my mother, I would play sonatas with Sigi, who was doing all right as a dentist. We never talked about Fritz anymore.

I was in Prague in the spring of 1945, during the intoxicating days following the rising of the people when the pictures of Beneš, Churchill, Roosevelt, and Stalin were displayed everywhere. When I returned to Prague two years later, the city seemed changed. In the national election of 1946, the Communists had polled thirty-eight percent of the popular vote, emerging as the strongest party, winning 114 out of 300 seats in Parliament. Beneš was still president and Jan Masaryk his foreign minister, but now the only pictures I saw prominently displayed were of Stalin and Klement Gottwald, the Communist Prime Minister. My homeland had become a Communist satellite. Quite legally too, a fact that is often ignored. The former stock exchange was now the new Parliament building. There was no need for the stock exchange, since all large enterprises had been nationalized. The former Parliament at the Rudolfinum was now used again as a concert hall, as before. It was there that I'd had a short, not particularly distinguished career in the early 1930's as parliamentary secretary to the two deputies of the tiny Jewish party. Czechoslovakia was the only country in Europe that had such a party.

We were the smallest among the seventeen political parties, but our influence far surpassed our numerical strength, since the Jewish party was affiliated with the powerful, large Social-Democrat party. We delivered relatively few votes, but one of our deputies, Dr. Angelo Goldstein, a noted Prague lawyer, enjoyed great personal prestige in the Lower Chamber, and I had direct access to the Social-Democrat members of the government. Dr. Goldstein's theory was that the strength of the Jewish party was based on ethics and ideals, rather than on votes and deals. President Masaryk, and after him President Beneš, fully agreed with this lofty political program. For a while I also helped to edit the Jewish party's weekly newspaper in Prague, *Selbstwehr* (*Self-Defense*). Its editor-in-chief was Dr. Felix Weltsch, the philosopher, one of the closest friends of Franz Kafka and Max Brod. His philosophical editorials were often quoted by the most influential Czech papers in Prague. Having since learned a few things about the dirty game of politics, I'm pleased at the thought that my own short excursion into the power game was based on philosophy and ethics rather than corruption and patronage.

In 1947, when Czechoslovakia had become a member of the Communist Bloc, the Jewish party was already part of history. The Communist party headquarters had been installed in the large, modernistic building of the former Czech Eskompte Bank, on Příkopy, next to the historical Prašna Brana (Powder Tower). Bankers were out, Marxists were in. The citadel of capitalism had become the citadel of Communism. Large black Tatra automobiles, symbols of power, were parked in front of the former bank building. And one of the largest limousines was assigned to "Cip" Geminder.

It was a fantastic story, but there was no doubt about it. I heard rumors in Prague that Premier Gottwald was "taking orders" from Bedřich (the Czech name for Fritz) Geminder. He was said to be the country's Gray Eminence. I carefully traced the facts, which were hard to get, since most people seemed afraid to mention Geminder's name.

After graduating from the Lenin School in Moscow, Geminder had been transferred to the Communist International, then the most important instrument of worldwide Communist expansion. During the Second World War, when the Comintern was formally dissolved, to appease the Western Allies, its machinery was incorporated in the International Section of the Secretariat of the All-Union Communist (Bolshevik) party. While working for the Comintern, Geminder used the pseudonym Bedřich Vltavský. ("Vltava" is the Czech word for Moldau; Vltavsky means "the man from the Moldau.")

During the Battle of Stalingrad, he was said to have distinguished himself as leader of a parachutist youth brigade, and was decorated for bravery. In Moscow, he attracted the attention of Georgi Malenkov, who was to become, briefly, Stalin's successor. Malenkov saw to it that Geminder was secretly trained to become the Kremlin's watchdog in Prague. His position in the Czechoslovak Communist party was anomalous and bewildered old party regulars. He was a member of neither the Central Committee nor of the elected party Presidium, but he took part in the top-secret meetings of both the Central Committee and the Presidium. During the party's general sessions, Geminder sat on the platform among the mighty ones. An editor of *Rudé Pravo*, whom I'd known for many years in Prague, confided to me that of all party leaders, only Gottwald and Geminder had direct access to the Kremlin. Gottwald was said to be the front man, but Geminder was running the show.

"We have orders not to print his picture in our paper," the editor said. I thought he looked slightly uncomfortable.

The nine-nation Communist Information Bureau (Cominform) was revived in 1947. Geminder became one of its master architects and Czechoslovakia's top delegate. He was also editor-in-chief of the Cominform journal, "For a Lasting Peace — For the People's Democracy," printed in Bucharest. In November, 1949, he co-authored the Cominform's call for the overthrow of Tito, and urged non-Communists to get behind the Communist "peace offensive," regardless of their political and religious affiliations.

The Kremlin's choice of Fritz Geminder from Ostrava was characteristically realistic. Gottwald had always been a Czech first and a Communist second; an ex-carpenter and proletarian, he at one time was quite popular with the masses in Czechoslovakia. Geminder, on the other hand, was Jewish, German-educated, of middle-class background, widely hated inside and outside the party. Anti-Semitism, not much of a problem during the Masaryk and Beneš regimes, had been successfully fomented during the Nazi occupation and lingered on ever since, though very few Jews had survived in the country. Unlike Gottwald, the Czech-trained Communist, Geminder was the typical Moscow-trained internationalist, a man without a homeland, whose allegiance and loyalty was solely to the party. His wife, Irene Falcone, was the former secretary of Dolores Ibarruri, Spain's famous "La Pasionaria." Geminder's official title was "Chief of the International Section of the Secretariat of the Central Committee of the Czechoslovak Communist Party." It was his job to make sure that the policies of the Czechoslovak Communist party were tied in with Moscow's interests. He was said to watch Rudolf Slanský, the party's general secretary. Originally close friends, Slanský and Geminder later became hostile to each other. I was told that Gottwald "was afraid of Geminder," who read the president's courier correspondence with all foreign countries.

I went to see "Cip" one morning early in 1948 at the Communist headquarters building on Prikopy. It was the era of dreary corridors and men wearing two-day beards and unpressed suits; only big shots could afford to wear ties. I had written to him requesting "a short, private meeting." I wouldn't attempt to discuss politics with him. I had never been able to outargue him in our student days. It was too late now. I wanted to find out what happened to Sigi, my piano partner.

I was taken into a large, bare waiting room on the second floor, and there I had a shock. Alexej Čepička, then the Minister of Justice (and also the son-in-law of President Gottwald), came out of Geminder's office. After a while the door was opened again, and this time Antonín Zápotocký came out of the office. He was then head of URO, the central trade-union organization, and after Gottwald's death became his successor as president.

I'd found it hard to believe the preposterous story of Fritz Geminder's rise to power in the Communist hierarchy, but now I was convinced. He *had* to be Czechoslovakia's Gray Eminence, if two powerful men, Čepička and Zápotocký, went to see him.

Geminder worked in a large, comfortable office. I remember pictures of Stalin and Gottwald, three telephones on his desk, books on the wall. He greeted me, cool and unsmiling, and this time he spoke Czech; in Ostrava we'd spoken German. His hair still fell onto his forehead, but he wasn't hunched forward anymore. His voice was soft but confident. He asked me where I'd been during the war. When I said, "In the American army," he nodded, showing no expression. He skillfully parried my questions. He'd been "away" for many years. Now he was doing a job, "just like everybody else — like the miners and workers and peasants in our country." Our talk went nowhere. I asked about Sigi. He said Sigi and his wife had gone to South America. The phone rang, and somebody came for me. We didn't shake hands. I was escorted out of the building.

In June, 1950, General Heliodor Pika, former deputy chief of staff of the Czechoslovak army, was executed in Prague's Pankrác Prison for "high treason." It was said that Gottwald had wanted to commute the sentence to life imprisonment, but Geminder had ruled that Pika must die.

Fourteen months later, a speaker at the Czechoslovak Youth Organization Conference in Prague referred to Geminder as a "traitor." On September 7, 1951, it was reported that Rudolf Slanský had been removed as the party's general secretary. On November 20, 1952, Slanský, Geminder, former Foreign Minister Vlado Clementis, and eleven other Communist leaders went on trial in Prague in the greatest Communist purge since the Moscow trials of 1936.

During the trial, Prague Radio every evening broadcast a commentary, interspersed with playbacks of tape recordings from the courtroom, where no Western correspondents were admitted. I listened to the broadcasts in Vienna, one hundred and twenty-five miles away.

Geminder was accused, among other things, of "high treason, espionage, sabotage, military treason, Trotskyism, Titoism, Zionism, and Jewish bourgeois nationalism." During the trial, I heard his voice several times. It was an expressionless voice, almost a dead voice. He made an abject confession. At one point he said, "I have never in my life been a true Communist." After a seven-day trial, eleven of the accused men were sentenced to die on the gallows. When Geminder was asked by the chairman of the Prague State Court whether he wanted to appeal the death sentence, he renounced his right to appeal. On December 3, 1952, Radio Prague announced at noon that "eleven former Communist leaders were executed earlier in the morning."

Sixteen years later, during the "Prague Spring" of 1968, after Alexander Dubček became head of the Czechoslovak Communist party and the Stalinists were removed from power, the eleven dead men were rehabilitated. Will they remain rehabilitated now that Dubček is gone, and, with him, his nation's hope for a better, more decent life?

In my sixth year at the *Gymnasium* (I was sixteen), I took part in a performance of Moritz Moszkowski's Spanish Dances no. 2 and no. 3, as my contribution to a show — the *Akademie* — that the student body put up at the end of the school year. The show was made up of various forms of entertainment, from classical German drama to dramatic feats of agility. The audience consisted of the families and friends of the performers who wouldn't have missed it for anything — and the families and friends of nonperformers who couldn't get out of it because each student had to sell five tickets. There was jealousy among the parents of performers, and bitterness among the parents of nonperformers. The *Akademie* invariably marked the end of many a beautiful friendship.

That year, there was a galaxy of actors, pantomimists, amateur magicians, and acrobats at the *Gymnasium*, and a scarcity of musicians. Only three of us played instruments that were acceptable to the school principal, a gruff old man with a white walrus mustache. Leopold Ludwig, one class below, played the piano; Fritz Pressburger and I played the violin. There were a couple of saxophonists, and one boy played the xylophone passably, but the Herr Direktor ruled that their instruments were fit only for nightclubs and not for the *Akademie*, which took place at eleven o'clock in the morning.

Unfortunately, the two-violins-and-piano combination has been neglected by many composers. We were bursting with temerity, and wanted to take on Bach's Double Concerto in D minor for two violins. I also suggested Mozart's Sinfonia Concertante, for violin, viola, and the piano, and volunteered to play the viola part. The year before, we had performed the beautiful Mozart work with Uncle Bruno and Aunt Grete for the seventieth birthday of my maternal grandmother. The family respectfully called her "the Empress" because of her dignity and the fact that she'd brought up thirteen children, only three less than the Empress Maria Theresa.

The Sinfonia Concertante was a great success with *our* Empress, though some of my uncles got restless and said it had been "nice but too long," not much of a compliment. Now the principal ruled that both the Bach and the Mozart were "too long" for the *Akademie*. Eleven minutes was allotted to the musical part of the program, just enough time to play the two Moszkowski dances. The principal taught Greek and believed in Spartan discipline.

Our rehearsals, held in Pressburger's home in the industrial suburb of Vitkovice, were chaotic affairs. Ludwig had a bad temper and a pianist's contempt for off-pitch violin playing. And there was physical violence on the part of Pressburger's younger brother Hansi, who hated music, off pitch or on. Once he attacked Ludwig's left shinbone with an andiron, and our pianist had to be bandaged up by the Pressburgers' father, a prominent physician. Ludwig's left shinbone remained a standing joke between us until one afternoon in postwar Berlin, in 1948, when Ludwig's shepherd dog Ajax attacked my right shinbone, and I had to be bandaged. Thereafter the joke was on the other shinbone.

There is a widespread belief among artists that bad rehearsals are always followed by a fine performance. This wasn't true in our case, perhaps because we weren't artists. Everything went wrong. Ours was the last act before the grand finale, which was a full-scale production of *Wallenstein's Lager*, by Friedrich Schiller. Four of Wallenstein's sturdiest warriors, all members of the class soccer team, had been assigned to push Ludwig's piano onstage, but when the time came, they were nowhere to be found. We had to go into the Moszkowski with Ludwig playing behind the scenes, while Pressburger and I fiddled forlornly in the middle of Schiller's martial landscape that had already been set up for Wallenstein's mercenaries.

In the wings, the mercenaries were spouting their lines and shuffling around, which drowned out our lovely *pianissimo*. Once a soldier got lost among the ramparts and stumbled out onto the stage. The audience started to giggle, and I heard my mother's jingling bracelets and knew that she was getting nervous. So was I. In its combination of sad music and low comedy, our performance had something in common with Richard Strauss's *Ariadne auf Naxos*. Somehow we got through the Spanish Dances, but by that time they sounded slightly Hungarian. It wasn't quite fair to Moszkowski, a German from Breslau with a Polish name, who died in Paris. There was less than a scattering of applause as we walked dejectedly offstage, and no one asked for an encore. Backstage, Ludwig had one of his tantrums, complaining that we'd lost contact in the Dance no. 3. The school principal didn't improve matters when he opened the cover of his large, round locomotive-engineer's watch and said, "Well done but half a minute too long!" The only cheerful comment was added by Uncle Bruno, who said, "Anyway, all three of you finished at the same time."

Ludwig still remembers that criticism as the most succinct he has ever received, and he has received a vast amount of professional criticism in the past forty years. He is *Generalmusikdirektor* of the State Opera in Hamburg, and conducts at the Vienna State Opera and in San Francisco.

He was an authentic *Wunderkind*, and knew it. He could play the *Fledermaus* waltz backward, and during the secret expeditions we used to make to the local dives, he might take over the piano, long after midnight, and amuse the customers by playing the *Aida* march with his left hand and Vincent Youmans's *Hallelujah!* with his right. He would clink a spoon against his beer glass and announce that the note was F-flat, or C-sharp, or whatever; he had absolutely perfect pitch.

As a boy, Ludwig often used to come to our house to play sonatas with me. This used to disturb my mother, because she was afraid that Ludwig would ruin the piano, which had been borrowed from Franzl Fried, our tenant. Two uprights in our town had already broken down under Ludwig's furioso sweep. He was tall and undernourished, with a mane of long blond hair, and someone had told him that with his large mouth and broad nose he bore a distinct resemblance to the young Ludwig van Beethoven. Our Ludwig tried to stress this by frowning and letting the corners of his mouth sag.

In our town it was against the law to make "unnecessary noise" after ten o'clock in the evening, but when Ludwig and I started playing, we often forgot all about the curfew. Around eleven we would be joined by Franzl, a fine pianist, whose specialty was to perform *Hallelujah!* in the style of Richard Wagner. At eleven o'clock one night, Frau Pick, a neighbor of ours, telephoned to ask us to stop the racket. Ludwig and Franzl responded by performing a deafening composition of their own, unrehearsed, four-handed. Before they had finished, the doorbell rang and a policeman came in. My mother quickly produced a bottle of *slivovitz*, an awful liquid made by Uncle Siegfried, the owner of a grocery and liquor store. Ludwig glided into a medley of Czech folk songs, played *pianissimo*. The policeman stayed and enjoyed the music until the bottle was empty.

At the *Gymnasium*, Ludwig, a Catholic, played the organ in the Catholic chapel at High Mass on Sunday morning. He also conducted the chapel's orchestra, consisting of an extremely nearsighted flutist, a cellist who knew only three positions, and of Pressburger and me, though this meant crossing denominational lines. Somehow Ludwig blended the five of us into a seraphic musical body, and our lugubrious presentation of the Bach-Gounod *Ave Maria* moved many worshippers to tears. One Sunday, Uncle Bruno attended the High Mass so he could listen to our performance. He created a minor disturbance when he refused to take off his hat because he was momentarily confused and thought he was in an orthodox synagogue. My mother wasn't surprised. "What can you expect from Bruno, who confuses toilet paper with onionskin?" she said.

Even in the chapel, Ludwig was not above a display of artistic temperament. Once, after an argument with Father Štancl, the instructor in Catholic religion, who celebrated the High Mass, Ludwig inserted a strain or two from Irving Berlin into the ecclesiastical music. Another time, he accompanied a Bach fugue with jazz rhythms, proving his musical theory that there was deep affinity between Bach and jazz. The congregation became restless, and the members of the orchestra were convulsed.

Once I accompanied Ludwig to the Reiss Bar, a local nightclub of doubtful reputation, where he performed from midnight to two A.M.

The establishment was off limits to students because it employed hostesses, among them a certain Ria-Rita who was popular among certain members of our class soccer team. That night Ludwig was found out by our gymnastics teacher, an unmusical man, who later explained that he'd dropped in only to make sure that no students were there. Ria-Rita knew better, and there was a scandal. Ludwig was expelled from school. He was overjoyed. At last, he said, he could go to Vienna and devote all his time to music. But his piano teacher, the great virtuoso Emil Paur, who was living in retirement in the nearby town of Mistek and gave Ludwig free lessons, took a different view of the matter. He insisted that Ludwig must first graduate from the *Gymnasium*, and he spoke to the principal, pointing out that the boy had turned his earnings over to his mother. Ludwig, to his disgust, was reinstated.

The incident came to the attention of Adolf Sonnenschein, the general manager of the Vitkovice Iron Works (then controlled by the Rothschilds in Vienna) who was known as "the General," for his word was law in Vitkovice. (At the Hamburg State Opera, *Generalmusikdirektor* Ludwig is now addressed as "General.") Sonnenschein had been a poor boy himself, and he knew that Ludwig's mother, a widow, was employed at the iron works as a telephone operator. Sonnenschein summoned Ludwig and asked him to give a piano recital in the dining room (which was also used as ballroom) of the Vitkovice Works Hotel, a depressing red-brick structure.

A few hours before the recital began, word reached the General that the hall wasn't sold out, so he sent word to his *Direktoren, Oberinspektoren, Inspektoren,* and the lower chains of management to show up exactly at seven-fifteen with their wives, and no excuse. Ludwig's classmates acted as ushers and checkroom attendants. I remained in the rear of the hall, organizing a claque. It was my first effort in a field in which I later became a success, when I was appointed as assistant to Joseph Schostal, the famous claque chef of the Vienna State Opera.

(A few years ago, *Who's Who in Music*, published by Burke's Peerage, Ltd, in London, notified me that I had been selected as a subject for a biography, and sent me a questionnaire. Among "honors and titles," I wrote, perhaps whimsically but truthfully, "Assistant Claque Chef, Vienna State Opera," and "Orchestra Leader, S.S. *Ile de France.*" The editors printed my honors and titles.)

Owing to the General's last-minute orders, our friend Otto Kriso, in charge of the box office, sold far more tickets than there were seats. Kriso later became a famous laryngologist in Vienna, where he treated the State Opera's most precious voices. The Ludwig recital was remembered locally for many years as "the night when even Frau Direktoren had to be content with standing room." Kriso spent much of the money on the purchase of an expensive death mask of Ludwig van Beethoven. At the end of the concert he carried it in and placed it on the piano, prompting many people to comment on the resemblance of the two Ludwigs.

Sonnenschein walked out on the stage, pumped Ludwig's hand, and slipped him several bills — enough, it turned out, to support Ludwig and his mother for a year. Then, with a stern glance at the audience, the General started to clap. His subordinates and their wives dutifully joined in, completely ruining my earlier strategy for "artistic" applause. They just clapped their hands in a thoroughly inartistic manner. When I told the story later to claque chef Schostal in Vienna, he said disgustedly, "That happens when applause is left in the hands of general managers."

In Vienna, after our graduation from the *Gymnasium,* I saw Ludwig often at night in the fourth gallery of the State Opera, where he and Kriso and I were active members of the claque. Even in our group, which enjoyed a city-wide reputation for artistic discrimination and audible enthusiasm, Ludwig was outstanding for his sheer exuberance. Applauding an opera was an exacting art then — not the production of vulgar noises at the wrong moment, often for the wrong singer, that it is nowadays. We had our cues, just as the singers had, and we would never have thought of breaking into applause when we weren't scheduled to. We wouldn't have applauded mere scenery, which is, I believe, a deplorable invention of matinee audiences at the Metropolitan Opera that has now spread to the other side of the ocean. We never applauded a singer making an entrance. Applause, as the Romans knew, is praise to be given *after* the performance. Schostal could be bought, but he could not be corrupted. If one of our "clients" didn't sing well, there would be no applause, even though the client had paid for it in advance, and the money would (or would not) be returned. We never committed the *claqueur*'s unpardonable crime — to start applause which is not taken up by the public and fizzles out ignominiously.

Many of us followed the performance with piano scores (all claque members had to prove they were able to read scores), but a piano score wasn't enough for Poldi Ludwig. He used to lug up the full orchestral score, sit down on the floor under one of the exit lights, and conduct an imaginary orchestra and cast with a baton that had been sandpapered by Kriso during a course in anatomy. The balance of his baton was even then as important to Ludwig as the balance of a violin bow is to a fiddler.

He showed scant respect for the State Opera in his conducting up there in the fourth gallery. He went along at his own tempo, which was seldom that of the other conductor, down in the pit. One evening, Richard Strauss conducted the Prelude to *Tristan und Isolde* too swiftly for Ludwig's taste, and Ludwig and his imaginary orchestra fell far behind. On other occasions, the performance was too slow for him, and he would finish triumphantly while the orchestra was still playing. Ludwig's conducting irritated some people in the fourth gallery — it was as if the sound track of a film were running a good bit ahead of or behind the action on the screen. But when anyone complained, Ludwig would point to the pit and retort that someday he would be "down there," conducting opera as opera should be conducted. Nobody considered these words to be prophetic.

In 1927, I left Vienna. During the next few years I played the violin in dives and aboard ships, and I was just as glad that my friends in Vienna didn't know how low I had fallen. Though there were brief moments of glory: on the *Ile de France* I once played the Bach Double Concerto with Jacques Thibaud, the great French violinist — the same concerto that the *Gymnasium* principal had not permitted us to play at the *Akademie.* After the fall of 1938, when my wife and I went to America, I lost touch with my friends in Europe, and then came the Second World War. In one of my mother's last letters to me (it was transmitted by the International Red Cross), she wrote that Ludwig had become First Conductor of the Vienna State Opera. So he'd made it after all, I thought, and I was pleased and not surprised. He was now sitting "down there," on the seat once occupied by Gustav Mahler, Franz Schalk, Richard Strauss, and was probably convinced that his *Tristan* was the best of all.

Two weeks after V-E Day, when I happened to be in Prague again, this time as an American soldier, I went to visit some friends. We turned on the radio at the moment when an announcer was saying that a concert just broadcast from Berlin had been conducted by Leopold Ludwig. There was a lot of "artistic" applause, and I regretted that we had not tuned in earlier. The following year, in Vienna, I met Otto Kriso. He told me that Ludwig, who was now married and *Generalmusikdirektor* in Hamburg, had been quite successful in Vienna but also remained the enfant terrible. He offended the musical bureaucrats and showed little respect for the sacrosanct members of the Vienna Philharmonic. He got into trouble with the Gestapo, when they found out that he was listening to the BBC London. Local Wagnerians were enraged when it became known that after conducting *Tristan* he would go to the nearby Moulin Rouge, a nightclub, or drive out to the gambling casino in Baden. (In Vienna, conducting *Tristan* is almost like celebrating a High Mass, but of course I remembered what Ludwig had done back home during the High Mass.) His financial affairs had been chaotic.

I'd seen him briefly in Berlin after the war though the intermezzo was marred by his shepherd dog's attack on my shinbone, but one day in the spring of 1954, I happened to drive through Hamburg, and then I read that he would conduct a *Meistersinger* performance that night. I called him and he was overjoyed, not stuffy at all, as one would expect a *Generalmusikdirektor* to be. He came to visit me prior to the performance, accompanied by an Irish setter called Lord. He waved his arms as though conducting "The Ride of the Valkyries," and laughed uproariously, and we embraced each other. We talked and talked, and he was almost late for his performance; there were so many things to talk about, mostly sad ones.

Later, I wrote an article about Ludwig which began with our *Akademie* and ended with *Die Meistersinger*, and Shawn published it as a profile in *The New Yorker*. There followed a cooling-off period in our relations, because some humorless citizens in Germany and elsewhere indicated to Ludwig and his wife that I hadn't written a very respectful story about the *Herr Generalmusikdirektor*. In Germany, and nowadays almost everywhere, all sorts of generals are considered sacrosanct, even musical generals. Today, many years later, Ludwig tells me that people still talk to him about the profile. They love it.

When he conducted at the San Francisco Opera, and the company went down for a few performances to Los Angeles, Ludwig paid a visit to Professor Fritz Landau, who was his and my violin teacher during our final years at the *Gymnasium* in Ostrava. Landau, a pupil of the great Otakar Ševčík in Pisek, was my last and best teacher, and he convinced me that if I really wanted always to love music, I should play the violin for pleasure and not professionally.

"In this business," he once told me, "nearly everybody hopes to become a new Kreisler, a new Heifetz, and then people wind up on the last stand of the second-violin section of a minor orchestra. They must play under conductors they don't respect. They must work so hard that the music comes out of their ears. I know quite a few who don't love music anymore, though they play it every day. This doesn't happen to a dilettante who loves music for the sake of music. Of course, there are exceptions — like Ludwig. They are different."

I followed Professor Landau's advice, God bless him. After living with my violins for half a century, I still love music.

My Connecticut Stradivari

LIKE MOST PEOPLE WHO PLAY the violin, I've always wanted to own a rare old Italian fiddle. Not everybody driving a car wants a Rolls-Royce or a Ferrari; I wouldn't take either one if you gave them to me. I know a lovely woman of impeccable taste who is not attracted by the cold fire of fine diamonds.

A violin is different. You don't hang it up on the wall. You can't show off with it as with a race horse, a Rolls, a Renoir, a yacht. You keep the violin in its case, and you don't open the case when you expect guests, as some people open their Steinway. A great violin is a powerful antistatus symbol, the extension of your voice and breath, almost a part of you, a very intimate possession. It is the only work of art that is truly appreciated only by one who practices the art. One can become a noted collector of paintings and sculpture without being a painter or sculptor, but to fully enjoy a rare old violin one has to be a violinist. A fiddle is strange and wonderful, not quite alive but not inanimate either. When I play my Stradivari, it sings out as though it were alive. To me, of course, it *is* alive.

There are great diamonds and great paintings all over the world, and new diamonds and paintings are created all the time, some of them perhaps great. But the number of great old Italian instruments is limited and shrinking. There are believed to be about two thousand of them, and perhaps there are three thousand more that are important though not great. (Half of them are now in the United States.) Their number decreases every year. Wars, catastrophes, accidents create irreplaceable losses. A great many string players will dream of an old Italian instrument but will never own one.

Some will be content with a good modern instrument. They claim that the fame of the great old Italian violins is a delusion. But the fact is that the golden period of violin making lasted only some two hundred years, and that the greatest experts have since tried to reproduce such instruments and have failed. The world's finest string instruments were made by less than a score of great masters, many of them in Cremona, a sleepy provincial town on the left bank of the River Po, with beautiful churches, palaces, squares. The largest square was the Piazza San Domenico, and nearby was the Contrada dei Coltellai, with a block of houses where generations of the great masters lived: the rich Amatis in their little palace, the run-down home of Guarneri del Gesù, the large houses of Antonio Stradivari and Carlo Bergonzi, the smaller ones of Francesco Rugeri and Lorenzo Storioni. Most of the world's great instruments come from Cremona; some come from Venice, Milan, Rome, Naples, the Tyrol.

The violin didn't develop gradually like other art works — there exist no "primitive" violins — but emerged almost from the very beginning in its final perfect form, a masterpiece of the laws of physics, acoustics, chemistry. We don't really know who invented it.

In the old days, the ratio between an artist's earnings and the price of a fine violin was in the artist's favor. In the summer of 1832, Nicolò Paganini earned eight thousand pounds in ten weeks for a series of fourteen concerts in London's Covent Garden — almost three thousand dollars, tax free, a concert. Yet he paid the equivalent of only a thousand dollars for his famous viola, made by Stradivari in 1731, the viola that led Hector Berlioz to compose *Harold in Italy*. "Paganini came to me and said, 'I have a marvellous viola, an admirable Stradivari, and I wish to play it in public but I have no music ad hoc. Will you write a solo piece for me? You are the only one I can trust for such a work.' " But after the solo piece was written, Paganini was displeased with it "because it contained too many rests for the viola." Today the Paganini viola would be worth close to a hundred thousand dollars.

Only successful artists and well-to-do collectors can now afford the greatest instruments. A violin should be played with love, or not at all. Some have been ruined by people who don't know better. The late Emil Herrmann, a great dealer-expert, used to say that the owners of fine instruments were merely trustees for future generations, whose owner-ship was temporary and whose duty it was to preserve their instruments for posterity. He thought the world was indebted to collectors for the preservation of great instruments. If all of them had been only in the hands of professionals, there would now be fewer of them. Some great artists — notably Heifetz, Menuhin, Milstein, Francescatti — are known to keep their violins in perfect condition; they clean them carefully and put them to bed after using them. But others expose them unnecessarily to the rigors of the climate, get them scratched, and neglect to remove rosin dust which eats into the varnish. One once famous artist, think-ing that something must be wrong with his Stradivari, had it taken apart so many times that it lost much of its quality. Every time a violin is opened, a little of the wood and varnish gets lost.

"Any time a man thinks something is wrong with his Stradivari, he ought to start wondering whether something isn't wrong with himself," Emil Herrmann told me.

When I started to play the fiddle, I wouldn't have dreamed that one day I would buy a Stradivari from Herrmann, who had sold to Heifetz and Menuhin, among many distinguished musicians, and who had known almost all the world's great instruments. I had started out with one of the cheap "factory" fiddles that are mass-produced in small towns in Bohemia, Bavaria, Saxony, and France, where bellies and back-pieces are cut by machines like patterns of garments. Women make fingerboards and children print beautiful labels — ANTONIUS STRADI-VARIUS FACIEBAT — that are worth as much as bank notes were during the inflation of the early 1920's. One of my early violins, an ugly-sounding instrument the color of a bloody mary, had such a label, and I thought it might be a Stradivari.

As a nightclub musician in Paris, I consumed several cheap violins. They had to be cheap. Once a drunk sat down on my fiddle, which I'd left on a chair. Another instrument perished during an argument with a Parisian *flic* (cop), during a police raid on our working place. The *flic* tried to hit me with his rubber truncheon. I held up the violin as a shield, in the manner of a medieval knight, but the violin was not made of armor. I also lost several bows in the line of duty. It was my duty to play solo in front of the curtained *chambres separées* for the customers inside. Afterwards I would put my bow into the slit between the curtains, expecting the gentleman to stick a bank note between the horsehair. In-stead, one customer, no gentleman, took my bow and broke it. Madame, who owned the establishment, refused to pay for my bow, calling it *vis major*, an act of God, and threatened to call the police.

As a ship's musician I needed a sturdy instrument. The salty sea air is healthier for people than for violins. During sudden storms, when I'd placed the fiddle on the piano in the grand salon, it slid off, which didn't improve its tonal quality. Once the ship's carpenter had to put it together. People said it sounded that way, too. The worst thing hap-pened one summer in the Red Sea. That was before the age of air-conditioning. The temperature on the promenade deck compared un-favorably with what modern cookbooks describe as a "moderate oven." Drops of water formed on my fiddle, and the fingerboard became a slide on which my hands performed involuntary cacophonous *glissandi*.

The atmosphere, and our entertainment, were strictly from Dante's *Inferno*.

I'd been warned to take special care of the instrument during the Red Sea passage, where the heat and humidity might be disastrous to the glue that holds a violin together. After work, I put the fiddle in a heavy oilcloth which I placed in the wooden case, and at night I carried the case down to the vegetable refrigeration chamber and stored it between heads of lettuce and spinach. In the morning the violin sounded as if the tones had been frozen.

One night, I became romantically involved with a lady passenger who ardently admired my performance of *La Berceuse de Jocelyn*, and forgot to take the violin down to the refrigeration chamber. I suspect I was in a hurry to join the admiring lady on the dark sundeck while her admiration was still ardent. The next morning, when I came on deck, my violin case was still lying on the piano. I opened it and saw a pile of thin wooden boards. During the hot night the glue had melted and the violin had fallen apart and reverted to its pre-assembly state. It wasn't much of a loss, but there was no ersatz instrument aboard, and the ship's carpenter, an alcoholic unanonymous, was unable to put it together. My boss, the purser, told me to get a violin at the next stop, which was Djibouti, or to get off the boat and lose my pay.

Djibouti was a free port where they had almost everything, cheap Scotch whiskey and French cognac, but no violins. I found one at last, in a cheap dive, where the fiddle player had left it lying on the piano, when he decided in a lucid moment, to take the next boat to Marseilles. Having seen Djibouti, I didn't blame him. The violin hadn't disintegrated in the hot, humid air, because it was held together by small nails. It had what you might call a hard, metallic sound, a quality much admired in tenor voices but not in fiddles.

It was a long way from the fiddle-with-the-nails to my Stradivari. I made it stage by stage. My first good violin was a Carlo Giuseppe

Testore which I bought in the early postwar years in Prague. I took it back to Hollywood where I showed it, foolishly, to Jascha Heifetz, who had bought from Emil Herrmann a wonderful Stradivari and a Guarneri del Gesù. Heifetz asked me, in his shy, offhand manner, whether I'd saved a little money, and advised me to see Herrmann on my next trip to New York. Emil Herrmann had a cathedral-like duplex study on West Fifty-seventh Street, close to Carnegie Hall. He was a spry man of medium size, with thick gray hair, a roughly angular face, and twinkling eyes, reminding me of a Bavarian woodcut.

I said I'd come to buy a fiddle. He gave me a shrewd glance, and asked me how much I would like to spend. He explained to me later that there was no sense in showing a person a thirty-thousand-dollar Stradivari when he had only three thousand dollars. After playing the better fiddle he wouldn't like the cheaper one, and Herrmann would lose a customer. He also asked me what I needed it for. To play at home for myself? In an orchestra? As a soloist or for chamber music? I didn't know that I, usually the interviewer, was being interviewed. He went into a vaultlike room and came back with three fiddles which he put down on the table. Instinctively, I picked up a golden-orange-brownish violin. Herrmann had watched me, and he seemed pleased.

"A very old violin," he said. "One of the oldest in existence. Made in Cremona, in 1608, by the brothers Antonio and Girolamo Amati. Their father was Andrea Amati, whom I believe to be the creator of the violin."

The violin had a sweet, soft sound. Herrmann said it wouldn't be powerful enough as a solo instrument but would be wonderful in the intimacy of a home. I tried it. Then I tried the next one, a louder but less beautiful-sounding Alessandro Gagliano. I got confused, and asked Herrmann whether I could take both violins home and try them out there. He agreed reluctantly, and later explained to me why a customer shouldn't take an instrument home and possibly have it played by a friend to hear "how it sounds." You just can't judge an instrument when it is played by someone else. You have to play it yourself to get the feel of it. Violin players disagree about violins as much as about women.

There followed weeks of indecision and excitement. The most exciting time about violins (and women) is when one tries to get to know them. I went back to Herrmann's study and tried more fiddles, but in the end I bought the violin which I'd first picked up from the table — the Amati. Herrmann wasn't surprised. He said most people are instinctively attracted by the violin which they like best.

Two years later, Herrmann moved to a large country place near Easton, Connecticut. In "Fiddledale," as he called the place, he built a beautiful large house with a combination office-and-study in the basement, and next to it a bombproof vault. There he kept his most valuable instruments, each in a velvet-lined compartment, resting on its side: the violins by Stradivari, the Guarneris, the Amatis, Bergonzi, and Montagnana. Elsewhere were the less important Guadagninis, Gaglianos, and Gofrillers, and others were stored on shelves. During the summer, an electric dehumidifier was put to work, and in winter a trayful of water was in the vault to moisten the air. Also in the vault was Herrmann's own register of the most important violins known to exist, listing the exact measurements and containing photographs of each instrument, describing the wood and color of the varnish, giving its history and ownership and whereabouts. With the help of this register, on which he'd worked all his life, he was able to identify and appraise all the great instruments in the world.

I'd become fascinated by violins as well as the violin business, and talked to Shawn about it. He agreed it would make a fine story, written as a profile around Emil Herrmann. We had moved from California to Connecticut, where we lived in a house near Bethel owned by a woman whose father, a Finnish lumber millionaire, had been a noted collector of old rare Italian instruments and a friend of Herrmann's. Another neighbor and Herrmann customer was Leopold Godowsky, the son of the great pianist. Leo owned a Stradivari violin and an Amati viola. He is the co-inventor, with Leopold Mannes, of Kodachrome, and could have bought half-a-dozen other instruments from Herrmann's vault. He too later became one of my profile subjects.

I would often drive over from Bethel to Herrmann's place nearby, doing research for the profile. It was one of the most fascinating research jobs I've ever done because it gave me a legitimate excuse to play on all the great fiddles in the Herrmann basement. Not that I needed an excuse; once a man had bought an instrument from Herrmann, he was automatically accepted as a bona fide member of the household, and permitted to have the run of the place and try any instrument in the vault. I didn't know that often customers would fall in love with a better, more expensive instrument.

The afternoons in Herrmann's study would begin with my trying to interview him, taking notes. But the steel door into the vault was open, and I felt myself magically attracted to the great instruments in the velvet-lined compartments. Every fiddler would have understood. So did Herrmann, a fiddler himself who loved his instruments.

"Go on, serve yourself," he would say. I would take an instrument at random and try it, enjoying its sound and trying to guess what it was. It was hopeless, though I learned to distinguish between the sweet nightingale tones of an Amati, the robust clarinet sounds of a Guarneri del Gesù, and the mellow oboe-like timbre of a Stradivari. Herrmann had spent his whole life with violins. His father had been a music teacher and dealer in Tauberbischofsheim, Germany, and life in the family had revolved around violins. At the dinner table, violins were discussed as wine is discussed at the tables of French *viticulteurs*. A violin was shown, and the boy was asked to describe it, and try to deduce the country it came from and its maker.

"If I cannot identify a good violin within a minute of looking at it, something is bound to be amiss," Herrmann told me one afternoon. "I begin to look at its back, examining the texture of the wood and the quality of the varnish. Next, I study the front, the *f*-holes, the sides, the ornamental purfling along the edges. Every prominent maker has certain peculiarities of design which are as obvious to the eye of the expert as the characteristics of a man's signature to a bank teller. Particularly the cutting of the scroll and the f-holes. Even aberrations sometimes provide a key. Stradivari's eyes grew weak in his eighties, and the curves and f-holes of his late violins lack the dynamic sweep of his earlier ones." Some violins display the touch of more than one maker. Some of the last instruments made by Nicolo Amati show the hand of his young apprentice Stradivari, and in some of Stradivari's last violins the co-operation of his sons Francesco and Omobono is evident. Labels too tell a story. Stradivari changed the typeface of his labels but never their wording. After 1729 he changed the Latin u in "Stradiuarius" to the Roman v.

It is an intricate science, and there are not more than a dozen people who can pass judgment on the authenticity and the merits of old violins, and make their judgment stick. People of taste and discernment who study their metier can become connoisseurs of paintings or old furniture, but an expert on fine old violins must have an academic knowledge, practical experience, an eye, and above all, a feeling for them, and he must have perception and absolute integrity.

Herrmann died in Switzerland in 1968, but I remember him and these wonderful afternoons in his basement study in "Fiddledale." Friends and customers would drop in under some pretext, and next thing they would try out fine violins. Most violinists' desire to own a wonderful violin exceeds their ability to pay for them. Next to owning a great Stradivari, the second best thing was to play one in Herrmann's study. Our behavior in the basement would have seemed somewhat lunatic to anyone but a violin-lover. Some people were so afraid of drop-ping a great fiddle that they could hardly put a bow to it. Some were awed that the small piece of varnished wood in their hands was worth more than a nice home. (In the 1950's, a great violin might cost sixty thousand dollars; today it is worth much more.) Some got that acquisitive gleam in their eyes that is familiar to croupiers in Monte Carlo, to bookies, and to salesmen at Tiffany's. Great violins have been stolen and some have never been recovered; perhaps the thieves keep them under their beds, since they wouldn't dare sell them.

On some afternoons, three or four of us would try out violins, milling around with fiddles under our chins, trying to outplay one another, or getting into a corner trying to hear how a violin sounded. The result was acoustic pandemonium as the air became filled with dissonant sounds and discordant opinions. Even celebrated violinists don't always sound as brilliant when they try out violins as they do on the concert stage. Very few players are able to make all violins sound right — even the good ones. The instrument is often overrated. A bad violinist sounds bad even when he's playing a great Stradivari, but there is no doubt that a great artist is helped by a fine instrument.

After a while the large study was filled with confusion. No one knew what violin he was playing. Some had the ecstatic expression of a Moslem pilgrim gazing for the first time on the minarets of Mecca. The violinistic orgy broke up only when Herrmann, who had been sitting quietly behind his desk, writing letters, or just watching us, smiling, suggested that we come up for a drink. Often we stayed for dinner. Mrs. Kira Herrmann, whose father had been a regimental commander in the czarist army in Sevastopol, was the only woman I know who kept homemade, precooked *pirozhki, kotlety Pozharski,* and beef Stroganoff in her freezer, always ready for an emergency. She knew we would be hungry. It must be the emotional experience of playing great violins that one is sure one will never be able to buy. There would be exciting dinner talk about the mysteries of the violin, especially the varnish. Everybody knows that varnish is a mixture of oils, gums, and alcohol, but no one knows the exact composition of Stradivari's varnish, whether it was cold or boiled. Analysis has not solved the mystery. Did he use, as some claim, "dragon's blood," a dark, red, gummy substance derived from the fruit of a Malayan palm tree that Marco Polo brought to Venice?

Some believe he used as many as four coats of varnish. If one is chipped away, there is another one underneath.

"Trustee in Fiddledale," the Emil Herrmann profile, turned out to be rather expensive for me. Until then, I'd been living happily with my Amati, which had a sweet, beautiful sound. Herrmann's own favorites were the Amati instruments. He once showed me a Nicolo Amati, made in 1656, with double purfling and tiny rubies and emeralds inlaid in the wood, that had an incredibly beautiful tone and almost, though not quite, as much carrying power as a very great Stradivari. When he had to sell it, being a businessman, he felt as though he'd lost a dear friend.

I'd also considered my Amati a dear friend, but now, after playing all the Stradivaris in Herrmann's basement, I began to have second thoughts. When I played chamber music with people who had cheaper, louder instruments, my Amati was often outplayed. I began to cautiously ask Herrmann about the prices of certain Stradivaris. The great ones were beyond my reach, but there were other fine instruments that had both tonal beauty and carrying power, the combination which makes Stradivari so expensive.

Herrmann discouraged me. He later told me he *wanted* me to keep my Amati. I went to Europe and I played much chamber music in Vienna. Unlike in California and Connecticut, where nearly everybody was playing on a fine Italian instrument, my fellow players in Vienna often played instruments that were not beautiful, but loud. While singing a first-violin melody, I was painfully shaken by the noisy *ta-ta* of my fellow players. I asked them to lower their voices, but their instruments were not built for *pianissimo*. The only solution would be to get a violin that could outplay them.

On my next visit to Connecticut, I asked Herrmann how much it would cost to graduate from my Amati to a middle-class Stradivari. He gave me a long, thoughtful look, and then he went into the vault and came out with a violin. He held it up for me. It had a beautiful one-piece back, and the orange-reddish-brown varnish was lovely.

"Even the label is genuine," Herrmann said. "But someone tampered with the year. It says 1716, which would make it one of the most expensive Stradivari violins, dating from the master's golden epoch. His masterpiece, the 'Messiah,' was made in 1716. I am pretty sure it was made around 1729 or 1730, when he was eighty-six. Somebody changed the date to get more money for the instrument. That happens often enough, the way ladies like to change their year of birth to stay younger."

He handed me the violin and a bow. The violin responded to the slightest pressure of the bow, and it sang like a human voice. Its tone was both soft and penetrating, sweet and forceful. With this violin I would no longer be outplayed by my *ta-ta*-ing fellow players. On the contrary; I hoped they would listen to its beautiful sound.

"Take it with you and see how you feel about it," he said. "But don't have it played for you by others as you did with your Amati, remember?" Again it struck me that he'd never been a high-pressure salesman but considered it his job to help each customer find the instrument that was best suited to him and to his means.

I kept the Stradivari, but it took me almost three years to court her and understand her. I think of my Stradivari as a woman. My violin can be capricious. It doesn't like sudden changes of temperature, hates heat, cold and humidity, bright lights and cigarette smoke. It doesn't like any kind of pressure, especially bow pressure. It doesn't want to be forced to do anything; the less power I use, the more I get out of her. We've shared some wonderful hours, and we hope to share some more. Sometimes I envy my Stradivari. At the age of two hundred and forty years, my Strad shows no signs of getting old.

A Visa for America

ONE DOESN'T BECOME A WRITER as one becomes a violin player. Few
writers start out as writers. They are teachers, accountants, civil servants,
housewives, bums, sailors, doctors, lumbermen, until they try to write.
If they are writers at heart, they keep writing; a real writer never stops
writing. The exceptions are the "talking writers" of Hollywood who
never write, and the nonwriters who hopefully talk of the novel they're
going to write someday. Somehow they never do.

Writers are born, though it may take them a long time to find out
what they were born for. In this country, some people seem to believe
that writers can be trained in school, but all the student writers learn
is technical facility and how to express themselves. Technique must
never become an end in itself.

In Europe, there were no schools for writers, no classes in journalism.
Writing wasn't considered a profession or a business but almost an art;
many people believed it should be an unprofitable art. Successful writers

would say that life is the writer's best education, provided that he finds out what he wants to write and that he cares deeply enough to write convincingly. In Germany, a writer who had published a few poems or a novel that was "seriously" reviewed was promoted to the rank of *Dichter*. The word doesn't exist in English. "Poet" comes close to it, but a poet usually writes poetry, and a *Dichter* often writes prose, preferably poetic prose. Promotion to *Dichter* included a ticket to fame, but sometimes a *Dichter*'s fame proved as perishable as the immortality of some members of the Academie Française who consider themselves immortal.

Paradoxically, Germany, the country of *Dichter und Denker* (poets and thinkers), rewarded its writers less generously than the allegedly uncivilized United States, and rated them socially inferior. In Europe, a writer who makes money is considered a somewhat dubious character, a sort of nouveau riche. There is an atavistic feeling that writers should be poor and bankers must be rich. Why? Because. A writer is expected to live in a garret, though the door handles may be gold-plated; *that* is "eccentric," and permitted. Poets should starve and love it. In Germany, the Group 47 that tried to monopolize the somewhat barren literary postwar landscape, during a feud with a commercially successful writer, called him a nonwriter because he owned two Mercedes and a motor yacht. In prewar Vienna, some coffeehouse poets who lived on other people's money were more respected than hardworking writers who honestly earned their royalties.

A curious distinction is made on the Continent between businessmen and artists, creative and re-creative performers. A successful art dealer may own a mansion, but not a successful painter, unless he is in the Picasso or Chagall class. Herbert von Karajan has a private jet and a Silver Cloud Rolls-Royce, but a serious composer would be criticized if he had a Rolls-Royce. Most modern composers couldn't afford one anyway. The German critics forgave Richard Strauss for writing second-rate music after his early masterpieces, but never for his candidly professed love of money.

I came to writing by way of journalism, the wrong way in the opinion of the critics in Central Europe who didn't know that some pretty good writers in English — Dickens, Macaulay, Johnson, Twain, Mencken — had once been journalists. On the Central European literary scene, the journalist was a low-species animal, living far below the Parnassian heights of *Dichter und Denker*. Among journalists, the reporter was the pariah. My European friends are shocked when I tell them that I am called a reporter in America. No use explaining to them that reporting occasionally reaches admirably high standards in the United States.

I began as a travel writer. Since Goethe went to Italy and wrote some poetic travel notes, this sort of writing was almost accepted by the critics, provided it was "serious." (A writer's life was damned serious in Europe.) Nearly every writer writing in German (the term includes Germans, Austrians, Swiss, and also Czechoslovaks, Hungarians, Rumanians, and others writing in German) has written on his travels. In France, most *hommes de lettres* occasionally write about some aspect of gastronomy, and the Elizabethan writers in England were expected to write about their Grand Tour — the leisurely trip through France, Flanders, the Low Countries, Switzerland, and always Italy, the country which Gibbon said "every scholar must long to see." "A man who has not been in Italy is always conscious of an inferiority complex," wrote Dr. Samuel Johnson, who missed the Grand Tour.

While the English and later the Americans became infatuated with Italy and France, the Central Europeans went back to the glory of ancient Hellas. At the *Gymnasium,* we accompanied Homer's Odysseus on his travels. We read the Latins, the Germans, the Russians, the French, but rarely the English. Except Shakespeare, whom our literature professor considered "almost a German *Dichter.*" My early knowledge of American literature was limited to Edgar Allan Poe, Mark Twain, James Fenimore Cooper, O. Henry. We had to recite by heart some second-rate ballads of Uhland and Wieland, but we didn't know the first-rate poetry of Burns, Keats, Shelley. Education is a strange, multifaced phenomenon. We knew that Hoffman von Fallersleben had written "Deutschland, Deutschland über Alles," but we never read the Gettysburg Address.

Years ago, I went to see William Somerset Maugham in his beautiful villa in Cap Ferrat, on the Riviera. I admired Maugham both for his style of writing and his style of life. He lived the life of a world-famous writer; he had a beautiful house filled with art treasures that he'd bought at the right moment, the park overlooking the Mediterranean, secluded yet half an hour's drive from Monte Carlo, and he went around the world, taking a detached, ironical view of its inhabitants. He told me that his early medical training had taught him much about human weakness, and we talked about Arthur Schnitzler, who had been a doctor and psychologically X-rayed his characters. Maugham said he'd never considered himself a *Dichter* (he used the German expression) but a "craftsman" and "storyteller."

He talked wryly about his struggles as a writer, and he didn't like the critics. "They call me an entertainer," he said. "Well, I've tried to be a *good* entertainer. I'm making my readers read and turn the pages of my books, not just skip them. That's a hard thing to do. My books are read. So many books are just leafed through."

Did he mind being imitated?

"On the contrary. I'm pleased. The time to worry is when they no longer steal from you."

As a young writer, he'd trained himself to write short sketches of people he'd just met. "A professional writer should be able to write a thousand-word essay on a person after talking to that person for fifteen minutes. He must use but never abuse his craft." Pointing around — to the paintings, the books, the trees — he said quietly, "All this I've earned with my pen."

He talked about the writer's artistic conscience. "The writer must artfully organize his material. Artlessness in writing is anarchy."

I went away, and wrote two thousand words about W. S. Maugham, by way of training myself. I concluded that Maugham "has a low opinion of mankind, doesn't like women, is not a kind man but a great craftsman who knows his worth. He never did anything in which he didn't believe."

After giving up the idea of being a professional violinist, I turned to writing. Words became a substitute for sounds. A sentence can be a melody. There are musical *and* written pieces in the major and minor keys. I never tried to write poetry. Even in moments of sorrow or exultation, when young Werthers all over the world escape into poetry, I stuck to prose. I never kept a diary. I never wrote letters for the thinly disguised purpose of having them collected and published. "This enervating correspondence will eventually be part of *Literaturgeschichte* (literary history)," the nineteen-year-old Hugo von Hofmannsthal wrote to a friend.

I once asked Thomas Mann whether he believed in inspiration.

The Herr Professor looked at me sternly. "Certainly not. Writing is hard labor." He pronounced both words — *"harte Arbeit"* — with equal emphasis. Mann kept regular working hours, every morning from eight-thirty to twelve-thirty.

"I am always at my desk, no matter how I feel, trying to put words on paper. . . . Sometimes they add up to something, and at other times they don't." At twelve-thirty, he would come out of his study. Lunch, a short nap, reading and writing letters. At four in the afternoon he would often read to his family and honored friends what he'd written in the morning. Walking and reading, and going to bed. Music, a lot of music.

"Yes," he said. "Day after day, week after week, year after year."

Mann and Maugham were lucky; *their* world didn't break down when they were in their teens. My journalistic *Wanderjahre* were con-

ditioned by a constantly shrinking world. The first language I wrote
in was German, which was then becoming the exclusive domain of the
"Aryans." Jews were not supposed to write German at all.

My first article was published in my hometown paper, the *Morgenzeitung*, whose publisher, Dr. Paul Fischel, was a friend of our family's.
The article was romantically titled "Mondnacht in Djibouti" ("Moon-
light in Djibouti"), a travel impression from a trip as a ship's musician
through the Red Sea. It won't make literary history but caused a mild
sensation in my hometown. No citizen had ever gone from Ostrava to
Djibouti, Shanghai, or New York, and *come back*. Those going to such
outlandish places had good reason never to return. Ostrava was known
for its pretty girls, charming embezzlers, and delightful crooks, for its
coal dust and amusing night life. People couldn't understand that I had
gone to faraway places "for no reason at all," and had returned.

Ostrava was a coal and steel town — some called it "little Pittsburgh"
— but my generation preferred "little Paris," because there was much
more going on in the hours of darkness than in the daytime. Ostrava was
a typical border town, close to Poland and Germany, and some dubious
characters were always coming and going, trying to avoid extradition.
Our coffeehouses, especially the Palace and Europe, were noted for their
splendor, high esprit and low morals. Life was never boring, and people
from as far away as Slovakia, Silesia, Hungary, Poland, Bohemia came
to Ostrava to have a good time. It got so bad that girls from good families were reluctant to tell their friends abroad that they were from
Ostrava, while we boys were as proud of it as if we had been born in
the Place Pigalle.

I began to send the *Morgenzeitung* my travel impressions, and became a very minor local celebrity; in order to live up to my early, undeserved fame, I went around in a black velvet jacket and a broad, black
Toulouse Lautrec hat, to convey the proper Place Pigalle impression.
Some people said the *Morgenzeitung* printed me only because the publisher was an old friend. Dr. Fischel was a tall, disjointed man who had
been an internationally famous soccer player before he got caught in

the newspaper business. He was working hard and was always tired. After directing the makeup of the paper's early evening edition, he would go to the local theater for a nap. He slept through the entire performance without snoring and when the curtain fell, he got up refreshed and went to supervise the final edition of the paper. He called the dramas of Ibsen and Strindberg, and several operettas, his favorite sleeping bills. I could contribute a long list of literary sedatives.

The *Morgenzeitung* belonged to the *Prager Tagblatt* concern. The *Tagblatt* made me an unsalaried "special correspondent" and published my articles from exotic places. When I moved to Prague, I doubled as a sportswriter and telephoned my hometown paper dramatic reports about the ice-hockey world championship in Prague. Next to soccer, ice hockey was the national sport in Czechoslovakia. Once our team beat Canada, and my report of the memorable event filled the entire front page of the *Morgenzeitung* and was more appreciated than the political news.

I began to write for several newspapers in Vienna and, with characteristically bad timing, made the distinguished *Vossische Zeitung* in Berlin, Germany's finest paper, on January 27, 1933 — three days before Adolf Hitler became German chancellor. That was the beginning and the end of my short-lived journalistic career in Germany.

Undaunted, I embarked upon a low-cost trip around the world and wrote a book, *Die Grosse Mauer (The Great Wall)* — a reference to the Great Wall of China, which I visited. To earn additional money, I took photographs and made commercial films, and collected economic information for several firms in Prague. My income from article writing was cut again when the Nazis took over Austria. *Die Grosse Mauer* was burned by the Nazis with all the other books they burned.

When I came back to Europe after the Second World War, I tried to find a copy of my book, but there was none. Not long ago, my tailor in Vienna, Mr. Šilhavý, discovered a copy of *Die Grosse Mauer* in a friend's house and got it for me. Now I have at least one.

When my wife and I left Prague for New York, late in September, 1938, we expected to be back by Christmas. Each of us had only a small suitcase. As an "experienced" world traveler, I'd told my wife that the wise man travels lightly. We took only a few things, and left all our belongings in our beautiful penthouse apartment in Prague, which had a large terrace overlooking the Moldau and Hradčany Castle. There was an oleander tree on the terrace, and somebody would come in to water the tree while we were gone. The penthouse was a luxury which we were hardly able to afford, but we were young and foolish.

I didn't turn out to be a wise man; it would have been wiser to take along a couple of trunks. But how was I to know that just as we were in mid-ocean aboard the French Line boat *Champlain,* the Munich Agreement would be signed, on September 29, that dismembered our homeland? Shortly after my arrival in New York, I went to the Czechoslovak Consulate General, on Broadway. The official photograph of President Beneš had already been removed from the wall. A lot of people were in a hurry to change loyalties. (Not much has changed since then.) A friendly consul advised me not to return home. I told him we'd come as tourists, and planned to be back by Christmas. It was by pure chance that we were in New York. A few months earlier, when the Sudeten German crisis erupted in Czechoslovakia, a man close to Prime Minister Milan Hodža who had known me since my days as a parliamentary secretary had asked me to go to the United States and give some lectures on the Sudeten German problem, "to influence public opinion in America." He said, "It's not like here where no one listens to what the people say. In America, public opinion may force the politicians to do things." I said my English was too poor for lectures. He said "Nonsense," and appealed to my patriotic feelings. I would get a small grant, hardly enough to pay for our tickets, "but you can write articles from America," and that was how we had come to New York.

The Czechoslovak consul listened, and then he said he couldn't tell me anything officially. But privately, "I wouldn't go back if I were you."

I said, "I am an officer in the Czechoslovak army."

He pointed at the white spot on the wall where Beneš's picture had hung. "Soon the commander in chief won't be there anymore. Don't have any illusions. It won't be long before the *Wehrmacht*. . . ."

He shrugged and didn't finish the sentence.

So that was that. A short, accidental journey to the United States became our emigration. There were problems. We'd been admitted for a limited time on a tourist visa. In order to immigrate, we would have to leave the country again and apply abroad for permanent immigration visas. Some refugees went to Mexico, and others to Cuba. We decided to go to Canada, mainly because it was close and less expensive. The little money we had was getting less.

We went to Montreal. Jaroslav Hnízdo, the Czechoslovak consul there, had been a friend of President Masaryk's. We sat around with him and other members of the Czechoslovak colony, commiserating about the tragedy of our homeland. We went through nervous hours in the waiting room of the American Consulate General. We had brought along an affidavit of support from a kindhearted businessman in New York. I'd told him our story, and he guaranteed for us, though he hardly knew us, declaring his assets and underwriting our uncertain future. Now, in Montreal, it turned out that we needed personal documents which we hadn't taken along. There were interviews, and there would be an investigation, and everything took a long time.

It was my first contact with the American bureaucracy. Even now I feel a slight constriction in my throat when I step into an American consulate and see the poor devils sitting there, waiting, perhaps silently praying. The American Consulate in Montreal had only two immigration-quota numbers per month for Czechoslovak citizens, and there were others ahead of us. In January, 1939, a sympathetic consul told us that our turn had come. A few days later we left the Consulate with two large envelopes containing many impressive documents with red seals,

large X-ray films proving that we had no TB, and other forms and
papers.

We entered the United States of America as full-fledged immigrants
at St. Albans, Vermont. I didn't know the name of the Saint, but considered it a good omen to arrive in our adopted country under divine
protection. In New York, we rented a furnished room on West Eighty-
ninth Street, near Riverside Drive. We soon learned to politely ignore the
other tenants in the red-brick house, but we couldn't avoid knowing
what they had for dinner: mostly fried pork chops, judging by the scent
that filled the staircase around six P.M.

The following weeks are a confused, unhappy memory. Legally, we
were future Americans; emotionally, we were former Czechoslovaks;
economically, we were nobodies. My wife found a job as a seamstress
at Charlie Le Maire, a friend of a friend of somebody in California. Her
weekly salary was eleven dollars. There was no point in lecturing on the
Sudeten German problem anymore. With the help of a friend, I wrote
a new lecture, "The Tragedy of Czechoslovakia," which I gave at
women's clubs and small Jewish organizations. My fees ranged from
four to seven dollars — more than my lecture was worth — and there
would be a free lunch, often chicken croquettes. Ever since, I've been
prejudiced against chicken croquettes and a vegetable known as peas-and-
carrots, an incompatible culinary mixture if there ever was one.

I spent many afternoons in the motion-picture theaters on upper
Broadway, sitting through the same films for two consecutive runs,
which seemed a better way of learning the sound of English than to
go to evening school with other refugees where everybody spoke German.

One afternoon I came out of a movie and saw a newsstand with the
evening papers. It was a high stack. I had a sudden, sickening feeling in
the pit of my stomach as I saw the picture on the front page: my hometown. There was the Rynek in Ostrava, the old town square, just one
block from the house where I'd spent all my youth. The baroque pesti-
lence column, a memorial after the plague that killed half the inhabitants

in the sixteenth and seventeenth centuries. The onion-like cupola of the Old Town Hall. Next to it, the corner building where my mother's stationery store had been. It seemed unreal to see my hometown square on the front page of a paper here on Broadway; it was also a reminder that no matter where you were, you couldn't get away from it.

I put down a nickel and took the paper. The dateline was March 15, 1939. The previous evening the German troops had occupied Ostrava. My mother was there, and my brother, and I wondered whether they were still safe. The German Gestapo would be there now, efficiently working round the clock, looking at their lists and arresting people, and they would be aided by many local Sudeten Germans who had well prepared the terrain in advance. I was thinking of relatives and friends, of what might happen to them, and in the end what did happen was worse than my fears.

I got busy the next day, but there was little I could do. I sent my mother and my brother affidavits of support from well-to-do American friends. I asked them to go to Prague and register right away with the American Consulate for visas. But the quota was small, and there were thousands ahead of them. My brother got out the following year, and went to Havana, and eventually he joined us in California. My mother waited too long. She wanted to take along some of her beloved paintings and rugs, the china and the silver. Special permits were needed, and that took time, and one day it was too late. The Jews in Ostrava were rounded up and most of them were sent to the Terezin concentration camp.

Ever since I've disliked possessions. Albert Einstein, a fellow refugee, called them *"ein Stein am Bein"* ("a stone around the leg"). They drag you down until you drown.

It was Czechoslovakia's first national tragedy in this century, after the earlier tragedy, the Battle on the White Mountain on November 8,

1620, which was the beginning of the Habsburg rule that lasted three hundred years.

One national tragedy ought to be enough in any man's life. But there was another one, on August 21, 1968, when the "fraternal" Soviet and Warsaw Pact countries occupied Czechoslovakia. One slogan in Prague said CAIN WAS ALSO A BROTHER.

The Battle on the White Mountain was followed by the Thirty Years' War. The Nazi occupation of Czechoslovakia in 1939 was followed by the Second World War. Will the Soviet occupation of 1968 be followed — sooner or later — by the Third World War?

Today, more than thirty years after I came to America, I don't pretend to know much about my fellow Americans. I am more puzzled than ever about their unfathomable ways. In 1939, after spending a few weeks in New York City, I thought I knew all about them. Like many other instant experts, I even wrote a book about them. It was published by Dr. Fischel in Ostrava, and became something of a best seller among worried Europeans who thought of emigrating to America. The book, an inexpensive paperback, earned me a couple of hundred dollars, a small fortune for me at that time, and to this day I don't know how the publisher managed to transfer the money legally to me in America.

The book was called *Visum für Amerika* (*Visa for America*). The cover showed the American colors. The word "Visum" was made up of blue stars, and "Amerika" of red stripes. Underneath was a photograph of our affidavit of support. I dedicated the book "to the helpful Americans and Canadians to whom so many European immigrants owe a debt of gratitude for assisting them to find a new home."

In the foreword I wrote, "There's nothing in this book about the longest bridge, the meanest kidnapper, the fanciest night club, nothing about Detroit, Wall Street, gangsters and G men. But you may find in it something about an immigrant's chances in America, how to start a new life in a New World, how to get affidavits and visas, how to live in

New York on little money, a subject on which I made first-hand research." The foreword ended, "Nearly everybody who comes to America sooner or later atones for his earlier, silly ideas about the country that is often described as cold-blooded and heartless. Nowhere in Europe have I found so many kind-hearted, helpful people as in the country of the 'tough, selfish Americans.' "

The book appeared in Czechoslovakia's bookstores in late March, 1939, two weeks after the Nazi invasion. It wasn't immediately seized — that came later. The new regime favored the emigration of unpersons, provided they left all belongings at home, taking along only five dollars. Many unpersons hopefully purchased my book. I hope I gave them emotional assistance and practical advice. I explained how to get an affidavit of support from an American, a document that often made the difference between being accepted or rejected by the American consul; how to find such a sponsor ("look up the local telephone directory for a person with your name"), and how to approach him ("tell him the truth"). I told the readers "to repay decency with decency — the Americans must never regret that they guaranteed for your future."

I advised my readers "to learn American, not English. . . . Your teacher told you never to use such expressions as 'damn!' or 'shut up!', but many Americans use them, though not in the presence of a lady." (I was still an optimist.) I told people to "talk, talk, talk . . . don't be afraid of your mistakes, of your thick accent." There were the mysteries of the U.S. immigration laws that kept out "idiots, alcoholics, criminals, polygamists, anarchists." (How many Americans wouldn't be admitted if they came as immigrants and told the truth?) I even told my readers what *not* to tell the immigration inspectors. ("Never tell them that somebody promised you a job.") Once a kindhearted immigration officer said to me, "In the old days the immigrants asked us what they might expect of America. Today we must ask them, 'What can America expect from you?' " (After President Kennedy's inaugural speech, I wondered whether his speechwriters had seen my book, but I doubt it, I doubt it very much.)

I seem to have known *everything* about this country. I told people where to look for a room, and how to order in a drugstore. I got mixed up idiomatically and called a hot dog a hamburger. I warned them against the fallacy of trying to live in America on European ideas:

People write me from Europe asking whether they could become legal advisers for emigrants. Others have plans to sell Prague sausages in Texas or to open a Viennese coffeehouse in the Middle West. . . . If they'd ever seen a town in the Middle West, with its mixture of gasoline-scented air and local patriotism, they would understand that the last thing needed there is a Viennese coffeehouse.

One chapter was called "Forget It!":

"Forget it" belongs to the slogans which the recently arrived immigrant should learn at once. Forget that you once had an eight-room apartment in the best residential district, and you may find your furnished room on the West Side quite comfortable. Forget your former title and you won't mind being addressed "Mr." Forget what you once were, and did. Americans are keen about their own history, but not about your personal history. The once famous Mr. So-and-so was a member of government. So what? Now he is just another immigrant looking for a job. Mr. Y. always traveled with a couple of secretaries; today you can see him at Horn and Hardart, deliberating whether to spend 30¢ or 40¢ on his lunch. The other day I saw there a former conductor of the Vienna Opera, a distinguished novelist, and a man who once controlled millions.

There was a chapter about my early personal experiences with Americans. Here are a few excerpts. They were not intended to be humorous.

Courtesy

American courtesy, a delicate subject, often complicates life for the new immigrants. A man doffing his hat in the street is probably a recently arrived European. The German saying, "With the hat in your hand you'll get through the land" is not valid in the United States. Americans greet you, "How are you?" without taking off their hat. They may do it in the presence of a lady, though not in Canada in wintertime, when it's too cold. You should take off your hat in the presence of a high-class lady. But who is a high-class lady? That, I'm afraid, you must decide yourself. All American ladies, high-class and otherwise, are pleased when a "charming" European takes off his hat and kisses their hands; most American males think it's silly.

The Customer Is Always Wrong

You've read about "Keep Smiling," the wonders of American service, but you'll soon discover in America that American service with a smile doesn't exist. No other country does less for the hapless customer. With the exception of a few luxury stores which you won't see inside anyway, the clerks are unfriendly everywhere. In the big department stores they've developed the technique of being rude. The salesgirls make the customers personally responsible for their lousy $15-a-week jobs when they think they ought to earn $5000 a week in Hollywood. The waiters in modest restaurants won't greet you politely, as they did in Vienna or Berlin where you were called Herr Doktor without being one, or even Herr Hofrat. Maybe the American waiter *was* once a Doktor or Hofrat himself in Europe, but he came earlier to America than you. Why should he be polite to you?

Appointments

They are the key to American business life. You can't just go and ask to see a man. Even if you happen to know that he doesn't do much work except keeping his feet on his desk, smoking a cigar, he won't see you without an appointment. Appointments, perhaps an invention of American Tel. & Tel., are made by telephone. (There goes another nickel.) To make an appointment by telephone is not easy. Authors of books about America have written about Roosevelt, the New Deal, the skyscrapers, Ford, Chicago, Hollywood but no one explains how to make a phone call. You dial. A sweet, girlish voice, unreal as in a Disney short, says "Good morning." Don't say, "Good morning." Give her your name. Pardon me . . . would you mind spelling your name? . . . Sorry, Sir, could you spell it once more? It is a hot summer day, and you are standing in a steaming phone booth. The ordeal of spelling one's name made many Europeans simplify and Americanize their names.

I didn't tell my readers that at one time I had Americanized my name when spelling W-e-c-h-s- ("How's that again?" the voice would interrupt, and I would grimly say, "See, age, ess") had been too much to bear. An American friend who meant well but knew little suggested "a good, old American name beginning with *W*, so you won't have to change the initials on your shirts." They were custom-made shirts, and I had ordered them in a fine men's store in Prague in an uncanny moment of acute foresight. Perhaps I sensed that these might be my last custom-made shirts for many years to come. I briefly called myself J. A. Waxmont, because "ekss" is easier to spell than "see, age, ess," but my friend suggested Warren, a fine, pre-Revolutionary name, he said. For a short time I became Joseph S. Warren. The *S* stood for "Siegfried," my father's first name.

"Warren" was easy to spell but hard to pronounce for me. The two *r*'s proved my phonetic undoing. Perhaps I should have emigrated to France, where a rolling *r* is an enunciative advantage. When I introduced myself as Warren in New York, people would give me a funny look. They thought I was a phony.

People in New York had looked at me that way already during my first weeks there, when I lectured on "How Czechoslovakia was Sold Down the River." I couldn't prevent being introduced as "Doctor Wechsberg, member of the Czechoslovak Parliament," though I'd made it clear that I had merely been a lowly secretary to a member. The man who introduced me would say this was the same thing, more or less. The introduction was the best part of the lecture, done with style and imagination, crediting me with strength of character and fine deeds that I had not carried out. What followed was a letdown. I'd learned my text phonetically and knew it by heart, like a singer performing a difficult part in a modern opera that he doesn't understand.

I'd been introduced to Mr. Feakins, a noted lecture agent and a kindly old gentleman who handled such lecture stars as Dorothy Thompson. Mr. Feakins said he would try to book me, and had some prospectus with my name and fictitious achievements printed, which he sent out. He said Americans were less interested in the subject of the lecture than in the personality of the lecturer. In my case, the magic of my personality didn't overcome the handicap of communicating with my audience. For about five minutes after I began to read my lecture, the poor people tried hard, and unsuccessfully, to understand what I attempted to say. Then they gave up, and a vague, bewildered expression settled down on their faces. For all they knew, I might be talking Mongolian or Swahili. They were too polite to look bored, but they *were* bored.

I didn't remain Warren long. Even the pretty, doll-faced receptionists seemed to resent my "American" name. I reverted to Wechsberg. Now I suffer in silence while my name is misspelled — Wechsbergh (like Lindbergh), Westberg, Wixberg, Fespert, Wexbarger, Wesber, Sexberg and Expert, to name just a few.

Very soon after I came to America, I decided that I was going to write for *The New Yorker*. This presented certain difficulties. I wasn't able to read the magazine I was going to write for. My English was limited to a couple of hundred words, most of which I was unable to pronounce correctly. Today I still miss the meaning of some stories and cartoons in *The New Yorker*, but I am not the only one. Harold Ross once told me that there were some things in his magazine even *he* didn't understand, and he gave an angry shrug. For a long time I wondered whether he'd meant it.

I must have been deeply attracted by the magazine which I couldn't read. I liked the way it looked — the mixture of serious and humorous elements, the grown-up, sophisticated way. Perhaps I instinctively sensed the style and taste, the cosmopolitan approach, the intellectual curiosity, the journalistic honesty. A magazine, unread, "speaks" to a writer as a Stradivari, unplayed, "sounds" to an expert. Perhaps I'd found something in *The New Yorker* again that I'd lost in Europe. Of the American magazines I saw, it seemed closest to the European spirit. As I began to feel my way through, I recognized certain things. It was like hearing a once familiar melody. The difference between "serious" and "light" music is as absurd as between "serious" and "light" writing. Music, or writing, is either good or bad. The music of *The New Yorker* often seemed light to me, like the bubbles in a glass of champagne, but it was good music. Vintage champagne.

In German writing, there exists a species called *Feuilleton*, which attained literary status a hundred years ago in the hands of its master practitioners. The *Feuilleton*, defined as "the bottom of a newspaper page, reserved for light literature or fiction," was rarely more than two thousand words, expressing an idea or commenting on an event, in lucid language and polished style, with a definite viewpoint. It was appreciated only by the cognoscenti; it was "caviar to the general." The critics called it *Kleinkunst* (a small genre of art). The *Feuilletonist* dispensed with bathos, passion, power. His ingredients were wit, innuendo, irony. Heine and Goethe wrote early masterpieces in this genre that became the literary fashion during the era of Liberalism in Vienna, toward the end of the nineteenth century. From there it was exported to Prague and Berlin, where the gentle stiletto experts practiced this civilized art form.

I'd written many *Feuilletons* in Europe. Now, trying to read *The New Yorker*'s "Talk of the Town," I felt that the anonymous writers were kinsmen of our *Feuilletonists*. They too practiced the intimate art of civilized detachment and sophisticated irony. They expressed a viewpoint but personally remained aloof. They refused to take anyone seriously, including themselves. And they knew that it is harder to make people chuckle than to make them laugh, that you can be serious without being earnest. The mood, the restraint, the discipline, the detachment, the artful yet casual formlessness were all there. Later I read that Ross called short pieces "casuals," for which there was no other classification.

Having made up my mind to write for *The New Yorker*, I decided to do it strictly on my own. No help wanted. I was going to start all over again. I would try to forget a great many things and to learn a great many more. I wouldn't ask anybody to help me with the editing of what I wrote. I wouldn't depend on translators. Translators were all right for the Manns, the Werfels, the Bunins, the Gides. The Olympians. We others who were closer to the ground had to comply with the rules of the earthly game. To write for an American magazine I would have to become an American writer.

English was the fourth language I was going to write in. Earlier, I'd written for publication in German, in Czech, in French. From the writer's point of view, English turned out to be the best and most practical language.

In German and in French, the written language is not identical with the colloquial language. No one in Germany speaks the prose of Thomas Mann. No one in France talks the way Marcel Proust writes. German and French writers-at-work become semantic schizophrenics, using metaphors and expressions they wouldn't use in their daily conversation.

(The Czech language is a special case. In modern Czech, the literary language is as close to the spoken idiom as in English. But Czech is much more difficult grammatically, with double negations, seven cases of the noun, and highly irregular verbs.)

The beauty of the English language is its simplicity. In English it is possible to convey deep thoughts simply. Lawyers, politicians, and public-relations apostles have tried to blunt the beautiful, sharp instrument by injecting pompous expressions and impressive-sounding words, but much as they try, they can't ruin the basic beauty of the English language. The best American prose writers write the way they talk. Good English is lucid English. In Germany, the literary language is rarely lucid. The German *Drang* toward mysticism and metaphysics prevents many German writers from writing lucid prose. And they are afraid of the literary critics, esoteric aesthetes, and pompous professors, who consider lucid writing simple or banal. The writers build up complicated word structures, contracting whole sentences into elongated words that terrify telegraph operators who must count the letters. In Vienna, the city of baroque titles, there exists the *Nebeneichamtsvize-präsident*, the-vice-president-of-the-other-gauging-office, and there was said to have been a *Donaudampfschiffahrtsgesellschaftskapitänswitwe*, the-widow-of-a-captain-of-the-Danube-Steam-Ship-Company, though I never met her and suppose she is a figment of a *Feuilletonist*'s imagination.

Mark Twain has made fun of it, but it was no fun to write the language. German writers often delight in vagueness and obscurantism, which is taken for profundity by their adepts. "The Germans," the late Wieland Wagner, the Master's grandson, once told me, "think they are profound when they are merely confused." Perhaps he was thinking of Grandfather Richard's unfathomable wisdom. (*"Zum Raum wird hier die Zeit"*; "Here time becomes space." Harold Ross, the perfectionist would have queried that statement, from *Parsifal*.)

Goethe wrote lucid German except when he *wanted* to be obscure, as in the second part of *Faust*, which exasperates *Professoren* and

Spiessbürger (philistines). Thomas Mann, a master of humor and clear prose, has written complex, esoteric pages in his late works that many readers don't understand, though few have the courage to admit it. Heine, a very great poet, wrote lucid essays and witty criticism. He could be logical in an illogical language. In German, there is a masculine apple (*der Apfel*), a feminine pear (*die Birne*), and both become neuter as fruit (*das Obst*) or compote (*das Kompott*). The foot (*der Fuss*) is masculine, the hand (*die Hand*) is feminine; and the heart (*das Herz*), the very symbol of life, is inanimate. (The wife, *das Weib*, is also neuter, and some husbands may agree.) Yet in this paradoxical wasteland there are meaningful signposts of truth: the manly head (*der Kopf*), the womanly soul (*die Seele*), the cold neuter brain (*das Gehirn*).

In order to write a foreign language, one must learn to think in it. The language is alive — in German, *die Sprache* (the language) is a woman — and translated words often lead an artificial, dormant existence. I thought I was making progress when I began to dream in English, but I didn't take it as Freudian proof of having the language absorbed subconsciously. I often dream in English, but I still count in German because I learned it in grammar school.

At our *Gymnasium* in Ostrava, the emphasis was on the humanities, while the *Realschule* specialized in the natural sciences. We studied Virgil and Ovid, Homer and Plato, and we would take a dim view of the *Realschule*'s poor semi-illiterates who learned nothing except mathematics, physics, and chemistry. Our intellectual arrogance toward the *Realschüler* was as bad as that shown by pure, abstract scientists toward applied scientists. I haven't changed my early belief in a humanistic education even in this technological age that devalues the knowledge of classical Greek. Besides Greek and Latin, our curriculum included German and Czech.

My French and English are entirely self-taught. My earlier knowledge of Latin and Greek was more helpful to me than what some people call the "musical ear." The written language is a structure of logical thought, not of melodious sound — except in some libretti of Verdi's operas that get away triumphantly with doubtful logic and beautiful melody. I wouldn't have been able to write in several languages without the knowledge of Latin sentence structure and Greek etymology.

As a teen-ager I went a few weeks to English evening courses in Ostrava but gave up because I didn't like the sound of English. No wonder, since the teacher spoke English with a thick German-Czech accent. This was my musical epoch, and I loved the more melodious languages, such as Italian and Russian. I disliked Czech, with words and whole sentences containing not a single vowel. The best known is "strč prst skrz krk," which is not a coded message but means "put the finger through the throat"— a feat almost as difficult to perform as to pronounce the sentence describing it, unless you were born in Bohemia or Moravia.

I might have changed my mind about English if I'd heard the language spoken by a great English actor, but I didn't go to England until rather late in life. At the *Gymnasium* we studied Shakespeare in the famous German translation by Tieck and Schlegel which our professor of literature, in one of his bizarre moments, called "superior to the English original." He claimed it wasn't really a translation but a *Nachdichtung*, a re-creation.

English was said to be the language you needed to go around the world, but when I made my global journey in 1936, I got along with a few words, and stock phrases. (As a ship's musician on French boats, I'd rarely spoken English, since most people seemed to speak French.) In the bars and bazaars of the Middle and Far East, a knowledge of the King's English was not required. On the banana boats and freighters which I took because they were inexpensive, some people knew even less English than I.

To increase my small income from European journalism, I'd agreed to "represent" an old Bohemian firm selling hops and malt to breweries all over the world. The owner, a friend, didn't ask me to sell anything, which I couldn't have done anyway. I was expected to drop in at big breweries in Colombo, Singapore, Shanghai, and Tokyo, and talk to the brewmasters, the firm's customers. They were red-faced heavy-built Czechs or Bavarians, and all of them were homesick for Prague or Munich. They drowned their sorrows in beer, while I listened to their tearful stories and drank with them. It was an ideal assignment. In the tropical latitudes I was always thirsty, and the beer was always cool.

There was no free beer in America, where the Bohemian firm was well represented. In the early summer of 1936, I'd arrived on the West Coast, coming from Japan on a steamer that served mostly raw fish for dinner. Though I wrote many articles for many newspapers in Europe, and illustrated them with my own photographs, I had little money — just enough to cross America by Greyhound bus. It was a fascinating experience. Exhausting, but I was young and didn't mind. I needed very few English words to cross the country. In the drugstores I would order hamburgers and apple pie, so there would be no misunderstanding. Also, I liked hamburgers and apple pie, and they were cheap. The difficulties begin only when one wants one's steak done a little more than medium-rare but not quite medium. This was no problem, since I couldn't afford steak.

I arrived in New York in June, 1936, and sailed for Europe. I was blissfully unaware that less than three years later I would be back in America — for good.

Fifteen Hundred Endless Days

LATE IN MARCH, 1939, we went from New York to California by Grey-hound. By now I was an old Greyhound hand and thought I knew my way around. "California" had a magic sound. We had friends there, the Karl Freunds (he was a celebrated cameraman) who wrote us we could rent a small house with a garden for sixty dollars a month, exactly what we'd paid for our room near Riverside Drive in New York. Sun-shine and flowers in the garden, free of charge. Informal clothes and informal manners. Also, I had dreams of glory, like almost everybody else who goes to Hollywood. I hoped to sell the movies a story for a million dollars.

We found a house with a garden in Laurel Canyon. There were flowers as long as my wife watered the garden twice a day. The empty lot next to the house was a weedy jungle. The climate was balmy but less than ideal for an unemployed, impecunious American would-be writer whose successful writer friends worked in the studios for a thou-sand dollars a week.

Hollywood seemed a clannish place. The "movie people," including both those who were trying to break in and others who had dropped out, rarely met "Los Angeles people," "Pasadena people," or just people. Place names had subtle meanings. "Pasadena" meant society, "L.A." was business, "Westwood" was the university crowd (UCLA). "Hollywood," where we lived, implied poor jerks who hadn't made it. "Beverly Hills," with a Crestview telephone number, indicated you were on your way, and in "Bel Air" you had arrived. "Santa Monica" could mean both a beachcomber's shack, or a movie-producer's mansion facing the Pacific. "Brentwood" was fine, but "North Hollywood" wasn't. "Culver City" was for carpenters, studio electricians, and guys getting union wages for not lifting a chair they weren't supposed to. "The Valley" was gaining social status, and "Encino" indicated you might be a neighbor of Clark Gable's though he certainly wouldn't know it.

In New York I'd noticed that Americans liked to talk about their "melting pot" but also liked to make sure the pot didn't run over when it started to boil. Until I came there, I'd never known that two adjacent city blocks might be a world apart. Snobs in New York were scholars in social topography. In Europe it mattered little where you lived, provided you had the right title. If you happened to be a university professor, a high-ranking civil servant, the member of an old though impoverished family, you could live anywhere. I'd never heard the expression "the wrong side of the tracks."

In Czechoslovakia it made no difference what school you went to, if you wound up with a degree. Nobody I knew was incredibly rich, and nobody was terribly poor. The aftermath of the First World War had upset all social norms. Famous scholars and members of once distinguished families were now impoverished. Scrap-metal dealers and *Schieber* (operators dealing in various commodities) were suddenly rich. At a performance at the Vienna State Opera in the early 1920's, I saw a nouveau-riche family in a nearby box. During intermission they dined on rolls with slices of sausage and threw the sausage skins into the auditorium. No one there seemed surprised.

In Czechoslovakia, then a young, true democracy, there was no
Establishment. There had been no time to groom an elite, though there
were political people in power. During the astronomical inflation, money
had lost all meaning. Money matters were always considered a man's
intimate sphere. No one would tell you how much he made or how
much he was worth, and not much has changed about that. A man's
bank account is still considered his secret, and not only in Switzerland.
I know more about the love lives of some of my close friends in Europe
than about their finances.

In Hollywood, the clans were divided vertically, by the size of the
weekly paycheck, and horizontally, by subtle ethnographic distinctions.
In a society where you were as good, or bad, as your last picture, it
took effort and ingenuity to stake out a social claim. The powerful people whose names were Hollywood household words would stick together, protecting each other against the hoi polloi. But even on the more
modest immigrant level, strict distinctions were made between this
morning's ins and last night's outs. The Hungarians and the Germans
had their tight little cliques and subcliques. The members of the invisible
but omnipresent Hungarian Club, a worldwide secret organization, told
terrible intrigues about each other but always helped one another. Every
Hungarian was automatically a club member through birth. The club
spirit was, and remains, strong. When a Hungarian attained a small
position of power in a Hollywood studio, he would surround himself
with a protective shield of fellow Hungarians. Some of them were said
to be quite gifted. Since few non-Hungarians understand Hungarian,
the Hungarians would amuse themselves by telling each other atrocious
stories about other people in the same room, who rarely knew that they
were the source of hilarity. Contrarily, the Germans never helped each
other, or anyone else. They were trying to become more American than
native Americans, yet they were never able to conceal their origin.
We drifted into a group of "Old Austrians," pliable survivors of

what had once been the Habsburg monarchy. All of them had a touch of nostalgia and a genius for compromise. The monarchy was finished, but everybody agreed it hadn't been a bad thing. In our small circle there were people from Vienna (the Vienna of Schnitzler and Karl Kraus), Prague (the Prague of Kafka and Jaroslav Hašek), Budapest (the Budapest of Molnár and Bartók). Jacques Kapralik came from Bucharest and was considered "almost Austrian." (He died early; the others are still alive. In writing this book I think of the dead more than of the living.)

Compared to the socially prominent British in Hollywood who treated the American natives with proper condescension, and the highly rated French, we Central Europeans were way down on the social ladder. At a dinner party in the house of a Hollywood producer (I seem to have been invited by a clerical error), the guest of honor was an English novelist whose minor literary talent was camouflaged by his major conceit. He was treated as though he'd won the Nobel Prize. Way down the table sat Thomas Mann, who *had* been awarded the Nobel Prize for Literature in 1929. He was ignored by the host and the hostess. Later, another movie mogul slapped Mann on the shoulder and called him "Tommy." Tommy! Who, by unanimous consent of the German *Literaturprofessoren,* was a saint.

My English was still primitive, and I amused my European friends in Hollywood with my delusions of grandeur, predicting that one day I was going to write for *The New Yorker.* I sounded like another writer who told everybody he was going to write *the* great novel of our emigration, or a man who claimed he had an appointment with Sam Goldwyn next week. A former habitué of the Café New York in Budapest advised me to be "realistic." He couldn't write a complete English sentence but had a writer's contract in a major studio where he was much admired for his wit. He spent his mornings in story conferences — in a singsong voice he pronounced the *o* in the word *story* like the *o* in *loan* — and was helping them with the "stoary line," whatever that meant. It meant, among other things, his weekly paycheck of twelve hundred and fifty dollars which his secretary brought him every Friday.

"*That*," he said to me, "is realistic. Why bother to write in English when you can be a twelve-hundred-and-fifty-dollar-a-week writer without writing a line?"

I asked him who wrote the lines. He gave a lofty shrug.

"Any jerk can write who went to public school," he said. "But how many people can think up a stoary line?"

I continued my lonely collision course with the English language. My enormous self-confidence was matched by my abysmal ignorance. Usually a pessimist, I firmly believed in my ultimate success as an American writer, though I knew little about America except what I'd seen of it from the window of a Greyhound bus.

I didn't bother to buy an English grammar. I still don't own one. Many writers feel comfortable surrounded by barricades of encyclopedias, dictionaries, almanacs, and other reference volumes. I decided right from the start on total independence — from men and books. Every writer needs books to look up things, but I trained myself to use them only if I didn't know the answer myself. The only reference book I own and use frequently is *Roget's International Thesaurus*. When I write letters in German, French, and Czech, I may have to look for a word in a small dictionary. I believe in linguistic rather than physical exercise.

Once in a while I am asked by people who hear me speak English whether I have somebody who fixes up my stuff. I can't blame them. My hairline is receding, but my accent is advancing. Happily, accent doesn't show in print. A writer is supposed to write, not to talk.

I am further handicapped by not being able to spell. I never learned spelling in school in Europe. German, Czech, and French don't present the baffling problems of spelling and pronunciation that schoolchildren in America and England learn to master early. How should one know whether "well" means "all right" or "spring," and whether "spring" is synonymous with "season," "source," "strength," "ship's rope," "recoil," "leap," "elasticity," "fountain," "motive," or "source of supply." (I'm quoting from my dear thesaurus. If it didn't exist, one would have to invent it.) Being unable to spell, I often have trouble writing down somebody's name which he spells for me. I give up and ask the man to please write it down for me. He complies, giving me a thoughtful glance. I know *exactly* what he is thinking.

Learning to write a new language at the age of thirty-two has its problems, but there are compensations. One doesn't make the beginner's mistakes of a grammar-school pupil. One takes nothing for granted. I knew the odds were against me, and I liked the challenge. I didn't learn, as in school, for the purpose of bringing home a report or passing a test. I learned so that I would be able to build a new life, and I knew the risks.

For over four years — fifteen hundred endless days — I kept writing, with no success and steadily diminishing hope. I wrote every day, including New Year's Day and the Jewish New Year, George Washington's birthday, Emperor Franz Joseph's birthday, President Masaryk's birthday, my own birthday, Saturday, and Sunday. Sunday remains my favorite writing day. People, children, and dogs have deserted the neighborhood scene. The painful noises of hammering and sawing have ceased. (The population explosion has reached my writing desk no matter where I am, and somebody is always building something nearby.)

The street is empty, the house is quiet. There is a lull between the storms. The pleasant, low-droning sound of a small private plane is in the sky. From somewhere comes the baritone humming of a lawn mower. Thank God, the grass is still growing, and it is always green, not violet or pink or black. There must be a Higher Order, though one sometimes tends to doubt it. There is the distant sound of a radio, and a faint echo of children's laughter. Until Poppy came along, children used to make me nervous, and I seemed to attract them magically. I might be the only passenger in a railroad coach, and soon families with small kids would gather around me, though there were empty seats elsewhere, and the little dear ones would be all over me. Now everything is different, and I enjoy the comforting sound of laughing children. Their laughter is what it should be — merry and true.

I never wrote less than six hours a day, and sometimes ten, winter and spring, summer and fall, in my good and bad moments, even during bleak moods of depression. When I say "I wrote," I don't mean that I put words down on paper for hours. I just tried to. Writing is a constant trial, a never-ending obstacle race. On a good day, I would make two or three hurdles; on a bad one, I couldn't even take the first. The working day was lost, but the therapeutic value remained. I liked the soothing, dark days of rain, which were rare in Hollywood. I began to loathe the glare of the sunlight, brilliant and unreal like many other things in Hollywood, where I learned to appreciate Venetian blinds. And now, in Vienna, where I write this, the skies remain dark and gray for weeks, and one gets as lonely for the sun as for the woman one loves.

In southern California, I missed the invigorating rhythm of the changing seasons. The glare gave the days and weeks and months a uniform, glossy look. After my writing hours, I would read — for study, not for escape. American and English prose, the great essayists, history, and biography.

I did foolish things. At one time I tried to write "short shorts" that I saw in some magazines. A successful writer told me that they paid a dollar a word. A dollar a word! The short shorts reminded me of Maupassant. I naively thought they were easy to write because they were short. I soon learned the bitter truth. The short shorts were put together as meticulously as a Swiss watch movement. Maupassant wouldn't have sold many short shorts to *Collier's* or *Liberty*.

In these long, sun-drenched years, I wrote thousands of pages. I don't know what happened to them, and I don't care. I've trained my-

self to forget as others train themselves to remember. I esteem the blessings of selective forgetfulness. Once in a while I discover an old manuscript in a dusty file. I don't remember having written it, but my name
is on it. I never reread anything I wrote a long time ago. I never look
through my books. They are the past. Better to think of the future, unwritten books.

Late in the afternoon I would walk down from our home in Westwood Village, where we then lived, to the post office, to mail my letters.
The short walk, maybe ten minutes, was an act of tradition. Europeans
are brought up to take a short walk every day (though now the tradition
goes to pieces under the devilish influence of the automobile). In Hollywood, walking was suspect; only the very poor and the very eccentric
walked. People wouldn't even cross the street. They would get into
their car, make a U-turn to the other side, and get out again.

The road to the post office descended slowly in two hairpin bends.
By the time I'd reached the second bend, there would often be a patrol
car coming up from behind. Westwood Village was well patrolled,
though not as well as neighboring Beverly Hills. The cops would stop
the car and give me a suspicious stare. Sometimes one of them would
ask me what I was doing, everything okay, son? I had an alibi, though:
a large manila envelope addressed to some magazine in New York. I
showed them the envelope as travelers at the border show their passport.
I said I was going to the post office to mail a manuscript.

"A *writer*," the cop said, giving his colleague a significant glance, as
though that explained everything. He looked like one of my uncles when
he'd told my mother, years ago, "What can you expect from a *writer*?"

The cops left in their car, their suspicion allayed but not quite
silenced. I went down and mailed the envelope. Several weeks later the
mailman would bring another large envelope, with the name of the
magazine in the upper left-hand corner. My manuscript and a printed
rejection slip would be inside. I know writers who like to say they could

have papered the walls of their office with their rejection slips. I could have redecorated a large mansion in the elegant Bel Air section if I had bothered to keep the slips. I didn't.

I gratefully remember a few writer friends, all of them American, who gave me moral support: Richard English, Jack Woodford, Robert Carson, Irving Wallace, Charles Brackett, Manny Seff. They couldn't tell me how to write, but they told me not to give up writing. Dick English, who had an adventurous career as a sailor, prizefighter, and jazz musician before he turned to writing, would say it was just a matter of sticking out all these rejections. The arrival of a rejection slip would be followed by an acute attack of melancholy, the writer's occupational disease. *Post rejectionem omne animal triste.* In novels, writers usually get drunk in such moments, but I couldn't afford it. In our early Hollywood days, our food-and-beverage budget was a dollar a day. Not as bad as it sounds now, but not enough to get drunk on. I briefly considered going out for a ride, or to a movie — but in the end I would completely close the Venetian blinds (every bit of bright sunshine and the successful world outside was particularly irritating in such moments) and would retrench behind my typewriter. A writer always seeks solace at his typewriter, which, paradoxically, is often the source of his trouble. He hates to write — but he hates even more *not* to write. He writes compulsively; he doesn't care what's going to happen; he writes though he is almost convinced he may never get published.

Somebody in the house on the hill above ours was playing the piano. Always Rachmaninoff's Second Concerto, the C minor; never anything else. Most of my rejection slips arrived accompanied by the beautiful lyric theme of the Second Concerto, which Abram Chasins calls "the most agonized-over tune in the whole concerto literature." To me it became the most agonizing tune. Whoever played up there on the hill played Rachmaninoff beautifully, with a faultless technique and rhapsodic lyricism. But I never want to hear the C-minor Concerto again. I firmly associate it with rejection slips in the dreary canyons of Hollywood.

It was a dangerous landscape. (This was before we moved on, and up in life, to Westwood Village.) We'd abandoned our first house, on a steep slope, that was literally falling to pieces, and had taken another house at the beginning of Laurel Canyon Boulevard. It belonged to a plumber who never charged us for repairs. Its attraction was a garden with a mimosa tree blooming every spring and reminding me that another year had gone by, and I was still a failure. The mimosa blooms lasted only a few weeks, but the black-widow spiders and poison ivy were there the whole year. One day I stepped in our living room and saw a vicious rattlesnake wriggling on the floor. The rattlesnake had come in through the chimney, though it wasn't the night before Christmas. I killed the snake with the fireplace tongs.

For about a week I was admired by my friends as a man of cold courage. Some seemed surprised; apparently writers are not generally identified with feats of heroism, a boomerang of the theory that the pen is mightier than the sword. As a matter of fact, a free-lance writer who lives solely on his wits needs the audacity of a racing driver, the nerves of a professional gambler, the equilibrium of a trapeze artist, and the optimism of a hospital nurse. A writer would be a hero to his valet if he could afford one.

I complained to our plumber landlord about the snake, and he assured me there would be no extra charge for it. Neither was there for the rats that occasionally visited our house. Perhaps these were symbolic visits — the ship wasn't sinking yet — but the significance was lost on me. The rats frightened me more than the black-widow spiders and the rattlesnake. Ann bravely set traps for the rats and burned them in the incinerator. Afterwards I went out and bought a bottle of Scotch, and the hell with the budget. This happened just a few hundred yards north of Schwab's Drugstore on Sunset Boulevard where some of the biggest Hollywood agents had their offices, and whom you couldn't burn in the incinerator.

At night we would listen to the gas concert, "Classical Music Presented by Your Southern California Gas Company." The gas people were crazy about Tchaikovsky, Sibelius, and, yes, the C-minor Rach-maninoff. Sometimes we went to a studio press preview. I got free invitations, as a bona fide member of the Foreign Press Corps in Hollywood, a distinguished-sounding group whose members couldn't afford any other entertainment. Once a month we were polled about the film of the month, and the results were printed in the *Hollywood Reporter*, the movie colony's Bible. Once I won the poll and saw my name in large letters in an ad in the "Bible." I would have preferred to see it in small letters on an inside page where every day the sales of stories were listed. Ten years later, when Twentieth Century Fox bought a story of mine, I lived in Europe, six thousand miles away from Hollywood.

My first regular "market" (a terrible expression that no writer should use) was a Canadian publication, the *Toronto Star Weekly*. I'd met George F. Rogers, the editor, when we'd been in Canada waiting for our American immigration visas. He'd been encouraging and asked me to send him something someday. Thanks to the checks from the *Toronto Star Weekly*, we were able to trade in our second-hand Chevrolet for a new Oldsmobile. We celebrated the event by going to Santa Barbara. Halfway I skidded onto the soft shoulder and banged into the car ahead of us, ruining the Oldsmobile's lovely new grille. That was the end of our celebration. I almost cried.

At that time, I began to experiment with slick, plotted short stories. Most of them came back, but then the *Saturday Evening Post* bought one, and two, and more. I didn't realize that the *Post* was not just a magazine but an American legend. Some of my American writer friends told me what it had meant to them when they had "made the *Post*." All of them felt devoted to the magazine which some of them had sold every week in their hometowns when they'd been little boys. The *Post* was a symbol to them, something nostalgic and dear to their hearts.

A writer who earned thousands of dollars a week at the studios and still wrote for the *Post* said to me, "It's not because I'm proud to write for a magazine for which Kipling, London, Ring Lardner, Fitzgerald, Faulkner and Hemingway have written. No — but the *Post* just remains part of my childhood, and you want to keep that part, don't you?"

Not long ago, I looked up some of my *Post* stories. They have cute titles: "Bathroom Baritone," "Don't Kiss Them on the Street," and "Happy Days Are Here Again." I tried to read one of them but gave up after a few paragraphs. They seem silly and dated. I wrote them for money. Naturally. Money has always stimulated the creative spirit. The letters of Joseph Haydn, one of the greatest creative spirits, addressed to the music publishing house of Artaria and Company in Vienna, show him as a shrewd man in financial matters. The late letters of Mozart, perhaps the greatest genius of all, reveal his constant preoccupation with money at the end of his short, tortured life. He doesn't write about the unfathomable masterpieces he was working on then; he needed another hundred ducats to pay his debts. He would have been happy to write *Gebrauchsmusik* ("utility music") for any occasion and any combination of instruments, if someone had given him a commission.

I studied the *Post*'s formula stories. They were a little like the Metro-Goldwyn-Mayer supercolossals that we saw at the free previews, creating a romantic never-never world for the American housewife, not very different from the silly dreamworld of the Austrian schmaltz-and-waltz operettas. Girl gets boy, money is the root of all wealth, roses are red but be careful of the thorns. This was before millions of men and women came home from the Second World War knowing that the Brave New World wasn't quite like the films and the stories.

Some readers wrote me letters complimenting me on certain characters whom they thought they recognized. I'd learned that one must write about people one knows in settings one knows. Perhaps my stories had a certain verisimilitude. I hope. Some took place in Gay Paree, always a surefire scene for Americans who love to read about the City of Light, though they should know now that Paree can be quite ungay. I wrote about beautiful European girls and occasionally about a Guerlain-perfumed femme fatale, though the femme fatale was a calculated risk with the editors of the *Post*, a family magazine. Once an editor told me, "Sure, lots of things happen in Omaha, Nebraska, but we don't have to advertise them." Did they have femmes fatales in Omaha? The editor said he hoped they did, though they might have another word for them.

Once I made the mistake of putting a lovely American girl into a story. It was a disaster. My experience with American girls was limited. Few lovelies seemed interested in a married, struggling, untitled refugee. If I'd had at least a "de" or "von" with my name, or was the black sheep of a noble British family. My American lovely created bewilderment and hilarity in the editorial offices of the *Saturday Evening Post*. I learned my lesson and kept away from lovely American girls. Especially in slick fiction.

On my first trip from Hollywood to New York, Paul R. Reynolds, my agent, introduced me to E. N. ("Erd") Brandt of the *Post*, who came to New York every Thursday morning to make the rounds of the prominent agents. Paul thought my bizarre expressions of Continental humor might become a salable commodity in Philadelphia. Erd Brandt was a skilled craftsman and a fine editor. He could take a short story apart like a Meccano toy and put it together again, and I realized that it had been upside down. My plotted stories had a schedule as exact as that of the Super-Chief (which is now a thing of the past, as is the *Post*). At certain points along the route, certain things would happen, there would be sudden halts and reverses, the train might be shifted to a siding — but four thousand words after the lead sentence, the story would arrive safely with its surprising denouement. Maybe it wasn't for the literary critics, but it was competently done, and sometimes it was even funny.

After the *Post* had published some of my stories and articles, Paul and I took a train to Philadelphia to lunch with Ben Hibbs, the editor, and Erd Brandt. We arrived in Independence Square, in front of the solid and solemn building of the Curtis Company, across from Independence Hall and Liberty Bell. I was awed. The spirit of Benjamin Franklin was all over the place. In Europe, I'd known him only as the inventor of the lightning rod, and here he'd also founded a magazine that paid millions of dollars for words. Like many other Americans, I firmly believed that the *Post* had been founded by Franklin in 1728. It said so on the masthead, and Franklin's profile and signature were there to prove it. Only after the death of the *Post* I read that the *Post*'s connection with Franklin was somewhat indirect; the *Pennsylvania Gazette*, which Franklin had edited, let the *Post* use its print shop in the early days, and one of the *Post*'s founders had been the partner of the grandson of Franklin's partner in the printing business.

The corridors of the Curtis building were gloomy, as though the late Franklin had planned to set up an undertaker's establishment and as an afterthought founded the magazine. I felt I had arrived in the innermost recesses of American history, and I understood at last why so many American writers wanted to "make the *Post*." *Aside* from the money. Ben Hibbs was tall and soft-spoken, gentle and honest, just the man to edit the *Post*. He and Erd Brandt were kind and made me feel at home there, as though I too had grown up in a small American town and had sold the *Post* from door to door as a youngster.

After a conventional conversational gambit in Ben Hibbs's office, we walked over to a restaurant in an adjoining building that seemed like the Philadelphia idea of an English club. It was a long walk, and our steps reverberated in the corridors. Hibbs, Brandt, and Reynolds were tall men, and I had trouble keeping in step with them. Hibbs and I walked in front, Brandt and Reynolds behind us. To any quiz contestant watching us, we might have looked like a couple of trust-company executives about to sign a multimillion-dollar deal. No one would have guessed that we were about to discuss the fine points of a word merger called "Bathroom Baritone." An autobiographical reflection, no doubt.

I always wanted to be a baritone in opera, but my limited vocal resources were good enough only for a completely tiled bathroom.

It was a pleasant lunch, and after the "Bathroom Baritone" had been done away with, Erd Brandt told us about the basement of his home, where he put together an old automobile engine which pleased him more than the construction of short stories. Everybody laughed. The stories, Erd said, were more complicated than the engine. Again everybody laughed. I once asked Erd, foolishly, whether he believed in these stories and the world that they created. He looked at me sadly, like a Saint Bernard dog, saying nothing. I never asked him again. Hibbs was often remote, saying little. Once, after reading an article I'd done on the plight of many parents behind the Iron Curtain who are afraid of their own children, he wrote me to say how deeply touched he'd been. The *Post's* editors respected writers. They wanted you to write articles about something you felt deeply about, and to write as you wanted to write. They would send me proofs, and never changed anything without my permission. They understood writers. The old *Post* was a fine magazine, and I had a sense of loss when it ceased to exist.

Late in 1942, I seem to have reached the conclusion, God knows why, that I was ready for *The New Yorker*. I mailed them a manuscript. *The New Yorker* was not ready for me. Weeks later, there was a large envelope with the manuscript and you-know-what. The next one was also returned, and so was the third. By that time we had moved from Laurel Canyon in Hollywood, playground of rats and rattlesnakes, poison ivy and black-widow spiders, to Midvale Avenue in Westwood Village. We'd made a small down payment on a six-unit apartment house. The neighbors called me "Doc," assuming I was teaching at UCLA. I did nothing to spoil their illusion; neither did I do anything to support it.

My wife had saved a little money from her earnings at a Beverly Hills dressmaking establishment, and I'd saved some money from my

sales to the *Post*. Taxes were low, and life was still cheap. Some invest-
ment-wise friends convinced us that if we rented five apartments in the
house, we could live "rent free" in the sixth. Four years after arriving
as impecunious immigrants in this blessed country, we joined the ranks
of proud house owners. We were full-fledged capitalists. The house was
only three years old, and there were neither rats nor rattlesnakes. But
most of our tenants had small children who cried a lot in the daytime.
At night they would fall out of their beds and cry again. One couldn't
miss the most inconsequential family crisis, for the walls were made of
cardboard. But no one was playing the Rachmaninoff Second Concerto.

One afternoon, when signs and posters all over Westwood Village
told everybody that there were only nineteen days left until Christmas,
I mailed another manila envelope, after the usual interception by the
local cops. Shortly before Christmas, the chimes sounded at the entrance
door. The mailman. He handed me a letter from *The New Yorker*. Not
a large manila envelope. *A letter!*

Perhaps my hands trembled as I opened it, but I don't remember.
I didn't watch myself with clinical detachment, as they do in novels.

The letter said that the editors had liked my piece "The Corsican
Express" and were buying it. They would be glad to consider more of
my work. The letter was signed in very small letters, "G. S. Lobrano."

Not long ago, I went into *The New Yorker*'s library on the nineteenth floor to look at some of my early contributions which I'd forgotten all about. There were the magazine's back issues, bound in big
volumes. I also saw some black-linen bound volumes containing the
pasted-up tearsheets of the contributors. Some of them had their own
volumes. I was surprised to see three thick volumes with my name in
big white letters. Miss Ebba Johnson, the librarian, said kindly, "But
you've written so much for the magazine," to make me feel easier. It
was hard to believe. I took out the earliest volume and read "The Corsican Express," published in the issue of June 19, 1943. (Nine, nineteen,

and twenty-nine are my lucky numbers.) Slowly, I began to remember. . . .

In the middle 1930's, before coming to America. I'd gone to Corsica to write some articles. Corsica was interesting, owing to Napoleon Bonaparte and some more recent bandits. Traveling on a small vintage railroad that made frequent, unscheduled stops between Bastia and Ajaccio, we had stopped somewhere in the mountains. The engineer said we would have to wait "until pressure in the locomotive builds up." I thought he wanted to visit with the owner of a nearby bar whose name was Philippe Fernande Colombo, a colorful character even by Corsican standards. After a few glasses of wine he told me, in strictest secrecy, that he was "the only direct descendant of Christopher Columbus." Many cities in Italy and Spain have claimed to be the birthplace of the Admiral of the Spanish Fleet and great discoverer. But according to Philippe Fernande Colombo, the real honor belonged to Ajaccio. He could give me no proof of his descendancy nor of his claim, but the editors of *The New Yorker*, thank heaven, had been amused.

At last. After fifteen-hundred-odd days of trying to write, of writing, sunshine, rats and rattlesnakes, rejections and the Second Rachmaninoff, and still more writing, I'd done it. Suddenly, I was terrified, convinced it could never happen again. Lightning never strikes twice, not in southern California, where thunderstorms are rare anyway. The letter, and the brief moment of exhilaration, were already an anticlimax.

Once again I had bad timing. Several weeks later I received "Greetings!" from my local draft board.

The Magic of the Uniform

A RECURRENT THEME SONG in Austrian and German entertainment, prior to 1914, was "Der Zauber der Montur" ("The Magic of the Uniform"). The magical, light blue uniform tunics were worn by dashing operetta officers who were as unreal as their uniforms. The officers were immensely popular with the readers of novels and the audiences of such operettas. My own ideas about the magic of the uniform were closer to those of Jaroslav Hašek's good soldier Schweik, the leading antihero of my generation. I was too young to remember the dashing young officers prior to the First World War, but I well remembered the pathetic human wrecks that came back from the war. I was unhappy when I was drafted for eighteen months of military service in the Czechoslovak army. I took a copy of Hašek's book with me when I went into the army but had to turn it over to our commanding officer. *Schweik* was too dangerous to be read and discussed in the barracks, "a demoralizing influence."

My mother was shocked when the army got hold of me. She was certain I would be rejected by the army doctors. For years she'd told everybody what a frail, green-faced boy I'd been, always suffering from colds and indigestion. Poor Pepi, as she called me, would refuse for weeks any food except wieners, which I washed down with cocoa. Always wieners with cocoa, or liverwurst with hot chocolate. My early gastronomic ideas were somewhat perverted. Or maybe I was just a spoiled brat.

The Czechoslovak army doctors weren't fooled for a moment. They looked at me and knew there was a *mens sana in corpore sano*. The chief doctor, a lieutenant colonel, cast a cursory glance at the protruding ribs of my naked torso and made a fateful check mark after the printed word *schopen* (Czech for "fit"). I was trapped. The checkup had lasted half a minute. It took place in a building that had once belonged to Grandfather Wechsberg. He would have been amused by this ironical twist.

Seventeen years later, the American army gave me a more thorough checkup in Los Angeles — a blood test, X rays of my lungs, and a long interview with an army psychiatrist that left me with many complexes. The psychiatrist had an unfair advantage over me. He was fully dressed; I was completely naked. The result, though, was exactly the same: once more I was fit for active duty.

In both cases the army doctors were absolutely right. I survived the Spartan exigencies of the Czechoslovak army, and my uncomfortable experiences in the American army during the Second World War. Once in a while I have a recurrent nightmare: again I am drafted for active service. I wake up in a cold sweat. I wouldn't be very surprised if it happened, confirming my pessimistic outlook on life.

The Czechoslovak army assigned me to the infantry, called the "queen of arms." We were told it was an honor, a privilege to serve in the "queen of arms." What else could they tell us after we'd crawled through mud-covered terrain or come back from an eighteen-mile march, carrying thirty-six pounds of useless equipment on our aching backs? We would have preferred to serve in a less prestigious, more comfortable outfit, sustained by motorized vehicles, or horses. I envied Uncle Eugen, my father's oldest brother, a captain in the cavalry, who walked around with shining boots and rattling spurs. He was suffering from diabetes, had been exempted from frontline service, and survived the war. Apparently, it was my fate to carry on my father's infantry tradition, while my younger brother Max served in the Czech cavalry and also walked around in shiny boots, carrying a swagger stick. But when Max arrived in America, as a refugee in 1940, he volunteered, and was assigned to a tank outfit at Ford Ord, California. He fought in North Africa with General Terry Allen's First Infantry Division.

The army of the United States, too, honored me by assigning me to the prestigious infantry. I loved ships and would have preferred to join the navy. But I was still a noncitizen, a second-class person. I went to see the navy recruitment people in Los Angeles. After ascertaining my nonstatus, they informed me, with no regret, that they were not interested. My only chance to serve in the United States navy would be in the Third World War, but I don't really care *that* much.

Serving in the queenly Czechoslovak infantry meant getting up at four A.M. in the summer and at five in the winter, marching for hours through rain and slush, lying all night long in the snow. Nowadays I'm told by some doctor friends that I should have more exercise, swim, walk, play golf. "It's good for you," they say. If they had walked half as much as I, they would give me better advice.

After returning to the barracks, wet and cold and dead tired, one had to clean — first one's gun, then clothes and equipment, and finally oneself. The gun, we were told, always came first. During the winter I expected to wind up momentarily at the hospital with double pneumonia and pleurisy, yet I never had so much as a head cold. It was claimed that the foul-smelling air in our barracks had a more salubrious effect than, say, the air up in the magic mountains of Davos, Switzerland. There were twenty-six of us sleeping in a large room. The windows were never opened all winter long, on the sound theory *lepši smradeček nez chladeček* (better a little stench than a little cold). A similar theory had been scientifically developed earlier, in Vienna's unaired literary coffee-houses, by some famous doctors and poets.

Our army equipment was simple and sturdy. We were not issued new shoes (as I was later in the American army) but had to wear shoes broken in by earlier generations of basic trainees. A good idea if the shoes had been the right size. Unfortunately, the quartermaster sergeant selected them for us, and his decision was wrong and final. It was forbidden to interchange the shoes. Each pair had a certain number. I finally found another soldier whose shoes fitted me while mine were good for him. We exchanged them furtively, like members of a conspiracy. In the wintertime we would rub the shoes with pork fat, which was said to make them waterproof. The luxury of socks was unknown. We were issued square pieces of hard gray linen. We learned to wrap these *fussakle* (foot rags) so well around our feet that we never suffered from corns and blisters, even after a ten-hour march. Later, in the American army, we were issued fancy woolen socks, and everybody had blisters.

The style of life in the Czechoslovak army was Spartan. We were trained for war. This was 1931. Hitler was not yet in power, but everybody in Czechoslovakia was convinced that sooner or later "it" was going to happen again; the entire system of the country's alliances — with France and England, and the "Little Entente," comprising also Yugoslavia and Rumania — was built for the ultimate showdown.

We had tough combat training. Among the twelve companies of each infantry regiment, the fourth, eighth, and twelfth companies were armed with heavy machine guns. To be attached to such a *kulometná rota* (heavy machine-gun company) was an extra-special honor even for a man serving in the "queen of arms." While my luckier friends wore only rifles, we particularly honored soldiers had to carry on our backs the cumbersome, weighty parts of the heavy Škoda machine guns. A famous weapon, used widely among revolutionary armies and military juntas in South America putsching to overthrow their governments. The heaviest part was the tripod, but the barrel was no fun either. Marching out with the company to the shooting range, I dreaded the moment when the man marching behind me would place the barrel on my right shoulder. The next five minutes seemed endless, but we had orders to sing "Kolíne, Kolíne," a melancholy folk song. When a man didn't sing loud enough, he had to carry the barrel an extra five minutes, by way of punishment.

During the summer maneuvers, the heavy machine guns were placed on two-wheel carts drawn by small horses. Ever since, I've stopped liking horses. They may well be noble animals, against the background of Ascot or Auteuil and maybe even in Ireland and Kentucky — but not the small, vicious Slovak horses with a mulish disposition that drew our carts. Later, as a second lieutenant and company commander, I always first looked after the horses, though, and then after the men. Those were my orders. It was a good army, with plenty of muscle and morale.

In the morning, after a *půlhodinka* (short half hour) of calisthenics in the courtyard — we were half naked even when it was freezing — we would line up with our tin cans at the kitchen. The cooks filled the cans with *káva* (coffee) and gave each soldier a piece of stale, dry bread. The inmates of the better federal prisons in the United States would certainly revolt after such a breakfast. The "coffee" was made from large bricks of an evil-smelling matter looking like the dry-mud bricks used for baths in health spas. When the bricks were dumped into hot water, they would dissolve into a witches' brew tasting of warmed-over asphalt. In the army of the United States, there would be much griping in the mess hall at breakfast because the eggs were not sunny-side up, the French toast wasn't French enough, and the milk wasn't cold. Similar problems didn't exist in the Czechoslovak army; eggs and toast and milk were unknown. They were only for civilians. "Civilian" was the worst swear word in our military lexicon. "You look like a civilian" meant that you were unsoldierly, sloppy, soft, a sissy, a good-for-nothing milk- or cocoa-drinker.

During the winter maneuvers, after we spent long nights lying on the icy ground worrying what the snow would do to our machine guns, which would have to be meticulously cleaned afterwards, something must have happened to the witches' brew. Long before dawn, the field kitchens would arrive, and we would hungrily line up for our rations of "coffee" and a piece of cold, hard bread. Suddenly the "coffee" tasted better than the finest blends of Colombian and Costa Rican coffees, and the dark bread was a gastronomic delicacy. It just goes to show you.

Life became ever harder at the officers candidates' school in Opava, a town in Silesia, where the food was bad *and* insufficient. I well remember the *spécialités de maison militaire*. On Tuesdays we had *beton* for lunch. *Beton* is the Czech word for cement, and that was exactly how it tasted — a gray heavy mass, rumored to be a mixture of excess barley, old potatos, stale bread, and other leftovers. Our food was considered a military secret; we were forbidden to write home about it. For supper we sometimes had a piece of sausage called *reklamni salám* (publicity salami), because sausage factories used it as giveaways when they couldn't sell it, owing to bad quality. The finest supper was *tvarušky*, small round cream cheeses smelling like Liederkranz in a late stage of decay. With it we were served a piece of margarine and a piece of dry bread.

After my promotion to second lieutenant, I was entitled to wear a saber. The last time I saw my father, late in August, 1914, when he left our home in Ostrava to report to his unit, he had worn his light blue tunic, darker blue pants, and his saber. He looked like an operetta hero, but he was real.

Our olive-drab uniform in the Czechoslovak army was more practical but less spectacular. No operetta producer would have hired us to radiate romance and virility from the stage. I liked the saber, though, and I was glad to share the officers' privilege of wearing civilian clothes after five P.M. Enlisted men must always wear their uniform.

I'm afraid I remained a civilian at heart. During the big parade on October 28, Czechoslovakia's Independence Day, when I marched through town leading my company, with saber drawn, while the drums rolled, I didn't feel elated by the admiration of kids and childlike women waving at us. I envied the citizens in their shabby civilian suits who stood along the street and stared at us coldly. Officers were no longer popular. The magic of the uniform had gone to hell. My civilian friends claimed that the uniform brought out the idiotic sides in a man's character.

As a reserve officer I was obliged to spend four weeks every year, during the summer maneuvers, with my company. We fought violent sham battles against imaginary foes, occupied peaceful villages, and stole genuine cherries and plums from the peasants' trees. Much of my time was spent trying to find suitable stables for the horses, quarters for my men, and finally a room for myself, preferably in the house of the local doctor or notary, if he had a young wife. The setting was as in a Flaubert novel, and the heroines sometimes reminded me of Madame Bovary. There were quite a few of them in the Moravian towns and villages.

The Czechoslovak army was in fine shape in the spring of 1938 when it was mobilized after Hitler's threats. I commanded my heavy-machine-gun company, occupying a sector of what was called the "little Maginot Line," the Czechoslovak border defenses facing the western borders of Bohemia. The defenses were never tested. The "little Maginot Line" turned out to be as useless as the real Maginot Line in France a few years later. One day, rumors reached our outfit from the rear that it was "all over." My men took their things and walked out of the trenches, following all the other men. I stayed there for a while, all alone in the cold, empty trench. Two young officers joined me. We sat down. No one spoke. We just sat there, feeling as foolish as actors on a stage on whom the whole audience has suddenly walked out in protest against a very bad play. We were shocked and desperate and a little ashamed; we understood the terrible meaning of what had happened. The war was over before it started. Afterwards there was no review nor a parade, as after a maneuver, no final commanders' meeting, no banquet at the officers' mess hall. The well-trained, well-indoctrinated army had disintegrated because the moral leadership was no longer there.

A few months later, the Munich Agreement was signed. It was the beginning of the end, and everybody knew it.

Early in 1943, when I received "Greetings!" from my draft board in Hollywood, California, I was thirty-six and married. They were reaching the bottom of the barrel. (In a barrel with caviar, the bottom is not worth a great deal.) I hoped I might not be drafted, having developed a "psychosomatic" stomach-and-gall-bladder disorder, probably as the result of all those rejection slips.

I went to consult Dr. Rosenthal, formerly from Oldenburg, Germany, a prominent Beverly Hills internist of high medical-literary standing in refugee circles. He was the *Hausarzt* of Professor Thomas ("Tommy") Mann, who lived in his "sanatorium" on a magic mountain overlooking Pacific Palisades. Dr. Rosenthal was a small, meticulous, stiff man who examined me carefully and said it was all in my mind, there was nothing wrong with me. He was too polite to call me a hypochondriac, but he expressed serious doubts as to the impression my illness would make on the army doctors. It made none. They thought that basic training in the company of teen-agers was just what I needed. Off I went to the induction center at Fort McArthur, near Los Angeles.

I made a last, desperate effort the first morning at breakfast. Each inductee received a metal tray with several compartments into which the cooks behind the counter poured mountains of scrambled eggs and layers of crisply fried bacon, a hunk of butter, and lots of toast. For years I had fearfully avoided scrambled eggs and fried bacon. Even Dr. Rosenthal admitted they might cause painful colic, and suggested instead cottage cheese and applesauce, the food of mental dwarves. (Perhaps it wasn't all in my mind, eh, Dr. Rosenthal?) I recklessly had my plate filled with scrambled eggs and fried bacon, and fearlessly ate the whole thing, feeling like Socrates drinking the cup of poison. I had coffee — "very bad," Dr. Rosenthal had said, "you should have tea," but I don't like tea. I also had half a pound of butter, toast, and then I went back for more eggs. It may have been the first attempted suicide in history by scrambled eggs. They were very good, and I was going to die anyway. I was looking for a convenient spot to collapse from a gall-bladder attack.

The attack never came. In fact, I felt fine, and by lunchtime I was hungry again. Clearly, this was what the German pagans called "*Gottesgericht*" ("the court of God"). I accepted the decision from Above. After all, the war against Hitler was my war too, and I joined it all the way.

I haven't changed my mind about "the magic of the uniform," though, the military life with its restrictions and controls, lack of freedom, and stupidity, its mindless methods of making you a faceless member of a uniformed society, its caste system and frequent injustices. I admit — reluctantly — that my two army careers were an important part of my education. Both the Czechoslovak army and the American army were seminaries in democracy. In Czechoslovakia, there were no special regiments for young men with inherited titles or new wealth, as in England or Austro-Hungary at the time of the Habsburgs. My father spoke, somewhat wistfully, I thought, of certain "aristocratic" regiments whose junior officers were involved in the bittersweet love affairs beautifully dramatized by Arthur Schnitzler. My father was a contemporary of Schnitzler. I've often wished I had lived at that time.

I learned much in my army lives that I wouldn't have learned otherwise. The American army was the only school I went to in the United States, and the best; a first-rate, postgraduate course after my earlier studies in Prague, Vienna, and the Sorbonne. I learned a great many things in the army I wouldn't have studied at Harvard, though several Harvard alumni I talked to failed to agree. They were very much aware of the proud history of their alma mater, founded in 1636. Very impressive, though perhaps not for an alumnus of Charles University in Prague, founded in 1348. Columbus's grandmother wasn't born yet.

The army of the United States taught me much about democracy in action, the brotherhood of men, the true meaning of the "melting pot," about American humor and Anglo-Saxon fairness, detachment and common sense, obscenity and four-letter words, a lack of suspicion and a sense of open-mindedness. These are truisms to a native American but not to a Central European who was brought up to believe in "authority," and had seen men thought to be guilty until they were proved innocent. (In Europe, small kids are still being told, "if you won't behave, the policeman will come and get you.") I realized how much I had learned in the army when I came back after the war and met my European friends who had been old enough, or lucky enough, not to be drafted. Some of them had become prosperous during the war. They knew little about America, perhaps because they thought they knew all about it. I suddenly sensed the abyss between us. I still knew little about this new country of mine, but at least I'd looked into it, and met people, and learned how Americans behave in certain situations.

At one point, the moment may come when a European becomes an American. Not just legally, by being sworn in as a citizen, but intellectually, emotionally, and subconsciously, when he reacts in a certain situation no longer as he would have done in his former life but realizes, with a sense of wonder, that he feels quite differently about it. With some people the mysterious metamorphosis never occurs. They remain steeped in the mixture as before.

I learned these things the hard way, during bull sessions in the barracks, and out in the field. After my artificial indoctrination in New York and Hollywood, I found out at last how Americans-at-large thought and dreamed and talked and acted. People I would never have met otherwise. The army supplied much of the practical equipment I needed when I began to write in American English for an American audience. I hereby give thanks to my erstwhile draft board (I've forgotten the number) in Hollywood, California.

The difference between my old army, in Czechoslovakia, and my new one, in the United States, was a basic one: in all European armies the soldier was taught that he must *not* think for himself. Thinking was the privilege, and the duty, of the officers. When a soldier prefaced an excuse with "I thought that —" he was interrupted and told that he wasn't *supposed* to think.

It came as a pleasant surprise to me that the American army expected, and trained, the GI to think for himself. The caste difference between enlisted men and officers was less important than between civilians-turned-soldiers and professional soldiers. As one of the oldest men in my outfit — I was older than most of the officers — and as a former army officer myself, I was able to see the situation from both the enlisted man's and the officer's point of view. The strength of the American army was its enlisted men. The cross section I met was a good one: surprisingly few were anti-refugee, anti-intellectual, anti-Semite, in fact anti-anything. They were a good bunch of men.

However, I wasn't in a typical outfit. The army mysteriously found out about my "special skills" and knowledge of languages, and even made use of them. That was another pleasant surprise. In my old army they told a standard joke, taken from the even older (Austrian) army, about the sergeant asking, "Who plays the piano?" Three men raise their hands and are told to carry up the piano for the lieutenant colonel's lady. The American army had such an elaborate system of ferreting out a man's hidden skills that it discovered some which the man hadn't even known about himself.

I was transferred from the queenly infantry to Intelligence, and sent to an (almost secret) camp, which gave me a chance of telling everybody about it. No army ever kept its secrets worse. My friends envied me for being trained as a double agent. Alas, the truth was prosaic: much of our "intelligence" was as dull as my earlier basic infantry training. My superior officers were mad about military secrets, stamping documents for no apparent reason as "classified" or "secret." Some would have loved to stamp even our toilet paper. The fine GI tissue, tangible proof of the high American standard of living, was a considerable improvement over my Czechoslovak army life, when we were told to use certain news-papers that were critical of the army.

Europeans have learned by bitter experience that there exist very few durable secrets. A secret, military and otherwise, is a transitory thing, like the sound of a melody, the taste of a dish, the scent of a rose. It doesn't last; sooner or later it evaporates, like sound or taste or smell. In the American army they thought that secrets were tangible and eternal, and they busily created secrets as sculptors shape forms.

I became a private, which is a euphemistic term. If there ever was anyone with no privacy at all, it is an army private. The German expression *gemein* (common, low, mean, vulgar) is closer to the truth. And what is first class, may I ask, about a private first class?

There is a cynical point of view claiming that the Allies made many mistakes but won the Second World War because the enemy made even more mistakes. This is hardly the impression one gains after reading the memoirs published by celebrated field commanders and military historians with inside information. If mistakes are admitted, they were always made by someone else. The picture would be clearer if some memoirs had been written by obscure enlisted men. Some have written memorable novels that tell the deeper truth; others tried to forget the war as quickly as possible. Thus it's mostly the victories and the grandeur that are remembered for posterity, while the defeats and stupidities have passed into merciful oblivion. Paris has no Waterloo Bridge and London no Dunkirk Square. Someday computers may figure out the difference between mistakes made by both sides — the difference between defeat and victory. But no computer will ever explain what happens to a man who puts on a uniform. He behaves dutifully, patriotically, perhaps even heroically. But something in him has changed. The uniform has turned him into a reluctant schizophrenic. He feels bound by the rules of a game that he may detest, and he blindly follows the statutes of a club that he wouldn't have joined on his own free will.

I spent a few months in Camp Ritchie, Maryland. It made me think of the Pieter Breughel painting *The Tower of Babel*, one of the glories of Vienna's Kunsthistorisches Museum. Ritchie was just as frightening. There were soldiers who spoke languages whose existence I hadn't even known and whose identities remained a permanent secret. The atmosphere was late Kafka, or rather, later-than-you-think Kafka. But the Babylonian camp did much for my linguistic self-confidence. I was no longer self-conscious about my rolling *r*'s and my deficient *th*'s. In Ritchie I learned that things could be much worse. There, and later in nearby Camp Sharpe, Gettysburg, it was almost a patent of nobility to have an improbable accent.

Camp Sharpe, more secluded and secretive even than Ritchie, was a short walk from the great battlefield. From the windows of our barracks we had a fine view of the farm that later became the home of General Eisenhower; ever since, many of us have had a good-neighborly feeling about the thirty-fourth President of the United States of America. In Camp Sharpe we were trained in the subtleties of what was vaguely known as psychological warfare, a new pseudo-science, a sophisticated blend of Goebbelsian persuasion and Lucky Strike — Madison Avenue methods. Some military leaders were said to take an exceedingly dim view of it. They dared claim that a well-placed machine gun was worth more than an outfit of "geniuses," as we were called by our own superior officers, many of whom were anti-psychological-warfare experts. Our aim was to confuse and soften up the enemy, make him come over and surrender. The antis said they'd come over all right if you shelled them long enough in the right spots — not because you showered them with leaflets.

Life in Camp Ritchie was not, as you might assume, a sort of profound meditation in an Institute of Advanced Military Thinking. It was a new version of the military game of "details." Having selected and tested, at considerable ingenuity, effort, and expense, a number of "specialists" and "experts" for Intelligence, the people in Camp Ritchie acted on the old-army "piano principle." They formed "details." In the peculiar army idiom, a detail is a menial task. KP (kitchen police) is the best-known, but not the worst, detail. There is shoveling coal, unpleasant in the wintertime, there is ash and trash, and latrine duty, unpleasant at any time. There are subtle subdivisions. In the kitchen, "pots and pans" was more unpopular than "peeling potatoes." The latrine detail had similar fine distinctions. The consensus among old detail hands was that to be a fireman was the worst detail of all, and if there was *any*thing worse, it was to be a *night* fireman.

I was a night fireman.

They said that any jerk could peel potatoes or clean a latrine. But to be a successful night fireman "you had to use your brains." I didn't like the theory; it smelled too much of the "piano principle." What crime had I committed, to be made a night fireman? I'd never volunteered for anything; not at my age. I wouldn't even admit to playing the violin. They might have ordered me out to fell maple or pine trees. (The back of a violin is made of maple, the belly of pine.)

The night firemen lived in splendid isolation in two large, secluded rooms at the end of a relatively quiet barracks. They slept in the day-time, like jazz musicians, nightclub waiters, and prosperous prostitutes. It was a strange place, even by Ritchie standards. Men were sleeping, some with eyeshades over their faces. A big sign said SILENCE. (Ritchie was a relatively polite camp.) According to a mimeographed sheet on the wall, the night fireman's turn of duty began at six P.M. and lasted until six A.M. On another list was my name, for once not misspelled; I couldn't claim it wasn't me. I was to report to "Area IV."

It was early January, and the smell of snow was in the air. Camp Ritchie was on a high-lying plateau, and there was a sharp, icy wind coming through. Area IV was a complex of two groups of three parallel barracks, with a courtyard in between. The boiler rooms were at the rear of the barracks. Near the furnace the air was hot and dry. There was an army number one magazine-type space heater connected with the electrically fanned, automatic heating system, and a small stove heating the water in the warm-water tank. A poster on the wall said, THE COAL YOU SAVE HELPS WIN THE WAR.

The day fireman was working in one of the boiler rooms, throwing a shovelful of coal into the big furnace. He was a strong Negro with melancholy eyes and a melodious voice. I remember him now as a sort of Joe Louis. He seemed surprised when I took off my overcoat and he saw my frail physique. I was certainly no Dempsey. I wasn't even Tunney, who likes books, music, and old clarets as I do.

The day fireman tried to cheer me up. He said the job wasn't as tough as it looked.

"There are six furnaces," he said. "You'll see two heaps of coal outside. Use soft, bituminous coal for the big furnace, and hard coal for the warm-water heater. The fires are in good shape. Check on them twice an hour. Don't fall asleep in the morning when you feel tired. Some guys sit down near the furnace, where it's cozy and warm, and fall asleep. First thing you know, the fire dies and there's hell to pay. It wouldn't matter if enlisted men lived in these barracks. But they are for senior officers who need plenty of heat, like babies. Watch out for number four. Nothing but lieutenant colonels and three chicken colonels."

He shrugged. "Keep the ashpit clean. Always clean it before you leave. Main thing is, keep the coal level with the bottom of the firing door. And check the fire bed for clinkers or hard crust. Open the clean-out door, and look into the furnace. And don't fuss around with the draft register if you know what's good for you. They all fuss around and shake good coal through the grate and leave the ashpit doors open. Those lazy guys, they put fresh coal on top of live coal. All they get is lots of smoke, and the heat goes down, and the people inside freeze."

Seeing the empty expression on my face, he said, "Jesus," and went for the shovel. He told me not to use the shovel too much. "Use the right-angle poker. Always poke for a minute before you shovel in fresh coal."

I asked, "How much coal do you put in at one time?"

He stared at me.

I said, "I mean, how many shovels?"

He gave me a speculative glance. "Never fired any of them?"

I shook my head. My knowledge of furnaces was limited to theory. Aboard the ocean liners on which I'd worked — not as a stoker but as a violin-playing member of the ship's orchestra — I'd sometimes gone down to the engine room. On the older ships they had used coal. I remember the half-naked, strong men, covered with coal dust and sweat, who seemed to have walked straight out of Dante's *Inferno*. The heat was fantastic. I wondered how they could work down there, especially in the Red Sea and in Indochina when even the grand salon upstairs had the temperature of a bakery oven.

"Didn't you have any stoves at home?" the Negro asked (in those days we didn't call Negroes "blacks").

I nodded. "Yes, but I had nothing to do with them." I added self-consciously, "We had a servant."

We'd lived on the fifth — and highest — floor of the Wechsberg family house. My paternal grandfather, practicing the judgment of Solomon, had allocated the floors to his three sons according to age: the oldest on the third floor, and my father (the youngest) on the top floor. The ground floor and second floor were occupied by the family bank, A. Wechsberg and Company. Around 1910, it was one of the most modern buildings in town, but it had no elevator. We had to climb one hundred and thirty-four steps. My brother Max and I didn't mind; and we were spared visits from unpleasant relatives who collapsed on the third floor and visited our poor cousins there.

A primitive windlass had been built on the outside of the house facing the small backyard. Baskets with anthracite were hoisted up from the cellar. The windlass often broke, and Marie, our old cook, had to go down and carry the heavy buckets with coal all the way from the cellar to the fifth floor. The coal was stored in a large crate on the "coal balcony" in the back of the house. Before Christmas, Marie would keep a goose on the balcony. The poor animal was forcefully fed. Marie stuffed *šlišky* (longish pieces of maize meal) down the goose's throat. It wasn't nice, but at Christmas we would have a beautiful goose liver, served cold.

In the wintertime, Marie would come into the "children's room" where my brother and I slept, at seven in the morning. I knew it was very cold outside when I saw lovely ice flowers on the window, in brilliant patterns, shutting out the outside world. When I exhaled I could see my breath form a white fog, and I would cuddle up under our high, feather-light eiderdowns, watching Marie, who knelt down by the white tile stove. She put down the old newspapers and kindling wood in her hand, and the coal bucket. First she collected the cold ashes left from the previous day, and put them into the paper. Then she made a large ball of another sheet of paper, put the matchwood inside, placed it into the stove, and lighted it with a match. For a minute she closed the stove door. I loved the pleasant sound of the fire, as the draft from the chimney fanned the flames. The matchwood made crackling noises, like walking over twigs in the autumn woods. Marie opened the stove door and carefully placed larger pieces of wood on top of the fire that was going merrily. At last she would put two or three small shovelfuls of anthracite on top. The "black coal," as we called it, came from the mine shafts that ran underneath our town. I liked to think that our coal came from our own private mine, a hundred meters or so underneath the cellar of our house. Marie would come back once or twice to put in more coal. Slowly, a soft mild warmth would fill the room — the sort of warmth that steam heating never gives you. Unfortunately, Marie insisted on leaving the window open for ten minutes. Her theory was that "the room will get warm more quickly when there is fresh air in it." Marie's theories were not always scientifically proven. When she had temperamental fits after standing the whole morning near the hot coal range in the kitchen — an occupational disease widespread among male and female cooks — she would tell us that "the heat from the range raises my blood pressure."

I was staring gloomily at the large black furnace in the cellar of barracks number three. There was nothing pleasant about it, as there had been about the white tile stove in our children's room. To tell the truth, it frightened me.

The Negro fireman asked me what I'd been in civilian life.

"Writer."

"I see," he said in his slow, meditative way, as though this explained everything. He gave a sigh.

"Above all, don't put in too much coal at a time. Might smother the fire. Make your rounds and put in, say, two shovels, depending on how the fire looks. After a while, you'll get the feel of it. The fires are built well and should last to the morning. It's all right to take off for coffee and something to eat, but don't stay away an hour. And be careful about number four. These colonels are murder."

He put on his overcoat and opened the cellar door leading into the courtyard, and he sniffed the air.

"Don't like it. Hope we don't get too much wind tonight. Wind is bad for the fires. Especially these small bastards. If you don't put in fresh coal often enough, they die of exhaustion, and if you put in too much, they choke to death. The first night I was here, it was really bad. I was running around in circles." He gave me an encouraging nod. "If there's trouble, come and wake me, I'm on bunk number seven." He left. He was a swell guy.

Alone and feeling lost, I began by inspecting my area. All six fires were going great. I put on the heavy gloves that my predecessor had left there, and tried to open the furnace door. It didn't open easily. I finally managed, but I hurt my hand and almost dropped my right glove into the fire. The gloves were much too large for me. I took the shovel. It was heavy, even with no coal on it. I filled the shovel and playfully tried to throw the coal into the fire. The shovel hit the rim of the door, and the coal pieces were scattered all over the cellar. I tried to collect them, leaving the door of the furnace open. This was a mistake, because the fire burned too fast.

I quickly closed the door, collected the rest of the coal, and tried again. This time I hit the fire all right. I threw in three small shovelfuls of coal, closed the furnace door, and put the shovel aside. My muscles hurt. I suddenly needed fresh air, and walked out across the courtyard into the cellar of number four, where the chicken colonels lived. The fire was not as bright and cheerful as number three, but a few shovelfuls of coal fixed that (I thought). I continued my round, inspecting the other furnaces. In cellar number two, a big piece of coal slid down from the shovel onto my shinbone. It hurt, and so did my upper arms.

It was half-past seven, and I was getting hungry. Dr. Rosenthal would have been pleased with my progress. No more gall-bladder attacks, psychosomatic or otherwise; just hungry. I went to the mess hall.

I came back twenty minutes later. A storm was coming up, and snow flurries were in the air. A nice night to sit in a cozy, warm room with a good mystery novel and no colonels around. Numbers one and two seemed all right, but number three was somewhat asthmatic. I tried to cure it by leaving the furnace door open for a while to get the draft through, and put more coal in, but perhaps my diagnosis was wrong; the fire didn't pick up strength. A lot of the coal I tried to get into the furnace was flying all around the cellar. I no longer collected it.

I walked up the stairway into barracks number three to test the temperature. The corridor was nice and warm. A major came out of a room. When he saw me with my thick gloves, he said, "Don't save coal tonight, soldier! It's bad outside, and I've got a cold." I didn't tell him that I might help to win the war by saving coal, and instead walked into the boiler room of number four. There it was, the big fire that seemed to have a cold. After I'd put some coal into the furnace, I realized it was the hard coal that was really for the stove. Well, it was too late now. I tried not to look inside the furnace. Numbers five and six were fine. I came back to number four. The fire was anemic. Don't put in too much at a time, my fireman friend had said. I wished I had some newspapers and kindling wood and could build a new fire, as Marie had done. On some days, when there was no draft from the chimney, the fire would die, and she had to try again, and then she would be in a bad mood all day long.

Outside, the storm was making ominous noises. I opened the cellar door and closed it quickly: the snow flurries had turned into what looked like a real blizzard. When I came out of number four and had to cross the courtyard to get to number three, I saw the imprints of my shoes in the fresh snow. They would have to have a special snow-shoveling detail. Well, that didn't concern me. All we students of military intelligence were thinking of in Camp Ritchie, was details.

By midnight, the blizzard was raging and I was in serious trouble with two of my six furnaces. Number three was still anemic, and number four — the chicken colonels' — was now on the critical list. My aching arms. I didn't understand it; I'd given the same loving care to all the fires, as a parent gives to all his children, but some children turn out worse (or better) than others. I worked hard on the children in barracks three and four, throwing in selected pieces by hand, which was more accurate than using the heavy shovel that was getting *too* heavy for me. By now I was hardly able to lift it. Maybe what number three needed was some of the coal dust lying on the floor. I threw a shovelful in.

The effect was unexpected; the flames momentarily disappeared under a cloud of black smoke. I smelled carbon dioxide. Remembering some mystery stories in which carbon dioxide was mentioned -— or was it a novel on suicide? — I quickly closed the furnace door and opened the door of the cellar. The snowflakes came in with a gust, almost to the very furnace. Throwing caution to the blizzard, I walked through the courtyard to number three. The fire seemed to have handed in its resignation. I remembered the right-angle poker, and tried to poke around for a minute, but it was no use. The fire was determined to die, and there was nothing I could do.

It was now very cold — I'd forgotten to close the cellar door — but perspiration was trickling down the back of my head. Perhaps the senior officers were all asleep. No one should sleep in a hot room anyway. Earlier, I'd heard heavy steps in the corridor above the cellar, but now all was quiet and peaceful.

Two o'clock. I was proud of my children one, two, five, and six. Not many parents of six children can say that. Number three was on the critical list. Dying. And number four had not recovered from the coal-dust treatment, though I carefully nursed what was left of the fire with selected coal pieces which I threw in, one by one. For a wild moment I thought of putting in a little oil or gasoline — but where would I get oil or gasoline at two in the morning? I watched the last small flames. They were licking at me playfully, kidding me, and then they were gone.

I stood there for a while, looking into the dark furnace. It was a sad sight — like an empty bottle of fine wine, or a darkened theater.

I listened. There was no sound above me. Thank God, the colonels were fast asleep. Outside, the wind was still howling. My earlier footsteps in the courtyard were again covered with fresh snow.

A man came down the stairs from the corridor. I hadn't heard him earlier. He wore dark gray woolen pajamas and an overcoat. I saw the silver eagles on his shoulder, and snapped to attention. I saluted smartly and dropped the shovel, unfortunately on *his* shinbone.

"Ouch!" said the colonel, and stepped back, holding his leg. "Are you crazy?"

"I — I apologize, sir," I said politely.

"What's the matter with you?" he shouted. "Don't talk like a goddam civilian. How long have you been in the army?"

"Seven weeks and three — no, four days."

"Why don't you look after the fire? Upstairs it's *freezing.*"

"Sorry, sir," I said. "The fire died on me."

"What's that?" He stepped to the furnace and opened the door. That was his mistake. A column of black smoke poured in his face.

Where there's smoke, there's fire, they say. But there was no fire in number four.

The colonel was furious. Must have been the carbon dioxide.

"I — I'm going to break you!" he yelled. "I'm going to break you if it's the last thing I do!"

"Sir," I said, standing at attention, "you cannot break me. I am a private." I should have told him that I was "unbreakable," but such highlights of smart repartee never occur to me in the heat of an argument. Especially when one argues with a colonel.

For a short moment I thought he would tell me to jump into the furnace. But even colonels are human — sometimes. He started to cough, put up the collar of his overcoat, and gave me a wild stare. He turned and was gone. I hoped he went back to sleep peacefully, but I doubted it.

I sat down on the coal heap, trying to reassess the tactical situation, as military leaders are wont to do. But there was nothing to be gained by catching cold. I was already unable to lift my arms. I quietly walked over to the mess hall, and had ham and eggs, with toast and butter, coffee, and fruit. A soldier came and asked whether I was the night fireman from the officers' barracks. I nodded and had more coffee.

"They're waiting for you there," he said. "On the double."

The duty sergeant was in the cellar of number four, with my friend the day fireman. My friend looked at me sadly, but he said nothing. He didn't seem surprised. I looked at my watch. It was half-past three. I said I was sorry they'd had to wake him up.

"That's all right," he said. "I told you these colonels are murder. He phoned the duty sergeant to get me out of bed. We'll build a new fire." We went to look after the other furnaces. He knew what they needed, a little draft here, a few shovels of coal there. Even number three made a beautiful comeback within an hour. By the time I went off duty, he had a fine fire going in number four.

"It isn't really difficult," he said, trying to comfort me. "If you know how."

"Yes," I said. I thanked him, went to my room, and fell asleep. They didn't let me sleep long. They woke me at eleven A.M. and told me to report to the top sergeant, on the double. The top sergeant said he was putting me on the latrine detail as of now, by order of the colonel.

There must have been some mysterious social significance about these details at Camp Ritchie. Consider, for instance, the latrine detail. Among its members was Prince de Chimay, a wild-looking Belgian nobleman who was the scion of an old family, and a first-rate crap-shooter. In the Gay Nineties a Princesse de Chimay had created a fine scandal by running off with a gypsy primas. There was Baron de Fernelmont, also the scion of an old family, who looked French and decadent even in fatigues, reminding me of the goutish gastronomes in Paris who wake up in the morning trying to decide whether to go for *sole Albert* at Maxim's, or *rognons jamais mieux at* Lapérouse. There was Count P., another aristocratic Frenchman, frail and delicate. His forebears were said to have laid siege to several towns near Avignon at the time when the Catholic Church had two Popes fighting one another. Another member of the elegant detail was Prince Bourbon-Parma, the youngest brother of former Empress Zita von Habsburg who would have been *the* Empress, except for certain deplorable events prior to 1918. Bourbon-Parma looked every millimeter the member of a centuries-old, almost-ruling house; he was superbly aloof toward members of the lesser aristocracy. Also present were little de Milhaud, soft-spoken and polite, who was said to be related to the late President William H. Taft, and Count Igor Cassini, known to his friends as "Ghighi" and to Hearst-newspaper readers as "Cholly Knickerbocker." He had black hair, always carefully brushed, and kept his sense of White-Russian humor even in moments of a minor crisis. Why I, a mere commoner, was made a member of the distinguished blue-blooded detail, I don't know. Cassini said it might be my (slightly) aristocratic profile, or because I spoke French. (The latrine detail conversed exclusively in the language of Marcel Proust.) Or maybe I was there because somebody didn't like me.

At eight in the morning, when other men were going to the classrooms, unless they too were on some detail, the members of the latrine detail met at the latrine, naturally. During the next two hours we put the place into top shape. This couldn't have happened in my old (Czechoslovak) army, where the latrines were dirty and unhygienic. At Camp Ritchie, the latrines were often inspected by visiting two-star generals from nearby Washington, D.C. They were showplaces of America's high hygienic, technological, and almost scientific latrine civilization. American plumbing is second to none; even Chairman Mao would have had to admit that. (The French members of our detail regretted the absence of bidets, however, which they called "the finest expression of the international plumbing spirit.") The latrines in Camp Ritchie were more elegant than in some European luxury hotels; they were also better taken care of. Americans do it with chemistry. We were issued various liquids, powders, and sprays; mops and brooms and other, more intimately shaped utensils. We were given all technical assistance that American know-how created. The rest was up to us.

Certain details of the operation were less pleasant than others, and we had established a just and fair system of rotation. Each of us had relatively light duties (mopping the floors, cleaning the walls) and more onerous ones (cleaning the seats, which are called "heads" in navy slang). For the enlightenment of my women readers who never had a chance to visit such a place as we had in Ritchie, I should explain that the leitmotiv was a total absence of privacy. Even in the Spartan Czechoslovak army they had understood that there are moments in a man's life when he likes to be alone. The American army, for reasons into which we don't want to go — please ask your analyst — did not encourage privacy. There were no cubicles, no partitions, no sidewalls even. The seats were placed next to each other. Theoretically, it would have been possible to hold a cabinet meeting there. (Members of the latrine detail referred to the latrine as *le cabinet*, which is the French expression.) Besides five seats for ordinary users, there was the sixth seat, set slightly apart, that was reserved for VD (venereal disease) cases. Never in my whole army life did I ever see anyone use it, but there was a deep-seated, though medically unfounded superstition, among the members of our detail that if you accidentally touched the sixth seat in the course of the cleaning activities, you might get infected. Another superstition, French no doubt, like the one claiming that you must always drink wine, not water, because water "makes frogs in your belly." Anyway, Cassini and I had evolved an intricate system permitting us to clean the feared contraption from a safe distance of about one yard.

With the help of our country's chemical industry, the job was finished in about two hours, with liberal intervals for rest and relaxation. If I remember correctly, the operation began with using a hose and spraying, continued with cleaning, spraying special disinfectants, and finally wiping the whole place, making it spic and span. "You could eat from the floor today," Fernelmont would say, as he surveyed the result of our Herculean labors.

No one was supposed to enter during the cleaning operation, and we were irritated when somebody came in because — as Wozzeck says in Georg Büchner's great drama — he was "overcome by Nature." We strongly discouraged such visitors, sending them to the officers' barracks instead.

We were a fine team. The conversation was animated and not influenced by the environment. By unspoken agreement, dirty words were avoided while we were on the job; they would have had no deeper meaning there.

In the Czechoslovak army, the week's supreme moment of terror came on Saturday afternoon at five o'clock, shortly before we were supposed to leave for the weekend. Our girl friends were already waiting for us at the gate. At five, the top sergeant or a young officer would inspect our room, which we had cleaned all afternoon. The sergeant who had advanced training in sadism would peek under the beds and behind the window frames for traces of dust. He would study the windowpanes that had been meticulously cleaned with old newspapers. He would open the small, wooden, black box that each soldier had standing at the foot of his bed. Inside there were small compartments for laundry, soap, shirts, toothbrush, forming a sort of soldier's still life; everything had to form part of a straight geometric pattern. And then, while we stopped breathing, the sergeant would put on a pair of white cotton gloves. (Caruso created a famous effect in the first act of *Rigoletto* when he nonchalantly put on his white gloves while singing the Duke's aria "Questa è quella.") Our sergeant had never heard of Caruso. He used his white gloves while he let his hand glide *inside* the iron stove. If the glove was black and dirty when he took out his hand, he would turn toward us and announce that the room was "restricted" for the weekend. The poor girls at the gate had to turn around and go home.

The American army was more sensible. We were told that we were cleaning the latrines for ourselves and our fellow soldiers; why not do it as well as it could be done? One two-star general said after an inspection they were the best-cleaned goddam latrines in the whole camp, maybe in the continental United States. My paternal grandfather, whose wisdom I like to quote occasionally, used to say, "One should know *every*thing but never need to do *any*thing." If the members of our exclusive detail should ever get back their châteaux, palaces, and estates that they lost during wars and revolutions, they'll be able to tell their servants exactly how these places should be cleaned. If servants still exist.

Everywhere Madness

JOSEPH WECHSBERG, PRIVATE, 39 716 066 — name, rank, serial number — arrived on the nineteenth floor of 25 West Forty-third Street somewhat as Parsifal arrived earlier on Monsalvat. Richard Wagner's *reiner Tor* (pure fool) knew nothing about the Holy Grail. I knew nothing about *The New Yorker*, its mystique and legends, though I'd learned to read the magazine and was writing for it. I was taken up one floor and through a bare, nondescript, gray corridor into a simply furnished office which didn't reflect the sophisticated luxury of the magazine's ads. No wood paneling, wall-to-wall carpet, smart-looking women wearing hats. A tall, diffident man wearing a tweed jacket got up and said, "I am Gus Lobrano." He had soft eyes and a shy smile.

Then I saw another man with a deeply lined face and sharp bright eyes who got up from a sofa where he'd been reading a manuscript.

"This is Wolcott Gibbs," Lobrano said. I felt as I had in my claque days at the Vienna State Opera, when we waited at the stage door for Richard Strauss or Franz Schalk, to ask for an autograph. I almost asked

Gibbs, my favorite parodist, for an autograph. Fortunately, he went out before I could give in to my silly impulse. Lobrano asked me politely, almost formally, to sit down. He was a Southern gentleman, a type I'd never met before. His politeness always put me on the defensive. He showed me the proof of one of my pieces and asked me gently, as though he were embarrassed, whether I would mind clearing up a few minor points.

The proof had scores of penciled marks and remarks and queries written in the margins. I'd never seen such painfully edited copy. At the *Prager Tagblatt*, I would bring my manuscripts to Rudi Thomas, the deputy editor with the debonair attitude and the red blazer. I'd come there in the early evening, after my work at the law offices of Adler and Pick, with an article I'd written at home the previous night. Rudi Thomas was rarely alone in his office, which was the *Tagblatt*'s unofficial coffeehouse, though no coffee was served. During the final two years, a dark-haired, attractive woman was often with him. He would kiss her nonchalantly, pretending to ignore the manuscript that I'd placed on his desk. In one corner a chess game was going on between the champion, who was also a stenographer, and three or four players, some of them obscure avant-garde poets. On the couch by the wall, a small group of people were discussing something modern, literature or music or philosophy. One evening I met George Szell there. He sat on the couch and talked about the premiere of *Katerina Ismailova* by Shostakovich, which he'd just conducted at the German Theatre. There had been a minor scandal. Szell analyzed the erotic interlude and told a funny though unprintable joke. Admirers of the stern, severe Maestro from Cleveland, Ohio, might now find this hard to believe.

Rudi Thomas would carry on with his beautiful brunette, who now sat on his lap while he gave a cursory glance at my manuscript. I'd learned to play the game. I would pretend not to look at him, just watching him out of the corner of my eyes for any sign of approval while he was reading my article, with a slightly bored expression. (Today I know better than to watch anyone reading something I wrote.) Rudi would kiss the girl in the nape, under her hair, saying, "You're the world's worst liar," meaning me, not her. Or he might say, "I never read such nonsense." Then I knew all was well. He made her get off his lap, reread and edited the manuscript, crossing out a few sentences, changing some words, and then he wrote *1* and circled it, on top. That was for tonight's edition. Or he would mark it *S,* for the Sunday paper. He would throw the manuscript into the out-basket and plant the beautiful brunette firmly back on his lap, and I knew I was dismissed. After a while, old Bečvář would come in, grabbing the pages in the out-basket as though they were dirty laundry to be taken to the washing machine. When Rudi Thomas became serious after reading the manuscript and said it was a good piece, there was trouble. Maybe they'd already bought something similar, or it was a good piece but maybe not good enough.

No one had ever discussed the fine points of a manuscript with me as Lobrano did during my first visit to *The New Yorker.* He asked me exactly what I'd meant by a certain phrase, and he smiled quietly when I said what he'd expected, and he would nod. He said we had to make everything as precise and simple and clear as possible. I've never forgotten. He suggested some minor changes, looking almost anxiously for me to agree, and now *I* became embarrassed. When we finished, he said he would like to take me to Mr. Ross. We got up. Lobrano said he envied me wearing my GI uniform. He'd tried to enlist at the beginning of the war; he felt strongly about it, and he was deeply disappointed when he'd been turned down for reasons of health. He'd gone down to the harbor, joining the longshoremen who were unloading war supplies, and for hours he carried heavy bags. He was a tall but frail man, and one day he collapsed, and the doctors warned him, and he complained to me because now he couldn't even help unload war supplies. Gus died in 1956, of cancer.

We walked down the stairway — his office was on the twentieth floor — and through a corridor to the last office on the left side. Lobrano introduced me to Harold W. Ross, and left. The editor of *The New Yorker* shook hands with me slowly and deliberately, as though it were a mental and physical effort. He seemed to be scowling at me, and said something in his rasping voice that I didn't understand. He brushed his unkempt hair off his forehead with the back of his right hand, and gave a sigh. He frightened me a little but not for long. When he noticed that I had trouble understanding him, he spoke more slowly, enunciating the words more carefully. I thought he was a kindhearted man who for some reason tried to look tough, and I've never changed my first impression. He wore a custom-made suit of an expensive material, but he looked as if he'd slept in it, and maybe he had. He walked toward the window, staring down gloomily, turning his back to me, and jingling some keys or coins in his right trouser pocket. Obviously he didn't know where to place me or what to do with me. Later he said, "I never met anyone from your part of the world." I'd told him I was from Moravia, and he shook his head slowly. Perhaps he thought Moravia was a wild country, with dark woods and aborigines, and he was puzzled to see me wearing a uniform. He didn't talk about the things I'd written for the magazine. He said he'd been a soldier himself, a goddam private first class, when he'd edited *Stars and Stripes* in Paris during the First World War.

"Just a goddam pfc., running a bunch of nuts," he said, gruffly. "Mind you, Wechsberg." Neither his profanity nor his snarling voice fooled me any longer. I liked him. I was sorry I could never get close to him, but it was a long way from Moravia to Colorado or wherever he came from. He took a protective interest in me because technically I was still a foreigner, and they'd drafted me. A helpless private in the army who wasn't even an American, without the citizen's constitutional rights. Something seemed wrong there to him. How come they hadn't made me a citizen before drafting me? He became quite angry.

"If you're good enough to be shot, they might as well make you a citizen," he said. I said we'd been told we would be sworn in as citizens before being shipped overseas.

"It could be much worse," I said. Foreigners serving in the British forces did not become citizens. If they were taken prisoners in action, they might be shot as civilian spies.

"How's that again?" Ross asked, looking at me. My heart sank. The editor of the magazine I would rather write for than for any other didn't understand my English. It had happened often enough with other people, but I was ashamed it had to happen with Harold Ross. Later I discovered that it didn't really matter. Ross sometimes puzzled over something I said, but he never asked me whether anybody had "fixed up" my stuff; *he* knew I'd written it all by myself. Once he said to me in his gruff way, "Don't worry, Wechsberg, you're always going to write because you are a natural writer. You can't help it, goddam it, so you'd better keep on writing." Exactly what I've done.

On our first day together he took me to lunch at "21." I no longer dined exclusively at Horn and Hardart, but my knowledge of elegant restaurants was limited. Ross was known and respected at "21." He was greeted with deferential familiarity by the doorman, by two of the Kriendler brothers, by a maître d'hôtel, and, most surprisingly, by our waiter. American waiters are rarely deferential. Perhaps the waiter was trying to write for *The New Yorker* in his spare time.

A brigadier general and a colonel were sitting nearby at the bar. Ross made a point of scowling at them. He had a theory that since the First World War there was a permanent conspiracy of the field-grade officers against the enlisted men, who did all the dirty work, and that colonels and general officers were "the worst." I have since come to the conclusion that he may have been right. He was pleased because I'd gone in as a private. He thought that with my background I could have got a commission in Washington, and he commended me for not even trying. He did not approve of my being in Camp Ritchie where they taught Intelligence, "a lot of nonsense. . . . They don't know a damn thing, and they pretend they know everything, which makes them dan-

gerous." Ross's statements sometimes seemed exaggerated when he uttered them in his angry voice, but some of them turned out to be
amazingly accurate. His evaluation of Intelligence was among them. A
great many times in the following months I was confronted with people
who pretended to know everything though they knew nothing.

During lunch, Ross made a lot of fuss, ordering special things and
asking me whether there was anything else I wanted. Several people
stopped by at our table, and I was introduced. My head was turning a
little; perhaps it was the second drink and the noise around us. At one
moment I wondered whether twenty-four hours ago I'd had chow in the
mess hall in Ritchie, wearing my fatigues that smelled of latrine. I told
Ross about latrine duty, and he became very interested and wanted to
know all the technical details. My report seemed to confirm his darkest
suspicions about army Intelligence.

He was angry with me only once. I came to say good-bye before
being shipped overseas. I'd just been promoted, straight from private, to
technical sergeant. Ross stared angrily at the five brand-new stripes on
my left arm, and snarled at me. How come a private could become a
tech sergeant, without first making pfc, corporal, sergeant, staff sergeant? Goddam it, Wechsberg, what is the army coming to when anybody (and he glared at me) could make a tech sergeant like that?

I tried to explain to him the vagaries of psychological warfare. That
was a mistake. "Psychological warfare" brought forth a wealth of Rossian choice profanity which I cannot render exactly because after a few
months in this man's army, my knowledge of American profanity, a
rich and mystical field, was still limited. What sort of warfare was I in,
he wanted to know, when unworldly writers could become tech sergeants overnight? For two years he'd edited Stars and Stripes in Paris,
and what had he been? A pfc.!

To this day I believe he was jealous. He wouldn't have minded if they'd commissioned me a captain or a major in Washington. He took a dim view of captains and majors generally. But he had an enlisted man's respect for the tech sergeant's rating, which was relatively rare. Anyway, I tried to change the delicate subject and told him they'd just made me a citizen. Chief Justice Fred C. Vinson of the Supreme Court himself had sworn in a group of us in Washington, in a highly emotional scene, during which the Chief Justice, after a moving speech, had cried, as he talked about "these fine, upstanding, new citizens" — us — who were going over to defend "the ideals of their new homeland." The Chief Justice wiped his eyes with a large, blue-white handkerchief. They said he had a son fighting abroad.

I succeeded in calming Ross down, and he took me for lunch to the Algonquin. He didn't mind my five stripes anymore but hoped I wouldn't come back with six, as a master sergeant. I didn't. Several months later, when I sent *The New Yorker* an article from Europe, it ran under the heading "Our Combattant Correspondents" and was signed "T/Sgt. Joseph Wechsberg," which was a euphemism, since I'd written from Paris about a meeting with old friends, under the title "Back to the Place Pigalle." During lunch, Ross, in one of his sudden, surprising changes of mood, wanted to know all about psychological warfare. His curiosity prevailed over his resentment. I told him about the collection of strange characters in our outfit.

He nodded gloomily. "Sounds almost as crazy as the office," he said. When we parted, he gave me his famous mixture of blessing and damning me, and he gave me the names of two *New Yorker* people who were over there. "If you are in trouble, get in touch with them," he said.

I thought a lot about his last words. Had he meant trouble with the enemy Germans, the allied Russians, the allegedly friendly French, with women and women spies, or, most probably, with some of our own general officers? His faith in the *New Yorker* people was touching; he was convinced they could take care of any trouble I got in over there. He was right about trouble, incidentally, but when I became involved with several generals, even Ross couldn't have helped me.

In wartime, troops don't travel but are shipped, like goods. On a hot summer night in 1944, the Fourth Mobile Radio Broadcasting Company left Camp Sharpe, Gettysburg, on its way to an "undisclosed destination." The operation was a military secret, but having become skilled psychological warriors, we'd found out that we were going to New York, on our way overseas. We'd notified our wives and girl friends to meet us in New York, which was, of course, strictly forbidden because officially we weren't even there.

The five mobile radio broadcasting companies that belonged to the Psychological Warfare Division were something new in the technique of military operations. Psychology as a weapon was not unknown to Xenophon, Caesar, Hannibal, Napoleon, Clausewitz. The Germans perfected it under the Hitler regime. Goebbels claimed that any lie, relentlessly repeated, will ultimately be accepted as truth. This too was not an original thought.

America's psychological warriors accepted the method but not the principle. Our ideals were not sacrificed; we were to spread the gospel of truth. Oddly, the Americans, masters of the hard sell when they dealt in big cars and soft drinks, failed when they tried to market the American way of life. Later, at Radio Luxembourg, where we wound up, our orders were to tell the truth and nothing but the truth. The Germans were losing the war, and we would tell it to them day after day, hoping they would believe us. Radio Luxembourg, a joint American-British operation, was a "white" station, declaring itself, telling the straight story. There was also a "black" station in town that pretended to be a German outfit, specializing in inside news, giving the names of people who had just been arrested by the Gestapo somewhere in Germany, or had been hurt yesterday in an Allied bombing raid in a certain street of a certain town. The German listeners couldn't help being impressed by the accuracy of these reports.

The mobile radio broadcasting companies did more than their name implied. Broadcasting was only part of the job. We also disseminated leaflets and newspapers which we'd printed; traveled along the enemy lines in jeeps and trucks equipped with loudspeakers, enticing the *Land-ser* (the German GI) to surrender; and used other communications media, trying to convince the enemy that it was useless to fight, so why not be smart and give up while they were still alive? Recent information gathered from prisoners of war was skillfully used to further undermine enemy morale. The complex operation relied on support from our own fighting troops who — theoretically — were to protect and help us. This created innumerable conflicts which the military bureaucrats love dearly, trying to figure out who outranks whom and how to sabotage the other guy. After the capture of prominent German prisoners, there was much infighting between various groups. Who would be the first to interrogate a captured *Waffen-SS* general? The commander of the outfit that had captured him? The Counter Intelligence Corps? Psychological Warfare? A powerful colonel on the staff of General Bradley?

The Fourth M.R.B., which Captain Goularte, in his irascible moments, called "a bunch of mad geniuses," included newspapermen, novelists, public-relations experts, editors, radio announcers, actors, artists, technicians, photographers, printers, entertainers, and others active in the not-so-beaux arts. Since the enemy had to be addressed in his own language, many psychological warriors were German-speaking recent-vintage *émigrés*. Some had been well-known novelists in Europe: Hans Habe, Stefan Heym, Klaus Mann.

We reached New York "under the cover of secrecy," and attended many not-secret good-bye parties. One night we boarded an elegant ocean liner in the harbor, which I instantly recognized as Cunard's *Mauretania*, though its name had been removed from the hull. No one was supposed to utter the name of the boat. Most secret, the British said. It wasn't the Cunard Line's old *Mauretania* that I'd often admired as a ship's musician when we passed it — a mobile ship with four funnels that had once held the Blue Ribbon. Our new *Mauretania* was modern, streamlined, faster, though it had only two funnels.

We were pleased, but not at all surprised, to cross the ocean on a luxury liner, in style, and not on a shabby Liberty ship. The Fourth M.R.B. Company was never suffering from a collective inferiority complex. On the contrary. One of our dukes expected to make the trip in a first-class stateroom. There was no chance of getting one of the *Mauretania's suites de grande luxe,* since several admirals and generals were aboard.

Somebody made a mistake about the travel arrangements, though. We went aboard and were taken from the promenade deck, where the deluxe suites were located, to A deck (first class) below, then to B deck (tourist class), down to C deck (third class, very bad), and farther down to D deck where the crew members slept. Our dukes, or *ducs,* were aghast. Farther down we went, to E deck, not fit for human habitation; in peacetime, automobiles were stored there. From E deck we descended on narrow, dangerous iron ladders to F deck, where the ship's water and fuel reserves were stored. In between the vast reservoirs, the *Mauretania's* builders had left some dark, damp dungeons that compared unfavorably with the famous cave near Marseilles where, according to Alexandre Dumas, the Count of Monte Cristo had been kept incommunicado. Our psychological-warfare experts instantly recognized the black holes on F deck as a sinister deterrent, created by orders of the evil Cunard management, to nip in the bud any attempt at mutiny. The Russians have Siberia, the French had Devil's Island, and the Cunard Line had F deck.

We were taken to the darkest, dampest, hottest dungeon of all. During the First World War, certain freight cars in Austria-Hungary had signs FOR 8 HORSES OR 48 MEN. Our dungeon was "For 8 Inmates of Hell or 108 Soldiers." There was practically no breathable air. The humidity was "above one hundred," in the opinion of one of our men, a meteorologist. Compared to the atmosphere in the dungeon, the sweltering New York heat-wave weather had indeed been balmy.

There were no bunks. We were told to lie down on the floor. Several men collapsed and had to be revived. We must have been a colorful group. Half-naked, covered with perspiration, our faces distorted with wrath and heat, we looked like a poster for Hugo's *Les Misérables*. Two dim bulbs hung down from the ceiling, casting ghostly half-shadows over our faces. In the middle of the cavernous hole, a big kettle was set up over a tripod into which British navy gremlins dumped their version of Boston baked beans once a day. The wine waiter of the *Mauretania* never showed up. The smell was bad and the sense of claustrophobia was worse. We agreed that we wouldn't survive the third day. Perhaps not even the second.

The Fourth Mobile reacted in style. A meeting was held, and I made one of my rare speeches. (I was the company's top-ranking noncom, and the second-oldest man; Francis Perkins, the *Herald Tribune*'s music critic, forty-two, was the oldest.) It was a short speech; no one would have stood for a long one. I said that this was an unusual situation which demanded unusual action. As experts in the devious devices of psychological warfare, we would now wage war — not against the enemy but against the powers aboard the *Mauretania* and, "if necessary, against the entire army of the United States." At this point, I seemed to have crossed the dangerous boundary from legitimate griping to criminal mutiny.

"Men," I said, "we shall survive against the enemy only if we don't lose the earlier battle against our superiors." (Protracted applause.) It was decided to send a delegation to the company commander "to make a last peaceful effort before resorting to desperate self-defense." But the company commander, a captain, couldn't help us. He was bawled out by a major who told him we should be glad to be on F deck. There were over twelve thousand troops aboard this ship that normally carried two thousand people. The major implied that things could be worse. Suppose we had to sleep near the propellers?

A short meeting was held on F deck. It was unanimously decided to put The Plan into action. It was simple and ingenious: trained in the modern communications media, we would start a dress rehearsal aboard. A delegation went to see the transport commander, a full colonel. We suggested, respectfully, that we might contribute to the morale of the troops by using the ship's facilities — the printing shop, the intercom network — putting out a daily newspaper, and broadcasting programs of news and entertainment.

The colonel was impressed. The ship was "crowded to suffocation." There was a morale problem. But, he said, the rules of security must be strictly observed.

"Above all, no mention of . . . well, you know what I mean."

We pretended to look astonished.

"Dammit, there's a war going on."

Still we pretended not to understand.

He gave a shrug and looked unhappy. "Submarines," he said, almost in a whisper. It is rare to hear a colonel whisper.

We'd wanted to call our newspaper *Zigzag News*, an allusion to the ship's erratic course, but under the circumstances decided to call it just the *News*. There would be fifteen hours of daily radio programs. The colonel was pleased. As he was about to dismiss us, I asked for passes.

It was his turn to be astonished. "Passes?"

"Sir," I said, "our men must have the run of the ship to be able to discharge their duties conscientiously."

Half an hour later, every member of the Fourth M.R.B. Company had a pass giving access to all decks including the captain's bridge where admirals, but no generals, were permitted. Another half an hour later, our dungeon on F deck was deserted.

That night I slept on the thick rug underneath the piano in the grand salon of the *Mauretania*. I was drawn toward the piano as a criminal is said to be drawn back to the place of the crime. I dreamed I was the orchestra leader aboard the *Mauretania*. Just as I played the *Merry Widow* waltz, I was rudely roused out of sweet slumber by two American military police. I showed them my pass, and they left, dumbfounded. The following night I slept on the sundeck between the two funnels where the air was cool and pleasant. A British navy policeman woke me and refused to recognize the transport commander's authority, even making some anti-American statements, but let me sleep when I promised to print his picture in our paper. Policemen love to have their pictures in the paper.

We set up editorial offices for the *News* in two small rooms strategically located next to the first-class bar. The *Mauretania* was crowded like a Chinese ferryboat during rush hour. Men were lying, squatting, sitting everywhere — on the decks, in the corridors, even in the lifeboats. Reporters doing their legwork stepping over so many legs had to be tactful. The soldiers had strict orders to stay where they were. Only the military police — and the men of the Fourth M.R.B. — were permitted to move around freely.

Our radio program was a great success. There was music (jazz) and news reports. Instead of commercials we broadcast the transport commander's orders. ("Keep your life vests on at all times!" "Don't light matches on deck after darkness!" "Don't discuss military matters!") One of our reporters talked to the transport commander. A photographer took his picture. Two men went up to the bridge, interviewing the captain. They spent two pleasant days on the bridge, enjoying the view. I went to see an admiral in his deluxe stateroom. I promised to run a short biography of the admiral, in installments. After the first installment, he was pleased and offered me a bath in his tub. Sweet water, too. I got three other men into the admiral's tub, under various pretexts.

The newspaper proved to be a smash hit. It contained news, the early boyhood story of the admiral, the picture of the transport commander, a sports page, soldiers' jokes, and a feature on how not to fall out of a hammock. Encouraged by the success, our men became more ambitious. One reporter discovered a group of WACs who were kept out of sight, and reach, in a hidden corridor on B deck. We printed the pictures of two good-looking girls, with plenty of leg. I wrote a short gastronomic essay on the British Boston baked beans, "the Germans' secret weapon aboard." One man, a society columnist in private life, wrote a gossip column with some piquant details about army and air-force rivalry aboard, including a dramatic incident in the first-class bar. People were beginning to fight for a copy of the *News*. Unfortunately, the print shop was short of paper.

The third issue was sensational. The admiral's biography had reached Annapolis. No mention was made of his low standing in his class. The society columnist had a story about two WACs who had been entertained in a deluxe suite — where else? — by a general and a colonel. Members of various troops and outfits had been interviewed about their travel impressions, which were not always flattering. I printed them; I'd read such stories in *Stars and Stripes* for years. Hadn't we been taught to tell the truth and nothing but the truth?

That was exactly what I told the transport commander who summoned the editors of the *News* to his office. He was in a state of impending apoplexy. He shouted that our activities were terminated "as of now." The men of the Fourth M.R.B. Company were ordered to turn in their passes and to proceed, on the double, to company quarters on F deck.

A proverb ascribed to Hungarians, Rumanians, and Bulgarians, all of whom decline to acknowledge authorship, says, "Lord, protect me against my friends; I can take care of my enemies." This accurately sums up my problems during the Second World War. The Almighty protected me against the Germans, but He did not support me against my superiors. As a former member of the officers' caste, I knew that its members often try to camouflage the scarcity of mental equipment with the grandeur of insignia and decorations. Especially professional soldiers, who consider all others mere second-class human beings.

Bureaucrats and military career men share absolute belief in their infallibility, contempt for lower-ranking personnel, and abject devotion to complex rules and regulations. In wartime, bureaucrats and military men merge into a military bureaucracy combining the evils of advanced red tape with the arrogance of the uniform. The system is built on the dogma that men are born to outrank each other.

I have no intention of contributing to the still-growing documentation of the Second World War. The following report is only a mini-marginal note to the dramatic counterattack launched by fifteen German divisions under General von Modell. It is remembered as the Ardennes Bulge, or the Rundstedt Offensive. It began on December 16, 1944. By December 19, the First U.S. Army was pushed out of Germany. On December 21, General Patton's Third U.S. Army rescued the besieged Americans in Bastogne. The desperate German gamble was stopped only on December 25, but it took over a month to wipe out the Bulge. American losses were estimated at 40,000. The Germans lost 220,000 men in dead and prisoners.

During the last two weeks preceding the German offensive, three American generals, abetted by large staffs, wasted their valuable time and energy fighting one another, instead of the Germans, as they argued for temporary possession of a certain technical sergeant.

At Radio Luxembourg I had a frustrating desk job, writing reports and features for our German-language broadcasts. Somehow I managed to get a pass to Paris, where I met several men working for *Stars and Stripes*. No other army ever dared publish a newspaper written by enlisted men that was often critical of the military establishment. In the Czechoslovak army it would have been unthinkable to publish such stories. The American army was big enough to afford some criticism, and to give a fine, worldwide demonstration of freedom of the press. The reporters for *Stars and Stripes* had some problems, to be sure, but they were still American reporters.

I was told that there might be a job for me, an ex-newspaperman who spoke German fluently. That one could "get a job" with an army paper was another revelation. I returned to Luxembourg City and talked to Captain Goularte, our company commander, a hell of a nice guy. He gave me travel orders to Paris, though I had no business being there. He said he was taking a chance, since our outfit, operating under SHAEF (Supreme Headquarters Allied Expeditionary Forces), had a very high priority.

"Priority" was the sesame that opened locked doors and neutralized many military secrets. Priority transcended rank; a private with high priority could ease a colonel with lower priority off a crowded military plane. *Stars and Stripes* had high priority, which its reporters needed to carry off their often delicate assignments. However, Psychological Warfare had even higher priority, being directly under SHAEF. We wore the crossed SHAEF swords with the flames on our arms, just like General Eisenhower.

At the *Herald Tribune* building in the Rue de Berri, in Paris, I met Igor Cassini, who had left the Fourth M.R.B. earlier and had been transferred out with the help of some friends in Washington. I thought of trying to find the *New Yorker* people Ross had told me about, but there was no time. My travel orders were limited. Cassini and I decided to "get jobs" at *Stars and Stripes*.

The building was filled with the dearly familiar smell of printer's ink and turpentine, which always does something to my blood pressure, and there was the faraway sound of the rotation presses, more beautiful than the melodious sounds of the waves in *La Mer* — and I love Debussy. We met a soldier wearing a shoulder patch, u.s. war correspondent, that seemed more desirable to me than a general's silver star. He took us to a friendly major in charge of personnel, wished us good luck, and left. We told the major why we'd come to see him. He looked skeptical. Here were two guys who wanted to work for *Stars and Stripes*, but they neither talked nor looked like American newspapermen. He asked us where we came from. We told him.

"Psychological Warfare," he said, and glanced at the SHAEF patches on our shoulders. He gave a shrug, and then he said he would give us a story assignment, and we had thirty minutes to write a thousand-word feature.

"If you pull it off, you're hired. If not, you'll be out of here in thirty seconds."

"Fair enough," I said, trying hard to look like a third-generation American newspaperman. We went off in search of two typewriters. Half an hour later, the major had his features, and we had our jobs.

"Incredible," he said, looking at the copy. "With *that* accent."

I told the major that there might be trouble. The Psychological Warfare people might want us back, and they had very high priority.

"Don't worry," the major said, temporarily assuming the pose of a major general. *"Stars and Stripes* has the highest priority."

Downstairs we bought U.S. war-correspondent shoulder patches, which we decided to wear on top of our SHAEF patches. The patches were later sewn on by a young lady whose name began with M — Michèle, Marguerite, Mirabelle, I'm not sure — though I do remember her throaty voice and the color of her hair, which made me think of slightly burned crêpes suzette. For a while I called her Suzette. We walked around proudly with our two shoulder patches, looking like General Eisenhower's private war correspondents. It seemed an unbeatable priority.

The following weeks remain one long dream of glory. I flew on assignments all over Europe. With our shoulder patches, it was easy to bum a ride everywhere in the European Theatre of Operations. Once I was fetched by a general's car driven by a WAC. I discovered that some generals were getting almost humble in the presence of a *Stars and Stripes* reporter. Everybody said the war was practically over and we would be at home around Easter.

In Paris, we didn't have to live at the official *Stars and Stripes* billet. Cassini and I shared a room in a hotel near the Place Pigalle, where I'd lived as a nightclub fiddler in the gay 1920's. The hotel's reputation was impeccable from the third floor up, where the rooms were rented on a monthly basis. The "transient" rooms on the second floor were available *pour un moment.* Our room was on the fourth floor.

The fat, old *patronne* who owned the establishment was still there, looking fatter and dirtier in a faded silk gown, smelling of garlic and Beaujolais, reading a *roman policier.* She complained bitterly about *ces soldats,* what they'd done to the furniture, and especially to the bidets.

I tried to comfort her. *"C'est la guerre, Madame. Les Boches, vous savez."*

Merde, she said, it wasn't *les Boches* but *ces Américains* that caused the damage. Totally unimpressed by the blessings of the Liberation, she asked us to pay for one month in advance. *Les affaires* were still *les affaires,* business is business.

Stars and Stripes had its own mess at Chez Mercier, a restaurant in Rue Lincoln on the other side of the Champs Elysées. Nowadays Chez Mercier has one star in the *Guide Michelin,* with *homard au gratin* and *caneton à l'orange* (on Thursday, Saturday, Sunday). We didn't get these *spécialités de la maison.* Our food was prepared from U.S. army supplies, but somehow it tasted much better than the chow made elsewhere by GI cooks. No wonder, perhaps, since the cooks at Chez Mercier were French. So were the waitresses. Waitresses, serving enlisted men! It was almost as good as the generals' mess at the Ritz, and much more fun, sitting next to Jimmy Cannon or Bill Mauldin. At night we had drinks with the civilian war correspondents at the Scribe. I ran into Joe Liebling and asked him to tell Ross that I'd made his old paper. It was a wonderful time. Cassini worked so hard that he lost two *Stars and Stripes* jeeps in five weeks — a record even among the paper's reporters.

One afternoon, I went back to my old haunt in the Place Pigalle. I'd wanted to go there for weeks but always put it off. I was afraid to go back to the past. Sixteen years ago, I had said farewell to Montmartre and its irresponsible ways, and now I was back as an American soldier. Life was much stranger than fiction.

Superficially, not much seemed to have changed. The accordionists were still playing their old javas, the tired sidewalk painters had their watercolors propped up against the trees on the Boulevard de Clichy, and the busy little ladies were patrolling up and down as of old, smiling, almost as chic as ever, in spite of three-year-old dresses and wooden shoes. The air had changed, though. It lacked the mingled smell of gasoline and perfume and good hot food that had always hovered over Montmartre.

The Café Aux Quat'z Arts, once the unofficial musicians' exchange, had disappeared. In its place there was now a couturière and a stationery shop. But the Café Pigalle was still there, with a new awning, facing the Métro entrance in the Place Pigalle. In the old days, we *artistes* had come there to meet the managers of movie theaters, nightclub operators, agents, headwaiters, and other people in search of musicians. In the early weeks when I wasn't known there, I carried my empty violin case under the arm so they would know what instrument I was playing. Pianists declared themselves by keeping a rolled piano score in their hands.

Inside, people were standing three deep at the bar. It was Friday, always a busy day for arranging *cachets*, temporary engagements during the weekend. My entrance caused a mild sensation. American soldiers had all but taken over Montmartre, but they never showed up at the businesslike Café Pigalle, preferring the hot spots La Lune Rousse or La Silhouette.

I heard somebody gasp, two strong arms enfolded me, and I was pressed against a dirty, deep-lined, unshaven face, while a familiar voice uttered curses of joy. I recognized Sapencu, a Rumanian violinist. In the summer of 1926, at the Moulin Rouge music hall, he and I had shared a stand in the orchestra of "The Blackbirds," an American all-Negro revue. They'd hired a white violin section. It was my first experience playing with a black orchestra, and quite bewildering. Sapencu and I had almost dropped our fiddles when the trumpets opened up during the refrain of the theme song, "I Can't Give You Anything But Love, Baby." It took us a long time to get used to their wild improvisations. We violinists earned much less than the black members of the orchestra, but we were also much less heard. Once I asked why they'd hired us. The conductor said he liked the sound of violins for the "romantic" Deep South scenes.

Sapencu hadn't been much of a fiddler, though he pretended to have been the favorite pupil of Georges Enesco. He had introduced me into the mysteries of gypsy playing, but I soon gave up because no man can pretend to be a gypsy fiddler who isn't born one. Like the real gypsy primas, Sapencu was always surrounded by beautiful women, and made good money selling a white powder which wasn't sugar and didn't taste like salt. Now he introduced me to a slim brunette of the forbidding femme fatale category. She had heavily shadowed eyes which she kept intriguingly half closed, and there was a permanent promise in her voice, though it wasn't certain exactly what she was promising. Sapencu said he didn't bother with cocaine anymore. There were much safer opportunities now. He asked me whether I could get him some army gasoline. He knew a *type* who was the friend of a *type* who would pay five thousand *balles* for a five-gallon can. I shook my head, and he went up to six and seven thousand francs. Switching to Czech (which presumably only we two among those present understood), he said he would be delighted to fix me up with the femme fatale, and he smiled at her and gallantly kissed her hand.

Two men pushed through the crowd and greeted me with enthusiasm. One was Carpentier, who once had sat next to me in the orchestra of the Folies Bergère (where we developed a dislike for Mistinguett because of her habit of kicking her legs out over our heads). The other was Gaston, a dark-haired Toulousain, formerly second violinist on various Messageries Maritimes liners on which I was orchestra leader. Carpentier right away offered me a *cachet* — Saturday and Sunday at a chic *boîte* on the Boulevard Montparnasse. A hundred francs an hour and a good supper. The place was patronized by Americans, he said, and I could tell them what was currently played in the States.

I said I couldn't do it, what with my shoulder patches.

"You always worried too much, mon petit Joseph-*et-son-caleçon*," he said. He'd christened me Joseph-*et-son-caleçon*. I would spend long hours sitting at my typewriter in the hot cabin, wearing only *caleçons* (shorts), because it was very hot in the Indian Ocean and in Indochina.

Once we had worked in a little *boîte* in the Rue Blanche, in Montmartre, where I was hired to play *à la tzigane*, in gypsy style, going from one table to the next.

"Oh, la, la," Carpentier said wistfully. "You worried that the *flics* would raid the place."

"But they did, and they closed it up."

"Yes, but it was fun while it lasted. You always worried too much. Remember Jeanne? You worried a lot about her."

I tried to remember Jeanne but couldn't, and gave up. Other men came to shake hands. I no longer knew their names but recognized their faces; we'd played together in *boîtes, bals, cinémas*. The barman offered me a drink and whispered, would I sell him some American cigarettes? Two Royal Air Force MPs came in, tall and stilted; they seemed shocked at the spectacle of a GI surrounded by so many odd-looking civilians, and went out again. The femme fatale pressed my elbow and offered me a big bottle of Chanel No. 5 that she had in her room. Did I know that it was practically unobtainable? Had I made any other plans for the night? And how about a few Hershey chocolate bars?

Around us was the familiar confusion I remembered so well — people exchanging addresses, writing *cachets* in their notebooks. It made me feel sixteen years younger. Business wasn't bad, they said, but it had been better when *les Boches* were in Paris. The Germans went all out for music.

"In a place on the Boulevard de Clichy," Gaston said, "a general came in one night with two SS blackshirts. They told a nice, quiet French couple to give up their table for them, and ordered us to play something *classique*. We played the Coronation March from Meyerbeer's *Le Prophète*. The blackshirts thought it was *ausgezeichnet* and gave me two hundred francs. They had as much money as they could print. The bills were always brand-new.

"Then our pianist had to open his mouth and say loudly, 'Too bad they can't play that march in Germany.' The blackshirts got suspicious, took out their revolvers, came up to the platform, and looked at the music. When they saw 'Meyerbeer,' they got mad as hell, and tried to round us up. The general wanted to intervene, but one SS man had the nerve to push him away. The next thing I knew, everybody got up and there was confusion. The general's monocle got broken in the scuffle, and someone turned out the lights. Great fun but not for me. The SS took me to Gestapo headquarters, and I spent two weeks there."

Under the Germans, American jazz was strictly *verboten*. Anyone playing a piece by Gershwin or Irving Berlin risked being taken into "protective custody." Once the Germans closed the Bal Musette because two girls had started dancing *le swing*.

The crowd was thinning out, most deals having been made, and I sat down at a table with my old *copains*, and we had aperitifs. I had forgotten about my uniform; it was — almost — like old times. I asked them what happened to Maurice Metzinger, who had been our cellist and the leader of the small orchestra aboard the French Line boat *La Bourdonnais*, on which I'd made my first trip to New York. It was the hot, crazy, wonderful summer of 1928. We'd been berthed at Pier Ninety-nine, at the foot of Fifty-ninth Street, in a dreary neighborhood of dirty lofts, chimneys, factories. I'd gone down the gangway and stepped on the soil of God's own country, carrying a list of telephone numbers which Maurice had handed to me. My orders were to call these numbers from a nearby drugstore (Maurice had explained to me what a drugstore was) and tell the people on the other end of the line, "The *Bourdonnais* is in town." I asked Maurice whether it was a code message. Yes, he said, don't worry. The people I called would know what it was all about.

They certainly did. Late in the afternoon they came to our two staterooms where Maurice had set up a private bar stocked with bottles of wine and brandy that we had saved from our meals, bought at a discount, or simply pilfered during the trip. Our customers were the sort of men whose pictures could be seen years later in *Fortune* — respectable executives, big businessmen, pillars of their communities. The pillars had met Maurice on earlier trips and kept up the valuable relationship.

We made more money on our illegal liquor sales during the ship's stay in New York than from our regular salary. I regret to confess that my first activities in America were not strictly legal, but this was Prohibition, and after all, I wasn't an American citizen then. And besides, all this took place on French territory. We were sorry when Repeal came and we were deprived of an interesting source of income.

Maurice had been a wonderful fellow, warm-hearted and exuberant. In the rare moments when he wasn't drunk, he played the cello beautifully; at one time he had worked with Casals. He was able to lead his bow quietly even when he was dead drunk, a remarkable feat. Maurice kept two separate, well-run households, in New York and in Paris, and he kept both ladies happy because they never knew of each other. I'm not sure whether he was married to either one; if I'm not mistaken, he had a wife somewhere in Alsace, where he came from. Carpentier said that Maurice had died the year before.

"Drank himself to death, literally. The collapse of France was more than he could stand. When *les Boches* marched into Paris, Maurice got drunk and stayed drunk."

This wouldn't prevent Maurice from working and doing strange things. He would get up in the middle of a piece, knock with his bow against the back of his cello, and raise his arm. (I nodded to myself; he had often done it aboard ship when he was seized by a wild idea.) People would stop dancing. Maurice would give a military salute, using his bow as a saber, and he would shout, *"Vive* Hector Berlioz!" or *"Vive* Claude Debussy, *musicien français!"*

The Germans in the audience were flabbergasted, but the audience caught on quickly, and there was a great demonstration for the great, late French composers whose names, in this connection, meant a great deal to the French people, even to those who didn't care about music. Maurice did some really crazy things. Around two A.M., when many German soldiers were more under than at the tables, Maurice, who spoke good German, would announce that the orchestra would play "Deutschland über Alles." The plastered Germans had to crawl out from under the tables, making an effort to stand at attention and salute, and naturally they fell flat on their faces. The French customers would start laughing, and in the end some SS men — there were always a few around — would call the nearest patrol and have the drunken Germans arrested.

"Maurice was personally responsible for the arrest and temporary putting out of action of at least a battalion of *Panzergrenadiere,"* Carpentier said. "Not bad for a cellist."

Carpentier said that Maurice's last master stroke was his original musical arrangement of combining the "Marseillaise" and the sentimental German lied "Ich hatt' einen Kameraden." Half the band played the "Marseillaise" and half played the German lied, and the whole thing was woven at the end into a fine, confusing counterpoint, along the lines of Wagner's *Meistersinger* Prelude. It fooled the Germans completely. When the band played the arrangement, with cello, trumpet, and cornet giving out with the martial melody of the "Marseillaise," the French in the audience would catch on, and there was a terrific ovation. This made the Gestapo and SS *types* reach for their guns. And then the "Marseillaise" section would play only *pianissimo*, while the violins and clarinets played "Ich hatt' einen Kameraden" with sentimental *tremolo*. Sometimes a tough *Oberfeldwebel* began to cry into his champagne glass.

"In the end, however, the 'Marseillaise' always came through," Carpentier said. He look ahead silently. Then he raised his glass. We nodded sadly, and drank to the memory of Maurice.

Shortly before Christmas, I was told to report to the major at *Stars and Stripes* who had hired us. He was furious. He said there was a war going on, there was trouble up in the Hürtgen Forest and all along the Siegfried Line, and three generals were arguing about a lousy tech sergeant, and then the people back home wondered why the war wasn't over yet. He said I would have to return to Luxembourg at once.

I said, "Sir, I thought *Stars and Stripes* had the highest priority."

"Maybe it's the second highest," he said grimly. "They've taken your case all the way up to — Oh, hell! Look, Joe, I tried my best. I never got bawled out as badly as last night since I joined this army. Serves me right for hiring a couple of characters from Psychological Warfare wearing SHAEF shoulder patches and speaking four languages, none of which I understand. Seems more like pathological warfare. . . . Your travel orders are ready, and a jeep and a driver are waiting downstairs. Get back to Luxembourg as fast as you can. You are in enough trouble the way things stand."

So that was that. I picked up my orders. My driver, a stoical Southerner with a sleepy disposition, had never heard of Luxembourg. He just wanted to get the damn war over with, and get home to Mom. We got a couple of extra gasoline cans, and I had my last lunch at Chez Mercier. Tomorrow, I thought, there would be no waitresses for me.

I went to say good-bye to all my friends — in Pigalle, at the Scribe, and somewhere I ran into the lady with the crêpe suzette-colored hair, and it was dawn when we left Paris.

We stopped in Reims, where I had friends in the champagne business. One champagne led to another, and we stayed for lunch, and then for dinner. We left Reims in the early morning of December 18, with half a dozen bottles of vintage *brut*. Soldiers always complained about lack of space in a jeep, but it holds a lot of champagne. I was tired, and dozed off. When I woke up and looked at my wristwatch, it was almost noon.

The highway was full of people — apparently refugees coming our way. My stoical Southerner said they'd been coming for hours, and that was why we were going slowly. I told him to stop, and talked to some people. There were wild rumors of a big German offensive. The Allies were said to be on the run. Somebody said the Germans had taken over Luxembourg City. Later, we met some American soldiers. They said it was true; a German offensive had started two days ago. They looked at my shoulder patch and asked whether I was going to cover the story. I didn't tell them that at *Stars and Stripes* they hadn't known about the offensive when we'd left on December 16.

The following two days were not dull. Twice we were stopped by our own military police, who were looking for German parachutists wearing captured American uniforms. When the MPs heard my accent, they were delighted.

"A Hun," one of them exclaimed.

I said I must have been the first Jewish Hun they'd met. This humorous aside was not appreciated. My driver saved me from being summarily shot. Then we ran into another MP patrol, and even he couldn't save me. A guy with a SHAEF patch and a U.S. war-correspondent patch speaking English with a German accent wasn't just a spy for the military police. Must be a double agent.

"Even carries German wine," one of the MPs said, looking at the label of the champagne. "Roederer. A Hun general."

I said the name was Roeder, and he was an admiral. "The dirty bastard," said the MP. I didn't know whether he meant me or Roederer-Roeder. They pointed their guns at me, asked me for name, rank, serial number, looked at my travel orders, and asked me where I was going. They weren't sure, though, and asked me who were the girls on the Bob Hope show and what about Jack Benny's valet. Fortunately they didn't ask me about the funnies and baseball. My Americanization had stopped short of these two phenomena. One asked me where I was living in the States, and when I said Westwood Village, he almost embraced me. He was from Brentwood. We celebrated with a bottle of champagne with the German general's name, reminiscing about events along Wilshire and Sunset Boulevard, and then we left. It took us three days to get to Luxembourg, normally a one-day drive from Paris. The main highways were jammed with military traffic. We had to drive over dirt roads and country lanes. We lived on K rations and champagne.

On the afternoon of December 21, I reported to Captain Goularte at the Fourth M.R.B. Company. At Radio Luxembourg, the scriptwriters and announcers wore steel helmets and had their guns lying near their desks. On the preceding afternoon, the Germans had come within three miles of the radio station. Writers, announcers, technicians, cooks, and drivers had been alerted and sent out there. Captain Goularte asked me how long it had taken me from Paris.

"Five days, sir."

He laughed. "I'm glad you didn't forget your psychological-warfare training in Gay Paree," he said.

The next morning the company was alerted again and sent toward the Siegfried Line to strengthen our defenses. Captain Goularte said that things must be tough all over when the "mad geniuses" were used along the front. I had my Christmas dinner in a cold foxhole with a fine view of an interesting sector of the Siegfried Line. Dinner was served at four in the afternoon, during a blizzard. I'd asked for white turkey meat and I got it, with sage dressing, sweet potatoes, and cranberry sauce. Everything was hot except the cranberry sauce. The turkey was delicious, not too dry, and they brought me seconds in the foxhole. I never understood how they managed to do these things, but this was one of the reasons why we won the war in the end. The Germans began to shoot at us again, but nobody cared.

The Germans were defeated, in spite of the psychological-warfare activities of the Fourth M.R.B. Company. On May 10, 1945, forty-eight hours after the end of the European phase of World War Two, I was on my way to Czechoslovakia.

I was then stationed in Bad Nauheim, near Frankfurt-am-Main, with a unit publishing German newspapers — the first democratic papers in Germany since Hitler came to power in 1933. I was on the staff of the earliest paper, *Kölnischer Kurier* in Cologne, which we put out while the Germans were still resisting in Deutz, on the other side of the Rhine. The first issue of the paper had a proclamation by General Eisenhower. The paper was distributed free of charge, compliments of the American army. Later, there was a whole chain of such papers all over occupied Germany. We tried to bring back democracy, but today I'm not sure that we succeeded.

V-E Day was a sunny May day in Bad Nauheim. I stood with Eric Winters, one of our editors, on the balcony of the elegant villa where we lived. I'd just come from Cologne, which was badly destroyed, and Bad Nauheim looked unreal to me with its white hotel façades and lovely parks. There was a scent of spring in the air, and the gardeners worked on the flowerbeds. All the spa needed to be perfect was solid burghers and their wives, taking the cure and walking in the park. Eric turned on the radio. There was fighting in Prague, where the Czechs had risen against the German occupiers in the streets. Suddenly, I had a terrible sense of urgency. I felt I *had* to go back to Prague. We Americans were not supposed to be there; the demarkation line between the American troops and the Red army was near Pilsen.

I went to see Major Patrick Dolan, a vigorous, sympathetic American with a sense of adventure. Pat is now a close friend of mine, but in Bad Nauheim he was just "the major" to me. He said he'd never been "in on any liberation," having barely missed the one in Paris, and he would come along. We would have to cross the Russian lines, and his gold leaves might facilitate the inevitable negotiations. He was a round-faced man with soft eyes and an upturned nose; he could have been a dark-haired Czech. He was a Madison Avenue man with a great appetite for excitement and food. We got hold of a jeep, several cans of gasoline, some boxes of K rations. I took along a small American flag which I intended to fly on the jeep while driving through the streets of Prague. I was having dreams of glory again.

The major and I left Bad Nauheim the next morning, drove through Nuremberg, which didn't quite look like the romantic medieval town that one sometimes sees in the second act of Wagner's *Meistersinger*, and later passed through Bayreuth. When I saw the Green Hill, I suggested we take a look at the *Festspielhaus*; I had never been there.

We parked the jeep and went in through the open stage door. A frightened old janitor sat inside, jumping to attention as he saw the holsters of our guns. We both carried Lugers, which were more fashionable with American troops than American weapons. I said I wanted to see the stage, that's an order. *"Natürlich, natürlich,"* he said, and switched on the lights.

The sets for the second act of *Die Meistersinger* were on the stage, the lovely vision of medieval Nuremberg. The janitor said it was in the middle of the last performance that *they* had come — and he pointed his forefinger significantly toward the sky. Well, said the major, *they* hadn't done any damage around here. I asked the major to sit down in one of the front rows, and proceeded to fulfill a lifelong ambition: to sing opera. I might as well start in the *Festspielhaus*, where many celebrated singers arrive only at the peak of their careers. I loved the part of Hans Sachs, the cobbler poet in *Die Meistersinger*. I sat down in the chair in front of Sachs's house, in the middle of the stage, and sang "Was duftet hold der Flieder." I thought my voice was not bad. The major applauded, and I sang the beginning of the *Wahn* monologue, "Madness, madness, everywhere madness," but halfway my voice gave out, and I walked off the stage. Many years later, I told Wieland Wagner about my debut at his *Festspielhaus*. He asked me to audition for him, but I declined, regretfully.

We took the highway to Pilsen and Prague. The road was crowded. There were many people on bicycles and horses and in haycarts and trucks. Many were walking. Some had a dazed expression, as though they couldn't believe the war was over. They all moved along at a steady pace, but when you asked them where they were going, most of them couldn't tell you exactly. Some were trying to get back to their countries and homes and families. Most were running away from something or somebody they were afraid of. There were German soldiers going west, looking stunned and bedraggled, and Czechs and Poles moving east. There were soldiers cut off from their units; gaunt, haggard people who had walked out of concentration camps; children looking for their parents; parents looking for their children.

As our jeep approached the frontier between Germany and Czechoslovakia, which runs along the crest of the Bohemian Forest, the highway was even more jammed than it had been earlier. We got through the crowds, however. The people moved aside when they saw our jeep with its American army markings. Some smiled and waved at us, and some stared at us with hate. But no matter whether they considered us liberators or conquerors, they took it for granted that we had the right of way. In order to ease military class distinctions, which in effect did not exist between the major and me anyway, and could only be a complicating factor on such a trip, I had taken off my sergeant's stripes and was wearing only the insignia of a war correspondent and my SHAEF patch. This confused many of the people we encountered. I hoped it would strengthen our authority. With the unpredictable Russians there, we were not sure we would be able to cross the borders.

I knew the region well. When I had been a law student in Prague, twenty years before, I often went there in the summer with my friends. The Bohemian Forest — called Šumava in Czech and Böhmerwald in German — which extends southward from the border of Bavaria and Bohemia, is only a few hours by fast train from Prague. It is a lovely, hilly region, with dense woods and clear trout streams, green meadows and fertile farms, pretty resorts and picturesque villages. In prewar days, most of the people were artisans who worked in their homes — woodcarvers, glass-blowers, makers of musical instruments.

Almost every village had its own home industry then. In Graslitz, for instance, thousands of cheap fiddles with nicely printed labels AN-TONIUS STRADIVARIUS were made. In other villages, the people made beautiful etched glass or painted china. Their sense of symmetry and color showed in their buildings as well as in their crafts. The small houses had red roofs with pointed gables, and gaily colored shutters. In the middle of each village was a church with a tall spire and with a graveyard behind it, and across the square from the church was the inn, or a couple of inns, with stained-glass windows and wood-paneled halls. On Sunday morning, after Mass, the men sat at the inn, drinking beer and playing cards, while the women went home to cook Sunday dinner.

We students went swimming in the streams or collected mushrooms and strawberries in the woods. The mushrooms there had a fine, strong flavor of earth and rain. Housewives cut them into small slices, dried them in the sun on flat stones or windowsills, put them into white stockings, and hung them in their pantries, where they retained much of their flavor all winter long. And many pantries were also stocked with hams and sides of cured pork, with fruit preserves and sacks of potatoes. Often there was a barrel of beer in the cellar — either a dark, sweet, heavy *Bräu* from a Bavarian brewery, or the light, pale, dry beer from Pilsen, recommended by the doctors against many internal ills.

As the major and I drove toward the Czechoslovak border, it was hard for me to remember that those days of plenty had actually existed and that these were the very places I'd once known. The countryside and the people had a tired, battered look. The houses were unpainted, the inns neglected, the church walls marked with bullet holes. There were bomb craters along the road. The traffic and the confusion continued to grow worse as we got nearer to the frontier. People coming away from the border said that all controls had been abolished. "No passports, no visas, no customs!" they would exclaim, shaking their heads in wonder. This had been one of the most difficult frontiers in Europe to get across, and the border officials on both sides had been feared. Before the war, people had spent hours standing in line to have their baggage examined. And now, for the first time in memory, all the barriers were gone. The border guards on both sides had disappeared, and their barracks and the customs officials' houses were deserted, the doors standing open.

As the road mounted, the air became sharper. The major and I were hungry. We'd had nothing to eat since breakfast, at dawn. We had the K rations, but we agreed that this was no day for K rations. The weather was lovely, the war was over, it was spring, and I was going back to my native land. We decided to celebrate with a real lunch, preferably served on a white tablecloth.

In those days, in Germany, you didn't bother to look for a restaurant and consult the menu cards posted beside its entrance. You just picked any place that looked as if it had good food, and went in and requisitioned a meal. If you felt generous, you left a few American cigarettes. The people you'd taken the meal from would thank you fervently, happy to get off so easily. It was high-handed, but the sense of victory was strong.

The major and I made sure that we were still in German territory, and then began to look for a good place. After a few more turns in the road, we saw a large Bavarian inn. The major looked at me, and I looked at him. This was it — a substantial, three-story building, the ground floor whitewashed stone, and the second and third floors of wood. The roof was pointed, like that of a Swiss chalet. Above the door was an inscription:

> *Grüss Gott, tritt ein,*
> *Bring Glück herein.*

That means God greet you, Come in, Bring Happiness.

In front of the inn was a flagstoned terrace offering an imposing view of valleys and forests. In back was a large beer garden, with tables and chairs shaded by old chestnut trees. I had never seen this particular inn during my hiking days, but I was sure it must have been popular with tourists. It was still well kept up. There was even a festive air about it. The windows were clean, the gravel walks were freshly raked, and from the roofs two flags were flying, both blue, yellow, and red in vertical stripes.

The major and I didn't know what country's flag this was. In the past two days we had seen a great many flags of all sorts. They cropped up everywhere. This was peace, and everybody was flying any flag he pleased, and we were all for it.

We got out of the jeep and walked toward a large gateway, next to the front door, that opened up on a cobblestoned courtyard. Through an open window came the sound of voices and a delicious aroma, which I recognized at once as that of fresh mushrooms frying in butter. The major stopped as we reached the courtyard, and inhaled deeply. His snub-nosed Irish face was transfigured.

"Oh, boy! That's for us," he said.

We crossed the cobblestones, our boots making a martial sound and the holsters of our guns flapping against our hips. We thought we looked suitably tough and formidable, like real conquerors. We found the kitchen door of the inn and went in, not bothering to take off our helmets.

The kitchen was large and bright. It had a tiled floor and white walls, two large ranges with iron pots on them, copper pans hanging from the ceiling, and several tables and sinks. About a dozen women, some of them wearing white coats, were cutting mushrooms, peeling potatoes, frying meat, cleaning brook trout, and baking cakes. We had heard a great deal of animated talking while we were outside, but when we appeared in the kitchen it stopped instantly. The only sound was of water running in one of the sinks.

It was important to make a strong first impression. I decided to insist on seeing the innkeeper.

"Wo ist der Wirt?" I asked, in what I hoped was an authoritative manner. *"Vortreten!"*

The major was standing next to me, his legs apart, his right hand on the holster. I thought we looked very impressive.

For a while, no one moved. Then we heard rapid steps, and a woman came out of an adjoining room. She was tall, dark-haired, and obviously a woman of the world. She wore a black silk dress that I was willing to bet had been made in Paris, and as she came up to us, a cloud of perfume that held memories even sweeter than the scent of fried mushrooms came with her. Molyneux No. 5, I thought.

She stopped in front of us. *"Qu'est-ce que vous désirez, monsieur?"* she asked me. Her tone was icy, and so was her stare, directed at my helmet.

I was so surprised at being addressed in perfect French by a lady in a black silk dress in the kitchen of a Bavarian inn on the German-Czechoslovak border that I forgot to be a conqueror, and removed my helmet automatically. So did the major, whose face was a study in bewilderment.

I explained, in French and somewhat meekly, that we would like to talk to the owner of the inn.

"The innkeeper and his wife have run away," the lady said. "Perhaps they had reason. What is it you want, *monsieur?* We're quite busy now, as you must see."

By now, I had overcome at least a part of my surprise and embarrassment. "In that case, who is in charge?" I asked.

"If you will enter the inn through the front door, *monsieur*, I'll ask the Minister whether or not he will see you," the lady said. "The kitchen is hardly an appropriate place for any conversation he may have with you."

She turned away and — this time speaking perfect German — told the women to go back to work. They did. The major and I left as we had entered, by way of the courtyard.

"Who do you suppose she is, anyway?" I asked.

The major wasn't curious, apparently. He was hungry. His Adam's apple was working in his throat.

"Fresh brook trout!" he said. "And did you see that cake? What are we out *here* for?" He hadn't quite followed the French conversation.

"All right," I said. "Come on. Maybe we'll be asked to lunch with the Minister. If I only knew what country he is from."

We went to the front of the inn once more and found a number of people crowded around our jeep. Some were obviously local Germans, wearing short leather pants, white shirts, and embroidered braces, or else breeches and checked shirts, and they looked at us with apprehension, trying to read in our faces whether or not our mission was punitive. But there were other people there who did not look German and were dressed like city dwellers. They wore small blue, yellow, and red flags in their lapels.

The major and I entered the inn through the front door. To our left was a small room that smelled of stale beer and was empty except for a zinc counter. To our right was a large hall with a platform at the far end, on which there were music racks and chairs. In the center of the hall, a large U-shaped table, covered with a white cloth, had been set up for an elaborate meal and decorated with blue, yellow, and red wild flowers. Near one of the hall's big windows was an improvised desk, made of three rough wooden tables pushed together. Behind it sat a gray-haired man, and behind him stood a large flag — blue, yellow, and red.

The man rose and came toward us, and we saw that he was tall and erect and that he wore striped trousers, a black jacket, and a gray tie with a pearl in it. He looked precisely like a senior career diplomat except that he wasn't shaved. He was holding a white silk handkerchief against his right cheek, which was swollen.

The man bowed and extended his hand. The major mumbled something indistinguishable but polite in tone, and shook hands. And so did I.

"Gentlemen," the man said in English, with a second bow, "I consider it an honor to welcome the representatives of the United States army. Please be seated."

He pointed to a pair of wooden chairs beside his desk. We sat down, and so did he.

"You must forgive my unusual appearance," he said, indicating the handkerchief. "As if I didn't have troubles enough already, I am now afflicted with an infected wisdom tooth. I sent the First Secretary to the village for a dentist, but there is none. The pain was so great this morning that I was unable to shave." He permitted himself a faint sigh.

We stared at him. I could think of nothing to say, and the major, too, appeared at a loss, which didn't happen often. The gentleman stared back at us. The silence seemed to last for ages. Outside, someone was playing with the horn of our jeep.

"You expressed the wish to talk to the proprietor of this inn," the gentleman said at last. "Unfortunately, we don't know where he is. When the legation staff arrived here, he and his family had disappeared."

"Thank you, sir," said the major, "You say the legation staff . . ." He groped a moment for the right approach, and then, dispensing with any attempt of diplomatic finesse, asked bluntly, "What government do you represent, sir?"

The gentleman seemed somewhat put out.

"But of course you know," he said, raising his eyebrows and pointing at the flag behind his chair, "that this is the legation of the Kingdom of Rumania."

I nodded vigorously, as though I'd known it all the time. The major hesitated and then said, "Yes, sir. Why, of course."

"The Rumanian legation that was formerly in Berlin?" I asked cautiously.

"No, no, *no!*" said the gentleman. "I am His Majesty's Minister Plenipotentiary to the government of Hungary. This" — he made a sweeping gesture to include the whole inn — "happens to be, temporarily, the Rumanian legation in Budapest. In a manner of speaking, of course. We fled west from Budapest to escape the Soviet occupation. It is a somewhat preposterous situation, but this location has its advantages. Sitting, as we were, on the fence between West and East, I feel that I may be able to safeguard my country's interests quite effectively. It has, however, been a great strain on our nerves."

"I imagine so, sir," said the major.

The Minister sighed and leaned back in his chair. "Sometimes I wake up in the night and am unable to remember where I am," he said. "I'm not going to bore you with a report of our absurd experiences during this last while. I'm beginning to doubt myself that they actually happened. Suffice it to say that, not being able to get back to Rumania, and not wanting to fall into the hands of any belligerents while the war lasted, my family and I, and my staff and their wives and children — forty-nine people in all — have been chased back and forth across Central Europe, first by the advancing Russians, then by the retreating Germans, then by the Czech and Slovak partisans, then by elements of General Vlassov's army, and finally" — he coughed delicately — "by the United States Third Army."

"We're sorry, Mr. Minister," said the major.

"No reason to apologize, sir," the Minister said. "Technically, you understand, *only* technically, a state of war still exists between your government and mine, no formal peace having ever been concluded. My nation has had the distinction of fighting against everybody during this war. We were on the side of the Axis powers from 1940 to 1944, and we fought *against* them from 1944 until a few months ago, when an armistice was signed between the Allies, including my government, and the government of Hungary. Had I been able to get back to Budapest . . ." He didn't finish the sentence but merely lifted both hands in a gesture of dismay.

"Well, Mr. Minister," the major said, "it's all over now. You'll be back in Budapest with your staff in no time. To tell the truth, we stopped in here only because it seemed a good place to have lunch." The major was fast becoming his brisk, cheerful self.

"I beg your pardon?" said the Minister.

Trying to be helpful, I explained that we were on our way to the Czech border, and had supposed the inn was still run by its owner. We had, I said, chanced to meet a lady in the kitchen, who . . .

"Oh, yes, indeed," the Minister said distractedly. He pressed the handkerchief against his cheek again. "My wife is a remarkable hostess, but she never had to cope with problems such as she has here. Almost the whole staff is out in the countryside trying to buy food. This happens to be a Rumanian national holiday, and my wife and I decided to give a little party for our staff, in spite of the unusual circumstances. How glad I would be to have you as my guests" — the major leaned forward, evidently to accept with great pleasure, but the Minister held up a hand to stop him, and continued — "but, of course, such an invitation might create an almost insoluble problem of protocol. As I have mentioned, there is still a state of war between our two countries."

He got up. So did we. The major looked deeply depressed. "I've confidence, though, gentlemen," the Minister continued, "that relations between our two great nations will soon be as cordial and mutually beneficial as they were prior to the start of this long and terrible war."

The Minister bowed, and so did we, and he led the way to the door.

"Gentlemen," he said, "this was indeed an honor. As soon as I am able to establish contact with my government, I shall report your visit on this great day when the people of Rumania celebrate the anniversary of their liberation."

I cast a last, wistful glance at the table, thinking how delicious brook trout are early in May, cooked just a few minutes in a court bouillon with vinegar, thyme, and laurel, and served with melted butter.

"Thank you, Mr. Minister," the major said, and shook hands with him again. "May I wish you a happy celebration of the anniversary of Rumania's liberation from the Germans?"

"You are very kind, sir," said the Minister. "As a matter of fact, it is *another* liberation we celebrate today. On May 10, 1877, during the Russo-Turkish War, the principalities of Moldavia and Walachia proclaimed their independence from Turkey. On that day, exactly sixty-eight years ago, our great nation was born."

A moment later, the door of the temporary Rumanian legation in Budapest closed behind us. We made our way to the jeep, which was still surrounded by people. The major seemed dazed. We got into the jeep, and I drove off as quickly as possible, but not before catching, once more, the aroma of frying mushrooms. I tried to put it out of my mind, but this was very difficult. The major sat beside me with closed eyes. Neither of us said anything.

A few minutes later, we crossed the border into Czechoslovakia. We were not asked for any papers. I pulled up the jeep under the first old chestnut tree I saw, and, still without speaking, we got out our K rations and opened them.

There was the smell of smoke and dead flesh in the streets of Prague, where some Gestapo murderers had been caught and burned alive, and sometimes there was the sound of shooting. Everybody was a little crazy. Once again, as so often in Prague's violent history, there was blood in the streets. Flowers were placed on the spots where the Germans, before getting out, had shot a few more Czech patriots. And now the murderers had been caught and were murdered.

The sight of the American flag on our jeep caused more excitement than we had expected. The American Third Army had orders to stay in Pilsen while Marshal Koniev's army had entered Prague. We knew it, but the people of Prague didn't. They thought we were the vanguard of the victorious Americans whom many people in town wanted to have there together with the victorious Soviets, as a sort of insurance premium. Others wanted the Americans much more than the Soviets. Prague's culture and civilization had always been orientated toward the West.

It was heartbreaking. We were cowards; we didn't have the guts to tell them that we were, and would remain, the only Americans in the capital of the liberated country. Several times I tried. Then I saw their elated faces, their hungry eyes, and I just smiled, shaking their outstretched hands. The history of Central Europe would be different today if we hadn't been the only American soldiers in Prague in May, 1945.

There was an unreal mood of exultation and despair in Prague, of death and getting drunk. Traitors were executed, and heroes were liberated. We had been received triumphantly by a colonel of the Czech Revolutionary Guards as the official representatives of the great and powerful United States of America. In no time we were installed in a swank apartment in Vinohrady that had just been vacated by a Nazi big shot. They must have surprised him while he was in the bathroom. The wet towels were still on the floor, and on the small table by the bed were his gold watch and glasses. He didn't have time to put on his glasses, or maybe they wouldn't let him. The Nazis had been six years in Prague, and they had killed hundreds of thousands of people in the country. We asked the Czech colonel what had happened to the owner of the glasses. He gave a short shrug. "He got what he had coming." He looked at me and said softly, in Czech, "He was a dog."

Three Czech women cleaned up the place, brought stacks of white linen, burned a picture of Hitler, and in its place hung up a picture of

President Beneš. I thought of the picture of Beneš which they had removed from the wall of the Czechoslovak Consulate in New York, when I went there in September, 1938. Seven years ago — or was it seven hundred? . . . From the windows of our Prague apartment we saw the graves of Olšany Cemetery. Some German suicide squads were holding out in the crypts, and there was a lot of shooting during the first two or three nights, until they were caught, and then the cemetery was quiet.

The colonel attached himself to us as a honorary aide-de-camp, though he outranked his guests of honor. He got us servants and an honest-to-goodness Czech chef named Bedřich (Frederick), who asked us to call him Fredrik. He'd previously worked for two ambassadors, the general manager of the Škoda Works, and at the celebrated Hotel Pupp in Karlovy Vary (Karlsbad). He brought along *his* personal staff — his wife, two nephews, several cousins, and their friends. He bartered our army rations of coffee and cigarettes for fresh eggs, butter, genuine Pilsen beer, and a wonderful fillet of beef. There were said to be only two fillets of beef in Prague. The second, Fredrik said, was for Marshal Koniev.

We never met the marshal, but we did meet nearly everybody else. I told the major we ought to pay our respects to the local commander of our victorious Allies, but for once he was reluctant. He said better not, since he happened to be attached to OSS. It might be hard to explain to the marshal that our trip to Prague was the result of a technical sergeant's sudden attack of homesickness, and not a sinister plot hatched by General "Wild Bill" Donovan's masterminds. Instead, the major said, we would keep up "a pretense of the American presence in Prague," which sounded to me a little like a Madison Avenue advertising campaign slogan. We entertained the country's political and military leaders. Word had got around that we kept the best table in the city, and everybody wanted to meet these Americans, who probably were not what they seemed. Sometimes I was flanked by two generals at the dinner table, which doesn't usually happen to sergeants. The major didn't understand Czech, and I played the part of interpreter and Gray Eminence.

Our prize exhibit was Václav Kopecký, the Minister of Information, one of the most brilliant Communist leaders. He was a Stalinist old-liner who had survived several purges. During the war, he and Klement Gottwald, who later became prime minister and finally president, had lived in the right place, Moscow, while Beneš and Jan Masaryk had been in the wrong one, London. The ideological contours were getting noticeable. Had we been more astute agents of imperialism, we might have flashed the word to the OSS. At that time, something could still have been done to prevent the loss of Central Europe. No one in Washington seemed to remember the old saying, ascribed to various people from Napoleon to Bismarck, that to dominate Bohemia is to dominate the heart of Europe. And Prague is the heartbeat of Bohemia. As late as 1947, some top American diplomats in Prague spent more time with some wealthy, insignificant people and riding-and-hunting ex-aristocrats, than with the leaders of Beneš's National-Socialists and the Social-Democrats, who badly needed support from the West. Once again our diplomacy had backed the wrong horse.

The Minister of Information, who was more powerful than his title implied, was a short, stocky man proudly wearing his steel teeth, the product of Moscow's dentistry. He was intelligent, polite, and dogmatic. He understood the major's position and once said to me, half joking, "Irish blood will tell," referring to both General Donovan's and Major Dolan's Irish ancestry. But the Minister was puzzled by an obscure sergeant, the son of a Jewish banker in Moravia who later went to America, and now had returned wearing the SHAEF patch and the war-correspondent patch. Obviously I was not to be trusted. I tried my best to live up to his dark suspicions, at the same time playing the naive, decadent Westerner. The Minister would accept a can of American coffee or a carton of cigarettes before leaving our apartment. Once or twice we went to visit him at his office, in one of the most beautiful baroque palaces in an aristocratic street in Malá Strana.

We were received in audience by President Beneš in Hradčany Castle. He did not ask us about the American Third Army; *he* knew that the Americans were not coming. Beneš had always been an optimist, but now he was tired, and he seemed to have lost his belief in his country's future. Instead we talked about the past — when he succeeded President Masaryk and I met him in Parliament. We shook hands and left. Three years later, in June, 1948, Beneš resigned, and in September he was dead.

Two days after arriving in Prague, I'd asked Dolan to come with me to the Terezín-Theresienstadt concentration camp, where the Jews from Bohemia and Moravia had been brought before being taken to their final destination. The SS guards had escaped and the gate was open, but most of the inmates were still there, too weak to leave. The Czechs had put up emergency hospital wards and kitchens. At the entrance, a sign warned visitors that there were cases of typhoid fever in the camp. I'd foolishly skipped the regularly prescribed shots that I got in the army, but we went in just the same. I'd known for some time that most of the inmates had been sent to Auschwitz back in 1943, but I was hoping against hope that a miracle might have happened, and I would find my mother there.

I didn't find her. A cousin told me she'd been on one of the last transports in 1943. She'd been cheerful, crying and laughing a little, as I remembered her, and perhaps she hadn't known where they were being sent. My cousin Hans, a doctor, survived because the SS guards needed him in their hospital, but his weight was down to ninety pounds and he was a walking skeleton. The most prominent camp inmate was Chief Rabbi Leo Baeck, who has been called "the last representative figure of German Jewry in Germany during the Nazi period." We brought him and a few others out. General Donovan thought they were important enough to be taken as quickly as possible to the Allied authorities in Germany, and he sent a Flying Fortress for them, and for us. It was the first time that a Flying Fortress had landed in Kbely, the military airport of Prague, and it created much interest among the Soviets. We had to ask our Czech friends to guard the plane during the night. We didn't sleep much that night; we were too worried the Russians might steal our Flying Fortress. We left in the morning. The Minister of Information with his steel teeth saw us off. I gave him our last carton of cigarettes, and he said, "Give my regards to your superspies in the OSS," and we shook hands. The major and I looked at each other as the plane taxied toward the runway. We hadn't been quite sure we would make it.

Hollywood's Devil's Island

I WROTE MY FIRST AMERICAN BOOK, *Looking for a Bluebird*, during basic training and latrine detail in the army. Writing my reminiscences as nightclub fiddler, ship's musician, *claqueur*, and croupier helped me to forget, for a few hours every night, my unfunny life as a fatigues soldier. I began to write in the barracks in Camp Ritchie, an uninspiring environment if there ever was one, and continued in a hotel room in Wainsborough, a short bus ride from Ritchie. My wife, who now had her own dressmaking establishment in Beverly Hills, had closed her *salon de couture* for a while and come east. I would catch the five-ten P.M. bus after retreat, arriving forty minutes later at the hotel in nearby Wainsborough.

The following three hours were carefully planned. I spent at least twenty minutes soaking in the bathtub to get the smell of latrine or KP detail out of my skin. Ann hung up my fatigues on a back balcony until some unpatriotic hotel guests complained about the stench; they should have worn them as I did. I put on a civilian suit, feeling almost like a civilian. After a simple meal in the antiseptic dining room, I wrote in our room for two hours. Around nine P.M., my head would fall down on my typewriter, and I knew it was time to go to bed. I had to get up at four-thirty to catch the first bus for Ritchie. On weekends I wrote most of the time when they didn't put me on duty or detail.

The New Yorker bought many of the stories that were later published in book form, and Arnold Gingrich, who edited *Esquire*, bought some. When a story was finished, I mailed it to Paul Reynolds, my agent in New York. A few days later Paul would write me that *The New Yorker* had bought the piece and after a few weeks it would be published. Somehow I found time to write even overseas. I saw some of my stories in print first in *The New Yorker*'s small pony edition that was put out only for the armed forces. In 1944, they published eleven of my pieces.

My American writer friends told me that you had to have an agent. I'd never had one in Europe but accepted this as another American peculiarity. In Hollywood, I'd met Gerald Drayson Adams, an agent who also worked occasionally as a writer in the studios. Gerry had sold several "originals" to the movies, and encouraged me to try some. I did, and he tried to "peddle" them, but no one wanted to pay a million dollars for one of my stories, or even one dollar. Gerry looked very English in his tweeds, with his pipe. He lived with his wife and half a dozen beautiful cats in Coldwater Canyon. They were from Canada.

Gerry represented a "literary" agent in New York, Paul R. Reynolds and Son. Apparently, agents in New York were literary and literate, while some Hollywood agents were rather illiterate. Not Gerry, who said he would send some of my efforts to New York. That was some time before I'd sold to any national magazine in America; my only source of income was the *Toronto Star Weekly*. My efforts were returned from New York, with a letter signed by Paul R. Reynolds, Jr. He didn't think he could sell me, and he wasn't interested in handling me. Gerry relit his pipe, which he did in moments of irritation. He said the Reynolds agency was one of the oldest and most distinguished, handling some big names, you know how it is. The vicious circle: the unknown writer needs an agent but can't get one, and the successful writer can get any agent but sometimes thinks he doesn't need one anymore.

It was a disappointment, but after I began selling my stories and articles to the national magazines, I wrote to Reynolds, and this time he was glad to handle me. I didn't regret it. It's harder to find the right agent than the right publisher. Publishers and magazines change their editors and policies, and when they become big they become faceless. The relationship between writer and agent must be personal to be successful. In Hollywood, I'd met several agents. Some were glorified messenger boys, just sending manuscripts to the studios' story departments. Others were glorified hold-up men, trying all sorts of dubious devices when they had a salable property. To me, an agent must be listener, sounding board, amateur analyst, father confessor. He should have a banker's reticence, a lawyer's sense of suspicion, a businessman's toughness, and he should understand his client's emotional makeup. Writers are said to be difficult, but who isn't?

I've been with Paul Reynolds since 1943, and we've become friends. We've often agreed to disagree, but there has never been any thought of divorce. I never signed a contract with my agent; it's a pleasantly old-fashioned relationship, a vague sort of gentlemen's agreement. The office is still on the eighth floor of the Scribner's Building on Fifth Avenue, the proper address for an outfit dealing in literature, and what purports to be literature. On the ground floor is the Scribner's bookstore. The building entrance is flanked by showcases displaying recently published books that the Scribner's people have hopes for. In this computerized age, much of the book-publishing business is still based, like roulette, on hope and a prayer. Some old-timers in the building remem-

ber "old Mr. Scribner" and Max Perkins, who edited Wolfe and Hemingway. Some also remember "old Mr. Reynolds." Paul's father was
the first literary agent in the United States when he opened his business
in 1893. I never met him. His picture at the office reminds me of Grandfather Wechsberg, who was honest and tough and had strict principles
that he applied to others *and* to himself. So did Reynolds *père*, I gather.
The picture shows him sitting at a desk covered with manuscripts. Some
of them may have been written by G. B. Shaw and H. G. Wells, whom
Paul's father represented in magazines. He wasn't interested in books.
He thought that publishers, contracts and royalty statements were a
nuisance. (He was right.) Today, books account for ninety percent of
the business. Letters from other immortal clients, Tolstoy and Zola,
hang on the wall of the outer office. Everything remains as I remember
it a quarter of a century ago — the uncomfortable black leather chairs,
the dark shelves with books and unpublished manuscripts; Paul still
uses his father's old rolltop desk. Business has expanded, the office has
spread to other rooms on the floor, partitions have been put in, but
there is still a flair of old-fashioned dignity about the place, even though
million-dollar deals are now arranged there as a matter of routine. The
most confidential dealings are carried on in a small chamber next to the
anteroom, while messengers, mailmen, and visitors come in. The door
is always open, though important financial deals may be discussed. The
office topography is based on the sacred principle that Gentlemen Don't
Listen.

I loved the conservative trappings long before I had hopes of having
my photograph hanging there, next to others, on one wall of the entrance, across from the framed letters of the immortals. These are the
photographs of some of the agency's clients. The pictures are mysteriously selected and shifted in a constantly changing pattern, perhaps
indicating secret ratings or higher preferences against which there is no
appeal. Or maybe they are just shifted every time the charwoman does
the dusting. Best-selling novelists with enormous incomes and tax problems hang next to what Paul calls "beautiful writers," an euphemism

for nice guys supplying modest commissions. The old-world charm reminds me of some merchant bankers in the City of London, such as Baring Brothers in Bishopsgate, founded in 1763, which is about what 1893 is on Fifth Avenue. The old merchant bankers are very much up-to-date in shrewd mergers and the strategy of finance, and so, in its own way, is the Reynolds agency. No one writes with quill pens. Someday a small computer will be installed there, discreetly hidden out of the clients' sight, checking up on the royalty statements of certain publishers. Business is bigger than ever, but there is no one in the Zola-Shaw-Tolstoy-Wells-Henry James class among the present clients.

It's unlikely that anyone would pick out Paul Reynolds in a police lineup as a successful literary agent. He looks more like an American actor playing a permanent undersecretary at the British Foreign Office. Tall, with silvery hair and a bushy mustache, he always tried to look older than his age, and succeeded admirably. He realized that an agent must convey a father image to his neurotic writer clients. He used to wear a waistcoat with a heavy watch chain, and would consult his old-fasioned grandfather's watch in ominous it's-later-than-you-think moments, but now some hippies wear such watches, and Paul does it only when he's certain there are no hippies around.

(When Paul R., for "Revere," Reynolds read the manuscript of this book and discovered that during my initial and foolish Americanization I'd once briefly called myself Joseph Warren, long before I met Paul, he wrote to me: "Paul Revere's closest friend was Joseph Warren who was killed at Bunker Hill. Paul Revere named his first son Joseph Warren Revere, who was my great-grandfather. His portrait, painted by an Italian painter, Gamba, now hangs over the couch in our living room where you often sat. . . .")

In Chappaqua, where Paul lives, he used to drive a car that had neither a radio nor a heater. I welcomed the absence of the radio, but a heater has its advantages in Westchester in the wintertime. Paul had other puritan ideas: he believed in awful sherry rather than good Scotch, and took a dim view of rich food. I've corrupted him. Nowadays he goes to Europe with his wife on French or Italian boats, enjoying both the cooking and the wines.

Alfred Knopf once said to me, in the presence of Paul, "He would sell his own grandmother," adding "but he would deliver her." High praise when one knows what Alfred was thinking of certain literary agents, and of certain Hungarians and Rumanians who were said to sell, but not to deliver, their grandmothers.

Looking for a Bluebird was published around Christmas, 1944, as a Houghton Mifflin Literary Fellowship book. The United States army was fighting the Germans on their own territory, and I was fighting a mafia of U.S. army generals in Paris. The book's dust jacket showed my picture with the caption "Made in Czechoslovakia." I was wearing a pilot's flight jacket with a white lamb collar, and a dashing officer's cap. I'd borrowed the outfit from a friendly Eighth Air Force pilot in a moment of alcoholic exuberance.

The jacket writer had skillfully blended pertinent with impertinent information. It said that I'd been "detained by the Italian Secret Police, thrown in jail by the Japanese Thought Police," which wasn't true but sounded distinguished, and that I'd "lived through an earthquake in the Philippines and a typhoon in Hong Kong," which was true but undistinguished.

The book was favorably reviewed. *Time* graced its review with a picture, showing the author wearing his M-1 rifle and steel helmet, standing guard, or ready for immediate action. It was closer to the truth than my picture as a would-be pilot, but it didn't quite tally with the reviewer's description of me. He called me "bland." I looked up "bland" in *Roget's International Thesaurus.* "Bland" was synonymous with "moderate," "hypocritical," "suave," and "flattering," leaving me wide open to interpretation.

Even Broadway and Hollywood became interested in *Bluebird.* S.N. Behrman, and later George S. Kaufman, thought of turning the book into a play, possibly a musical comedy. Oscar Karlweis, who'd had a great success with the Werfel-Behrman comedy *Jacobowsky and the Colonel* talked to Behrman about the book; he hoped to play the lead. Nothing came of this, but I spent pleasant hours with Behrman and Kaufman, and I saw much of Karlweis until his early death, in 1953.

In Hollywood, William Pereira, the noted architect who was then a producer at RKO, became intrigued by *Looking for a Bluebird,* but he quit the celluloid business before doing anything about the book, and went back to building structures of more durable material in California. Then Paramount took an option on the movie rights. Fortunately, I was in Europe as a soldier, and didn't know about all this. Later, Paramount didn't buy the book but offered my agent a six-month writer's contract at their Hollywood studios, with the usual options. I was to report for work "after demobilization."

I got the news in Luxembourg City, on a bad day when the Germans were getting uncomfortably close to the radio station and everybody had orders to wear weapons and helmets. The typeface on the small, photographed V-mail letter from Paul Reynolds was so small that I needed a magnifying glass to read the letter. The paragraph concerning the financial arrangements of my Hollywood contract was partly blotted out by the copying machine, and I didn't believe the terms, but a later letter from my agent confirmed them. I would make more money per week than I'd ever earned in any previous week of my life, and this Elysian state of affairs would last twenty-six weeks. If Paramount decided to pick up my options during the following seven years, I might be richer than my paternal grandfather ever was.

Paradoxically, my first reaction was resentment rather than joy. Earlier, when I'd lived in Hollywood, the contract would have made a lot of difference. Now it meant nothing. The war was going badly and might last a long time. Hollywood was further away than the other side of the moon, and just about as real. Perhaps it was true, as they used to say there, that in order to be discovered by Hollywood you must not live there. I put the whole movie business out of my mind.

One day in September, 1945, I arrived at the separation center in Fort Dix, New Jersey. Neither the climate nor the landscape were inspiring, but I was glad to be there. My elation was short-lived, though; they couldn't find my army records. My personal file had been sent from the Fourth M.R.B. Company in Europe to the OSS in Washington but got lost in transit (as I did earlier). A lieutenant at the separation center told me that so far as they were concerned, I didn't exist. I was a nonperson at Fort Dix. I had become Joseph W., a second cousin, strangely removed, to Kafka's Josef K.

Unlike my poor cousin in Kafkaland, I'd learned my lessons in the jungle of the army bureaucracy. I called Pat Dolan in Washington, and he called some people in high circles. Even a general was approached who said I certainly had existed; he remembered indeed that son of a bitch from Paris. The separation specialists in Fort Dix had to let me out of the army, though they still claimed I'd never been in it. I was given an honorable discharge. I always carry a laminated miniature copy in my wallet — just in case.

Paul Reynolds was upset about my Hollywood contract. He said it was nonsense for a man to work in a Hollywood studio when his first book had made the best-seller lists and he could write for *The New Yorker*. He implied, darkly, that many good writers had gone out to Hollywood and were never heard of again. In his reticent Bostonian style, Paul mentioned no names.

A few days later, Ross, just as displeased but less reticent, didn't hesitate to mention a few names who had found nothing but oblivion in Hollywood. I told Ross I wasn't as prominent as the names he'd mentioned.

He said, "Dammit, Wechsberg, maybe you are not prominent, but you are certainly naive." He pronounced "naive" with the emphasis on the *i*, making it sound like an obscenity. He said good writers had been finished in no time "out there." He didn't mind when "they" bought something *The New Yorker* had published, so the writers made dough, but he didn't like his writers to get lost there.

"It's bad, Wechsberg," he said. "It's much worse than you think."

To cheer him up, I told him about my short, happy life with *Stars and Stripes*, and how it had ended, when the powers of darkness got me back into Psychological Warfare. I thought he'd forgotten about Hollywood, but when I got up, he said, "Dammit, Wechsberg, you shouldn't go there," and he did not give me his blessing.

For about two weeks, in Hollywood, I enjoyed the unfamiliar sensation of being the returning hero. I'd been the only soldier in our "Old Austrian" refugee clique. They were disappointed because I hadn't any orders or decorations; Austrians love titles and orders. At a party I had to put on my uniform with my three campaign ribbons. I shouldn't have told them that everybody got a campaign ribbon who had been in a certain theater of operations during a certain time. It was quite a letdown. One Hungarian remarked that one of *their* men had come back with lots of decorations, and he said, "At least you should have bought some, to please your friends." He pronounced "bought" like "boat," (or "stoary"). He'd just sold a "stoary" to MGM.

Gerry Adams came to see me. He said Paramount had already called him about me; they were eager to have me start working, and how about next Monday?

"Probably have a hell of an assignment for you," Gerry said, lighting his pipe.

He picked me up on Monday morning. The sun was shining; *that* hadn't changed. The white houses in Westwood Village seemed whiter than I remembered them. In front of Sears, Roebuck, a long streamer said GLAD YOU'RE BACK. They *would* think of everything. The long shiny cars were longer and shinier; at least I thought so. Maybe I'd seen too many jeeps in the recent past. I tried not to think of the past. I was now a member of the Screen Writers' Guild, going to the Paramount Studio, accompanied by my agent.

Gerry parked his Buick, and we went through the studio gate with the sign PARAMOUNT PICTURES, INC. and the little Matterhorn. I'd been there before, on some evenings, as an impecunious foreign-press correspondent, attending a preview. You sat in a producer's comfortable armchair in one of the private projection rooms where, in the late afternoon, the great men watched the daily rushes, and you wished you had a percentage of the producer's income. But now, I thought proudly, I was part of Paramount. I was a small cog in this world-famous company that had entertained millions of people since Hollywood's ice age. Jesse Lasky, Ernst Lubitsch, Marlene Dietrich, Maurice Chevalier, Billy Wilder, Bob Hope, Bing Crosby. And now, Joseph Wechsberg.

Something went wrong, though. We stepped into the charming little bungalow with the sign STORY DEPARTMENT, and Gerry introduced me. There seemed to be a cold draft of embarrassment all around, as though it was a ghastly mistake. They didn't know who I was or what to do with me. After five uncomfortable minutes, we left. Outside, Gerry nervously lighted his pipe and said that the man who'd hired me had been fired and was now with another studio.

"Happens all the time in this town," Gerry said. Naturally, the *new* story editor took a dim view of all people hired by his predecessor. As we walked toward the gate, a man behind me whistled exactly as Bing Crosby did in his pictures. I turned around. It *was* Bing Crosby.

They assigned me a small office on the top floor of the writers' building. It looked like a cell in a progressive penitentiary, though less comfortable. From the window I had a fine view of the executive parking lot, filled with more Lincoln Continentals and Cadillacs than I'd ever seen together in one spot. The view was more interesting than the interior of my cell, which wasn't much to look at. A writing desk, a small table with a typewriter, a swivel chair, a guest chair, and a large wastebasket, the most important single piece of equipment, the graveyard of many unfilmed epics. There was a couch, as in the offices of the unforgotten *Prager Tagblatt*, where every editor had a couch, not necessarily for sleeping. My Paramount-writer neighbor on the left side occasionally made stimulating use of his couch, usually during lunchtime, when everybody was downstairs at the commissary. I once saw a pretty girl come out of his room, who looked much spicier than most of the dishes served at the commissary. My neighbor had the better lunch, and more power to him.

In the cell on the other side, two men were talking quietly. Suddenly there was a gale of laughter, and then, just as suddenly, the voices would resume their quiet talk. A few minutes later there might be another violent outburst of mirth, and again, abruptly, silence. Sometimes they were talking for a long time, and I was getting impatient for their laughter, but it never came. It was nerve-wrecking.

Later, I met my neighbors at the writers' table in the commissary. They were serious men, looking tense. One had milk with his food, and the other didn't even dare drink milk. He had a small bottle of pills next to the ketchup. They were writing one of the "Road" pictures for Crosby and Hope, and were trying out their gags on each other. The "Road" pictures were high-budgeted and important, and the two gag writers looked as though they had nothing to laugh about. One told me that they laughed only during working hours.

"We're getting paid for it, you see? Laughter by appointment to Paramount Pictures, Inc. Ha, ha, ha!" He stopped laughing as suddenly as he'd started, and took another pill. He was said to earn three thousand dollars a week, and he deserved every thousand of it.

I went back to my cell, lay down and read the *Hollywood Reporter*.

Or I looked out of the window at the executive parking lot. One day I drove in with my Chevrolet, just for the hell of it, and was told to beat it.

I was the forgotten man on the fourth floor. No one called. On the fifth day, when I'd already earned almost my entire weekly salary, feeling slightly guilty about it, I timidly called Central Switchboard and asked whether they had my name and extension.

A crisp woman's voice said, "But of *course* we do, Mr. Wechsberg," and gave me the number of my extension, and there was an angry click. She sounded like a duchess who had been asked to submit proof of her ancestry.

On Friday morning, an upholstered blonde who claimed to be my secretary brought me my paycheck. In the afternoon I took it to the bank. I was so thrilled by the picture on it of the Paramount Matterhorn that I forgot to endorse it.

"Sign here," the teller said.

I signed. That was the only writing I'd done all week.

At the end of the next week, I called Gerry Adams. Should I go down to the story department? Maybe they'd forgotten about me?

There was a pause. Gerry was probably cleaning, or lighting his pipe. He said that would be all wrong.

"I heard they're negotiating a couple of big properties right now. Might be something for you, something *really* important."

The third week came and went. I knew already the exact hues of all the Cadillacs in the executive parking lot, though I am color-blind. On Friday, payday, somebody knocked at my door. A loose-jointed man came in. He walked like the sailors in the books by Joseph Conrad, swaying slightly, his arms hanging down by his sides, and he seemed to fall out of his tweeds. He had a reddish face with a sad, long nose and a small mustache. His eyes were bright and smiling.

"I'm John McNulty," he said. We became friends at once. We shared many things — our loneliness on Paramount's fourth floor, and our devotion to *The New Yorker*. McNulty had been one of the earliest *New Yorker* writers. He'd been close to Ross and Thurber and White in the legendary days, when the magazine had been put out week after week almost on an experimental basis. He was Irish: emotional, either funny or sad, but mostly sad, sweet and warmhearted, except when he drank too much. Until I got into the American army, I'd never met any Irishmen. They were irascible, unpredictable, softhearted, and mystic-minded, never dull. They would have belonged in the Old Jewish Town in Prague, where the legends of the Sippurim, the Golem, the great Rabbi Loew, were still alive. Some of my Irish friends are Jewish in their souls, in spite of their Catholic superstructure.

McNulty had been on the Paramount payroll for three months. He came to the studio only on Friday, to get his check. They'd bought one of his *New Yorker* pieces and hired him, on the theory that "no one else could turn it into a screenplay." It sounded too good to be true. When he arrived in Hollywood, they gave him the silent treatment for a few weeks, and then they assigned two other writers to his story, on the theory that McNulty was "too close to it." For a while he consoled himself with his paychecks, but now he was getting homesick for the streets of New York, *The New Yorker*, and his Third Avenue friends at Tim Costello's. When he was depressed, he would call up Thurber or Lobrano or Tim Costello, at Paramount's expense. He'd figured out a way of doing it, claiming it was part of a "long-distance story conference."

McNulty had the true humorist's incurable sadness. When he was low, he asked me to come with him to the Playboy. The Playboy (this was long before the word became a symbol in some strata of the American subcivilization) was a bar installed in a small, pseudo-Moorish plaster structure near the executive parking lot, which may have been put there by Sears, Roebuck ("Glad You're Back") for the benefit of homesick Irishmen. When we came in from the outside glare, it seemed pitch-dark inside. McNulty said he was beginning to see the light around the third drink.

We spent many afternoons there. McNulty was talking, mostly to himself. I often regretted that we didn't have a tape recorder installed underneath the counter. McNulty told me many unwritten *New Yorker* stories that needed no editing. He sat there on a high stool with his legs dangling down, speaking exactly as the characters in his stories did. He was a wonderful mimic, and he would chuckle when he said something that seemed funny to him. He did all the rewriting and revising in his head. By the time he sat down at his typewriter, the story was done, down to the last comma. I envied him. I'm mentally lazier and have to do all my rewriting on paper, sometimes half a dozen drafts, and I'm never satisfied. I dread the moment when I take the manuscript to the post office, because it's gone and I can no longer improve it. Once McNulty had it on paper, he was finished with it and didn't worry.

He loved to talk about his early newspaper days. Newspapermen all over the world have an affinity for each other and mysteriously recognize one another, like trombone players or hotel managers. Contrarily, headwaiters and violinists distrust each other violently. The stories McNulty told about his newspaper adventures in Columbus, Ohio, or New York very much resembled my experiences in Ostrava and Prague. He reminisced nostalgically about the triumph of gifted dilettantism in the early days of *The New Yorker*, and he hated the phony professionalism on the top floor of Devil's Island. He called Paramount's writers' building "Devil's Island."

"What are we doing here anyway?" he would ask. It was a rhetorical question which no one could answer. McNulty had another drink and began crying softly. He asked the barkeep for paper and a pencil. Drinking and crying, he put down some figures. He said he was going to compute how much his crying spell cost Paramount Pictures, Inc.

"One hour leading up to it, another half hour until I calm down, and in between, a good twenty-minute cry," he said, and was no longer crying. He added it up, in the nonchalant fashion of certain headwaiters in Vienna who put an extra tip on top of the fifteen percent service charge. He figured that his emotional outburst cost the "factory" (Paramount) one hundred and thirty-nine bucks. That cheered us up, we had one for the road, and the afternoon ended on a note of eighty-six proof optimism. McNulty said since we lived in an unreal place, we had to live an unreal life in order to create some reality, somewhat as minus plus minus makes plus.

When he drank too much, his Irish temper showed through, and when the wrong people were around, or even the right people saying the wrong thing, there might be trouble. I heard him say some terrible things about Paramount Pictures, Inc., to some top studio executives. He was right, but they didn't appreciate the truth. McNulty was a real writer. He didn't want to understand that the inmates of Devil's Island didn't have to be writers; many of them were highly skilled construction men. They created "plot structures" that didn't pretend to have any relation to reality and life; the "characters" that they thought up had to fit the "plot structures." Any similarity to human beings was strictly coincidental. Sometimes a real writer was brought in "to make the characters alive," but he was up against the unholy alliance of the construction men and the financially-minded producers who cared more about the box office than top quality. Only a few truly creative people did get away with making the films they wanted to make, and often produced very fine movies.

At the commissary, McNulty and I moved away — rather demonstratively, I'm afraid — from the long writers' table where the habitués told each other about the ingenious twists of their plot structures, or were so bored that they played boyish games, with the loser paying the lunch check. Some of them were pompous old-timers who acted as though they belonged there. They thought they were writers, but they behaved like bureaucrats in the musty government offices of Central Europe. Some had been there so long that they had acquired prestige through seniority, like some members of the United States Senate. They *must* be able, otherwise how could they have been around so long?

It was no secret that producers, directors, stars, prominent cameramen formed tight little cliques in Hollywood, talking only to each other and their analysts, but it surprised me that there were three-thousand-dollar-a-week writers who would talk only to other three-thousand-dollar-a-week writers, or maybe to God, when they got lost in the labyrinths of their plot structure. The studio was a hothouse of Byzantine intrigue. It is often said that no one has yet written the true story of Hollywood. Perhaps not the complete story — but many who wrote about it, Scott Fitzgerald and Ben Hecht and Evelyn Waugh and Budd Schulberg, have contributed much valid material. Perhaps the problem of writing about Hollywood is that its unreality exceeds even the boundlessness of fictional fantasy.

On the rare days when McNulty came to the studio, to pick up his paycheck or to offend somebody, we would lunch at a small table at the wrong side of the commissary, where the secretaries and carpenters sat. McNulty thought of putting on the table a small flag of *The New Yorker*. He called up Ross in New York to have a flag designed, showing "the magazine's true colors" and a picture of Eustace Tilley, the bemonocled patron saint. But *The New Yorker*, in spite of its long-standing literary sovereignty didn't have its own flag, though it did more for civilization than Andorra or Monte Carlo or San Marino or Albania. Ross later told Lobrano that things must be really bad "out there" in Hollywood — as he had known all along. McNulty and I had bad timing. We were protesters long before protest became *the* thing to do.

At long last, somebody at the story ("stoary") department decided to give me an assignment. I was to write a synopsis called "The Adventures of a Ballad Hunter," a film for Bing Crosby based on John A. Lomax's search for truly American folk songs. ("It was a logical assignment," Virginia Wright wrote in the Los Angeles *Daily News*. "Wechsberg has been a musician.") The locale of the film was Texas, where I'd never been. Somehow I'd missed the Lone Star State on my Greyhound bus peregrinations. And I knew nothing about American folk songs.

The story editor, whose first name was Dick and whose last name I shall mercifully not reveal, considered my ignorance a definite advantage. "It'll help you to approach the story with an unprejudiced mind," he said, with (I only now realize) the quintessence of Hollywood logic anno 1946. The film was going to be a Bing Crosby "vehicle." He would sing all these beautiful folk songs.

Gerry Adams said it was quite a break to be assigned to a Crosby picture. "I might get your salary doubled when they pick up your option," he said, and happily lighted his pipe.

There was another writer on the top floor of Devil's Island who was working on a film called *Saigon*. He happened to be from Texas and had never been in Saigon. I knew Saigon rather well from my earlier travels as a ship's musician; the Messageries Maritimes liners would stop there for a week before they went on either to Haiphong (that was called the Indochina run) or to Hong Kong, Shanghai, Yokohama (the China-Japan run). Usually we members of the ship's orchestra made a little extra money playing at aperitif time at the sidewalk café in front of the Majestic Hotel. Later we would spend the money all over town and in Cholon.

And so, one afternoon, the writer assigned to *Saigon*, and I went down together to see the story editor. We suggested that he let us switch our assignments. The writer from Texas thought he could do an inside job on Texas and Lomax; I believed I might at least contribute "authentic color" about Saigon. I'd heard about "authentic color" at the writers' table where they constantly talked about it.

Our suggestion was listened to politely and rejected unequivocally. We were told that maybe that's what they would do at another major studio. But not at Paramount where, thank God, they still favored the "unspoiled approach."

"If everybody would write only about the things he knows, we would soon be in a rut," Dick said. When he uttered these words, they didn't sound as idiotic to me as now, when I write them down. We were told to go back to work, fellows, let that be a lesson to you.

I have no recollection of the Lomax story which I wrote, but I did write it. I remember the blond, upholstered secretary going back and forth with the pages, beautifully typed in quintuplicate, with the proper margins. An important-looking manuscript if there ever was one. I don't think anyone of importance read it, and if anyone did, he never told me. It was very bad, I'm sure. And I'd been given the kiss of death long before, though I didn't know it. During my last weeks on Devil's Island, I forgot about Paramount and began working on a long piece for *The New Yorker*.

I'd wanted to write for some time about my return to my hometown, as an American soldier, shortly after V-E Day. Long before the Americans reached Czechoslovak territory, I'd hoped to be the first American soldier coming back to Ostrava. As I later wrote, "Entering the town in triumph, showered with flowers by strangers, kissed by relatives and friends whom I had come to liberate." It didn't turn out that way, though.

When I began to write the story, it was mostly about my trip from Prague to Ostrava on one of the first trains running after the end of the war. I was in a badly damaged third-class coach, with some former inmates of German concentration camps, mostly Poles from Buchenwald trying to get back home, and with many Russian soldiers. The Russians didn't like the overcrowded compartments and climbed up on top of the coaches. They lay down on the roof, rolled themselves into their heavy blankets, and in no time were fast asleep. Sometimes one of them would fall down, or was hurt by a tunnel or a low bridge. The Czech conductor told me it happened so often that they no longer stopped the train. "Those Russians!' he said, shaking his head in wonder and admiration. "That's why they won the war." The soldiers were full of laughter, and of vodka. Some smiled at me, but as we got farther east, the soldiers in the stations stared at me with suspicion. In Přerov a captain said to me, "Don't mind them. They've never seen an American soldier in the flesh. You must be the first damn *Amerikanski* east of Prague."

I didn't tell the Russian captain that I had not informed the military attaché at the American Embassy in Prague of my trip. He would have had to stop me. But the Russian was no fool. He asked me, casually, how come I traveled alone and, less casually, did I have *dokumenty*? Sure, I said. Could he see them?

I showed him the special pass I'd been given by Czechoslovakia's Prime Minister Fierlinger in Prague. Written in Czech and Russian, it said I had the right "to travel everywhere in Czechoslovakia," and asked all officials "to extend their help and courtesies." The *dokument* had an engraved seal below the official signature, and my photograph. The captain touched the seal with two fingers and ran them over it as a blind man would read Braille, and then he studied the paper, his lips moving, as he read the Russian text.

"*Khorosho*," he said. Good. He took me to the kitchen car of his unit's military train that stood on a siding, and filled two mess gears, for himself and me, with soup and stew. Later, he went off and came back with a heavyset, broad-shouldered, grim colonel of the gangbuster type, whom he introduced as "*Pan Polkovnik*," ("Sir Colonel"), the regimental commander. The colonel addressed the captain as "*Tovarish*" ("Comrade"). Very large glasses and a bottle of vodka were brought. *Pan Polkovnik* filled them to the rim, and shouted, "President Trumán! Marshal Stalin!"

I tossed off my glass. The murderous concoction tasted like a rare blend of nitroglycerin, sulphuric acid, and plain fire, with a seasoning of atomic matter. That's how I described it, sitting up there in my cell in Devil's Island.

The railroad trip was the main part of my story. It ended with an anticlimax: my homecoming, which was not heroic but heartbreaking. The houses with the memories but without the people I'd known. The streets filled with people with strange faces. The slow, painful discovery that there was almost no one left — that I was going home nowhere.

I wrote the piece, and *The New Yorker* bought it. On my next trip to New York, William Shawn, who was then in charge of the fact (nonfiction) department, wanted to talk to me about the article and took me to lunch at the Algonquin.

Shawn looked almost as he does today; he hasn't changed much. He was gentle and soft-spoken, strong in his beliefs and sure of his judgment. He knew exactly what was wrong with my piece, and he made it quite clear to me. Had he been an internist or analyst, he would have been a great diagnostician. It was miraculous, like getting lost in a dark tunnel and suddenly somebody taking me by the hand and guiding me out. That was the first but not the last time that Bill Shawn helped me to get out of my self-created confusion. He said the emphasis was all wrong. The train ride was interesting, but it was merely leading up to the real story — my coming back to something that was no longer there. He told me to write about my wife's parents and how I found them, and how I didn't find so many other people in my hometown.

("I had met nine people in my home town. Nine out of a thousand I had once known. I had discovered that there was no bridge leading from the past to the present. No way back. Nothing left but the dingy houses, the grimy streets, the coal dust, the fog. The grayness and sadness. No one else was left of the town I had known, and I knew that I was really going home now. . . . Home to America.")

That *was* the story, as I so well know today, but Bill Shawn made me see it. There is a hairbreadth line between light and darkness in the writer's mind, and often he is unable to cross that line unless he's lucky to have an editor who helps him.

When Ross died, on December 6, 1951, and Shawn became his successor, Janet Flanner said to me, "We've lost two great editors. We lost Ross. And now we've lost Shawn, who won't have time to edit our work anymore." Once in a while Shawn still takes time out to edit one of my pieces. He doesn't tell me — that's not done — but I can see the fine Shawnian hand. His touch is more gentle yet more effective than anyone else's. The best editor does the most with the least.

"Going Home" was a two-part Reporter-at-Large piece. Earlier, Alfred Knopf read the manuscript and decided to publish it. The book was well received by the critics but didn't sell. Alfred later told me it was badly timed, it came out too early. I took a dim view of the Russians, who were still our great friends then. Some people called me a "reactionary." Some of them later called me an "arch-liberal." One cannot please even some of the people some of the time.

I'd written a considerable part of "Going Home" up on Devil's Island, so perhaps my exile on the Paramount lot was not a total loss. Financially, it was. I invested most of my Paramount earnings in the common stock of the Packard Motor Company. An old friend who had become a multimillionaire in Prague, where he was said to have the Midas touch, was now living in Hollywood. He gave me a hot inside tip: Packard. He'd made his large fortune on inside tips; in Prague, not in America. I bought Packard at twelve dollars. I was smart; I sold out when they were three dollars. My friend, who had told me to hold onto the shares, kept them until they were no longer quoted.

I ought to be grateful, though, to Paramount Pictures, Inc. Suppose they had picked up my option. Why, I might have wound up with a mansion and a kidney-shaped swimming pool in Beverly Hills, three cars and three lawyers, an analyst and the delusion that someday I was really going to write what I wanted to write. Someday, when I would be "between assignments." I can think of worse ways of making a living — but not much worse.

One day toward the end of my exile, the phone rang in my cell, which didn't happen often.

A voice said, "Ross." An unmistakably snarling voice that could be nobody else. The editor of *The New Yorker* said he was all lost downstairs, and could I come and rescue him from this goddam place, and where was McNulty? I told him McNulty had gone back to New York a few days earlier, and went down. Ross stood near one of the sound stages, looking utterly lost. He wore an elegant, rumpled, dark blue suit, and snapped his red suspenders in frustration. He said his wife was working here in a picture directed by Elliott Nugent and he'd been supposed to see them but apparently he'd got his dates mixed up, and now he'd come here but the company was on location or something, and he said, "Nobody tells me anything," as he used to say at the office, on West Forty-third Street, where he (and I) wished we were this very minute.

Abruptly he shrugged and said, "Let's go. We'll have lunch at Dave Chasen's."

He was relaxed there. He was very fond of Dave Chasen. He said this was the only place out of which he'd made some real dough in his whole life. I thought this was a Rossian exaggeration, but later I read in Thurber's book that Ross made close to a quarter of a million dollars on his original investment of a few thousand dollars in Chasen's. At lunch, we talked about *Stars and Stripes*, during the First World War when he'd been the editor, and in the Second World War when the editor had to let me go because three generals were after me. Ross shrugged. He didn't approve of his successor.

"Couldn't have happened while I was there," he said. "No goddam general would get a reporter away from *me*."

The next morning he called me early at home and said he would like to take my wife and me to lunch. We picked him up in a big house in Beverly Hills that his wife had rented. He seemed lost there too. He said he'd talked to his wife on the phone. The company was still on location. He was returning to New York that night. The very thought cheered him up. I expected we would go to Chasen's, but he asked me to drive over to Chasen's competitor, Mike Romanoff. There was the usual palaver with the haughty attendants in the restaurant's parking lot who thought my Chevrolet did not belong among all the Cadillacs, but I told them, probably emboldened by the presence of H. W. Ross, to leave it there. If they didn't like it, go see Mike. I said "Mike" as though I were an intimate of Mr. Romanoff's.

We sat at a table outside, in front of the white building. Mike Romanoff, looking more improbable than an actor playing the part of Romanoff, came to greet Ross, and there was considerable commotion. The maître d'hôtel issued secret orders, three special waiters were summoned, and a wagon with hors d'oeuvres was rolled up to our table. Quite obviously, Ross was treated as a very VIP. He was a charming host, and enjoyed himself hugely. He told us that he liked the food, and then he called Mike Romanoff and bitterly complained about it. I began to understand why he'd taken us there. Romanoff lost much of his sangfroid, and what was left of it went to pieces, when Ross asked for the check and discovered that he had no money. I took out my wallet, but Ross said, "Don't you dare," in a conspiratorial whisper.

Mr. Romanoff said, rather pointedly, I thought, to the headwaiter that there was *of course* no check for Mr. Ross. That was exactly what Ross had been waiting for. He said he hadn't come to this joint to eat on the house. He spoke loudly, and some people looked at us, among them a columnist of doubtful reputation. Romanoff, reduced to the shadow of a Brooklyn duke, said if Mr. Ross insisted, he might want to sign a check, and he handed Ross a golden fountain pen that looked to me like twenty-nine karat.

Ross breathed heavily and said he couldn't sign a check. He was already overdrawn at the bank. "They wouldn't let me sign any checks anymore," he said dejectedly, implying that he was out on parole. He enjoyed himself hugely. He said he was sorry, he shouldn't have come here in the first place, and he wouldn't be surprised at all if Romanoff called the police now, right away.

"Tell you what we'll do," he said. "Dave Chasen's going to send you a check. That all right?"

My dealings at *The New Yorker* were with Lobrano about fiction and Shawn about fact pieces, a situation which Ross called "fairly unusual." He never interfered editorially. I'd begun to go to Europe on extended trips, and did all sorts of pieces for them, and once in a while Ross would write me, usually about some money matters, or to comment on my work, or both. This letter belongs in the "both" category:

June 25, 1948

Dear Wechsberg:

You were told that you would probably have some more money coming. What we have done is send a check to Paul R. Reynolds and Son for $1657.50, which is in payment of a bonus of twenty-five per cent for the bills paid for previously. This is the usual quantity bonus, as we call it, for turning in more than six pieces in a twelve-month period. This bonus will also be paid on the pieces you have pending at present with Mr. Shawn when they are edited and put through, on the grounds that you did these pieces within a year's time, even though they haven't gone through yet.

All in all, we're proud of the work you did abroad for us. It was fine, and has been so adjudged not only by people around the office but by readers of the magazine. I've heard considerable about the pieces, although I don't get around much. I can speak for Mr. Shawn in saying that we'll be glad to talk business when you think of going abroad again, and I can speak for Mr. Lobrano in saying that we wish that, meantime, you would get in some fiction pieces.

I'm sending the check out on behalf of the Messrs. Shawn

and Lobrano, because it represents payment for both fact and fiction pieces, a fairly unusual situation — and, anyhow, Mr. Lobrano is gone for the day, and I will be gone too in a moment.

As ever,

Ross

When Ross liked one of my pieces very much, he might send me a short "well done" letter. He understood writers, and he knew how important such letters can be; they help you to carry on during the bad spells which every writer has. My favorite Ross letter is dated June 28, 1948. I'd gone to Cremona, the birthplace of the world's greatest violins, feeling like a pilgrim on his first trip to Mecca. I talked to lots of people and was delighted to discover that an *avvocato* (lawyer) named Mario Stradivari lived in town, who turned out to be a genuine, sixth-generation descendant of the immortal Antonio Stradivari, the most celebrated violin-maker of all. The *avvocato* was a wonderful Renaissance character who looked like a Michelangelo sculpture come to life. He couldn't care less about his great-great-great-great-grandfather, but he loved music and especially opera — his father had been a close friend of Puccini's — and he had composed two operas that were performed successfully in Italy.

We had a wonderful time, with much wine and much talk. In the early morning hours we wound up at the entrance to the local opera house. Stradivari woke up the janitor, an old friend and client of his, and we walked up onto the stage. The curtain was up. The sets had been left there from the fourth act of *Rigoletto*, which had been performed the night before. Stradivari, his friend Renzio Bacchetta, the town's outstanding expert on the (immortal) Stradivari, and I performed excerpts from *Rigoletto*, carried away by artistic enthusiasm and the effect of three bottles of cheap local wine. We even sang the beautiful quartet from the fourth act, with the assistance of the old janitor, Bacchetta and myself taking the women's parts.

After each number, the janitor would switch on the house lights, Bacchetta would let down the curtain, "and then the four of us would step in front of the footlights, bowing proudly to the frenetic, if inaudible, applause of an enthusiastic, if invisible, audience."

Ross wrote me:

June 28, 1948

Dear Wechsberg:

I hadn't read your piece on Stradivari when I wrote you on the sordid subject of money. I have since read it, over the weekend, and will say that it is a lulu. You outdid yourself on this one. It's the first time the author of a Reporter piece has ever confessed in print to getting drunk on the job, but I think that even the members of clergy among our readers will overlook that under the circumstances.

Every once in a while I get a pleasant surprise like this, and it encourages me to carry on.

As ever,

H. W. Ross

The last time I saw Ross was early in 1951. Once again I was on my way to Europe, and Ross talked to me in his office about pieces "you might do for us." I remember that we'd talked at length about an idea of mine that we'd discussed earlier: I wanted to write a profile of my Swiss wristwatch. Most profiles are about human beings, and that's exactly the way I wanted to treat my watch. A good watch has qualities — reliability, precision, punctuality, sturdiness, even character — that are sadly lacking in many human beings. I thought the profile would begin with the watch being conceived and assembled, and would end when the watch was beginning to live, and to click, making its first noises, like a newborn baby.

Ross liked the idea, the mixture of abstract and concrete elements, and the larger concept of time behind the watch, "the seconds clicking away." That day he took me to lunch at the Stork Club, and told me much about his friend Raymond Schindler, the famous detective.

On the way back to the office, I admired his new shoes. He said they were imported from England, sixty bucks. When I said good-bye to him, he gave me his blessing and asked me to do the watch piece "promptly." Other things interfered, as always happens, and the watch piece was still in the project stage when Shawn sent me a cable to Europe that Ross had died in Boston. I wrote the profile only eight years later. In July, 1959, Shawn cabled me: THE WATCH PIECE IS A BEAUTY AND EYE GUESS ONE MUST SAY DEFINITE. SAD THAT ROSS COULD NOT READ IT AFTER ALL THESE YEARS.

Caviar for the Digest

AFTER MY RELEASE from Paramount's Devil's Island, I occasionally wrote for the *Reader's Digest*. I'd met the late Robert Littell, then a senior editor of the *Digest*, in New York. The Littells loved music; Mrs. Littell, the former Anita Damrosch, had been brought up on good music. My *Digest* articles were on musical subjects. I interviewed Yehudi Menuhin, who talked more about yoga than music. I wrote an article on film music, reaching the sorry conclusion that when the audience gets aware of the musical accompaniment in a picture, it's probably the wrong music. This didn't endear me to several composers of film music in Hollywood. They thought they were real composers, perhaps because they made more money in four weeks at a studio than Mozart had made all his life. The good Hollywood composers were fine craftsmen who were not kidding themselves about their "art." The bad ones thought they could write "serious" music, music not for films, any time they felt like it, though somehow they never felt like it. They talked about their celebrated local colleagues, Arnold Schönberg and Igor Stravinsky, whom they ignored otherwise. Schönberg died in Los Angeles, a lonely, bitter man. Some Hollywood composers were friends of great virtuosos who made their home in southern California: Jascha Heifetz, Gregor Piatigorsky, Artur Rubinstein. A studio composer told me he'd written a violin concerto "for Heifetz." He sounded a little like Brahms, who had shown *his* violin concerto to Joseph Joachim and asked for the artist's advice.

Hollywood, to paraphrase the late Fred Allen, is a better place for oranges than for composers. The local composers wanted both pay-checks and immortality, but perhaps the climate was too mild for im-mortality. Some ambitious composers wrote symphonies which they con-ducted. The symphonies sounded distressingly like the sound track of a major epic. Any moment Clark Gable and Greta Garbo might appear out of the blue horizon.

Beethoven found inspiration in Heiligenstadt and Baden, near Vi-enna. Brahms composed music in his head while walking through the lovely landscape near Pörtschach, Carinthia. Wagner wrote much of *Tristan und Isolde,* the most passionate love music of all, in the unerotic countryside overlooking Lake Lucerne in Switzerland. Mahler created his musical weltschmerz in the dramatic mountain scenery of the Dolo-mites. I wondered what *they* would have written if they had lived in palatial mansions in Bel Air.

I love music, but I don't write about music per se; I leave the field to the experts and musicologists. (I've written a book about music for young people, mainly to try to get them interested in the beauty of music.) I've always been interested in how great musical performers practice their art and how they perform. Unfortunately, this is a subject many celebrated artists don't like to discuss. There is a widespread belief that a great musician is also a man of unusual intellect, and that virtuosity is matched by wisdom. But this is the exception rather than the rule. The great performers are blessed with great talent, and they work hard. Somewhere in their career there is nearly always the element of good timing and good luck. They are able to project their personalities far beyond the boundaries of their art, and they become identified as "great musicians." But many of them are unable to analyze the secret of their art, or they are afraid to do so, because they consider analytic knowledge the deadly enemy of artistic intuition. Some of the world's greatest singers cannot explain how they produce the wonderful tones that thrill their audiences. They don't understand the function of the diaphragm or the workings of the vocal chords, and have only the vaguest ideas about breath control. "I don't *want* to know," a very famous singer once told me. "I might become self-conscious. How could I sing a high C in front of three thousand people if I worried about my vocal chords contracting ever so slightly?"

I once spent a frustrating afternoon in a second-floor room of a Beverly Hills home with Jascha Heifetz, the greatest violinist I've known. (Some people may disagree, but everybody is entitled to his opinion. The trouble with many music critics is their irritating habit of tossing off objective-sounding statements, such as "the world's greatest violinist," instead of calling him the greatest so far as *they* are concerned.) I was doing an article on Heifetz, whom I called "Fiddler's Fiddler." Many famous fiddlers agree.

Heifetz was shy and uncooperative. I'd heard people say that he was a "dull" person. But when you try to find out what makes a person, what he really is like, even allegedly "dull" people become interesting. I tried to talk about Heifetz's great art; I wanted to know how he did it. But I didn't get very far. He seemed quite consciously to avoid the heart of the matter. I believe he felt that he gave away his innermost secrets when he performed, and he saw no need to express them in words. Every time I probed beyond points of technique — we agreed that technique was taken for granted — and tried to pry into the mysterious secrets of re-creating the music, I faced a blank wall. His magnificent

Guarneri del Gesù was lying in its case on a table. I thought it would be nice if Heifetz would just play something for me, instead of my asking him questions he didn't feel like answering. I didn't dare ask him to play for me. In Detroit, the late Henry Ford had once invited the young Heifetz to his home. Heifetz was to give a concert that night. Ford had two Stradivari violins there that he considered buying — he was fascinated with the violin as a "miracle of man-made perfection," as he called it — and he asked Heifetz to play something, to hear how they sounded. Heifetz refused. He said he never played a violin he wasn't used to a few hours prior to a concert. Ford understood; he respected the young perfectionist.

I'd secretly hoped to talk with Heifetz about some blessed moments of his performances, when he played with such unearthly beauty that he brought tears to my eyes. But somehow we drifted off again into a purely technical discussion. (He told me something I've never forgotten. "During the physical and nervous strain of the concert performance, what with the heat and the problematic acoustics of the hall, a part of what you are trying to do always gets lost. That means that you've got to be better than you'll eventually sound. You've got to be prepared one hundred and thirty percent so that when thirty percent gets lost, the audience will still get a hundred percent, and be satisfied. If you played only a hundred percent, you wouldn't give them enough." To me, this has always been the explanation for Jascha Heifetz's "perfection.")

At one point, I remember, Heifetz was trying to explain to me exactly how he played a certain, extremely difficult phrase. I looked at him uncomprehendingly. Suddenly he took his violin and his bow, and played the phrase for me.

"See what I mean?" he said, looking at me. I stared at him blankly. A fast run, with double stops, going over three octaves. Heifetz hadn't even bothered to tune his violin, but he played the virtuoso passage with his customary perfection. He could play on an instrument that was slightly out of tune by making his fingers perform infinitesimal adjustments with lightninglike speed.

"Would you mind showing it to me once more?" I said. (I didn't dare ask him, "Please play it slowly, I'm just an ordinary mortal.")

"Sure," Heifetz said. This time he held up his violin toward me, so I could watch his left hand while he played the incredible passage again. God and Heifetz alone knew how he did it. I didn't. This wasn't violin playing, but the sort of black magic that made Paganini's impressionable contemporaries claim that he had a secret deal with the devil.

If Heifetz ever had a deal, it was with the Almighty; his playing sounded more of heaven than hell. I later carefully studied the phrase, but to this day I don't know how he did it. Which is perhaps as it ought to be. We know practically nothing about the mysterious working of the creative mind. Hundreds of volumes have been written about Mozart, but no one has been able to explain the unfathomable enigma of Mozart's genius. Perhaps it is also impossible to explain the last secrets of the great re-creators.

One day in the early 1950's, Paul Reynolds and I went to Chappaqua, New York, to lunch with the editors of the *Reader's Digest* — a ritual, I was told, that was considered part of a contributor's duties. The *Digest*'s headquarters, a complex of several ornamental buildings located in a beautiful part of Westchester, looked as though they had been put up on the Paramount lot for a Bing Crosby–Bob Hope "vehicle" called *The Road to Chappaqua*. The interior decorations were chintzy and cheerful, in Early-American-Optimism style. Life can be beautiful even if you have gallstones and no money at all. The receptionist smiled, the curtains smiled, the senior editors smiled, and so did the junior waitresses. The only man who could afford not to smile was DeWitt Wallace, who invented, and with his wife owns, the *Digest*, the most commercially successful magazine on earth.

"Wally," as his senior editors called him, is a tall, shy man, gentle and reticent. He spoke softly. I never heard him raise his voice above *mezzo piano*. He didn't have to; when he said something, everybody listened respectfully. He had warm, thoughtful eyes, and moved with slow, hesitant gestures, giving the impression that he felt ill at ease in the presence of outsiders. He looked like the son of a Protestant missionary (which he was). If he'd been a Catholic, he would have made an imposing cardinal. Fortunately, his dignity was tempered by a genuine sense of humor.

I'm convinced that Wallace believes in the philosophy (if you want to call it that) of his magazine. He is also a great businessman and a shrewd judge of human nature. He must know a lot about people, otherwise the *Digest* couldn't be such a hit everywhere — not only among Americans, whom he knows well, but also among Norwegians, Japanese, Germans, Spaniards, and Arabs, who are very different from DeWitt Wallace. Perhaps he senses that on a certain level the common denominators are the same everywhere. Tens of millions of frustrated, dissatisfied, lonely, depressed, unhappy people all over the world are cheered up to read, once a month, that life can be beautiful. Nowadays the great leveller is sex, but Wallace originally performed his publishing miracle without the help of sex. When I wrote for the *Digest*, sex hadn't been discovered yet in Chappaqua. Today it's different.

Lunch at the *Digest* was as strict a ritual as in any secret society. The smiling receptionist announced us, and a smiling girl took us to the office of the senior editor who had worked, perhaps unsmilingly, on my last articles. The antiseptic corridors belonged in a Swiss sanitarium for rich people suffering from often imagined but always expensive nervous breakdowns. The editorial rooms didn't have the smell and feel of magazine offices. Rather, they made me think of a literary clinic, where teams of surgeons and nurses were getting ready for their operations, preparing their scissors and sandpapers, waiting for the patient — the writer and his manuscript — to be wheeled in. Only the rubber gloves were missing.

No business was to be discussed, or even mentioned, at the senior editor's office before lunch; that was rule number one. The conversation was innocuous and general, always on a jocular note. Laughter is the best medicine, even for a *Digest* editor, who had just taken a couple of

Alka-Seltzers to get over his hangover. After a while we left the office and stepped out into the beautifully landscaped grounds. Just across the highway there was a small shack with a bar in it. I was told that the *Digest* didn't officially believe in the blessings of alcohol, except for rubbing purposes, but it was all right to have a couple of drinks in the no-man's-land across the street. I was much cheered by this healthy display of post-Prohibition cynicism. It was, I soon discovered, not restricted to the pre-lunch drinks.

After a while we walked back, already in a more relaxed mood, into dry Early-Optimism America. Our arrival at the entrance to the executive dining room was carefully timed to coincide with the arrival of DeWitt Wallace and his top editorial generals who had been summoned to lunch. I was introduced to everybody, and there were more smiles. Wallace and his generals had had no drinks before lunch and seemed more restrained than our cheerful group from across the road.

Lunch was dedicated to the proposition that writers should be seen and heard. I happen to believe that they ought to be read. DeWitt Wallace sat down at one end of the long table, and I was asked to sit down at the other end. The other editors were seated in definite though often changing patterns, somewhat like the Soviet Politburo leaders overlooking Moscow's Red Square during the First-of-May Parade, which makes "usually well-informed sources" and "veteran Western observers" speculate endlessly about the precarious positions of power inside the Kremlin.

Lunch around the table was organized like a center-court game in Wimbledon. DeWitt Wallace started serving the conversational ball to the writer at the other end of the table, who was supposed to come up with some fast backhand repartee. Between the two of us, the spectators (and maybe referees) along the sidelines would turn their heads uniformly right or left, as the words were flying. Wallace, the champion, was never going to make a double fault. It was tough on the challenger — the writer — who was expected to come up with strong volleys of article ideas. That was the official purpose of the lunch. The writer was also expected to entertain his audience, telling amusing stories about his harrowing experiences in the wide world-at-large outside Chappaqua. In my case, it was the world outside the continental United States where no God-fearing, red-blooded American citizen had any business being, except on a *Digest* assignment.

It took me a while to learn the subtle touches of the *Digest* lunch game. During my first two or three visits, I hardly managed to eat anything because I was busy serving, parrying, backhanding, lobbying all the time. After Wallace had finished eating and put down his fork, the plates were quickly removed, not unlike at the Habsburg court, where no one was supposed to eat after His Majesty, the Emperor, had finished. This was especially hard for the hungry, young archdukes way down the table who had been served last. His Majesty was a fast eater.

Fortunately, the food prepared at the *Digest*'s own kitchen, while not rating so much as half a *Guide Michelin* star, was, like much of the *Digest*'s editorial content, carefully predigested and easy to swallow. There were mostly soft things — fruit salad, mashed potatoes, beautifully colored Jell-O. The trick was to quickly swallow a bite between two bright aphorisms, and then swallow another one while everybody laughed. They were a grateful audience and laughed a great deal.

By that time the purpose of the lunch seemed to have been forgotten. No one was talking about articles anymore. And then we got up. DeWitt Wallace, his eyes still sparkling with mirth, would thank me for coming out, and I realized, dolefully, that I hadn't sold them a single article idea.

Slowly we walked back through the long, clean corridors, in twos, as after a pleasant funeral. I was never able to prevent DeWitt Wallace, a very polite man, from escorting me, the guest of dishonor, on my left side. In front of his office he might say good-bye to us. Paul and I would walk back to a senior editor's office where we tried, with no smiles at all, to "come up with something." Unfortunately, they often knew what they didn't want, but they rarely knew what they wanted. They were shrewd judges of *Digest* material, and made a sharp distinction between a writer's abilities as contributor and raconteur.

One day — I'd just returned from Europe — I told them at lunch how four American foreign correspondents, of whom I was one, had been arrested by the People's Police in Leipzig, during the Trade Fair, in March, 1951. It hadn't been funny at all when it happened but may have sounded that way when I told the story. There was much laughter that day around the center court, and I managed to eat nearly my whole lunch. And while we walked back, Wallace suggested to me, in his off-hand, hesitant manner, "You ought to write the story exactly as you told it to us."

I looked at him in surprise. The suggestion had never occurred to me. Fellow writers will understand. We often don't see the stories closest to us.

My three traveling companions had been Joseph Alsop (I described him as "a dapper fastidious man who had always managed to get his daily, ice-cold bath in the Japanese prison camp near Hong Kong where he'd been interned in 1941, and he liked to have a valet around to press his clothes. There were said to be few bathrooms in Leipzig, and practically no valets.") ; William Attwood, then working for the New York *Post*, now editor-in-chief of *Look*; and Don Cook, who worked for the New York *Herald Tribune* and today runs the Paris bureau of the Los Angeles *Times*. Our trip had been improvised in the dining room of the Hotel Neva in East Berlin. Surrounded by ruins and rubble, the building had been spared by the bombs. The dining room looked like a ludicrous set for a *belle époque* film, with red plush curtains, bronze chandeliers, and large potted palm trees. I'd stumbled upon this nightmare decoration one day when I searched for caviar. The Neva, an Intourist establishment, offered Beluga caviar from the Soviet part of the Caspian Sea, excellent Wódka Wyborowa from Poland, white toast and sweet butter from East Germany, and an obliging East German waiter (probably working for the East German secret police) who was willing to take "cheap, lovely East marks," as Alsop described them, in lieu of payment.

There were no lemons available. We brought them with us from West Berlin.

Our caviar-and-vodka feasts began around four P.M., when many people ate lunch at the Neva, and lasted until night. In the end, the bill always surpassed our supply of cheap, lovely East marks, and we had to make up the difference in unlovely, expensive American Express travelers checks. Once, when the caviar had been exceptionally mild, soft, and delicate, our combined dollar assets were not sufficient. Fortunately, we were bailed out by Adlai Stevenson, whom Attwood had brought along: he was then a presidential candidate in search of practical political erudition going around the world. Fortunately, Stevenson was not recognized by the habitués of the dining room — Communist Party big shots, Marxist amazons, and dubious-looking "neutral" businessmen and other black marketeers who could afford to eat there.

Our trip to Leipzig, that had been decided at the Neva the night before, began in characteristic style. At the Potsdam Bridge, Joe Alsop ("looking impeccable in a Savile Row suit of brown gabardine and a blue topcoat, carrying Xenophon's *Anabasis,* since he claimed to be going there as a 'student of history' ") broke into Homeric laughter at the sight of a benign likeness of pipe-smoking Joseph Stalin, whom a large sign caption called "the Best Friend of the German People." In Washington, D.C., Alsop's hoarse, hollow laugh is feared in High Establishment circles, where it is associated with the fateful sound of the Erinyes. A Soviet sentry at the Potsdam Bridge took a firm grip on his tommy gun. That would have been the moment to turn around, as they write, with hindsight, in prestigious military histories. Instead, we drove on. In Dessau, we went off the autobahn, which was strictly forbidden. The student of history wanted to see the famous Junkers aircraft factory. He said, loftily, that we would remain "inconspicuous." I am afraid Cook's Chevrolet with its American license plate was as inconspicuous in Dessau as a Soviet submarine would be on New York's Fifth Avenue.

In Leipzig, the student of history launched his private Point Four

Program by handing out chocolates to pale children and cigarettes to grateful grown-ups. We had been assigned quarters in a suburban apartment house where Alsop made arrangements to have the hot-water stove lighted in the building's only functioning bathroom, and assigned various *Hausfrauen* to the duties of pressing his clothes, shining his shoes, and boiling his breakfast eggs "exactly three and a half minutes." The *Hausfrauen* loved "Herr Aslop" [sic] and hung over his bed a framed piece of embroidery saying *"Hab'Sonne im Herzen"* ("Have Sunshine in Your Heart.")

We spent the next days walking all over Leipzig, then a reporter's dream town, never going near the Fair. We were constantly shadowed by Soviet secret police, "inconspicuous" in their long leather coats and yellow scarves. In Auerbach's Keller, the fourteen-hundred-year-old beer hall known as the setting of a memorable scene in Goethe's *Faust*, we turned the tables on our pursuers. Alsop went over and invited them to sit with us, "to facilitate matters." We went reluctantly to the Fair only on the morning of our last day, to have our papers stamped, which was mandatory before leaving Leipzig. The most impressive exhibit was the Soviet Union Hall with a twenty-five-foot-high red plaster statue of "the Best Friend of the German People." Alsop shattered the church-like silence in the large hall by his Oxford, clipped *basso profundo*.

"Quite appropriate," he boomed. "Statues of dear old Joe. The principal export of the Union of the Soviet Socialist Republics." As we three deserted the two Joes and ran out, we heard his hollow laughter reverberated by the walls of the large mausoleum.

Attwood took a few photographs of interesting sights. We went for the last time to Auerbach's Keller, where we had become respected caviar comrades. Before leaving Leipzig, we went to the Church of Saint Thomas, where its erstwhile choir leader, Johann Sebastian Bach, lies buried. Alsop, totally uninterested in musical matters, remained sitting in the car. As we came out, we were arrested by a Vopo and one of the civilians wearing a leather coat and yellow scarf. Alsop tried to explain "to these agents of Justinian and Theodorus" that he was an American citizen, as though the whole matter didn't concern him *at all*. The man with the yellow scarf, who spoke German with a thick Russian accent, asked who this man (Alsop) was. He was told by Attwood that the gentleman was a noted student of classical history. The student immersed himself in Xenophon's *Anabasis,* which he always carried around. He loftily ignored the hostile outside world.

We were taken to the Police Presidium, and walked up five flights of stairs. I silently counted the broad steps, as they do in detective novels, wondering gloomily whether I would ever walk down these steps again, a free man. Sinister characters in leather coats were standing around. Two heavily armed Vopos separated Attwood from his camera. One said we were being held "under suspicion of espionage." They were going to develop Attwood's film to see "whether it showed objects of military importance," assuring him there would be no charge for developing.

"By the way, my dear fellow," Alsop said, turning to Attwood, "what sort of pictures did you take here?"

"That," Attwood said, "I've been trying to remember for the past half hour."

The Vopos knew all about us. They said we'd allegedly come to Leipzig to see the Fair, where we'd spent exactly twenty-three minutes; that we made derogatory remarks at the sight of Comrade Stalin's picture near the Potsdam Bridge, that at Auerbach's Keller —

"For heaven's sakes," Alsop said impatiently, "must you go on like this? I hate discussing politics with policemen."

A splendid military figure appeared, tall, towering, and booted, with pompous shoulder insignia, who was called "General." He asked us who we were. By way of returning his curiosity, we asked him his name, rank and what his shoulder insignia were. He called us *Dummköpfe* (idiots), and stalked away. He was the People's Police President of Leipzig. The student of history said matter-of-factly that now everything was lost. "I suppose I should have listened to my brother," he said. "He warned me not to go to Leipzig."

Why we were released as suddenly as we had been arrested, we've never found out. Cook's theory is that the Russians took a secret liking to the student of history who read Xenophon in Leipzig. Out on the street, the student, once again his magnanimous self, invited one of our ex-captors for a vodka before we took off. We wound up in a cozy black-market place serving excellent vodka. After five glasses, the Vopo became quite friendly and assured us, quoting a mysterious Kremlin source, that the Russians would never attack the West. Speaking un-officially for the White House, "Herr Aslop" assured him that the West would never attack the Soviet Union.

This time the student of history didn't ask Cook to get off the autobahn. It was nobody's fault that the Chevrolet had a flat tire, and that this had to happen within sight of a supposedly secret Soviet airfield. While Cook fixed the tire, I made sure that Attwood didn't take any pictures. The student of history remained sitting in the car, reading Xenophon, totally unperturbed.

Around midnight we arrived at the Berlin Press Club, where we had already been given up for lost. Herr Alsop ordered champagne for every-body, and summed it all up. "I daresay, there is nothing like getting arrested to find out about the People's Police."

"Caviar for the Comrades" ("Four debonair American journalists have a ludicrous time in Communist Germany") was the lead article in the May, 1953, issue of the *Reader's Digest*. I keep few letters nowadays, but I've kept the one DeWitt Wallace wrote me earlier, after reading the manuscript:

March 2, 1953

Dear Joe:

For once in my life, I have been out of commission (hepa-titis) for two months. But I'm back on the job to get the best thrill in a long time after reading *Caviar for the Comrades*.

It is a masterpiece!

May your inspired words continue to pour forth from your typewriter!

All best wishes,

Wally

After the *Digest* published my story, the syndicated Have-Sunshine-in-Your-Heart columnist didn't talk to me for two years. I regretted it because I was fond of him, but these are the hazards of the journalistic profession. Eventually Alsop mellowed, hearing so many compliments about his courage above and beyond the call of duty in Leipzig, and I'm glad to report that we are friends again. The four of us no longer go to East Berlin on caviar expeditions. Under the circumstances there, we wouldn't enjoy even the finest Beluga. Our friendship has endured, though. Good caviar does that to people.

Not all of my *Digest* luncheons ended on such a cheerful note. Once DeWitt Wallace kept me in a state of suspense during lunch while he remained cryptic about an article I'd done for the *Digest*. Some senior editors liked it and some did not, and "now it is up to Wally," I was told.

After lunch, Wallace gravely invited Paul Reynolds and me to his large corner office with fine, old American furniture and not-so-fine, new American books that the *Digest* might condense in "permanent" booklet form. I didn't like the invitation and my forebodings proved right. Wallace told us reluctantly that he'd decided not to buy the article. He looked almost as dejected as I did. He said this was no criticism, it was a fine piece, it just "didn't fit in" at the present moment. Exactly what Rudi Thomas, wearing his red blazer, had said twenty years earlier at the *Prager Tagblatt* when he reluctantly rejected a manuscript.

Wallace looked very unhappy. To show how he felt about it, he suggested a settlement of half the price. I nodded; I thought this was very fair. We said good-bye. At the door, Wallace asked Paul to stay on for a moment. I thought the tactful editor didn't want to discuss the distressing financial details in front of the sensitive writer.

After a while, Paul came out looking puzzled, which doesn't happen often. As we walked out of the citadel of American optimism, Paul told me that Wallace had given him two checks. One for half the price of the article. The other, in the same amount, as a "bonus."

"A bonus for what?" I asked.

"That's what I've been trying to figure out," Paul said, sounding like a character in my *Digest* "masterpiece."

Later, Paul sold the article to the *Atlantic Monthly* and sent the money, a fraction of the *Digest* rate, to DeWitt Wallace. One good turn deserves another.

When Wallace more or less retired from being the editor, I stopped writing for the *Digest*. Bob Littell had died. Two other friends, who happened to be senior editors, had been shifted to other "departments." The *Reader's Digest*, like so many other successful operations, had become hopelessly departmentalized. No department seemed to know what the other department was doing. Committees voted on article ideas. An editorial bureaucracy developed, and everything was done by channels, as in Washington, D.C., or at the Time-Life Building, the Valhalla of group journalism.

Wallace's brilliant idea has been imitated all over the world. He was the first to realize that people are too lazy to think for themselves, and like to have their reading matter selected and prepared for them. Haven't they also their books chosen by others, in the book clubs, and their opinions shaped by columnists? It's not an ideal situation, but things could be worse. Suppose these wizards in Chappaqua would start digesting and condensing the world's great paintings, showing selected details from the masterpieces of Rembrandt and Renoir? Perhaps just the two main characters in Rembrandt's *Night Watch*, or the lovely couple dancing in the forefront of Renoir's *Moulin de la Galette*? Suppose they started to produce mini-editions of the enormous works of Richard Wagner? *Tristan und Isolde*, that masterpiece of masterpieces, condensed, in permanent form, from five hours down to fifty minutes — just the beautiful Prelude, boy-meets-Isolde, boy-loves-Isolde, Isolde's *Liebestod*. None of the interminable monologues and dialogues in between, that keep only certified Wagnerians happy. Who knows, they may be working on the project right now.

Gambling

THOUGH I'VE NEVER BEEN A GAMBLER, I became an assistant croupier
in a Riviera casino during my early, irresponsible life. My aversion to
gambling may have been the result of a story that my mother often told
when we had guests. She had gone with my father on a holiday to
Monte Carlo in the spring of 1908, when I was eight months old and
a noisy baby. They left me at home. I don't blame them.

Monte Carlo must have been beautiful during the last years prior
to the First World War. My mother loved to reminisce about the
beautifully kept flowerbeds around the Casino, the Monegasque carabinieri (oversized lead soldiers in their tall helmets, red and royal-blue
uniforms, and heavy epaulets), and the ancient landaus, smelling of
horse and nostalgia, debouching fragile, white-haired English ladies in
front of the Casino. *Concours d'élégance* and flower parades . . .

My mother would sigh wistfully. They didn't get near the Casino.
My father was afraid my mother might lose her head and his money
around the roulette tables. And he was a little afraid of his father. Grand-

father Wechsberg disapproved of gambling, not on moral grounds but because "you can't win against the bank." A successful banker, Grandfather knew the odds. Only on the last day, shortly before they were to leave, my father took my mother to the Casino, perhaps in a moment of guilt or because it seemed safe now, and gave her a gold coin, a napoleon.

My mother, with feminine intuition, put the coin recklessly on number twenty-nine. August 29 happened to be the baby's (my) birthday. The croupier said, *"Rien ne va plus,"* spinning the wheel which circled the rim, and fell into the slot marked nine. The croupier said, *"Neuf: rouge, impair et manque,"* and raked in the losing stakes, including my mother's napoleon. My father smiled and gave her another gold coin, telling her to try the twenty-nine once more. My mother shook her head. The ivory ball spun again, and the twenty-nine came out. Had my mother repeated her bet, she would have won thirty-five napoleons. She broke into tears, and when she saw that my father was rather amused, she got mad and walked out.

"He was glad because I'd learned my lesson," my mother would finish her moral tale. "And I was angry because he was right. God knows what might have happened if I'd *won!*"

Paradoxically, I've never really cared about roulette or card games or betting on horses, though I am a gambler in my private and professional life. I've often taken foolish chances. A writer living on his wits is always gambling. Each manuscript is just another bet. We authors are creatures of contradiction. I wouldn't bet a thousand dollars in a card game where the odds against me are three to one, but I'm cheerfully betting a year of my life on a book that may never pay off. I jealously protect my private life, but I share my private thoughts with my readers, the more the better. While my boyhood friends played "God's Blessing at Kohn's House," our local version of what Americans call blackjack, I was more interested in girls, which involves far greater risks than any card game. In Paris, I once spent a night in the home of a rich man who had a private roulette wheel in a back room. I gambled a little, watching myself clinically. My blood pressure didn't go up. Even in the American army, I never learned to shoot dice. And yet, I was an assistant croupier in the Casino Municipal in Nice.

During the particularly cold, damp winter of 1929, I worked as a nightclub musician in Paris, and didn't see the sun for three months. It was still dark when I came home from work in the early morning, and it was dark again when I left my hotel in the evening. I got so depressed by the darkness that one day I quit my lucrative job and went down to the Côte d'Azur. I wanted to see whether the sky was as azure as on the preposterous travel folders. It was. I had a brief moment of glory when I managed to give a solo appearance with the orchestra of the Casino de la Jetée, an ugly structure built out over the sea on steel piles. Everybody in Nice was glad when it was bombed out of existence during the Second World War.

My concert appearance was attended by old ladies, noisy kids, and bored tourists. I stood on the stage, surrounded by potted trees that had been left there after a previous attraction, perhaps looking not unlike the emperor who fiddled while Rome burned. I tried hard but not always successfully to keep in touch with the accompanying orchestra down in the pit. I was blinded by an idiotically placed spotlight, and couldn't see the conductor. It was a miracle that the orchestra and I reached the end of the Mendelssohn violin concerto at approximately the same time.

There was mild applause. I hastily played an encore, Sarasate's "Romance Andalouse," before the audience changed their minds. The local paper, *L'Eclaireur de Nice et du Sud-Ouest*, gave me a friendly review. Somehow I didn't get paid, though, for my performance, and what with travel expenses and the cost of living on the Riviera, I owed the rent to Monsieur Zapletal, a countryman from Moravia. I lived in a small room in his apartment in the old Riquier district. He worked as croupier at the Casino Municipal in the Place Massena. When I failed to find a job in a local nightclub, he offered me work as an assistant croupier. There was an epidemic of the flu among the croupiers, and they were short of men anyway.

I told him I knew nothing about the croupier's work and was weak on arithmetic. Zapletal shrugged and said, *"Nevadi"* ("Doesn't matter"). We conversed in French, German, and Czech. Zapletal spoke Czech when he was homesick for the dark gray skies of his native Moravia. He hated the sunny skies of the Côte d'Azur.

"You've got a double-breasted blue suit and a serious face," he said. "The assistant croupier is there mainly to keep people from cheating. You'll earn less money than your French colleagues, but you know how it is." Yes, I knew.

My indoctrination lasted about ten minutes. Zapletal introduced me to the head croupier, who looked forbidding, with X-ray eyes and a Lenin beard. They gave me a blitz course in how to observe the players' faces while the croupier observed their hands. I learned the finger signals between croupier and assistant croupier. Left forefinger pointed down meant "Attention!" Small forefinger of left hand pointed at a player was "Watch this person!" And so on. The signals were changed every month because the players always caught on after a while.

The Casino Municipal in Nice was a very poor relation of the celebrated establishment in Monte Carlo, where they had a croupier on each side of the wheel and one at each end of the table, and also a head croupier behind the wheel croupiers. In Nice, each table had only the croupier who spun the wheel and paid out the winnings, and the assistant croupier at the other end of the table. At that time the Casino Municipal had ten tables of boule and several roulette tables. Zapletal and I were assigned to a boule table. Boule is known as "roulette's bad little sister." It's a terrible gyp racket. There are only nine (red and black) numbers. The payoff is seven for one; the odds are $11\frac{1}{9}$ against the player. I wonder what Grandfather Wechsberg would have said to *that*.

In European roulette, which has thirty-six numbers and zero, the odds against the player are $2\frac{26}{37}$. In American roulette, where the wheel has two zeros, the odds are $5\frac{5}{19}$ percent. I found this out only years later. Neither the head croupier nor Zapletal bothered to discuss such delicate matters. I soon learned, though, that a croupier's life is one long running fight against optimists trying to beat the law of averages. Sometimes the optimists are trying a bit too hard. The croupier's job is to discourage them.

At the Casino Municipal, the admission fee was small and the minimum stake was one franc, then four cents. Our clientele consisted of shabby tourists and small-fry suckers who wanted the thrill and couldn't afford Monte Carlo.

After a couple of days, I felt quite at home at the boule table. I helped the players make their bets, glared at them sternly, hoping to discourage them from claiming other people's winnings, and in general conveyed a forbidding impression, but perhaps not forbidding enough. Almost every night there was trouble with players who would wait until the last second and then would surreptitiously move their bet from one number to the next. When the former number came out, they said it had been there, it was all a mistake. I soon learned why croupiers take a dim view of their fellow creatures. A gaming table is not the place to fall in love with the human race. Eventually, my career ended on an ignominious note, when I made the wrong decision in a dispute between two players — a faux pas that led to a free-for-all at our boule table, and to my instantaneous dismissal.

I've remained interested — theoretically — in gambling, from the croupier's point of view. It's like having been a member of the claque; in opera houses all over the world, I always study people's applause. On several visits to the Casino in Monte Carlo, I watched the croupiers there with the fervent respect that members of amateur orchestras pay to the Cleveland Orchestra. In the early postwar years we lived for a while in Monte Carlo. It still had a certain sense of unreality, with an operetta quality much of its own. There were no skyscrapers yet, no American movie queens and Greek shipping billionaires. The place was elegant, though a little shiny at the elbows, like the croupiers' dinner jackets. Antiquated Rolls-Royce taxis, once the cars of optimistic plungers, were parked in front of the imposing entrance of the Hotel de Paris; before the last war, Monte Carlo had the largest number of Rolls-Royces, per capita, of any country in the world. We stayed at the Hermitage Hotel, which was to the Hotel de Paris what the Bentley is to the Rolls-Royce. My room was in a round tower. Underneath the windows were the railroad tracks that went right through Monte Carlo. Every time a fast train went by, my room trembled sympathetically. When the trembling assumed the proportions of a minor earthquake, I knew the Train Bleu, the world's oldest all-sleeper train, was going by, as it has done every day since 1883, despite wars, occupations, and other catastrophes, a durable symbol of a more romantic past.

I rarely went to the Casino, and when I did, it was only to watch the gamblers. I'd learned that the best way to win is not to gamble at all. I came to know some of the local habitual gamblers, old ladies and gentlemen who lived on a low budget, setting a little money aside for their living expenses and spending the rest of their allowance at the Casino. They were *systémiers* (system players), men in threadbare suits and women in dresses that had plainly been made over several times. They would rush into the Casino every morning when the doors were opened to the gaming rooms, at five minutes to ten, each heading for a particular seat at a particular table. They would put down their notebooks, diagrams, and pencils, and finger their ties, cigarette cases, rabbits' feet, coins, or other tokens of luck. No one spoke. Most systems depend on the outcome of the day's first spin of the wheel. The *systémiers* knew that in order to stay in the game against the immutable mathematical disadvantage for any length of time, they must play cautiously. They wouldn't have bet on one number, *en plein*, as my mother did. If they succeeded in making *la matérielle*, as much as they considered necessary to sustain life for a day or two, they went home. If they lost, they might stop eating for the day, until they could scratch together another smattering of capital. They lived in small, furnished rooms a long way from the rococo suites of the Hermitage Hotel. Fundamentally, they were less interested in getting rich than in proving that once they got the proper sequence of numbers and colors lined up, their system was infallible. In 1939, at the beginning of the war, the Casino had been closed for three months, and frustrated *systémiers* were seen staggering around the town like movie alcoholics in search of a bottle.

Exactly at ten o'clock, the *chef de partie* said, *"Messieurs, faites vos jeux."* No one at the table even picked up a chip. The first round is rarely played by any *systémier*. But after the first round, depending on the number that had come out, they would hurriedly consult their tabulations, and then they began to bet in a cautious way, playing the simple chances, *rouge* or *noir*, odd or even, or bet a *douzaine*, a vertical column of twelve numbers paying three times the stake.

It was rather pathetic. It made me think of the patients in a TB sanatorium in Davos who were lying on the terrace in the bright winter sunshine, knowing they were going to die, just trying to postpone it for a while. Some would spend the whole day at the Casino, just rushing out for a bite to eat, afraid that a certain magical sequence of numbers might come up and they would miss it. They knew that *rouge* once came up twenty-three times without a break, and that both twenty-two and thirty-two had turned up six times in succession. Others would leave after a few minutes if it wasn't the "right" day. The most popular system was doubling the bet after a loss, and a form of doubling called the flat-stake system. Few *systémiers* had enough capital to afford a long run of doubling up. A player starting out with a fifty-franc bet on *rouge* who lost twelve times in succession, would have to bet 204,800 francs — and twelve consecutive rolls of the same color are not uncommon.

To become a croupier in Monte Carlo, one needed more than a double-breasted blue suit and a serious face. I watched my celebrated colleagues, virtuosos of the gaming table, and admired their skill, elegance, and imperturbability. In those early postwar years, the Casino was somewhat shabby and could have done with a new coat of gold leaf, but there was nothing shabby about the croupiers. They would spin the wheel with éclat; make neat, quick stacks of exactly twenty chips, something I'd tried but never achieved; place bets and toss the chips with such precision that they fell directly on the desired number; pay off a distant player with a cascade of chips that landed right in front of him. When I tried it once, the chips landed on the floor, which would be grounds for dismissal in Monte Carlo. They raked in losing stakes without disturbing the winning ones, watched the players' faces *and* hands (how about that, Zapletal?), memorized the patterns of bets, and multiplied in a fraction of a second the number of winning chips by thirty-five, seventeen, eleven, or eight, depending on whether they had been put on a number, on the line between two numbers (*à cheval*), on three numbers across the board (*transversale*), or on the intersection of four numbers (*en carré*). They performed these feats with the impeccable sangfroid of a chief of protocol directing a diplomatic dinner in a foreign ministry.

I suggested the profile of a croupier to *The New Yorker*. They liked the idea. Ross was something of a compulsive gambler, though he knew little about roulette. He pronounced it with the accent on the first syllable, making it sound like "rolled." It was a somewhat unusual profile because the croupier had to remain anonymous, which was against *New Yorker* policy. Croupiers in Monte Carlo were not supposed to mix socially with nonresidents of the principality, an injunction going back to the old days when dishonest croupiers would join forces with a gambler, pay him fake winnings, and later split the take. It was a surefire way of cheating, but it wouldn't work now, since croupiers, on and off duty, are always watched by the Casino's almost-secret police. To outwit the police, the croupier (whom I called Gaston Raymond) and

I would meet in a small bistro on a steep, narrow street in La Con-
damine, the harbor section of Monaco, where he lived. Though we
became friendly, he never invited me to his home. The Monegasque
standards of hospitality were lower even than those of France, which
are low enough. Raymond was an interesting man. He might pay out
millions of francs' worth of the Casino's chips in the course of a day's
work, but remained a penurious *petit bourgeois* in his private finances.
Some Swiss bank cashiers are like that. During working hours, M. Raymond rarely smiled except when a player threw a *pourboire* chip to one
end of the table, where an assistant croupier picked it up, nodded his
thanks, and put it into the croupiers' slot, called by old-timers number
thirty-seven.

M. Raymond was a third-generation resident of Monaco but not yet
a citizen. The local naturalization laws, tougher than the membership
bylaws of some very exclusive clubs, barred anyone from applying unless his family had resided in the principality for four generations.
M. Raymond's father had been a croupier, and he hoped his son would
be one. In his sentimental moments, he spoke of the Casino as *"la
maison,"* but when he complained about his low salary he called it
"le Casino." He'd started as attendant, went to a special school, became
a croupier, and hoped to become *chef de partie*, sitting in the high chair.
He was expected to photograph in his mind the layout of the chips on
his table before the ball was rolled out. Some croupiers were able to
carry the complete pattern of as many as three tables in their head, he
said. There might be forty or fifty people betting at the same time, but
he would know not only how much each of them had staked on a certain
number or combination of numbers, but also their methods, whims, and
frailties. Unlike a certain assistant croupier at the Casino Municipal in
Nice, M. Raymond would make the right decision in a dispute among
the players.

M. Raymond reminisced about his father, a great *chef de partie*
who once ruled that J. P. Morgan must not play over the maximum
stake, then twelve thousand francs on a plain number. Of course. Even

la maison couldn't afford to play against Mr. Morgan. M. Raymond *fils* served a two-year apprenticeship before he became an *aspirant* (candidate for croupier). Among other chores, he had to pick up chips that had fallen on the floor. No real gambler would ever bet such a chip again because it's supposed to bring bad luck, but there might be a poor sport around who would try to hide a chip under his foot and pick it up when M. Raymond wasn't looking. Eventually he had to present himself before a commission of casino officials who examined the candidates for appearance, education, knowledge of foreign languages, and the ability to calculate rapidly. Croupiers were also expected to have long, supple fingers. I might have passed on fingers but would have failed in calculation.

At the Casino's school for croupiers he was taught by veteran croupiers, and after class he would practice finger exercises, counting chips, rolling the ball with thumb and forefinger only, and spinning the wheel with the forefinger and middle finger. In Nice, Zapletal had used five fingers to spin the wheel. I brought up my past in Nice only once but never again when I noticed that M. Raymond took an exceedingly dim view of his *confrères* there. He also told me that the players were always addressed as *Messieurs*, even if there were only women around the table — a tradition stemming from the days when ladies were not supposed to have any association with gambling. M. Raymond wished those days were back. "Women around a gambling table," he said, "shorten a croupier's life expectancy." And he was bitter about another tradition, that his dinner jacket must have no side pockets.

I learned a great many tricks of the trade from M. Raymond while working on the profile. The wheel must be in motion while the betting goes on. After each play, it must be spun in the opposite direction. The ball must be rolled *against* the direction of the wheel's rotation with enough momentum to circle the rim from seven to nine times before falling into one of the ivory-and-rosewood slots. The chips must be thrown so that they fall down, never roll.

"Watch old ladies with trembling hands," said M. Raymond. "They may tremble so much that you don't notice that she is playing *la pous-sette*, staking her chips between *manque* (one to eighteen) and *impair* (odd), and giving them a little push to the appropriate side whenever *manque* or *impair* come out. And be on your guard when there is an *avocat* at your table, the fellow who always waits until a number comes up on which a lot of people have staked a bet, and then claims that one of the chips on the number is his." He told me that every morning the Casino's mechanics interchanged the parts of all roulette tables. Each table has minute physical irregularities, tiny scratches, an almost imper-ceptible unevenness. A smart gambler watching the tables for a long time might notice that certain numbers came up more frequently than others. An English engineer once won nine million francs, gold-standard francs, in three weeks, until the frantic Casino authorities discovered that he'd made a study-in-depth of that particular table.

M. Raymond's most interesting customer had been an American who thought he'd found the solution to end all other solutions. He figured that the trouble with all gamblers was that they wanted to win, and in the end they always lost. "Suppose a gambler *wanted* to lose, then he ought to win, eh?" he said to M. Raymond. The croupier admitted it sounded logical enough, but where was the man who wanted to lose?

The American had an answer for that. He said, "Suppose the man doesn't gamble with his own money. Then he might want to lose." He hired a fellow and gave him two thousand francs, with instructions to lose it as quickly as possible. For this chore, the man would get two hundred francs. The American's capital was fifty thousand francs, and he intended to try out his plan for three weeks.

"What happened?" I asked.

"You should have seen the American's agent bet! He threw his em-ployer's money all over the table. The first day, he was cleaned out in twenty minutes. The following day, he lost his daily stake in eighteen minutes. The third and fourth days, he lost quickly, too. The fifth day, believe it or not, he won sixty thousand francs. The American, who had been watching, came to the table and quickly took the chips. He gave a thousand francs to the fellow who had gambled, and a thousand-franc tip to the croupier, and left. He was a smart *type*. Never came back."

Years later, I continued my croupier's researches in Las Vegas, Nevada, where everything was bigger, though not necessarily better, than in Monte Carlo. The "21" Club, the gambling casino of the Hotel Last Frontier, never closed. They didn't have croupiers but "dealers," which sounds less elegant. They worked in three shifts around the clock. They wore no dinner jackets without side pockets because they had no dinner jackets, but garishly checkered shirts. But they were much friendlier than the Monte Carlo croupiers. Especially Russell A. Walker, a blackjack dealer whom I came to know well.

Like M. Raymond, "Pete," as they called him, was a virtuoso of his profession. He shuffled the deck rapidly to keep the players from seeing the faces of the cards, dealt with automatic precision with his right hand, and took in cards and chips with his left, all the time talking to the players. He could tell the exact value of a stack of silver dollars simply by its weight, and the number of chips in a stack by its height. Speed was his keynote, and rapid turnover his aim. In twenty-one, or blackjack, the object is to accumulate cards totaling a maximum of twenty-one points, or at least closer to twenty-one than the dealer. An ace counts either one or eleven, as desired; the king, queen, and jack have the value of ten; the values of the rest of the cards are determined by the number of spots on them.

Pete looked quite different from M. Raymond, but his philosophy was remarkably similar. He too needed the patience of Job and the politeness of Chesterfield, the accuracy of a mechanical brain, and a detective's powers of observation. Working from seven P.M. to three A.M., he knew that lots of people stayed up all night trying to figure out new ways of cheating him.

He told me that he'd learned to watch the tendons on the back of a man's hand. They would tell him whether a player was trying to crease his card along the edge, or whether the man was a bend player, trying to bend a card between thumb and forefinger. He told me of a cold-decker who, when asked to cut the shuffled cards, nimbly substitutes his own "cold" deck of marked cards for the dealer's deck. Cold-deckers work in pairs and are hard to catch. There were also "nailers," who make a tiny dent with their thumbnail in the edge of the cards; and "daubers," who use paint or chalk on their fingers to gimmick the backs of the cards; and "machine players," who can pull a card up their sleeve with the aid of a rubber band that stretches all the way down their body and is operated by moving the leg. Monte Carlo was never like that.

Pete agreed that it was important to watch a man's face. He sensed a player was up to no good when his lips got thin and his facial muscles got taut. The most dangerous opponents in blackjack were those who "cased the deck." They would memorize each card that was played out until only a few cards remained in the dealer's hand.

"Suppose that many of the low cards have been drawn after a few games and I'm still holding a relatively high number of face cards, tens, and aces. Since the rule is that the dealer must hit [draw up to] sixteen, and stand [draw no more cards] on seventeen, the deck-caser knows there is a better-than-even chance that the dealer will go bust. So the deck-caser will stand on an unusually low hand. It takes concentration and memory. What a shame those guys don't use their brains in a more productive line of work! I gather that something's up when players, after betting five or ten bucks, suddenly start to bet fifty and a hundred. Then I know it's time to shuffle the cards."

Pete liked women because they gambled instinctively. "Men are too logical and conservative. They rarely draw another card when they hit eighteen. They know the chances are about three to one that if you try to better a card count of even seventeen, you'll go over twenty-one. But tell that to a woman. She'll draw when she holds eighteen, and she'll draw a two or three. Of course, most players lose not because they draw too little but because they draw too many cards and go bust."

In one respect there was no difference between Monte Carlo and

Las Vegas: no player ever knew when to quit. One of Pete's friends, also a blackjack dealer, one night after work stopped at another hall. He started with ten dollars, and a couple of hours later he had twenty-two thousand dollars, which he took home. But a week later he'd lost it all — plus his latest paycheck.

"All gamblers are alike," Pete said philosophically. "They say the best thing in the world is to gamble and win. The next best thing is to gamble and lose."

I wrote Pete's story for *Collier's*. A few years later, *Collier's* gambled and lost. So did *Liberty* (reading time: three minutes, nineteen seconds) and even the *Saturday Evening Post*. Magazines die a lonely death. No one goes to their funerals.

"To Delight and Satisfy"

THE DURABILITY OF *The New Yorker* astonishes its readers and advertisers, its enemies and admirers, and sometimes even its editors and staff members. *The New Yorker* has managed to keep its identity in spite of constant changes, and there has been a continuity through all the years from the very first issue. Not long ago, Shawn said, "We have always got out the magazine that was an honest expression of ourselves, and was something we truly believed in. We hoped to find and hold readers, but we didn't think about what readers wanted, or even try to figure out who they were. We just edited a magazine to delight and satisfy ourselves, and hoped that what we did would find readers."

To me the changes are often less noticeable than to an outsider because I am too close to the magazine. I couldn't exactly define the changes, though I am aware of them and subconsciously adjust; otherwise I couldn't write for *The New Yorker* anymore. Every February I am comforted to see Eustace Tilley, the dandy looking through his monocle at a butterfly, on the anniversary cover, the symbol of continuity. *The New Yorker* is still created by people who want "to delight and satisfy" themselves. Which is more than can be said of most people in this country working for the communications media.

Much of *The New Yorker*'s operation is a matter of osmosis. *Fingerspitzengefühl* (supreme sensitivity) is needed to feel, often instinctively, that certain things are done, or not done, at certain times. In 1968, in the only interview-in-depth Shawn ever gave, he analyzed the magazine's constant changes. "It's grown deeper, I think. It's also broadened in its intellectual range, and even, I'd say, in its emotional range." Emotion is no longer taboo on the nineteenth floor, as it was when I first came there.

Some changes are hard to explain, and harder even to translate into one's work. Nowadays we write longer, more technical, perhaps more complex nonfiction pieces than before. They may contain facts as well as ideas. Many of my pieces are too long, but I can't forget Ross's telling me, "People want to know everything about a subject," perhaps because *he* wanted to know everything about it. I often get deeply involved in a subject and want to know all about it. Intellectual curiosity can be a dangerous thing.

We try to explain the often inexplicable. Once I asked George Szell, a deeply intellectual musician, about the mysteries of the conductor's art. He shrugged and said, *"Nicht den Blütenstaub wegblasen"* ("Don't blow away the pollen."). That wouldn't have satisfied Ross, who took nothing for granted. In the second part of a two-part article, one must not refer to something or somebody mentioned in the first part without briefly explaining it again. "Suppose nobody read the first part," Ross once said in a gloomy moment. Such habits are hard to get rid of.

I've written for *The New Yorker* about elusive and abstract subjects that would interest few other magazines. The abstract subjects are fascinating, perhaps because so many concrete subjects have already been done. I've written about the mysteries of light and darkness, the meaning of time and of silence. People are the protagonists in these pieces, but the core of the story is the abstract idea. The writers' ideas for *New Yorker* pieces are getting more complex, and so is the writing, because both reflect the world around us, which is getting more complex all the time. Yet the basic characteristics of *The New Yorker*'s reporting haven't changed. Shawn once defined them as being "as close an approximation of objectivity as we could humanly manage, straightforwardness, thoroughness, fairness, clarity, truthfulness, and accuracy." But he admitted, "There is more to it than that." You can never quite get away from *The New Yorker*'s mystique.

Writing is an intellectual effort. Writing for *The New Yorker* is also, for me, an emotional effort. I get personally involved, though my involvement and emotion must never — never! — show in the writing. When I write something not intended for *The New Yorker*, I always write as though it were for *The New Yorker*, but somehow I seem to succeed best when I actually do write for the magazine. This again gets me into the mystique of the magazine, and I wouldn't even try to analyze it. Writing for *The New Yorker* is an intensely personal effort. Though I speak only for myself, I have a hunch that quite a few *New Yorker* writers would agree with me. I never discussed it with anybody; I suppose that's one of the things that isn't done up there.

Shawn, of course, senses my personal involvement. After reading my profile of Madame Point, who owns and runs the Pyramide in Vienne, the world's greatest restaurant, Shawn cabled me: CLEARLY WRITTEN WITH LOVE. I hadn't been aware of this, but then I realized that I *did* write it with love. Another time, after reading my long profile of Prague, Shawn cabled: CERTAINLY NO ONE ELSE COULD HAVE DONE IT, expressing exactly what I'd subconsciously tried to do. What sense was there in writing about Prague unless, owing to my past and background, I could do something special? Writing for *The New Yorker* carries a strong sense of responsibility: to the magazine, its integrity, its quality, its editor, and above all, to myself. Writing is always hard, but writing for *The New Yorker* is harder because instinctively one makes it harder for oneself.

One of the world's greatest violinists once told me that the most difficult thing for him was not to perform two technically strenuous violin concertos in Carnegie Hall, but to play in a string quartet or trio before a small audience of chamber-music addicts, each of whom knew exactly what it was all about. Writing for *The New Yorker* is almost like playing chamber music for an audience of chamber-music players. There must be no tricks, no clichés, no pretense, no effect; it's pure music and must be performed purely. Very, very difficult. The striving for near-perfection remains. (*New Yorker* writers know that "perfection" does not exist.)

The New Yorker has often, but always unsuccessfully, been imitated. Not surprisingly, many people resent the magazine's continuing success. Some who strongly criticize it don't read it thoroughly; they just look at it. In Europe, where the magazine is handed around among members of the intellectual community and people who still admire America (which is not necessarily the same thing), the men first look at the cartoons and the women look at the ads. They are surprised that the magazine can be serious, and how! People love or hate *The New Yorker*, but they are rarely indifferent to it. Fortunately, because indifference is dangerous.

Gustav Mahler, during his ten-year tenure as *Direktor* of the Vienna Court Opera, the opera-house-with-a-soul, would say that it was a miracle to achieve one excellent performance every ten evenings or so. How many excellent performances can a magazine have that performs fifty-two times a year? The readers of *The New Yorker* remind me of the aficionados of the Vienna Opera. Because they love it, they always praise or condemn, they are frequently upset about it, but wouldn't want to miss it. They are fond of backstage gossip, often more interested in the private lives than in the public performances of the artists. The readers have been with the magazine so long that they feel they've become part owners, who may not own stock but have the vote and the right to gripe. Herbert von Karajan, as *Direktor* of the Vienna Opera, once complained to me that he had to run the house with the unsolicited advice of 1,700,-000 Viennese, most of whom had never been inside the Opera at a performance. Perhaps Shawn, the *Direktor* of *The New Yorker*, feels that way about the half-million subscribers of the magazine, each of whom has definite ideas of what it should be. I'm convinced that *The New Yorker* is the magazine-with-a-soul, though I wouldn't say so on the nineteenth floor. *That* isn't done up there.

I spend much time in Europe now; I live there physically, though not always spiritually. Like any damn fool, I go back and forth by plane. Flying may be the fastest, most practical way of travel, but it is also the most exhausting and uncivilized. Everybody wishes to get it over with as quickly as possible, which seems a poor inducement for going places. In the stateroom of a boat or in the compartment of a fast train, I enjoy privacy. On the plane, there is no elbowroom, even in first class; it's a waste of money to go first class. (On a boat, it pays to go first class.) Going west or east by plane, the abrupt change of time affects me for days after my arrival. In New York, I fall asleep in the middle of the day and I wake up long before dawn, listening to the sounds of Manhattan. They go on forever, like the breakers of the ocean, but are much less soothing. Buses screech to a stop and start off again in low gear. Cars sound their horns. There is a siren and the clanging bells of a fire engine. The city is asleep, but tragedy remains awake.

If I arrive by boat, I can slide imperceptibly into the invigorating rhythm of New York. I can sleep after getting there. Somerset Maugham once told me that the only place where he felt completely relaxed was aboard ship, as soon as the soft trembling under his feet indicated they were off, and the coast, and the people and their problems, were receding into a haze, and there was the wonderful feeling of being lost in time and space. I've always loved ships, and I feel I am betraying an old love whenever I take a transatlantic plane. I tell myself that the boat trip takes "too long," but why am I in a hurry? I'm afraid of "getting restless" on a boat, but when I fly across the ocean, I look down and I wish I were there instead of up in the air. I'm afraid of eating too much on a boat, but nobody forces me to eat every meal. My defense crumbles as it often did when I was a young lawyer in Prague. Having convinced myself at last that I ought to take a boat, I hurriedly phone for my airplane reservation, any plane, and I begin to fret about the discomforts awaiting me. Delayed departures, cool voices from loudspeakers apologizing with no regret for mysterious delays, waiting in unfriendly transit lounges. At last, a human sardine squeezed in between fellow sardines. Inflight meals served at absurd times. Circling ominously through dark clouds before the pilot gets permission to land. Wondering whether one's suitcase will show up on the moving rubber band, and then having to carry it past the customs officers. Great fun.

The welcome that the world's greatest city (I mean New York) accords to its arrivals, unless they happen to get special treatment, like the Beatles and Mrs. Onassis, is calculated to break down the strongest ego, reminding us that all airplane travelers are born equal. My friend Herman Elkon once had to hand over his small basket with *fraises de bois* that he'd hopefully brought along from Paris. The customs men considered the wild strawberries a worse health hazard to New York City than the garbage collectors' strike.

It is Sunday. I like to arrive in New York on Sunday afternoon, when the city's blood pressure is low. It's easier to get acclimatized. Well-dressed people strolling on Park Avenue; enormous, shining cars; empty, peaceful crosstown streets; in front of a fire station, two firemen are sitting on folding chairs. An idyllic place, New York City. Who said this place wasn't safe anymore? No siren sounds, no police cars, no thugs. Tragedy has taken off for this Sunday afternoon. Or so I'm telling myself.

The unostentatious entrance of the Waldorf Towers with its tall, ostentatious doorman; one mustn't carry unobtrusiveness too far. In my room I sit down in the armchair by the window, looking out at New York, and already I'm feeling much better. I'm beginning to enjoy New York. A couple of dark new skyscrapers — this year the new ones are all dark — have gone up in front of the window since my last visit. It's getting more difficult than before to catch a glimpse of New York from up high. I get up, bending hard and stretching my neck, and now I can see a tiny sample of the East River. It's still there. Down below is a slice of Park Avenue, with the flower arrangements in the middle strip. Millions of dollars' worth of real estate spent for decorative purposes. Now comes the magic hour, when the lights go on in the windows, almost as arranged by computers. New York is a wonderful place — from the twenty-fifth floor. The trouble starts when one gets down to street level and gets involved with noise and traffic-jams and no taxis and dirt and rats (last year they had lots of rats down there), with cinders in your eyes, with problems and people.

I unpack, and get into the tub to get the smell and feel of airplane and travel out of my system. From the tub I have a fine view of the tall buildings of Manhattan. In India, I once saw a maharaja's tub made of black stone, with gold-plated faucets, but I prefer the tub with the view of Manhattan. The chimes of a nearby church sound six o'clock. It's midnight in Europe, and that's the way I feel. I get out of the tub and get dressed. I dial a Lehigh number. Shawn may be at home, working.

When I happen to arrive in New York on a weekday, I call the *New Yorker* office after checking in at the hotel, and then I walk over to Forty-third Street. I walk slowly, enjoying every moment of my first walk. I notice a hundred things that I'll take for granted the day after tomorrow. The new colors of the cars. The new shapes of the women's dresses, or un-dresses. The very short (or very long) coats. All men wearing the same sort of suit, the same sort of hat, with a narrower brim than I saw in Europe, where they are always a little behind in hatbrims, and other things. Several clowns playing Con Ed men cheerfully creating an improbable traffic jam with a roped-off hole in the pavement, in the middle of the street. The clowns laugh, enjoying themselves more than their public. The liquor stores with each bottle in the window having a price tag. No sense bringing in a bottle duty-free on the plane; it's almost as cheap here. New banks looking like restaurants, and new restaurants looking like banks. And everywhere, perfectly good buildings being torn down.

The receptionist at *The New Yorker* office hardly looks my way, taking me for granted. The black bulletin board with a typed notice: "Furnished Four-Room Apartment in the Village. Reasonable." A notice signed by William Shawn, about the office being closed on Thanksgiving Day. At the water cooler, I turn left. The photograph of Harold Ross on the wall; he is immensely alive, looking at me in his scowling way, probably telling me something I try hard to understand. At the end of the corridor, I walk into the last office on the right side, and there is Bill Shawn.

We shake hands a little formally, in the European manner. We never slap each others' backs, in the American manner. We never tell each other "Good to see you," because it's *really* good to see one another. I sit down in the hard chair by his desk, and now I feel back home, as though I hadn't been away at all.

We never seem to have trouble picking up where we left off, though I may have been away a year. There is no moment of sudden embarrassment, as there is sometimes between former friends or classmates who happen to run into each other and have nothing to say because there is nothing to be said. While I was abroad, I've remained in touch with Shawn, by cable. Years ago, we silently agreed (our agreements are unspoken, only the disagreements are discussed) to dispense with the hazards of transatlantic telephone calls, which leave in their wake doubts and misunderstandings. I'm bound to say the wrong things in such moments and to forget to mention the right ones, that will occur to me a minute after the call is completed. I wonder whether I expressed myself accurately, and I worry about the inflection of the voice at the other end.

The uttered word can never be revised; *semper aliquid haeret.* A cable can be rewritten before it is sent off. Cables are like manuscripts — to be pondered, drafted, revised, perhaps finally thrown away. No one can throw away a telephone conversation. Cables often contain mechanical errors that occur in transmission, as stubborn as the strange mistakes in books that proofreaders and editors overlook, and certainly the author, who is slightly blinded by the brilliance of his wit and wisdom and fails to notice the vast, empty stretches between the wit and the wisdom. In this age of Telstar and marvelous communications, Shawn's last cable said, COLD, and I know he didn't mean COLD. He didn't mean SOLD or TOLD either. Did he mean COULD or HOLD, or possibly BOLD, CALL, or PULL? He might have meant CANT. I hope he didn't.

In all these years, Shawn and I have managed to keep up our mutual enthusiams by cable. Enthusiasm is a tender, delicate thing, like freshly plucked *fraises de bois* that ought to be eaten at once, otherwise they lose their fragrance. Today's enthusiasm may be tomorrow's tedium. Enthusiasm is rare in these days of cold-blooded relationships between editors and writers, when ideas are contrived, assigned, produced, and bought like any other commodity. To make someone three thousand miles away share your enthusiasm about a new idea is getting increasingly difficult in our era of "perfect" communications. You can't "sell an idea" to Shawn as you sell it to a producer in Hollywood. You must convey your enthusiasm and the sources thereof.

Unfortunately, my own enthusiasm is often diffuse. I hopefully have an idea in search of a direction. Shawn not only senses my enthusiasm but knows exactly in which direction it should go. Once I told him at lunch I wanted to write about the London fog, its terrifying aspects, what fog does to people, how helpless they become. Shawn listened and nodded thoughtfully, looking down at his plate of Rice Krispies. We frequently lunch on breakfast food. He didn't see the Rice Krispies, though. He saw the dense, dirty, deluding London fog.

"Yes." He seemed to be talking to himself. "The lore and fascination of it. Turner and Whistler, Sherlock Holmes in Baker Street, Wilde, Galsworthy, Eliot. There is a fine description of the fog in Dickens's *Bleak House,* I think. . . . The story should have the beauty of the fog, and some of the dread." That was the way my fog piece eventually emerged, going in more than one direction. Shawn has belief in his enthusiasm, and he trusts his writers.

"If I couldn't get enthusiastic anymore, there would be no use going on," he once said.

Though Shawn rarely leaves his office at *The New Yorker* for any length of time — even when he is elsewhere, he remains at his office spiritually — he seems to instinctively sense much of what is going on not only in New York and its extended suburbs (Paris, London, Washington), but all over the world. I've heard people complain that *The New Yorker* runs too many European pieces. (I happen to think that they run too many Asiatic pieces.) Some say the magazine should be more concerned with New York. Shawn feels that what happens in Moscow, New Delhi, Prague, the Vatican City, and Berlin may affect New Yorkers more deeply than what happens in the Bronx or Westchester. (Ross admitted this to me at the end of the war, saying, "Editorial isolationism is finished.") Shawn publishes what "delights and satisfies" *him.*

Sitting with his back toward the windows, wearing warm clothes even during the New York summer, facing the white walls of his office, he is deeply aware of what happens in other parts of the world, of the emotional and intellectual climates there. He senses the innermost connections and the deeper truths which so many American correspondents and diplomats don't understand after staying abroad for years, because they really never left home.

Some editors go abroad periodically to get the "feel" of faraway places, but after their return they publish so much rubbish that I wonder what sort of feel they picked up. Shawn does his traveling in the up-holstered swivel chair in his office, a large corner room facing east and south, with few executive trimmings, rather a workshop of journalistic alchemy. The alchemist keeps law and order at the office. His desk is uncluttered; sometimes a new proof is lying there. Two towerlike files with manuscripts, letters, and proofs form the ramparts on his desk, and there are other impenetrable fortifications built of editorial material. The editor feels comfortable behind the defenses of his literary-journalistic castle. He doesn't mind the disturbing height of the towers, and works them down, page by page. He reads up to five hundred pages on a quiet weekend at home. He reads everywhere, just as a writer must write everywhere, and no excuse.

Piles of books are stacked high on a large table by the wall. A television set on a rolling stand is sometimes there, facing the desk. Along the left wall is a tan-striped sofa. At Shawn's right elbow is a typewriter, and the Second Edition of Merriam-Webster's New International Dictionary, on a small stand behind his chair. There are paperweights and jars with pencils on the desk, drawings and caricatures on the walls, and a picture painted by a child, inscribed "To Daddy from Wallace." Notably missing is the artificial sense of disorder that some publishers like to give their offices to convey what they think is an atmosphere of "literature."

The New Yorker might be a different magazine today if it had been founded in 1955 instead of 1925, but would it be a better magazine? "More provocative," a young man said to me the other day. He believes in New Journalism. To be with it. I asked him what New Journalism will be like at *The New Yorker*'s age. Will the New Journalists try to be interesting and thought-provoking week after week, occasionally long-winded and musty, to be sure, but then again, once in a while, inspiring and humorous? It is more effective to appear young and violent than middle-aged and mild. Provocative precocity now ranks higher with the readers than mellow maturity. At a time when style, value and quality have become almost dirty words, *The New Yorker* valiantly tries to present style, value and quality week after week.

The present trend is against its basic philosophy. The book publishers who considered publishing an occupation for civilized gentlemen are gone or were swallowed up by the giants. The greatest newspaper in New York and perhaps in the world is no longer what it was. Other symbols of quality — Harvard, the great foundations, the Metropolitan Opera, great old companies and great stores — have their problems, because they are The Establishment. They are not with it and popular support is no longer with them. *The New Yorker* keeps its image but there is no doubt that it is fighting a rearguard action against new communications media that are not devoted to style and quality, good writing and good editing. Instead they supply their customers with what is considered sensation, argument, sex, violence, lack of taste and cheapness.

Shawn regrets that he cannot print more humor in what was always a magazine of humor. Humor remains elusive. There is humor all over the country, but it gets increasingly harder to get it into a magazine. Today's humor is volatile, going into films, television, nightclub comedy. The editor wistfully thinks of the magazine's *belle époque* of humor, when Benchley, Perelman, Sullivan, Gibbs, Thurber, and White were writing at the same time. Rudolf Bing of the Metropolitan Opera feels that way about the Vienna Opera of his youth, when they had half a dozen great tenors there, around each of whom one could now build a season. No comparison is intended between humorists and tenors, who are among the most humorless people on earth. Both Bing and Shawn have been called "museum curators" for the way they run their respective institutions. At least, they are *nice* museums.

One of *The New Yorker*'s old contributors told me the other day, with some acerbity, that he'd never met Mr. Shawn. Shawn is disarmingly polite (Janet Flanner says that no one was ever able to go through a revolving door after Shawn), but he tries hard not to meet people. He has a passion for anonymity which is almost incompatible with the semipublic function of running *The New Yorker*. The editor's name appears only once a year, in very small print in the magazine's Statement of Ownership. He is not an officer or director or a consequential stockholder. He believes it's "psychologically better for an editor not to be financially involved." Occasionally, the editor's picture, and a story about *The New Yorker*, appear in a newsweekly such as *Time*, possibly with malice toward all. The citadel of group journalism is not lovingly disposed, corporationwise, toward the lofty castle of individual journalism, although many *Time*sters — privately — admire *The New Yorker*. Quite a few prominent writers for *Time* later left the magazine and became *New Yorker* contributors. No one of importance has gone in the opposite direction for any length of time.

Shawn doesn't attend cocktail parties, Truman Capote balls, "April in Paris," gastronomic dinners, or other splendid manifestations of the contemporary social spirit in New York. When he goes to a nightclub, it's mostly for music; he is a serious student of jazz. He doesn't believe in standing up with a glass in hand, listening to disjointed monologues; he likes old-fashioned conversation. At home in the Shawns' living room, we still talk with each other, not past one another. There are just a few friends, most of them connected with *The New Yorker*. Everybody is seated. It's unfashionable, nice, and not musty at all. Two walls of the living room are lined with bookshelves. One contains books by *New Yorker* authors, many of them dedicated to Shawn. There is a complete edition of bound *New Yorker* volumes, beginning with the first issue in 1925. Along the third wall is the piano, and a varying collection of musical instruments. The last time I was there a bass fiddle was leaning against the piano, and a violin was on it, and on the floor was a set of drums. Books and music, words and sounds are important in the Shawn home. A self-taught pianist who doesn't read music, Shawn plays the piano very well. Playing the piano relaxes him after reading close to a hundred thousand words a day, reading them with a deep sense of responsibility, knowing that each word was written with a little heart blood. Wallace, the older son, is an able violinist. Allen, the younger one, studies composition at Harvard. As a teen-ager, he was a musical *Wunderkind*, playing with me, often by sight, a sonata by Brahms, Debussy, César Franck.

During my annual visit to New York, we usually have an evening of music. My Stradivari doesn't like airplane travel, and Mrs. Shawn borrows a violin for me at Wurlitzer's. Sometimes she gets a beautiful old Italian fiddle, possibly Mrs. Wurlitzer's tribute to the editor's publishing my articles about beautiful old Italian fiddles. When Allen is in town, we play sonatas and something for two violins and piano, often ad hoc composed by Allen. I have more difficulty sight reading the modern composition than my two fellow players. Without Allen, we are restricted to duos for two violins. The literature is limited. The last time Wallace brought home some beautiful duos by Haydn that I hadn't known. Haydn could do anything he wanted. In one of the duos there was a lovely gypsy rhythm in the finale, very appropriate, since two of the friends present had just got married in the afternoon, and Haydn's gypsy tunes went well with the champagne.

Years ago, after *The New Yorker* published Geoffrey Hellman's profile of Alfred Knopf, Knopf invited Shawn for lunch. Later, Alfred Knopf, then my publisher, told me he'd crossed Shawn off his list because the editor had failed to heed the Olympian summons. Having reached myself a point of no return in social life where I was crossed off many lists, all the way from Vienna to Los Angeles, because I failed to heed summonses, I naturally sympathized with the editor. I told Knopf that Shawn doesn't like to come to dinner either. He once called us off, on short notice, and my wife was upset, having baked her special chocolate cake for him. Once the Shawns came to lunch, on a Sunday, when we briefly resided at our sixteen-acre estate in Redding Ridge, Connecticut, the only estate I ever owned. I sold it, being unable to cope with the problems of absentee ownership. Much of the sixteen acres was primeval Connecticut woodland with frogs, skunks, and snakes. I would love to keep half a dozen estates in as many countries, like Mr. Getty, a fellow contributor to *Playboy*, but as a writer (and financier) I am not quite in Mr. Getty's class.

We were about to leave for Europe, and Shawn implied that the Sunday lunch was a one-time thing, as they say around *The New Yorker* in the case of a certain bonus, "not necessarily to be repeated." It was a nice lunch. Afterwards the editor spoke dreamily about Ann's chocolate cake. Years later, when Shawn and I celebrated our conveniently close, late-August birthdays in a house in Bronxville, that the Shawns rent every summer, we took another chocolate cake along, which was a seasonal mistake. The cake melted on the floor of the car.

I wistfully remember our estate in Connecticut. A fine house, and a beautiful front lawn bordered by a stone fence. The address was Sunset Hill Road, which sounds better for an Edwardian novelist than for a *New Yorker* reporter. From my second-floor bedroom-study I had a beautiful view of the Blue Hills that Mark Twain had loved.

The front lawn looked Ye Merry Old England when it had just been mowed, but after a couple of weeks it reverted to not-so-merry New England. I tried to cut the lawn myself but didn't get along with the mower. We had to phone a man called Ben, who asked more money for the job than the head gardener of Louis XIV had been paid in Versailles.

I understood why you have to be a writer of Mr. Getty's (financial) standing to afford several homes with large front lawns. Something was wrong with the front porch, which was sagging a few inches every year. An expert came, told us there were termites in the wooden beams, left a bill, and departed. A friend who spent a night in the guest room was bitten by a squirrel that had come in through the window. Anyway, that was what his lawyer wrote. We lost a friend and had no houseguests afterwards.

The squirrel must have come from the woods in the rear of the house, where I rarely went, and only in daytime. We had privacy — one could barely see the next house — but paid for it dearly. Something was wrong with the cesspool, or with the water pump, or with the electric current, which was whimsical, to say the least. A locally respected expert on pumps once explained to me that our water pump was too close to the cesspool (if I understood him correctly) until no one knew what was what. I asked him whether that meant that the cesspool was diverted in our water system. He asked me what I did for a living.

"I'm a writer," I said.

"Oh," he said, looking exactly like my uncles in Ostrava and the cops in Westwood Village. Once a writer, always a writer.

Another expert whom I asked about the bizarre behavior of our electricity shrugged and said maybe the skunks were playing with the wires. *He* knew I was a writer, and didn't even try to make sense. I wished Mark Twain were still around. He would know what to do. I sadly concluded I wasn't made for country life in New England.

I couldn't get acclimatized to the rhythm of social life in Fairfield County, which fluctuated between solitude from Monday to Friday and togetherness from Friday night to Monday morning. Solitude meant puritanism, while togetherness was strictly abandon. I was afraid to wind up writing about the local Madison Avenue gentry, which other writers could do much better. I finally decided to give up the pleasures of a country squire in New England and go back to Europe as a correspondent for *The New Yorker*, which was really my field.

Shawn avoids meeting people whose profiles he published. He feels he knows them better from the manuscript than after a personal acquaintance, which shows his trust in his writers. The explanation wouldn't convince Alfred Knopf or anybody else whose profile was published, but Shawn was right. A successful profile often tells more about a person than the person might want to know about himself. It isn't a question of doing an inside job, or getting the skeletons out of the closet. In the upper corridors of 25 West Forty-third Street it is a foregone conclusion that there is a skeleton in practically everybody's closet, so why bother? The profile writer must be an interested listener, a thorough reporter, and something of an analyst; and he should be able to write a story.

Once Shawn didn't mind meeting a man whose profile I'd written. The subject of the profile, incidentally, had some difficulty reading it because his English was limited. I hope this isn't going to upset Alfred Knopf, whose English is unlimited. Shawn had asked me to do a profile on Henri Soulé, the proprietor of New York's Le Pavillon, possibly the best restaurant that has ever existed in New York, the United States, and the western hemisphere, owing to Soulé's exacting standards of ambiance, service, and gastronomy. Though Le Pavillon was very French, it was also very American. Shawn and I had talked about "bridge" pieces, touching upon the cultures of both Old Europe and Young America, and about people building such bridges. Soulé was a bridge builder. He'd been born in the Basque country near the French-Spanish border, learned his exacting profession in Paris, came to this country to manage the French Pavilion at the New York World's Fair in March, 1939, and eventually opened *his* Pavillon in 1941, blending French elegance and his know-how of food and wine with American wealth and sophistication.

When I first met Soulé, he treated me with the characteristic arrogance he displayed toward the richest, most powerful people in America who bothered him for a good table. He soon changed, though, when he realized that I knew something about his profession. He had a pro's respect for a fellow pro. We saw each other after the profile had been published and became friends, and he told me many good stories that should have been in the profile. One gets some of the best stories *after* the profiles are published.

A few weeks after the publication of "The Ambassador at the Sanctuary" — Soulé being the "ambassador of French cuisine in New York," and the "sanctuary" the small front room whose seven tables were socially the most desirable in the whole restaurant — Soulé drove up one Sunday morning in front of our house in Connecticut, by non-invitation. He didn't wear his tuxedo uniform, and looked unfamiliar. He wore a broadly checkered English tweed jacket, a French trenchcoat with a belt tightly fastened around his expanding middle, and a hat with a tiny brim that he wore at a rakish angle, as many Parisians do after bumping into other Parisians in the Métro. In fact, he looked exactly what he once was — a noted maître d'hôtel from the unforgettable Café de Paris at 41, Avenue de l'Opéra, where he'd taken a post-graduate course in his profession.

A liveried chauffeur opened the long black Cadillac limousine, and Soulé got out, royally surveying the countryside. The chauffeur opened the trunk. Soulé came in, followed by the chauffeur, and watched like a benevolent Oriental potentate as his gifts were displayed on the floor of the living room. A magnificent doll for Poppy; unfortunately, the doll was taller than Poppy, then four years old, and somehow Poppy never got over her fear of "Annabelle." A small lapel watch for my wife. A case of Château Cheval Blanc 1937 and a case of Pommery champagne for me.

Having deposited his offerings, the chauffeur departed. Soulé took off his trenchcoat and sat down in the living room that was filled with a mixture of surprise, pleasure, and embarrassment. I didn't dare explain to him that *The New Yorker*'s policy against pre- or post-profile gifts was stricter even than President Eisenhower's in Washington after the affair of Governor Adams. There you may still accept an Easter ham or a Christmas turkey, but not up on the nineteenth floor.

Soulé stayed for lunch — there was another chocolate cake, which he enjoyed — and departed in the limousine, after his legs had been carefully wrapped in a camel's-hair blanket. He often reminded me of another great Frenchman. He had, in fact, once ended a labor dispute with a union unilaterally by proclaiming, "Le Pavillon, *c'est moi!*," and arrogantly stalked out of the meeting.

I took my problem to Shawn. He decided that it would unnecessarily hurt and anger Soulé if the gifts were returned. They couldn't be considered accessorial bribery after the fact, since the story was already published. Shawn further eased my guilty conscience when he sipped a little of Soulé's champagne during the memorable lunch at our house. The champagne is gone, but I still have two bottles of the magnificent Château Cheval Blanc in my mini-cellar in Vienna, as I write this.

Later, the Shawns went to dinner with us at Le Pavillon. The editor was impressed by the ambassador who was haughty toward people of wealth and social position but often warmhearted toward his less prominent friends. Shawn noticed the thoroughly professional manner in which Soulé ran his place — his efficiency and judgment, taste and tact, attention to detail and sense of perfection. Both Soulé and Shawn were trying, each in his own way, to do the best they could. Like Shawn, Soulé knew a lot about human nature; otherwise he couldn't have gone that far in his profession.

During the years that followed, Soulé often asked me to drop in at Le Pavillon as though it were a place where one dropped in, and when I refused because he wouldn't let me pay my bill, he was angry. I liked to go for dinner at his home, on Sunday night, when the restaurant was closed. He lived in a small apartment on Park Avenue. There was no dining room because he didn't need one. He would set up a table in the small entrance hall, next to the kitchen. Le Pavillon's habitués wouldn't have recognized the feared ambassador. He wore an apron and had his shirt sleeves rolled up, as he was lovingly basting a large fillet of beef in the oven. A fine fragrance of butter drifted out of the kitchen.

He had brought from Le Pavillon a choice tin of caviar which we called *"le caviar du commandant,"* as on a boat where the finest caviar is reserved for the captain's table at the captain's dinner. Soulé was the toughest caviar buyer in America, and drove his suppliers to drink. The caviar would be mellow, almost unsalted, delicately flavored, each egg separately defined. There is nothing wrong with eating such caviar in a tiny entrance hall. There was chilled Polish vodka. Soulé ate a lot of caviar; he said that only people who loved caviar could buy and serve it properly. With the meat he served a baked potato which, he knew, I couldn't get in Europe. A fine Château Cheval Blanc or Château Pétrus, often in magnum, was served with it. It was a dinner fit for a king.

Soulé died in 1966, after surveying the lunch service at his Côte Basque, formerly the "original" Pavillon. He died right next to the sanctuary, like a great actor dying on the stage. Shawn sorrowfully cabled me the sad news.

The Making of a New Yorker Profile

EVERY *New Yorker* PROFILE opens up a new world for its writer. Profiles are not mere articles but books skillfully condensed into article form. The world of Henri Soulé, the restaurateur, is different from the world of George Szell, the conductor; of Emil Herrmann, who knew so much about violins, and Abe Feder, who does miracles with light; of Fritz Frey, who owns his private little empire on a mountaintop in Switzerland, and of Mario Buccellati, the twentieth-century Benvenuto Cellini in Milan, who died before his profile was published; of the world of Vienna, the city of the baroque, and of Prague, the mystical city. These ideas, and others, grew out of my curiosity and enthusiasm. Some were suggested by Shawn or were evolved mutually. Our interests are catholic, and we are both fascinated by unusual projects. (An idea remains a "project" until it becomes a "manuscript.")

New Yorker profile subjects are suggested by writers or staff members and outlined in "the book," one of the few office secrets I was permitted to see. A profile remains "reserved" for a writer who gets the go-ahead from Shawn, even if he doesn't work on it for years. Only if the writer releases "his" subject, it may be assigned to another writer. Some very prominent citizens would be shocked to know how many years they remained in cold storage.

Not all manuscripts that are accepted and paid for get published; a drawback of our insecure profession. (Another painful drawback in the life of a foreign correspondent is a sense of unsplendid isolation as he waits with mounting concern for the word from New York and gets nothing but editorial silence that soon takes on an ominous dimension. It doesn't help to rationalize that the editor is probably busy with another of his hundred writers or thousand problems.) Being only human, we writers like to get paid *and* published, but we are defeated by the mechanics of magazine life. A topical piece gets overtaken by the events, the protagonist fades into oblivion, or the editor is no longer as enthusiastic about the piece as he was when he bought it. Writers are haunted by the fear of drying out and having no more ideas. Editors are haunted by the nightmare of having nothing to print in their next issue. They protect themselves by building up a backlog (a "bank") of material. Unfortunately, manuscripts, unlike precocious children and young wines, do not improve with age.

Many of my ideas developed into "projects" during lunch with Shawn. At one time we would escape into the relative serenity of the Ritz-Carlton, but nowadays Manhattan traffic precludes the pleasant excursion from West Forty-third to East Sixty-third Street. We walk across West Forty-fourth into the dim, noisy dining room of the Algonquin Hotel (the Rose Room), an odd place to work up enthusiasm, in spite of its historical associations with *The New Yorker*. I try hard but not always successfully to disregard the disturbing voices around me. I haven't been able to acquire the denizen's protective deafness toward distracting noises. The waiters are members of the secret antiliterary underground who always interfere at a crucial moment. The menu is

thrust against my chest, or I am offered more coffee just as we approach
a subtle meeting of minds. Disconcerting fumes — garlic or poison gas
— drift over from a neighboring table. Once we couldn't stand it, got
up, and escaped into the hall. Things have worked out over the years,
but I wonder what we could come up with if we could miraculously
escape for lunch into a sunlit Italian piazza or the terrace of an inn overlooking the Alps. Nowadays we are trying to beat the system, and the
noise at the Algonquin, by going to lunch at two-fifteen, when we are
almost alone and the headwaiter is lunching at a nearby table.

In the late 1950's, Shawn would sometimes talk about the moral and
political crisis of the Western world, and encouraged me to think of
profile subjects, MEN WHO COULD START FROM SCRATCH AND BUILD A
NEW AND BETTER WORLD, as he once cabled. They would have to be
idealistic realists, or realistic idealists, WHO ARE SPRINGING UP ALL OVER
THE WORLD TO COPE WITH THE CRISIS WE ARE GOING THROUGH.

I found several constructive idealists in and around Vienna. There
was Hermann Gmeiner, an impoverished medical student from Vorarl-
berg who became deeply concerned about the world's many homeless
children. He built a vision and forty-two dollars into the SOS Children's
Villages all over the world. Two years after my *New Yorker* profile, "A
House Called Peace," had been published, Gmeiner told me happily that
he'd received "at least a couple of million dollars" from rich people who
had read it. Several years later, I wrote about a constructive idealist
from America, the late Maurice Pate, then the head of UNICEF, the
United Nations International Children's Emergency Fund; Herbert
Hoover had called him "the most efficient human angel I ever met." In
Vienna I met Otto Molden, who in 1945 founded the European Forum
in the secluded Tyrolean village of Alpbach, which is still one of the
most important intellectual meeting places on the Continent. An idealist
of a different kind was Helmut Qualtinger, playwright, actor, philosopher, nonconformist, and Austria's greatest living satirist, who helped
to create and performed the character of "Herr Karl,"

. . . a scoundrel with a macabre charm that many Austrians and many foreigners as well find irresistible. He is at once dangerous and deplorable, fascinating and pathetic, and is literally a poor devil — poor and a devil. Outwardly easygoing and *gemütlich*, he is filled with pity for himself but has none to spare for others.

Not surprisingly, perhaps, Qualtinger is not *persona grata* in official Vienna, and neither am I now. Professional patriots accused us of trying to destroy the legend of "the golden Viennese heart," but many young people wrote to tell me their approval.

Alfred Knopf, the wine expert, introduced me to Alexis Lichine, whom he called "an expert among experts." Lichine was then the only American who owned a vineyard in Burgundy and controlled some châteaux in Bordeaux. He was obsessed with wine, and was an amusing raconteur. I suggested a profile but Shawn hesitated, cabling: THE SUBJECT OF WINE HAS BECOME A LITTLE TEDIOUS. Wine was becoming a popular topic of conversation, and men exchanged vintage cards instead of girls' telephone numbers. Several months later, I wrote to Shawn that I'd had several letters from Lichine, and still believed he would make a good story. He knew many things about wine that I'd never read anywhere. Shawn, never dogmatic, cabled: YES YOU HAVE CONVINCED ME THAT LICHINE COULD BE A DIFFERENT KIND OF WINE STORY AND A GOOD ONE, and told me to go ahead, and I did:

Lichine often forgets faces and places, but he never forgets wines; he can recall exactly what wines were served at a certain dinner party years ago, though for the life of him he can't remember the name of his hostess, or what she looked like. . . . He talks, thinks and drinks wine all day and he dreams wine when he finally falls asleep.

At a dinner party of local wine growers in Bordeaux, Lichine had been given an unlabeled bottle of wine, was told only that it was "true and a great year," and was asked to guess the wine. He took a deep breath. He knew his personal prestige and the prestige of the United States of America was at stake.

> I identified this wine first as Bordeaux, then as a Médoc, and then a Saint-Estèphe. You start with the region and work down through the district to the commune. Then I turned to the question of the year. It wasn't one of the '40s or '50s — that was elementary — and I knew it wasn't a '34 or '37, the two great years of that decade. It just didn't have the right characteristics. And gradually I became convinced that it could only be from one of the four great years of the '20s — a '24, a '26, a '28, or a '29. I eliminated '26 and '28 because the wines of those years have a pronounced hardness and this wine didn't. It might be a weak '24 or a soft '29. I tasted again. The wine was full and round and slowly dying out, which is typical of the '29, so I eliminated the '24. Now, then, where did it come from, exactly? There are only three great châteaux in the commune of Saint-Estèphe — Château Calon-Ségur, Château Montrose, and Château Cos-d'Estournel. In a second I eliminated Montrose. Thirty seconds more and I eliminated Calon-Ségur. I can't really explain what goes on in my head at such times. My brain is filled with names and years, and the ones I eliminate just drop out, as if they were falling through a strainer, and in the end only one name and one year remain. So I said, "This is a Cos-d'Estournel '29." And it was.

My love of music made me explore the mystery of the human voice (the subject of the profile was George London), the enigmatic profession of conducting (done around George Szell), the secrets of an orchestra (the Cleveland), the art of the pianist (Artur Rubinstein) and of the violinist (Isaac Stern). I sat in the orchestra pit during a Broadway performance of *My Fair Lady*, conducted by Franz Allers, who became a profile. I made a pilgrimage to Eisenstadt, in the Austrian Burgenland, where Joseph Haydn had spent thirty years in the service of Prince Esterházy. In Zelazowa Wola, near Warsaw, I heard Chopin's music played in the house where he'd once lived, and I understood why his music became a political and national force in Poland. I went to Verdi's home in Sant' Agatha and stood in the sunlit room with the piano where he'd written the incredibly beautiful music of *Otello*. At the house Wahnfried in Bayreuth, there was the piano used by Richard Wagner who wrote, at about the same time, his *Parsifal*.

My reminiscences as a member of the claque at the Vienna State Opera were among my first stories that *The New Yorker* published. After the Second World War, in Vienna, I wrote about the last days of the opera house, that had been set afire by five American bombs, on March 12, 1945, and the astonishing renaissance of opera in the cold, hungry city. The reopening of the rebuilt Vienna Opera, in 1955, gave me a chance to analyze the mysterious science of acoustics that still baffles the experts. (If money could buy good acoustics, there would be better sound in New York's Philharmonic Hall.) In Barcelona, I heard a group of artists from the Vienna Opera who put on a performance of my favorite Mozart masterpiece, *The Marriage of Figaro*, at the Gran Teatro del Liceo, that began at ten P.M. before an empty auditorium and ended after two in the morning, with some aficionados sitting in their inherited boxes on the stage *behind* the curtain. I went to Bayreuth, where they perform Wagner at four in the afternoon. And eventually, I became curious about the business of running the world's largest opera house, and wrote about Rudolf Bing, the Metropolitan's general manager. In writing for *The New Yorker*, as in life, one thing leads to another.

I have always loved ships, possibly because I come from a landlocked country. *The New Yorker* published my reminiscences as a ship's musician, which became part of *Looking for a Bluebird*, my first book in America. Among the ships I'd worked on was the *de Grasse*,

> . . . celebrated for the lightheartedness of her atmosphere and the sturdiness of her action. During the summer of 1929, when I was the second violinist in the vessel's five-man orchestra, . . . I remember particularly a westbound crossing that was just one big party. Passengers were gambling, singing, drinking champagne at breakfast, running around in various stages of disarray all day long and most of the night, and joyfully weaving about in other people's cabins.

When I boarded the rejuvenated *de Grasse* after the war, in 1948, this time as a passenger, Robert Bellet, formerly the assistant purser and the orchestra's boss, had become the chief purser. There were other crew members who had started their careers in the late 1920's and had now reached positions of rank. If I'd remained a ship's musician, I might now be the French Line's *Generalmusikdirektor*, a sort of itinerant Karajan. Tony Prothès, once a colleague of mine, was in charge now, playing the double bass and the drums. One night I sat down with the orchestra, and we played all the old tunes again — "Always," "Singin' in the Rain," "Valencia!," and "I Can't Give You Anything But Love, Baby" — in an orgy of nostalgia.

It was quite a crossing. Ted and Vera Patrick were aboard. He was the editor of *Holiday* and liked to have *New Yorker* writers do an occasional article for him, and one night, in the bar, we talked about ideas. Everybody was in the bar much of the time during that trip, or we were in the stateroom of Ted Patrick's neighbors from Quogue, the Edwin J. Harragans, who had two five-gallon containers there, such as were then used in gas stations. They didn't contain gasoline, though. One was filled with martini cocktail, the other with manhattan — useful good-bye presents left by some friends. Eventually the containers were empty, but the bar of the *de Grasse* wasn't. Vincent, the barman, officially closed at midnight, but business-as-unusual went on in the small room behind the bar. Elliot Paul was there, reminiscing about the last time he saw Paris, and Freddie McEvoy, who later went down at sea with his boat. Vincent brought silver platters with small sandwiches arranged in artful patterns that the French Line offered to late drinkers as a public service. As I said, it was quite a crossing, and some people (I am one of them) think of it with a sense of nostalgia and intense regret. Maybe someday I'll write a book about it. Or maybe better not.

The *de Grasse* was then the only French Line boat doing the New York–Le Havre run, and the company was training its choice personnel that would later take over the *Ile de France* and the *Liberté*. Former maîtres d'hôtel were working as waiters. The library steward was the former *chef de reception* from the *Normandie*. The *saucier* had been chef on the *Ile de France*; there was no doubt about it after tasting his sauces. It was as if Heifetz, Oistrakh, and Milstein would play in the first-violin section of the New York Philharmonic.

The atmosphere was faintly reminiscent of the summer of 1929. Some people were again drinking champagne at breakfast and all day long, and others were "joyfully weaving about" in other people's cabins. (I'm quoting myself.) How I managed to take notes I don't remember, but I later wrote an article about the memorable trip which some people, including myself, have since tried hard to forget. In 1951, I was on the newly refitted *Ile de France*, making her postwar maiden voyage from Le Havre to New York. John O'Reilly, of the *Herald Tribune*, wrote, "For some undefined reason, the *Ile de France* has always evoked more sentiment than any of the other great liners which have entered the Port of New York."

I could have given O'Reilly half a dozen good reasons. I'd been aboard twenty-two years earlier, on the *Ile*'s maiden voyage, when she was called the Rue de la Paix of the Atlantic, and her suites, cuisine, and passenger list were the envy of all other shipping companies. We'd played very little music then. There was no need to create a joyful mood. The *Ile de France* had its ambiance built in, "a blend of broad good humor and the charm and excitement of a champagne picnic."

In 1957, I was aboard the *Liberté*, doing a profile of my old friend Robert Bellet, a five-star man in his profession, who was then the chief purser of the French Line's flagship, and the reason why many people chose the *Liberté*. Bellet was unsurpassed in his ability to create an indefinable something that we used to call *l'atmosphère Transat*, "as intangible yet as unmistakable as the tang of salt in the air." Tony Prothès, with whom I'd worked in ship's orchestras, was also aboard, as the *Liberté*'s musical director, with three orchestras under his command. He'd just shelled out a fortune for orchestrations of the *My Fair Lady* music, but he said they were still playing the old hits we'd played together.

"Imagine, kids who weren't even born in 1928 have come around and asked us to play 'I Can't Give You Anything But Love, Baby,' " Tony said. He looked into space. "Somehow it makes me happy. You know what I mean, *mon vieux?*" Yes, I did.

For many years I wanted to write the profile of a symphony orchestra, "the most beautiful, most sensitive, and also the most complex, most mysterious musical instrument."

Ideally, a perfectly co-ordinated orchestra is the supreme achievement of teamwork, an integrated organism that breathes, emotes, acts and re-acts like *one* human being — a super-human being with one hundred hearts and minds devoted to the spirit of the music and with two hundred arms bringing alive its sound. The orchestra players may be different in their intellectual outlook and emotional approach to the music; they don't agree with each other on personal, political, social and musical matters; they may envy, dislike, hate one another. Not all of them are technically or musically on the same level. Some are idealistic and think first of the music while others think primarily of making money. But when they sit down to make beautiful music together, they mysteriously become one heart and one soul, a triumph of Western civilization: an orchestra.

It is difficult enough for any one musician to play every note of his complicated part at the right time in the right place at the right length in the right pitch with the right tonal power. It is miraculous when this is done simultaneously by one hundred players. Intellectual concentration, emotional discipline and muscular prowess are needed. The orchestra musician must have talent and skill, self-denial and self-control. For brief periods of time he suddenly emerges as a "momentary protagonist" with a personality of his own, and just as suddenly he must give up his personality and submerge into the orchestra's collective life. Some very good instrumentalists are unable to make this adjustment. They will never become good orchestra musicians. The players must understand what the conductor wants, and be able to execute his demands; but not everybody has the ability of putting himself into somebody else's mood at the flip of a stick.

Shawn liked the idea very much. Ideally, it should be an abstract piece on *the* orchestra, an anonymous body, but this might create a problem of unreality. We agreed that it would combine abstract and concrete elements. I'd thought of doing the piece around the Berlin Philharmonic, which Herbert von Karajan molded into one of the great orchestras of the world, but this might involve me in German profundities and metaphysical exercises. And I wasn't sure whether Karajan, a brilliant conductor with a sense of personal splendor, might not be more interested in himself, the orchestra builder, than in the orchestra he'd built. My final choice was the Cleveland Orchestra, which musicians all over the world consider an orchestras' orchestra. After over twenty years under George Szell, the Cleveland had become a completely integrated group of virtuoso players, combining some of the finest things in American music with a deep understanding of European music making. Above all, I could count on the understanding and assistance of George Szell. Not all profiles are done with the cooperation of the people to be profiled; sometimes one encounters considerable resistance.

I arrived in Cleveland one night from Europe and met Szell the next morning, a Tuesday, at nine o'clock in his office at Severance Hall. The first orchestra rehearsal for the week's subscription concert, on Thursday night, would begin at ten o'clock. I told Szell I would try to finish my research by Thursday night.

He seemed surprised. I explained to him that I didn't want to stay too long. I had to do the story while my powers of observation were sharpened and my sense of excitement alive. I suggested to him that I attend every rehearsal. In between I would talk to a cross section of the orchestra musicians, asking them, "What *is* an orchestra?" He said he would suggest several players who were especially articulate, but I was free to talk to anyone else.

I soon realized that I hadn't anticipated the main problem: many musicians seemed unable to analyze their work. They couldn't explain *why* they did a certain thing at a certain moment. They expressed themselves clearly about their craft and their instruments, but couldn't answer certain questions. I asked them what happened, for instance, at the beginning of Beethoven's Fifth Symphony, when the conductor gives the preparatory beat and the orchestra comes in, simultaneously and miraculously, with its ta-ta-ta-*tah*. Exactly *when* did they come in? Under Wilhelm Furtwängler, a great musician with an erratic beat, the members of the Berlin Philharmonic would say, "We come in when Furtwängler's downbeat reaches the second button of his white vest."

The truth was that because Furtwängler was a powerful personality, they all came in beautifully, at the same split second.

One of the old-timers in the Cleveland Orchestra, Hyman Schandler, a member of the second-violin section, thought it over. He said, "At the beginning of Beethoven's Fifth, Szell gives his upbeat, and somehow we all come in at the same time."

Could he elaborate on "somehow"?

He seemed puzzled. "I never tried to analyze it. We've worked together so many years and are so well integrated, and listen to each other, until we *feel* each other. . . . When you think of a hundred players doing it with absolute precision at the same moment, it staggers the imagination."

"Do you think it's intuition, a mystery?"

He shook his head. "No. It is a sudden occurrence, the result of hard work and playing together for years. . . ."

Later, I talked with many other men, building the mosaic-like parts of my story. No one could convincingly explain the mystery of the ta-ta-ta-*tah*. Szell said, "Many elements of conducting defy rational explanation, such as the simultaneous attack by a hundred players."

The most important piece on the week's program was Richard Strauss's tone poem *Don Quixote,* a beautiful and demanding work that is a real test for a great orchestra and a great conductor. During the rehearsals, I watched with a mounting sense of fascination how Szell created the complex musical structure, blending all details into a whole until he had built "a cathedral out of pebbles," as he defined it. During the general rehearsal on Thursday morning, I sat among the musicians in the rear of the orchestra to get the frog's-eye view. By that time I was filled with music and excitement, and was completely immersed in the orchestra's inner life.

I listened to the Thursday night concert in the conductor's box, with

Mrs. Szell. When Szell lowered his arms after the final *pianissimo* chords of *Don Quixote*, there was a long moment of breathless silence in the hall — a greater tribute to the work and to the performers than a sudden cascade of applause. I knew that I had learned much about "the most complex musical instrument."

There was much additional research, reading and studying, until I started writing the piece. It took more than two months. After several drafts and revisions, I had one hundred and twenty-seven pages — more than *The New Yorker* could use. Shawn liked the profile. I had some second thoughts, however. The efficient checkers at *The New Yorker* would do a thorough and occasionally exasperating job, but this was a highly technical subject. No one knew as much about it as George Szell, who has been called "the most intellectual among today's conductors." I suggested showing the manuscript to Szell for the sake of accuracy. I knew that Szell would not attempt to exercise censorship. He has too much respect for the writer's craft. Shawn agreed.

In the summer of 1968, Szell came to Salzburg to conduct at the festival. I called him from Vienna and asked him to read the manuscript, and could I mail it to him? He called me two days later and called the piece "a work of art." Praise from Szell, a perfectionist, doesn't come easy, but he tempered my satisfaction, saying there were "quite a few matters that needed to be corrected," and promised to write me. This is his letter:

20th August 1968

My dear Joe,

I am returning herewith the photostat of your Orchestra Profile, with my comments, written in ordinary lead pencil on separate sheets. As I have not used reference numbers and as I have made those notes primarily as an "aide-memoire" for myself to be used at our next meeting, I would prefer it if you would just keep them as well as the copy of your piece locked away until we meet in November and can deal with the matter at leisure.

As I told you over the phone, your original contribution is quite remarkable in its insight, sensitivity and happy formulation. It might conceivably be the best or one of the best things you have written. Just for this reason I find it imperative that it should not be marred by inaccuracies, mistakes, misquotes, confused compilation of source material etc. etc. Of these there are plenty. All this must be carefully and rigorously corrected and cleansed, otherwise there is a tremendous danger of your outstanding work being virtually invalidated by statements which can be challenged easily and successfully. I shall not accept the rejoinder that you are writing for the public at large and not for the expert. In the first place, the public has a right to be informed accurately, in the second place it would not take experts to point out many things which are simply not so. Furthermore, words put into the mouth of people they never uttered, are a dangerous thing. This, alas, can happen when statements are notated with half an ear listening or when a compilation is made of a number of statements which amounts to a contraction. I do believe in absolute accuracy — especially if statements are quoted verbatim, between quotes. Any change or transcription of the order of words has to be checked most carefully whether they modify, convert or subvert the intended meaning.

Generally speaking, I find most impressive those sections where you write from immediate, personal experience, including your talks with various people, whereas I find the middle section where you go into general matters, quoting or paraphrasing existing literature, weakest and in need of most serious scrutiny — or perhaps even of wholesale omission.

I hope you won't mind my being so completely candid. I feel
I owe it to a real friend whom I admire sincerely.

My best to you, as always.

Ever fondly

George

Szell returned the manuscript with seven pages of penciled notes.
Some were mere additions and clarifications. ("On page 5, after your
sentence, 'It takes years to build up an orchestra and decades to make
it great,' I would add, 'and it can be ruined in a fortnight.' ") On page
forty-one I'd written, "Scientific research has established that the educated human ear hears any imprecision lasting longer than fifty milli-
seconds, one twentieth of a second." Szell wrote, "This must be re-
phrased. As it stands, it does not make sense. Suggest '. . . that the
educated human ear accepts as simultaneous what is not further apart
than fifty milli-seconds.' " If he were not a great conductor, he might
be a fine editor.

When I called Szell "a first-chair conductor who addresses himself
during rehearsal mainly to the first-chair men, expecting them to explain
his wishes to the rest of the men," Szell wrote, "Incorrect, although
perhaps said by some." My sentence "There are more fiddlers than
oboists available," was called "a dangerous misstatement!!" Another
sentence was "partly incorrect, partly incomplete, partly irrelevant,
some essentials missing." Maybe he wouldn't be only a fine editor but
a severe critic. By the time I'd studied Szell's notes, I felt exactly as
generations of suffering orchestra musicians have felt during rehearsals
under Szell, when they fervently wished they were elsewhere, though
they knew he was right.

Several months later, I talked to George Szell in Vienna about the
manuscript. He said *now* he was satisfied with it.

Obviously, writing a *New Yorker* profile is always an experience, and sometimes more. At best, it may lead to a permanent friendship between the profile subject and the writer — a considerable bonus for a reserved man of middle age who doesn't make friends easily anymore. It happened to me several times in the past twenty years, possibly because I never attempted to write about people whom I instinctively dislike. I gave up several projects when I was unable to establish psychological contact with my subject. I leave the negative approach to the stiletto experts. The most brilliant of them was Wolcott Gibbs, who wrote his profile of Henry Luce in *Time* style, with the sentences running backward.

Only one man has made a point of not talking to me since his profile was published. I regret it because I like Artur Rubinstein as a human being and admire him as an artist. The experience taught me never to show a person galley proofs before publication. Many people are afflicted with proof fright at the sight of galleys with their name on them. The printed words seem sinister and inexorable to them, and they regret they let themselves become involved, and now it's too late, and fate, or whatever it is, will take its course. . . .

Working on the Rubinstein profile had been an unmitigated delight. I went to see him in Paris, and spent a fine day in his beautiful house (next to the villa where Claude Debussy died). Mrs. Rubinstein, a first-rate cook, had prepared a fine lunch; I remember the delicious mushroom soup, a Polish specialty. Rubinstein, in great form, ate a lot and talked amusingly, and he had several glasses of champagne, though he had a concert that night. In the afternoon, he took a nap. Mrs. Rubinstein and I went to the food market to do some shopping for the party after his concert. In the evening, on our way to the Théâtre des Champs-Elysées, something went wrong with the windshield wiper of the car. Mrs. Rubinstein, who was driving, got out to fix the wiper, asking Rubinstein and me to stay in the car. It was very cold, and the heater didn't work very well, and Rubinstein had forgotten his gloves. He was to play in half an hour. The very thought made me nervous, but he was perfectly relaxed, sitting quietly and a little remote, an angelic expression on his face. Perhaps he was already in the music. I offered him my gloves, but he smiled and shook his head.

When we arrived at the theater, it was rather late, and everybody backstage was nervous except Artur Rubinstein. He rubbed his hands, and greeted a few people, and a few minutes later he walked out on the stage, sat down at the piano, and began to play. He played like an angel, assuming that there is such a wonderful pianist among the angels up there. The final selection on the program was Chopin's Andante Spianato et Grande Polonaise, opus 22, and as he played the andante, one of Chopin's loveliest compositions, I got the feeling that the vast auditorium had shrunk to the size of a living room, and that Rubinstein was playing his cherished Chopin for a few intimate friends instead of twenty-seven hundred people. With parted lips and head thrown back, he gazed upward like a man in a trance. Then the music stopped, and for some time there was silence, while the audience groped its way back to reality. When at last the spell was broken, the place fairly exploded with applause.

Afterwards, Rubinstein's house on the Square du Bois de Boulogne was illuminated by floodlights. About a dozen guests had already gathered in the drawing room, and while Mrs. Rubinstein greeted them, her husband went upstairs to change. More and more of the "intimate friends" kept arriving, until there were about sixty people. A large buffet had been set up in the dining room, prominently displaying Mrs. Rubinstein's specialties, and on every table were bottles of champagne.

Rubinstein reappeared, wearing a dinner jacket and looking as spruce and rested as if he'd just waked up from a long nap. All the guests stood up and raised their glasses to him — a scene out of the romantic past. Rubinstein was enjoying himself immensely, his food, his champagne, his cigar, and especially his friends, as he moved from one table to the next, talking, laughing, hand-kissing. (He was then sixty-nine years old.) He was still going strong at four-fifteen, when he reluctantly said good-bye to the last batch of guests, asking me to stay for "one more glass of champagne, as a nightcap."

After Shawn had read and accepted the profile, I showed the manuscript to Rubinstein to be sure I'd made no technical mistakes about the art of piano playing. Not many people know as much about the subject as he does. Later, I had a charming letter from Mrs. Rubinstein; they'd liked the profile. I thought all was well.

When the profile was scheduled, I was in America. *The New York-er*'s checkers got busy and called up Rubinstein in Paris, clearing up some minor points. Rubinstein got more nervous than before playing five concerts in twelve days in Carnegie Hall — an incredible *tour de force* that he brought off — and asked to see the final proof, which was considerably shorter than my manuscript. It seems that he became annoyed when he noticed that he'd been cut; a sensitive artist and proud Pole doesn't like to be cut down by *any*one, even editorially. There was some last-minute don't-dare-publish-this-or-else unhappiness.

The profile was published as scheduled, and I heard much favorable comment on it. Except from Rubinstein's five thousand intimate friends, who remained eloquently silent. So did he.

I had better luck with another great artist. One dismal November evening, back in 1932, I was walking aimlessly through the streets of Aarau, a dull town in central Switzerland. I was between trains, not due to leave until midnight. A slow rain was falling, and I felt lonely and rather lost. As I passed the late-Gothic Stadtkirche, I heard the organ being played inside, Bach's Great Fugue in G minor. I could tell at once that the organist was a master. The main entrance to the church was closed, but a small side door stood open, and I went in.

The church was dark, except for a dim light from the organ loft, and empty. I sat down in a pew near the door and closed my eyes, and suddenly the drab, damp streets of Aarau began to seem a long way off. The organist was performing with understanding and authority, conveying all of Bach's sweep and grandeur, without sacrificing, as so many organists do, his fascinating detail. His phrasing was intimate and his legato was beautifully lucid. After the fugue, he played the moving chorale prelude "Nun danket alle Gott." The church seemed to be ringing with a multitude of exquisite voices.

When the music came to an end, I continued to sit quietly in the pew, with the sound of the fine organ still in my ears. After a while I heard the sound of steps, and a man came down from the loft and walked swiftly toward the door. As he passed through a patch of light, I could see that he was perhaps sixty years old and carried himself with remarkable vigor. His face was deeply lined, he had an aquiline nose, and a bushy mustache drooped around the corners of his mouth. I stood up as he approached, and he raised a hand in greeting.

"I played the chorale too fast, didn't I?" he asked, and nodded vigorously, as though in answer to his own question. He spoke German with an Alsatian accent. I apologized for having come in without permission, but he didn't seem to be listening. He asked me whether I liked Bach. I said I did, but that as a student of the violin, I had never felt as close to Bach as an organist would.

He shook his head. "You mustn't say that," he told me firmly. "Bach was an accomplished violinist. He knew a lot about the technique of violin playing. If he didn't, how could he have written all that great polyphonic music in his violin sonatas and partitas? Many of his works for the organ demand a violinist's phrasing and modulation. Have you ever played the chaconne that concludes the Second Partita?"

I said I had tried to.

"An astonishing work," the organist said. "One doesn't know what to admire most — the wealth of the variations, the development, or the polyphony." He smiled, raised his hand again, and left.

A minute later, an elderly man came and told me gruffly, in his Swiss German voice, that the church was now closed. I asked him who the organist was.

He gave me an odd look. "You mean to say you don't know Albert Schweitzer?" he said.

As a matter of fact, at that time I knew next to nothing about Albert Schweitzer. He wasn't, of course, as celebrated as later on. I bought his autobiography, *Out of My Life and Thought,* and I was impressed by its modesty and its clarity of style. I tried to read everything I could lay my hands on by and about Schweitzer — Schweitzer the organ builder, the organist, the interpreter of Bach and Goethe, the architect, the philosopher, the minister, the theologian, the apostle of the universal spirit, the lumberman, and the doctor or, as his African patients called him "the fetishman."

Twenty-two years later, when I was once again in Switzerland, I read that Schweitzer, as the winner of the Nobel Peace Prize in 1952, had attended a meeting of Nobel Prize winners in Lindau, on Lake Constance, and was now in the small Alsatian village of Gunsbach, where he made his home when he was in Europe. I wrote to him, asking if I might see him there, but I received a prompt reply from Mme. Emmy Martin, his private secretary, expressing her regrets. Dr. Schweitzer was going through a fatigue crisis, had to concentrate on a special manuscript, and had called off all his lectures. "Please try to understand. . . ." There was a postscript in German, written in a small, vertical hand: "Please forgive a man who is so tired and swamped with work that he cannot fulfill your request. For the first time in my life, I must try to live as quietly as possible." This was signed "Albert Schweitzer."

Two months later, I happened to lunch with friends at the Maison des Têtes, in Colmar. While we were waiting for our lunch, I glanced at the map of the region. Eleven miles from Colmar, on Route N-417 to Munster, was Gunsbach. I went to the phone and put in a call to

Schweitzer, and after a nip-and-tuck struggle with the whimsicalities of the French long-distance telephone service, I was connected with Mme. Martin. She remembered my letter.

"I knew you would call someday," she said, with a sigh. "If I ask you to come at three o'clock, will you promise not to stay too long?"

I met Schweitzer that afternoon in his house. He was then seventy-nine, but he had the sparkle of a young man. His hair was white, the lines in his face had deepened, and his mustache still drooped. He made me think of an Alsatian woodcut. He was wearing the clothes of a country doctor or a pastor — black trousers, a black coat, a black waistcoat, and a high wing collar with a black bow tie. He autographed a book for a young girl, and said he was going to the church. He said to me he was going to practice some Bach chorales that he would record next week, and asked me to come along.

Mme. Martin, the secretary, said, "Dr. Schweitzer needs no practice. He knows three-quarters of Bach by heart."

"These chorales belong to the fourth quarter," Schweitzer said, and laughed — a fresh, youthful laugh.

He went upstairs and came back after a while, wearing a somewhat battered felt hat and carrying a white linen bag in one hand and a folder of sheet music in the other. He took my arm, and we moved off up the road toward the church. We met several villagers who greeted him in German or French. Schweitzer smiled and shook hands, inquiring about their children. I was reminded of the familiar description of him as "a combination of Goethe and Saint Francis of Assisi."

We went on. Suddenly he stopped, looked me straight in the eye, and asked, "Do you still play the violin?"

I was taken aback. I hadn't mentioned Aarau in my letter.

"That night in Aarau, we talked about Bach the violinist, didn't we?" he continued as we walked on.

I said it was astounding that he should remember.

"I've trained myself to remember. Now, are you still playing the violin?"

"Sometimes, for pleasure. Mostly chamber music."

"Chamber music is the finest music of all, better even than organ music," Schweitzer said. "Bach played the viola in small groups. He liked to sit in the middle, so that he could hear what was going on on both sides." He went on talking about Bach. His knowledge was encyclopedic. He waved to three women in the street, stopped again, turned toward me, and said, with finality, "You will stay for dinner."

At the entrance to the church, there were several people and quite a few children. Schweitzer walked quickly up the steep, creaking wooden stairs to the organ loft, and I followed him. Most of the people remained downstairs and sat in the pews. Schweitzer removed his shoes, opened the white linen bag, and took out a pair of organist's shoes, with soft rubber soles. More people slipped into the church; word had got around that Schweitzer was going to play. He told me to sit down next to him, and put on a pair of spectacles.

"Careful!" he said softly. "Don't touch the pedals with your feet. Turn the pages for me. I'll tell you exactly when." He lowered his head, as if in silent prayer, and sat motionless for a minute or so. There was great stillness in the church. Then he raised his head, set the manuals, and began to play.

He started with "An Wasserflüssen Babylon." The organ had a sweet, soft, almost tender sound. When the time to turn a page drew near, Schweitzer whispered, "Wait," and then, "Now." After he finished, he sat staring hard at the music.

"I'm afraid I played too fast," he said, shaking his head. "I always feel I play the chorales too fast. So much detail of Bach's magnificent architecture comes to light only when you play the music slowly."

He played another chorale, "Allein Gott in der Höh' sei Ehr'," and then "Schmücke dich, O liebe Seele," one of those Bach compositions in which the structure is hidden behind a lovely haze of melody. Schumann once wrote that Mendelssohn had told him that "if all hope and faith were taken out of your life, this chorale alone would be enough to restore them to you." Schweitzer played it with deep feeling. He repeated the second part of the chorale, and then complained once more that he had played too fast. He took down the score and said, "Now I don't need my glasses."

He laid them aside, removed his jacket, adjusted the stops, and after a few seconds, during which he seemed to completely withdraw into himself, plunged into the magnificent chords of the great D-minor Toccata and Fugue. For me, this has always been one of the most dramatic of Bach's works, and now I was overwhelmed by it. I closed my eyes. . . . When I opened them, as the music ended with a majestic fortissimo, the sun had fallen below the level of the windows. No one stirred, not even the children. It was Schweitzer who broke the spell. He put down the organ lid resolutely, locked it, and turned off the light.

Schweitzer looked for a moment toward the windows and the sun.

"At this hour, I make my last rounds of the wards in Lambaréné," he said. "Let's go back to the house."

Sometimes a story just happens to a writer, unexpected and unplanned, a gift from the gods. The trick is to see it and hold it, or it may be gone.

One autumn afternoon several years ago, I drove from Switzerland to Austria over the Arlberg Pass and was coming down the steep highway toward the Tyrolean village of St. Anton-am-Arlberg. I've been afraid of this road ever since I came down one day in my Buick, and the brakes were getting hot, and failed. The car was getting out of control just as I noticed a dirt road going up on the left side of the road. I was lucky — no car was oncoming — and sharply swerved the wheel to the left. The car went up the dirt road and came to a stop, not two seconds too late.

This time I was stopped at the outskirts of St. Anton by a herd of cattle that was crossing the road with exasperating sluggishness. The cows had spent the summer on the high Alpine pastures called *Almen* and were being driven home for the winter. There is no point in disturbing or rushing the cows, I've learned. I pulled up at the side of the road. Just below, the railroad tracks disappeared into the eastern portal of the Arlberg Tunnel. Above the entrance I saw the imperial Habsburg coat of arms, the inscription "Franz Joseph I," and the date "1884," the year the tunnel was completed. The Arlberg Tunnel is one of the oldest and longest railroad tunnels on earth — six miles and nineteen hundred feet — and there is not a single light in it. I must have traveled through it at least fifty times on the Arlberg Express. After the beautiful ride up the Inn Valley to St. Anton, at an elevation of 4,277 feet, the tunnel ride is a climactic thrill. I like both railroads and tunnels, and a fast trip through a long tunnel is a mysterious adventure. The noise of the wheels is amplified as it reverberates against the great square stones of the tunnel walls. They are so close that you think you could reach out and touch them, but then mist begins to form on the windows, which have to be kept closed because the air in the tunnel is bad. I remember one ride when the lights in my compartment had gone out, leaving me in absolute darkness. I was thinking what could happen if, . . . and suddenly there was a cannon shot, a sharp blast rattled the windows, and a train shot by the other way. It took the Arlberg Express nine minutes to go through the tunnel. Then there was bright, blinding sunshine, and the train stopped at Langen, at the western end of the tunnel.

I was thinking about that, while the cows ambled in front of my car, and then I saw a man coming out of the tunnel. He wore blue overalls, a short jacket, and the long-billed cap that is worn by mountaineers in the region. He carried a rucksack on his back and a large monkey wrench in his hand, and an old-fashioned carbide lamp, like the coal miners back home in Ostrava, a mining town. He walked down the center of one of the two tracks, looking sharply at the rails until he reached a wooden shack, not far from the tunnel entrance. He unlocked the door and went inside.

I got out of the car and went to see the man in the shack. His name was Johann Raffeiner, and he was the *Streckenbegeher* (the man walking the tracks). Six times a week, looking for breaks in the rails, an eight hours' walk, stepping from tie to tie, sixteen thousand ties a day. One day he walked track one, from here to Langen, and the next day he walked the other track. Quite a few times he'd asked people, "Want to walk through with me?" and a few had tried, but no one had done it yet. Once a newspaperman from Vienna started out bravely, but after a couple of hours he couldn't take the darkness and the foul air and being closed in under the mountain. Raffeiner had to call for a motor rail car, and they came and took the man out. Raffeiner shook his head and said, "The tunnel is no place for fools." Some of his predecessors, who were by no means fools, had been killed in the tunnel because they were careless just for one moment.

There was my story. I had to get special permission in Vienna, which wasn't easy; I had to sign a paper releasing the Austrian Railroads from all obligations, if something should happen. One morning, weeks later, I walked into the tunnel at St. Anton behind Raffeiner. I had expected the foul air, the darkness, the sense of isolation — but not the shock of the first train coming by while we were hiding in one of the niches that were built in the walls every hundred meters. Suddenly the headlights were close, there was thunder, and the train seemed to leap out of the darkness and flash past us. There was a tremendous noise, and a strong current of air, smelling of hot metal, pushed me back against the wall. I had a short, nightmarish vision of lighted windows and of people behind them. Then the train was gone. My eyes were full of dust and tears, and my knees were a little shaky.

Raffeiner taught me how to "feel" when a train had entered the tunnel; there would be an almost imperceptible pressure in the ears. He explained to me that when there was no pressure in his ears, it might mean that there was no train in the tunnel — or that *two* trains were in it, neutralizing the drafts. Right now, he said, was such a moment. There were two trains in the tunnel, and he walked on. I asked him whether we shouldn't hide in the nearby niche. He shrugged.

"The trains are still two kilometers away. We've got time to make the next niche. . . . One feels these things. Experience, I guess."

It was an eerie feeling, walking through the darkness and wondering whether the first train would come at us from behind or toward us. I remember a stone plate in the wall, at the spot where one of Raffeiner's predecessors had been killed by a train, although he must have been experienced.

Eight hours later, I stumbled and almost fell down when we reached the western exit at Langen. I stared at the lovely picture of blue skies and white clouds, of mountains and trees and colors, framed by the tunnel portal. Walking through a long, dark tunnel may be a poor substitute for an astronaut's walk through space, but to me it was a little like getting back to earth. Outside the portal I deeply and gratefully inhaled the brisk air, the scent of trees and mushrooms and resin and wet earth. The air was as wonderful as the bouquet of an old claret, and the colors were brilliant. Fellow mortals, if you ever get bored with life on earth, walk through a long tunnel.

No Publisher Is a Gentleman
to His Author

PUBLISHING HAS BEEN CALLED an occupation for gentlemen, but there are moments when no publisher is a gentleman to his author. I believe an author should have a personal relationship with his publisher, but that is now considered an outdated notion among the bright promoters of the great publishing combines. They consider a book "a title," or worse. The author considers his book his child. The publisher, the child's godfather, might at least sympathize with the father. Hah.

In the prewar days in Europe, the *ménage* between an author and his publisher was dissolved only by the author's death or the publisher's bankruptcy. The publisher would publish anything his author wrote, even if he was certain he couldn't sell it. Few publishers today can afford such generosity.

Authors always had problems with their publishers, and publishers with their authors, but everything was less complicated. Homer, Shakespeare, Dante, and Goethe didn't have to worry about subsidiary rights, book clubs, motion-picture deals, and splitting their income for tax purposes. Instead of spending time trying to decode hieroglyphic contracts, they carried out the writer's task, which is to write. Homer was doing pretty well without a literary agent. Today's best-selling novelist is surrounded by cohorts of agents, lawyers, copyright experts, tax specialists, accountants, and managers trying to "protect" their client — at considerable expense to the client. The successful novelist has become a corporation. No one talks of a "child" or even a "title." It's a "property." A best-selling book is a valuable property; a book that doesn't sell is just a book.

Contracts have become complex documents which few authors even try to understand. They are drawn up by jurisprudent masterminds with a penchant for ambiguity who feel happily at home in the dim jungle between legality and hocus-pocus. These modern Machiavellis would soon be out of business if contracts were written in the lucid style of a *New Yorker* article. Even *The New Yorker*'s Summary of Retirement Annuity Plan is partly written in obscure legalese with cabalistic undertones. "Annuity payments starting at a deferred commencing date will be in a somewhat increased amount, depending upon the employee's age at such a date, actuarially equivalent to the annuity payments as due at his normal retirement date. . . ."

Such seventeeth-floor business-office prose would not be tolerated in the editorial offices higher up.

I don't believe in change for change's sake — in love, marriage, friendship, or business. I've had the same banker, the same tailor, the same lawyer, the same barber, the same agent, the same editor, for almost three decades. I might still have the same bookstore and delicatessen if they hadn't gone broke. I have some silk shirts made by Y. Omiya and Company at the Imperial Hotel Arcade in Tokyo when I was there in 1936. My shirts have survived the Imperial Hotel. I still wear some dress shirts bought after the Second World War in London's Old Bond

Street. They were expensive and worth every guinea; this is a matter of philosophy rather than economy. I was in a Fifth Avenue discount store only once in my life, to buy some records for Poppy, and I don't intend to ever go there again. The experience left me slightly bruised, minus a button of my overcoat. At home, I love to wear shirts that are frayed with old age and comfortable to the skin, while I work, and I've distressed unannounced visitors who glance at my shabby appearance and think I'm insolvent.

Once in a while, in moments of sartorial splendor, I wear a suit made in London's Savile Row in 1949, when I went through a period of emotional irresponsibility and financial recklessness. Poppy now calls it "the gangster suit." It has a broad chalk stripe that she's seen in some old gangster films, perhaps worn by Humphrey Bogart or George Raft. She sort of likes the idea that I might have been a gangster too, at least in appearance; it proves that our generation wasn't really so different from hers, though the skirts are shorter now and the sideburns longer. I wore long sideburns before the Beatles were born, though some ladies now think that I wear them as a symbol of delayed protest. (To tell the truth, I imitated Clemens Krauss, the great conductor and *Direktor* of the Vienna Staatsoper, who in turn imitated one of *his* boyhood heroes.) I tried to explain to my daughter that in the City of London such chalk-stripe suits are now worn by eminently respectable bankers whom even their best enemies would not publicly call gangsters, though privately they may consider them as such, but she wasn't convinced. I happen to know some of the great merchant bankers — owing to my profession, not to exalted financial circumstances. I wrote several *New Yorker* profiles, and later a book about them. I wouldn't dare, though, ask for a checking account with N. M. Rothschild and Sons, much as I would like it. The wife of a friend in London once had a checkbook from Hambros Bank but was asked to return it when they noticed that she used the checks with the hallowed name of the firm to pay her grocer's and laundry bills. They suggested that Barclays Bank was better equipped for that sort of thing.

It is easier to keep the same suit for twenty years than the same publisher. This, the publishers will tell you, is the fault of the greedy authors, who always want more money, more publicity, more of everything. They say that authors have no loyalty nowadays. But loyalty is a two-way street. One of my publishers I'm fond of, repeatedly assured me that he would gladly publish the telephone directory if I wrote it. This didn't prevent him from turning down a couple of my manuscripts, which I consider superior to his hometown's telephone directory. Maybe he meant another directory, perhaps the Vienna telephone directory, which has a certain mystique since the most important subscribers, of whom I am one, are not listed in it. We have secret numbers and pay a large extra fee for the privilege of anonymity.

Another publisher, after making money on one of my books, immediately turned down the next because he was afraid to lose money on it. That was the end of another beautiful friendship. All publishers dislike to discuss money, though they think of it much of the time. They accuse us of the same thing, but many writers are actually embarrassed to discuss money matters. A prominent broker friend in Wall Street tells me that next to doctors and scientists, writers are the most unworldly fools about investments. No writer has yet achieved the distinction of having his shares listed at the New York Stock Exchange, but you are welcome to speculate in the stock of several publishing firms.

My first American publisher was Houghton Mifflin in Boston. Paul Reynolds sold them *Looking for a Bluebird*, which became a Houghton Mifflin Fellowship Book. I was then with the American Army in Europe, and I knew little about American publishers and fellowships. I hoped to meet Mr. Houghton and Mr. Mifflin one day. I didn't know that in present-day Boston, as in old London, some firms are still named after the original founders. After the war, I went to Boston. I liked the city; it reminded me of London, with a better orchestra and a better climate. Boston and San Francisco remain my favorite American cities. The

offices of Houghton Mifflin needed just a little more dust to have that
authentic Bloomsbury look. Paul Reynolds had told me that my book
had done pretty well, but that wasn't the impression I got in Boston.
No one called me "Joe" or "honey," as in Hollywood. No one gave me
a cocktail party, thank God. An assistant woman editor took me to
lunch at a nearby cafeteria. Today some authors might switch publishers
after such an indignity. A famous novelist I know stays at a luxurious
suite at the Plaza, at his publisher's expense, when he deigns to visit
New York.

It was a good cafeteria, though, and I ordered swordfish steak for
the first time in my life. Delicious. There was a lot of human fish in
Boston, some of it cold. I was told that Bostonians for generations have
trained that cold-fish look — reticence, honesty, dignity. Paul Brooks,
the editor of Houghton Mifflin, whom I liked, also cultivated that look.
I once referred to him in my correspondence with Reynolds as "the iceman cometh," and thereafter ICEMAN became a code word in our top-
secret cables. We have other code words for our publishers, but I see
no need to break the code here.

I remember a nice though somewhat arduous weekend in Paul
Brooks's country home, near Boston. After lunch he suggested a walk
through the charming New England countryside. I accepted, not knowing what I was up against. Brooks was an ardent outdoorsman who
loved walking. I had done so much forced walking in the infantries of
both Czechoslovakia and the United States that I'd become strictly an
indoorsman; I've had all the exercise I need for the rest of my life. Brooks
didn't walk; he strode with long powerful steps, and I couldn't keep up
with him. I'm fated with men of long stride. In Hollywood, during an
interview with the late Gary Cooper, I had to accompany him all over
the Paramount lot, and was so busy keeping in step with his stride that
I couldn't follow his monosyllabic utterances, and got nothing out of the
interview. If you should be on New York's Fifth Avenue, around lunchtime, between Forty-third and Forty-eighth streets, and you should pass
a tall silver-haired man accompanied by a tense fellow with a receding

hairline, trying desperately and unsuccessfully to keep in step with the tall man, you've just seen Paul Reynolds — also an enthusiastic walker and outdoorsman from New England — with the writer of this sentence. ·

My cross-country walk with Brooks ended on an undignified note. Trying to follow his example, I jumped across a barbed-wire fence and tore a large hole in my pants. I barely avoided falling into a brook (no pun intended) which he insisted on crossing. It may have been the Rubicon, metaphysically speaking. A couple of years afterwards I was no longer with Houghton Mifflin. I was with Knopf.

Alfred A. Knopf had been a friend of Paul Reynolds's father, and spoke admiringly of the dean of literary agents in America. Alfred, I soon discovered, didn't speak admiringly of many literary agents, literary men, or men, for that matter. Paul Reynolds had sent him my manuscript of "Going Home" which *The New Yorker* was going to publish. Alfred, whom I'd never met, wrote, "Dear Mr. Wechsberg, You write like an angel," and said he was going to publish "Going Home" as a book. I was happy. I'd heard of the House of Knopf in Europe, where it enjoyed greater prestige even than in America. European authors were keen on having a publisher with a literary reputation, while many American authors were more interested in the number of copies of their books sold than in the publisher's imprint, even if it should be a Borzoi.

I never had any walking problems with Alfred and Blanche Knopf. Alfred's idea of a nice Sunday walk was to leisurely perambulate through his beautiful garden in Purchase, New York, looking at his fine flowers and rare trees. That was the kind of walk I like. I shared other things with the Knopfs. With Alfred it was our common love of stimulating people, good writing, nice things, fine food, rare vintages. With Blanche, whose idea of a good lunch was a couple of selected salad leaves, it was our common interest in Europe, especially in France.

Blanche insisted on talking to me in French, which occasionally irritated Alfred. When Blanche talked about Paris, where she spent much time at the Ritz every year talking to authors and trying to get their manuscripts, Alfred countered with stories about America's national parks, which he visited regularly. It took advanced diplomatic skill to move in the literary no-man's-land between the Paris Ritz and Yellowstone National Park. I got along well with both Alfred and Blanche, *and* with Alfred, Jr. (Pat), now one of the owners of Atheneum Publishers. It was a complicated family, but which family isn't, and how many families have published so many beautiful books?

Sunday lunch at Alfred's house in Purchase was a memorable experience. To an author a summons to Purchase was what an invitation to the Queen's Buckingham Palace garden party is to the mother of an American debutante. At the deplorable White Plains railroad station, after the ride on the terrible commuters' train, we would be fetched by Alfred's man, and instantly the atmosphere would change from the drabness of a bankrupt railroad to the opulence of a solvent gentleman-publisher. I wasn't the first one to notice the Olympian image that Alfred conveys; if Goethe, the great Olympian, had been alive, he would have been published by Knopf. Alfred is what a world-famous publisher should be. He has a beautiful home, venerable first editions, is on a first-name basis with several Nobel Prize winners, has a great many titles *honoris causa,* and is aware of having created a distinguished record in American publishing history.

He was also trying to create the impression of a slightly eccentric Man of Distinction — in speech, dress, and behavior. He had always the right dog and what he (but not many others) considered the right taste in vividly colored shirts. He knew that people would talk about the unorthodox hues of his shirts. I never quite understood why Alfred would care whether anybody was talking about him.

Other publishers have tried to imitate Alfred's Olympian image, and failed, though they spared no expense. They surround themselves with Persian rugs and post-Impressionists, trying hard to *épater* the world-at-large and specifically their authors, but they don't succeed. The message is clear. "If you weren't such a poor schnook and would publish books instead of merely writing them, you too could live like a king."

Instead of being impressed, the author can't help wondering why the publisher was so stingy about the last contract. If he happens to be one of the publisher's successful authors, he quietly decides to ask for more money the next time, or else; and he is mad at having partly financed all that luxury.

Alfred's man would put us into the station wagon, and off we went. That was before Alfred bought a Rolls-Royce. I like to think that nowadays authors are fetched by the Rolls-Royce. Some of my best friends drive Bentleys, but it takes a man of courage as well as of distinction to be seen in a Rolls. When we arrived, there would be *chère* Blanche and dear Alfred, and after a warm, bilingual welcome there would be the ritual walk through the garden. Alfred would give us a conducted tour of the rare trees sent down to him from Harvard. He talked with great delight about his trees, especially after he noticed that I had not the slightest idea what he was talking about. I love trees, but I know nothing about them. In addition to being color-blind, I seem to be tree-blind. I don't know the difference between an elm, a maple, and an oak. The only thing I know about maple is that the wood is used for the back of violins.

I didn't know that they were growing trees too at Harvard, and I wondered whether a Harvard tree feels as superior toward other trees as certain Harvard graduates feel toward the rest of mankind. Alfred thought of his garden as a botanical library full of rare editions. When my wife once asked him, rather impetuously, whether she might take along "a few flowers," Alfred said succinctly, "Certainly not!" in the manner of Monty Woolley playing Alfred Knopf. She didn't understand: she'd thought they were *flowers*.

After the walk through the garden, there would be a glass of white wine, usually a fine Moselle vintage, on the sunny terrace. Alfred knew better than to serve vulgar cocktails, American style, pretentious sherries, English style, or a Dubonnet, French style. He had published so many fine German *Dichter* that he liked to identify himself with a German *Denker*. With the Moselle, or Mosel, there was excellent Nova Scotia smoked salmon, which Blanche referred to as *saumon fumé*, with the accent on the first syllable, as the Swiss pronounce it. Alfred said nonsense, it was smoked salmon, and there followed a lengthy argument. I assured them that lox, the Yiddish version of the German word *Lachs*, was fine. After watching me at lunch in Purchase, the State Department's protocol people might have offered me a good job.

Lunch was beautifully cooked, and served in elegant style. Alfred still had "couples" — a butler and his wife, who was a good cook — when other millionaires were glad to have a woman come in twice a week. Blanche had only a cook in her New York apartment, but she was a genuine Frenchwoman who accentuated many American words on the last syllable, like "Connecticut." There was only one thing missing at Alfred's table. The very-Early-American benches had no backs, and I could not lean back, in moments of exultation, after tasting a particularly noble vintage. Once I got so excited about an elegant, fruity, well-rounded Richebourg that I almost fell off the bench. It may have been all right for the Puritans. *They* were never tempted by Alfred's vintages. Alfred was more a Burgundy lover (though he emphasized that he was a man of all wines), while I was strictly a Bordeaux partisan. To add a tantalizing note, he would serve such fine Burgundies that he almost made me betray Bordeaux.

There was much wine talk, with connoisseurs' observations and learned jargon. But after a few meals, during which Alfred served us his choicest vintages, he made the disturbing discovery that I didn't know as much about wines as he'd expected from the author of *Blue Trout and Black Truffles: The Peregrinations of an Epicure*, published in 1953 by Alfred A. Knopf. The subtitle had been Alfred's idea. It worried him a lot. Here he had promoted me to epicure under the august Borzoi sign, and I'd slipped up on a Close de Perrières, which is not a mineral water but a fine Meursault. Years later, a friend of mine who is also a friend of Alfred's told me in strictest confidence that one day Alfred had asked him for lunch and, after an uncharacteristic period of avoiding grim reality, had said to him, "You know, I believe that Joe doesn't really know much about wines." Again, years later, *another* man who is very close to Alfred confided to *me*, in strictest secrecy, "You know, Alfred knows a lot about wines, but I suspect he doesn't know as much about food."

Alfred was absolutely right. In 1953, I didn't know as much about wine as you would expect from a Knopf-promoted epicure. I had even told Alfred that I didn't like white wines because they didn't agree with me. He'd asked me sardonically whether I liked some inky Chianti with my fish. I said thanks, I would have nothing with the fish, but for Alfred I was what the French (and Blanche) called *fini, foutu,* through, *erledigt.*

With wines I feel as with women and Chinese politics. In the beginning one thinks one knows all about them, but gradually, as one begins to learn, one's knowledge diminishes. My vinicultural education started late in life. As a child I loved hot cocoa and hated milk. I had a theory, later confirmed by many Frenchmen, that "milk contains germs," though I began to like milk in America, where it tasted quite differently; America is a milk and liquor country. As a student in Vienna, I agreed with the Viennese that Vienna's *Hochquell* water was the world's best. It came from springs high up in the mountains, a hundred kilometers away, and tasted like fresh spring water on a beautiful spring morning. Big signs said: "What does the Viennese enjoy most after returning from his summer vacation? The water." Unfortunately, the good water is a thing of the past, since the United States forces in Austria taught the "natives" to put in chlorine. "To drink the so-called Viennese spring water is to take one's life into one's hands," an American surgeon general declared after the war in Vienna. So now most Viennese drink cheap, young wine which the Americans have not yet chlorinated.

Czechoslovakia is a beer country. The good soldier Schweik drinks beer, and so did his creator, Jaroslav Hašek. Beer was the official beverage at the editorial offices of the *Prager Jagblatt.* Even poets drank beer in Prague instead of the proverbial nectar, and we ordered beer for the ladies, with many physical attributes and few moral inhibitions, whom we invited, after the final edition of the paper had come off the presses.

I began to drink wine in the cheap *prix fixe* restaurants in Paris in my early twenties because half a carafe was included in the price, but it wasn't the kind of wine the connoisseurs talk about. It arrived in large tank cars from the Midi and was distinguished only for its total lack of distinction. As a ship's musician on French Line and Messageries Maritimes liners, I had free wine with my meals. My experienced French colleagues called it damned cheap *pinard.* No one ever sent us a fine bottle in recognition of our performance, as the beautiful people do in the films. In fact, I discovered that a great many French citizens knew little about wines.

I first suspected that Alfred didn't know as much about food as about wine one beautiful day several years after the publication of my book. Alfred and Blanche had met us for lunch at the Pyramide in Vienne, which had been the final chapter, and the climax, of my epicurean peregrinations. We had a magnificent lunch at Madame Point's table, but somehow it wasn't a complete success. Blanche would get up between courses and disappear for a few minutes. Afterwards she confessed to me that she had to have a cigarette and had been embarrassed to smoke during the meal because I had written it wasn't done at the Pyramide. Alfred criticized certain things, not because he disliked them but because he was fond of dissenting with the rest of us. He said the warm pâté was too rich and the exquisite *gratin de queues d'écrevisses* was too salted. Blanche talked only French, and Alfred was in a particularly Francophobic mood, not the right disposition for the enjoyment of *la grande cuisine*, which is strictly a French art. Ever since, Alfred has cautioned people against the Pyramide and most other three-star restaurants in France, though he was very fond of Alexandre Dumaine's in Saulieu. I once told him that Dumaine himself had considered the Pyramide *"la plus grande table de France."* Alfred pretended not to hear what he didn't want to hear. Instead he would suggest some other restaurants that he had discovered.

Not long ago, Pat, Alfred's son, went to Europe with his wife and planned to have a meal at the Pyramide. I advised him to have lunch there, which is the important meal at all temples of French gastronomy. They couldn't make it for lunch, but later Pat wrote me, "Our dinner at the Pyramide was a triumph. Madame Point took care of everything to perfection. . . . It couldn't have been better, in spite of the fact that Alfred told us we wouldn't find it very good."

As a host, Alfred couldn't be better. One day, when he invited me for dinner, he left his office in midmorning, and did the shopping himself. He walked over to Sixth Avenue to the establishment of the late Arsène Tinguaud, which the late Lucius Beebe once called "the Cartier's of baby lamb." Beebe, an expert both on baby lamb and Cartier's, knew what he was talking about. (Soulé bought all his lamb, veal and sweetbreads at Tinguaud's.) Alfred selected a tender fillet of veal, had it wrapped, bought some delicious asparagus nearby, and carried his purchases to his office on Madison Avenue. Not many publishers of Nobel Prize winners would do that for an author whose name the Nobel Prize Committee in Stockholm had never heard.

I've learned a little about wines, and I hope to convince Alfred someday that I've worked up at last to his exalted standards of a Borzoi epicure. My friend Alexis Lichine says that the only way to learn about wines is to drink them judiciously and enjoy them. In recent years I've passed some hard tests at the Pyramide. Madame Point serves a simple Beaujolais — simple from the Pyramide's point of view. Every year she and Louis Tommasi, her trusted sommelier, drive to the nearby Beaujolais country and taste their way through the young wines of the year. A tricky business, because young Beaujolais is often hard on the tongue and may start "working" around Easter, a few months after it was bought. As in the case of a baby, one is never certain how it will turn out, but Madame Point, whom her husband considered an outstanding expert, always seems to select the finest wines of the year.

When I'm there, Louis asks me to guess both the commune and the year of a Beaujolais in an unlabeled bottle. The neighboring communes (villages) of Chénas, Fleuri, Juliénas, Moulin-à-Vent, are small, and the differences in the wines' tastes are often very subtle. During the past three years I've guessed right the first time, both the village and the year. I wished Alfred had been there.

In the end it was neither wine nor *Weltanschauung* nor our different opinions on world literature or vintages that caused a cooling period in our friendship, but what Harold Ross called "the sordid subject of money." Pat, then an executive of Alfred A. Knopf, Inc., liked my book *Avalanche!*, a blow-by-blow account of what happened to the people of a small village in western Austria that had been completely obliterated by a terrifying avalanche in January, 1954. Originally, this had been a Reporter-at-Large piece in *The New Yorker*. Pat gave Paul Reynolds a good contract and, in Alfred's opinion, far too much money. Pat said it was a good book. Alfred said sure it was a good book, but it wouldn't sell, just wait.

Sitting between two chairs has been called "civilized man's forced position." I fell through between the two chairs of Knopf senior and Knopf junior. Once again Alfred was right. Most critics said that *Avalanche!* was a good book, but it didn't sell.

For a few years I missed Alfred's colored shirts and rare trees, his wit and wines, and above all, the good laughs we'd had together. In 1965, Alfred A. Knopf, Inc., celebrated its fiftieth anniversary with the publication of a beautiful volume, "Fifty Years — Being a Retrospective Collection of Novels, Novellas, Tales, Drama, Poetry, and Reportage and Essays (Whether Literary, Musical, Contemplative, Historical, Biographical, Argumentative, or Gastronomical) . . . All Drawn from Volumes Issued during the Last Half-Century by Alfred and Blanche

Knopf." The selection was made by Clifton Fadiman from among more than twenty-five hundred authors. Included as a gastronomical afterthought was my *New Yorker* profile about Fernand Point of the Pyramide, which became the final chapter in *Blue Trout and Black Truffles*.

I was uncomfortable but not unhappy to be published among the titans — D. H. Lawrence, Gide, Eliot, Cather, E. M. Forster, Camus, Sartre, Mann, Conrad, Romains, Bunin, Mansfield, Mencken, Unamuno, and others — and I wrote to Alfred. He answered, in his unsentimental style, "All right, let's just take up where we left off," and we did.

I once made the mistake of visiting the Frankfurt Book Fair. Willy Droemer, the German publisher of some of my books, had asked several of his authors to help him drum up in Frankfurt a little enthusiasm for our children. It was a bewildering experience. The Frankfurt Fair is the world's largest concentration of books. That year, one hundred eighty thousand different books were displayed in enormous halls that were usually filled with textiles or agricultural machines. Over sixty thousand of the books had been published during the past year all over the world. That meant, roughly, seventeen hundred a day, seventy an hour, more than one new book every minute of the day and night. . . .

Trying to find the Droemer booth that was said to be in the rear, I had to walk through a large forest of books, with each book-tree growing out of hopes and tears, sweat and disappointment. It seemed preposterous that people would bother to look at all these books, let alone buy them, and I got more depressed by the minute.

As I approached the Droemer booth, I saw a lot of people milling around, though many other booths were completely ignored. My mood improved. I hoped they'd all come to look at my book, which was lying there among a dozen other new books. But most people didn't bother to look at the books. They'd come to collect pamphlets and publicity material that all publishers gave away free. Some visitors carried large shopping bags filled with collections of printed matter. No one stopped to look at my book or at me, and no one recognized me, though my enlarged photograph was on the wall next to those of my fellow authors. The publisher's employees (Droemer wasn't there) greeted me "correctly." No one seemed pleased to see me. On the contrary, I had the impression that I was considered a damn nuisance — an impression that was shared by my fellow authors, as I soon found out.

The literary climate was glacial. I hid behind a large display of a book with a sex angle that was the firm's current best-seller and created quite a stir. I was joined by two other Droemer authors.

"That's all they care about," one said gloomily, and pointed at the sex book. "The author didn't even bother to come to Frankfurt. Probably much too busy to count his royalties." The third author, who was in a state of advanced melancholia, said that Herr Droemer didn't feel well, having been at a large party until the morning hours.

"They either give or attend parties," he said. "The whole thing makes me sick. The triumph of commercialization. *Eine Schweinerei.*"

Two girls came to ask whether we'd seen Herr Günter Grass. The melancholy author who was reaching the manic-depressive stage said, "No, and neither have we seen Hemingway or Pasternak, but you might meet Doctor Zhivago in the Rowohlt booth over there." The girls looked frightened and walked quickly away.

Two arrogant television men appeared, followed by some husky fellows carrying lights, cables, equipment, cameras. We moved closer, hopefully. One of the TV men asked us not to stand in the way, and they set up their lights and photographed the sex-book display, with one TV man giving an excited commentary. Then they took their equipment and left. A man wanted to know where he could get a pair of hot sausages that are called wieners in Frankfurt, and frankfurters in Wien (Vienna). A dirty old man pointed at the sex book and said that was for kids. He'd just been at the booth of the Olympia Press, oh boy! "That's the place to see real pornography," he said in a confidential voice, as though giving a hot tip on IBM. A girl asked whether these books were for sale. I shook my head. She pinched a book, right in front of me, and walked off.

"These idiots think we're working for Droemer as clerks or traveling salesmen," the melancholy author said bitterly.

"Did anyone ask you for your autograph?" the other author asked. We shook our heads disconsolately. "I saw Ludwig Erhard a while ago, signing dozens of copies of his book. One ought to be a former Federal Chancellor, not a writer."

That night, Herr and Frau Droemer gave a large reception in the ballroom of the Frankfurter Hof. We were asked to stand near the Droemers, welcoming the people in the reception line. Having attended many diplomatic receptions where I was queued up to shake the ambassador's hand, it was a novel experience to play the ambassador's part, and I tried to live up to it, pretending how pleased I was to meet these people I hoped never to see again. The pleasant sensation didn't last long, though. Quite a few people broke out of the reception line when suckling pigs were served on the large tables in the middle of the ballroom. We ambassadors of goodwill and literature looked frustrated. I asked an underling whether I could have a drink. He shrugged regretfully.

"*Um Himmelswillen,*" he said. "What would the booksellers say?"

"The booksellers?"

"The *important* people in Frankfurt are the booksellers," he said, staring hard at me to drive home the point. "See that fellow coming up with the fat woman? They own eleven bookstores in the Rhineland. Be nice to them."

The bookseller, a dyspeptic character who seemed to hate the world and world literature, nonchalantly shook hands with the Droemers and ignored us. His wife shook hands with me and addressed me by the name of a successful author who stood next to me. She said she'd loved my last book, especially the part about the man going to bed with the two tennis girls who had just won the women's doubles at Wimbledon.

"Are you still playing tennis?" she asked me, and moved on, without waiting for my answer.

It was a swell party. The big ballroom was so crowded that it was impossible to get away from some bores who seemed to move in on me from various directions. Short conversational tidbits reached my ears.

"I hear his book doesn't sell either."

"I'm exhausted and I've got to go to two more parties tonight."

"You're telling me. I've used up all my Alka-Seltzers."

"Droemer's suckling pig is always first-rate, but at Rowohlt's there's more to drink."

"Has Günter Grass been here?"

"Some British publishers serve Scotch in their booths."

"Molden and Weidenfeld had lunch today. What are they up to?"

"Watch the Czechs, they're big this year."

"There's a Japanese publisher who'll pay sight unseen for any novel with a castration in it."

"Keep away from that guy. If you don't look out, he steals your fingernails."

Word spread that real caviar was served at another party, across the corridor, and the crowd thinned out. I got a drink at last by walking into the pantry where the waiters enjoyed what remained of a suckling pig. The melancholy fellow author said never again, he wouldn't come to Frankfurt even if he were number one on the best-seller lists. I agreed. We both felt very noble. We knew, of course, we would never make number one on the best-seller lists.

In London, I was first published by the late Michael Joseph, a gentleman-publisher, and later by the unique Victor Gollancz, whose violent preferences and prejudices surprised even me. He would take me for lunch to the Ivy Restaurant to discuss projects, but instead he talked about Richard Wagner, the Guilt of the Germans, Socialism, the Doom of Opera.

I am now published by another enthusiastic nonconformist, the one and only George Weidenfeld. No one in London remains unruffled at the mention of George Weidenfeld, and some people get quite ruffled. I never met him until the early 1950's, but we share memories and associations of good and bad — mostly of bad — days. George is Viennese. I am not from Vienna, though many people believe I am. But there are many parallels we never talk about — the aftermath of the First World War, poverty, the advent of Nazism, the educational experience of our emigration. European refugees found it harder to be accepted in England than in the United States, though England is believed to be part of Europe. Once in a while when George discusses a grandiose project, he brings up a name in Vienna, a street, a character in a Hofmannsthal play, the pastry at Demel's, and we knowingly look at each other, and understand. Another song without words.

Back in 1947, George would walk in Hyde Park with my friend Patrick Dolan, building castles in the sky. Pat had forgotten about the castles by the time he got home, but a week later George would call him that he'd now found the money to finance the castle, at least he hoped so. Both have made a success since, in the millionaire class. The advantage of having millionaire friends is that they never ask you for money. After you've convinced them that you won't ask *them* for money, they'll love you for what you are, not what you can do for them.

George came to see me in Vienna one day in the early 1950's. If the phrase "brimming over with ideas" didn't exist, it would have to be invented for George, a man of instant enthusiasms. When he discusses ideas, he speaks so fast that his voice cannot keep up with the supersonic flight of his thoughts. He becomes incoherent, unable to finish sentences, and he swallows the endings of long words, and breathes in gasps, like a swimmer coming up for air after a long dive. This is the moment when I'm getting cautious. George has told me six different ideas in less than six minutes. The question is whether the ideas will still be good the next morning or the next month. He seems to take it for granted that many ideas will evaporate, but one may remain that might strike gold. In such moments, George switches from high-class English to upper-bourgeois Viennese. The business details are spelled out in English, and the romantic details of the ideas in German, in the ambiguous, bittersweet code of soft Viennese German, which is not identical with the cold German German. During his soliloquies, George is alternately moody, exuberant, cynical, depressed, trustful, warmhearted, dangerous, bewitching. The subtle changes of his inner self would be difficult to describe even for Arthur Schnitzler, the poet and observer of the Viennese soul.

George has made a conspicuous career in London in the past twenty years, but he is not one of the boys — never will be — and there is envy and jealousy. The conservative tweedy types are not fond of him. He's too "clever," and he's "trying too hard," and all that. He's introduced the hard sell among the apostles of the soft sell. He has revitalized British publishing and he works hard, which doesn't please people who never were used to working hard. I wonder how the tweedy types would be doing if history had gone the other way, and the British empire, instead of the Habsburg empire, had collapsed and they had been forced to emigrate to Vienna, or Prague, or Budapest. George hasn't made it easier for himself by his inclination to be difficult and often vague in business matters, as well as very ambitious in his private life. A while ago he was knighted, and the first thing some people said was that Sir George wasn't happy because he'd hoped to become Lord Weidenfeld. Personally I was delighted with the ex-refugee who had become a gallant knight.

He is an extrovert's extrovert and finds it hard to understand introverts. My idea of a good evening is to be quietly alone with someone I'm very fond of. George's idea is to throw an enormous party, to have one hundred celebrities-of-the-moment gathered in his living room. His parties are a matter of public knowledge. I attended one by accident. I'd arrived in the early afternoon from the Continent, and George called me up and said he had a few people in, would I come? The few people turned out to be the most interesting cross section of Londoners since

G. B. Shaw invented the cast of *Pygmalion*. I remember a duchess, a famous philosopher, two Conservative and three Labor politicians. (George may be a capitalist now, but his heart belongs to Socialism in the Viennese tradition of Viktor Adler.) There were Zionists and stiff Germans, pretty girls and unpretty editors, a genuine Rothschild, scientists and people under contract to George, writers and hopeful writers, and people who hoped it might help their credit rating to be seen talking to a Rothschild. Everybody in the large room disliked at least somebody else, but everybody had a good time. George, the improbable catalyst, had done it again. He stepped over people sitting on the floor, carefully avoiding stepping on their toes. It was a black-tie party, and I was among the few who didn't have a tuxedo. Joe Alsop once told me he never travels without his dinner jacket; he would rather leave his pajamas at home. But I wouldn't like to sleep in my dinner jacket. It didn't matter, though; after eleven P.M. nothing seemed to matter, when the party took on many aspects of unreality.

I've had my problems with George, but now I never discuss business with him — I leave this to my agent — and everything works out well. I've learned to live with his enthusiasms by putting them in cold storage for a while. He convinced me for years that a book about the great merchant bankers might be interesting, and he was right. He is said to love projects that will make him rich, but few publishers, in London or elsewhere, like projects that make them poor. When George really loves a project, he will move mountains. The clue to George Weidenfeld which many of his very best friends-of-the-moment ignore is that he is basically a baroque Viennese. I didn't think of him when I wrote, in the beginning of my book *Sounds of Vienna*, which he later published,

The Viennese are essentially a baroque people. . . . Life to the Viennese is nothing but a play. They will often tailor reality to fit their imagination. The Viennese is a born character author who performs with considerable skill the part that life has assigned to him. People fight too, but are soon friends again — after all, they have only played a scene. In his verse play, Arthur Schnitzler writes, "We all act parts and wise is he who knows it. . . ." The baroque schizophrenia of the Viennese is the essence of their *Lebenskunst*, their way of life, and their philosophy.

That's George.

Silence Is Golden

FOR SOME UNFATHOMABLE REASON, a great many people are interested in the writer's craft as though there were some magic about it. They wouldn't ask a surgeon or a pawnbroker what he's working on now, but they will ask a writer. A painful question. The writer is not really sure what he's working on; at best he's hopefully trying, but he may be superstitious, and doesn't like to talk about an unborn child. People don't care whether their lawyer uses a dictaphone and their analyst a pencil or fountain pen, but they want to know whether the writer types or writes longhand or uses a tape recorder. Does he use file cards for his characters, with specimens of their idiosyncrasies and conversation? How and when and where does he get his ideas? This is a tough one. Even other writers don't hesitate to ask you, though they ought to know better. I give them the silent treatment, and in an emergency I say the first thing that comes to my mind: when I shave, when I read the news-paper, when I sleep, when I sit in a train, looking out.

It makes no difference whether one writes lying in bed, sitting at a desk, or standing up — as long as one writes. In an interview, Len Deighton said he stands up while he types on an IBM computerized typewriter, using a telex roll. When the roll gets to the floor, he knows he's written four thousand words. He also uses video tape, cameras, and other machines. I was deeply impressed until I read the sentence "All the gadgets don't make me write any better," and he summed it up: "There isn't any magic about writing." Exactly. But what about the "light touch," that charming, amusing piece you must have dashed off between drinks and dinner? Yes, the "light touch" is the result of five or six painful drafts until it gives the impression of a happy moment of inspiration, instead of the hard labor which it was. There are exceptions; there are always exceptions. Some writers hammer out a piece on their typewriter, and it's good; they have done their thinking, revising, re-writing in their head, before they actually sit down to write. Some work at night and others in daytime, fast or slow, surrounded by silence or noise. Proust wrote in a cork-lined study, and Molnár wrote *Liliom*, a masterpiece, at a table in Budapest's Café New York, while a brass band was playing. In the end, nothing counts but what one puts down on paper.

When I am on a reporting assignment, the early stage is important. I perceive things clearly, and the contours are sharpened. After a while, the impressions become hazy; that's the time to stop. I try to approach people with deceivingly polite persistence. Since I no longer rely on memory when I interview them, I have to make notes. Some people get acute notebook fright that can be as bad as stage fright or mike fright. They stare hypnotized at my liquid-lead pencil as though it had a nu-clear writing head, and start acting in the manner of minor statesmen talking for publication.

To put them at ease, I ask whether they object to my taking notes for the sake of accuracy. I try to establish a psychological rapport, and after a while they relax and almost get used to my notebook. Everybody has his own technique of interviewing; the best technique is the one that gets the best results. Many people instinctively distrust a reporter. I try to make people trust me. Most people love to talk about themselves, if they feel you are really interested in them. The writer's task is to get underneath the surface. Good writers get very deeply into human beings. Sigmund Freud, who knew a great deal about the dark abyss of human nature, in 1906 wrote to Arthur Schnitzler, the great Viennese poet and playwright:

> I have often asked myself, wonderingly, from where you were able to draw the secret knowledge which I have had to acquire through laborious investigation of the subject, and in the end I have come to envy the poet whom I had only admired before.

Sometimes I work on a story, talking to people and taking notes, but it's all dull and pedestrian, and I'm beginning to wonder whether I wasn't wrong about the story — whether there *is* a story at all. I seem to be up against an invisible wall, and I feel, unhappily, that it just doesn't work. There is no inner excitement. If I am not fascinated, how can I convey my fascination to others? I've wasted my time, and I can't even write it off to experience.

And then, suddenly and inexplicably, it happens. Something sparks inside me, I've established a secret connection with the other person who tells me what I hoped all along he would. The story is there, and it's an exciting story, and I have a sense of exhilaration. My blood pressure goes up, my hands begin to tremble. I write fast now, much too fast; sometimes I'm later unable to decode my own notes. It is like the sensation I noticed around the roulette table when a gambler has a winning streak. Unless he keeps a cool head, it may all be gone. The gambling writer, too, is afraid of losing the story, of not being able to hold it. One needs discipline and a sense of self-control, to remain intent and alert until one feels that one has got the story.

Now all you have to do is to write it.

A writer has his failures and successes, and sometimes the failures are more important than the successes. Late in October, 1956, when we in Vienna heard of the people's revolution in Budapest against the Russians, I drove out to the Austrian-Hungarian border near the village of Nickelsdorf. The barrier was up, and refugees were coming in, exhausted but exhilarated to be in a free country at last. Women carried small children. Men had a vacant look in their faces. Many seemed unable to comprehend what had happened. The Soviet soldiers were said to be in control of the highway to Budapest. Only Red Cross vehicles, carrying medical supplies and children's food, were said to get through to Budapest.

A convoy of white-colored trucks with large Red Cross signs was forming near the barrier. I asked a Red Cross official to take me along. He shrugged.

"If the Soviets discover that you are an American journalist, they might stop the convoy. We can't take the chance. We carry blood plasma and penicillin that might save people's lives."

I couldn't insist. No story is worth the price of a human life, or serious danger to human life. I've lost a few good stories because I wouldn't be able to conceal my sources if the story was published, and no one knew what might happen to my sources.

I hoped there might be another chance of getting through to Budapest, but there wasn't. My friend the late John McCormac, then the Vienna correspondent for the *New York Times*, had gone to Budapest a few days earlier, and I wished I'd gone with him. He later wrote the best eyewitness report of the revolution.

In Vienna, I talked to several refugees who told me exciting stories. I cabled to Shawn, suggesting a Budapest piece done around some of the refugees in Vienna, and he told me to go ahead. I'd brought it off once before, after the East German uprising of June 17, 1953, when the workers all over the Soviet Zone revolted against the Ulbricht regime, until the Soviet tanks came. In West Berlin I'd met one of the *Barrikadenstürmer* (barricade fighters) who told me what had happened at the Leuna Works in Merseburg, near Leipzig. Shawn had been enthusiastic about my report "The Seventeenth of June," which later got the Sidney Hillman Award for the year's outstanding magazine article.

The Budapest piece didn't work out. It lacked the smell and the feel of the on-the-spot report. The dimension of reality was missing. Shawn suggested that I come to New York and try to revise the piece. But the revision failed too. I was bitterly disappointed. Budapest was an important story. I felt I'd let the magazine down. Several weeks later, Shawn wrote me that another writer had gone to Austria to make a television film for Hungarian Relief, had met a Hungarian refugee and written a piece that *The New Yorker* would run.

> I write you now because I want you to know I feel distressed that when, after all your efforts, we do run a Hungarian piece, it will turn out to be done by another author. It's extremely painful to me to have to add this ironic turn to your disappointment. I wish the Hungarian piece we publish were a Wechsberg. However, that's only one piece, and there will be, I hope, a hundred wonderful Wechsbergs after it. . . .

It was a depressing experience but a healthy one, in the long run. The writer-editor relationship must be a two-way loyalty. Not many such loyalties exist in the cold, competitive climate of America's magazine world.

Writers complain about their lonely profession, but they would rather remain lonely than give up writing. The woman one loves, the understanding editor, the helpful agent may hold the writer's hand, guiding him part of the way, but in the final stretch the writer remains all by himself. He is strictly on his own. It is the final stretch that proves whether he makes it.

All writers suffer from their loneliness, especially those who won't admit it. Some try hard, giving the impression of being gregarious people to conceal their loneliness. Some learn to live with it, and others accept it as the writer's permanent occupational disease. They talk about the problem with other writers, like hospital patients meeting in the corridors and telling each other the symptoms of their ailments, each hoping that the other patient is worse off. In Europe, writers congregate in literary cafés, feuding with one another and bolstering their egos, to cover up their loneliness. In Vienna I'm considered a strange animal, or worse, because I don't mix with the Viennese writers. Many of them have become provincial-minded, basking in their local celebrity.

Writers, being incorrigible individualists, rarely agree on anything, but most of them admit the need for self-discipline. A writer is much envied because he has "no office hours," may "work whenever he wants," and so on. True enough, but there is another side of the coin. A writer must write when it's raining for weeks, which depresses him, or when the sun shines day after day, which may depress him even more. He must write while listening to barking dogs and crying children, noisy motorcycles, nagging wives, and neighbors fond of blaring radios. No wonder that the writer feels he is up against a worldwide, antiwriter conspiracy. Its members, often invisible, always sinister, are secretly sworn to make the writer's life hell. Poets have a theory that they must suffer in order to write good poetry, but why does it have to happen to reporters too?

The writer wakes up one bright morning after a good night's sleep, eager to start work. It's a blessed day. No headache, no problems, no inexplicable depression. (Depressions are always inexplicable, otherwise one could get rid of them by rationalizing.) While the writer shaves, ideas fly toward him out of space. The coffee is strong, the toast is warm, the butter is ice-cold. Swell.

The writer sits down at his typewriter, all set to go. And then it happens. The conspiracy. In the apartment upstairs somebody begins to knock down a wall. The writer's agent calls with bad news. There is a letter from his accountant, whose very sight makes him uneasy, though he won't open the letter until after lunch. In the nearby house a little boy starts practicing the violin, the awful Ševčík scales. His wife bursts in to complain that something went wrong again with the water heater, and what was the number of the repair firm? All this would be unimportant in the afternoon, at the end of a working day, but now, at the crucial moment when the writer tries to start on his flight toward creation, it is a major crisis. He cannot get off into space. The earth's gravitational pull is too strong. The ideas have evaporated. He feels drained and low.

If he were a bureaucrat or a waiter, he could take it out on his customers, but a writer can take it out on nobody but himself. There he sits, staring disconsolately at the blank page, trying to produce insight, wit, suspense, charm, originality, stream of consciousness, dialogue, description — maybe even salable pornography thinly disguised as religious inspiration. If his words will form sentences and paragraphs that make sense, or proper non-sense, he will be famous and rich (well, maybe not rich; remember the accountant's letter that is still there, unopened?). And if the words are not good, they are worth less than the yellow paper on which they are typed.

The intimate memoirs of sensitive writers convey the impression that they were extremely vulnerable, susceptible to cold stares and cold drafts — human mimosae. In point of fact, most writers are hard crabs underneath their soft shells. They have to be tough and resilient to function; they cannot afford self-pity. Proust, Kafka, Joyce permitted themselves an occasional sigh, but they were not sorry for themselves. Knowing that he is all alone, the writer builds himself his private little spaceship, equipped with the most useful and absurd devices, and there he goes, hoping to conquer yet another universe.

The United States has the best mass communications media on earth; Americans are the world's best informed people. Right? Wrong? Check one.

Better not. Americans certainly know more about their own country than the citizens of most (but not all) other countries know about theirs. But Americans don't know as much about the rest of the world as they like to imagine. They are sometimes badly informed, or misinformed, about those parts of the world now screened off by various curtains.

My work as a foreign correspondent for *The New Yorker* is different from working for a newspaper or news magazine, radio or television. I am not interested in journalistic scoops, not rushed by tonight's deadline. I don't work with one eye glancing at my wristwatch, and I have no excuse for jumping to premature conclusions. I can't compete with my fellow correspondents for speed but can outdo them in depth. I have time to check on the all-important details; I have all the freedom and almost all the space I need. I can afford the luxury of establishing the mood of a certain situation, which is often important for its interpretation. Some of my Letters from foreign countries run to twenty thousand words. Some Reporter-at-Large pieces later became books, with little material added.

Such a report must tell more than the facts that are already known from the press, newsweeklies, radio, TV. Shawn once said in an interview that in reporting for *The New Yorker* one tries, whenever possible, "to let the facts implicitly convey the writer's interpretation and point of view." This is more complicated to do than it sounds. The facts must not just be used to fit the writer's (or, God forbid, the magazine's) point of view — though this has been done elsewhere. Ideally, a *New Yorker* report should be objective but not impersonal, humanly truthful but not coldly analytical. We take it for granted that pure objectivity does not exist, but we try to come close to it "as humanly as possible." Even a topical report should have an inner timelessness. It should not be dated as yesterday's newspaper but remain valuable for months, or years, after the event.

After watching my American fellow correspondents for a long time in the journalistic inferno behind the Iron Curtain, I've concluded that most of them are able reporters but many of them were the wrong people for their job or were working in the wrong place.

The people behind the curtains live political lives. (I can speak only for the Iron Curtain countries, not having worked in the Bamboo Curtain area.) The air they breathe is composed of oxygen and politics. They cannot afford the luxury of escaping into a never-never world where they are left alone. Many people there have paid the penalty for neglecting political realities. The citizens must keep up with the fluctuations of political power, or they may find themselves one early morning deeply in trouble. They don't have to read the party paper every day, unless they are party people, managers, journalists, men making decisions. But they cannot ignore the mainstreams of political thinking.

A pro-Western East German friend whom I've known for many years explained to me recently in East Berlin why he must think, and live, politically.

"My job and my family's existence depend on politics. My wife and I think politically, and our children have learned this even before going to school. They know they're growing up into a political world and have to cope with it. How will your hippies and flower children and romanticists be able to face the realities of the late twentieth century when they wake up from their daydreams?"

It is impossible to get at the deeper political truth in the Communist world without speaking the language of the people who live there. Even the U.S. State Department, not always an institution of revolutionary reform, has quietly acknowledged this fact of political life by sending its younger officers to foreign-language schools before assigning them abroad. Washington, the capital of a nation of immigrants, neglected to avail itself of the large pool of former immigrants, many of whom could be useful in the complex development of America's foreign relations. (Henry Kissinger is the exception, and maybe a beginning.) We former immigrants are no longer second-class citizens. The Supreme

Court changed that a few years ago. Now I get my passport renewed as easily as a native-born American, no questions asked. But in the upper levels of High Bureaucracy, a stigma remains attached to Americans born abroad. Many believe that naturalized Americans should not serve the United States in their former homeland. I was told by very high bureaucrats that such people might face a "conflict of loyalty" abroad, or that they might "get involved and be in trouble." A State Department officer of Czechoslovak origin who speaks Czech, Russian, German, French, and English spent several years in South America, where his widely known abilities were wasted; he is not the only one.

Unless one gets "involved" anywhere today, one doesn't find out the truth. And in order to get involved, one must speak the local language. Even that is no longer sufficient. It's one thing to speak the language, and another to understand the complex ambiguities of local thinking — to interpret the subtle inflections and hidden meanings of the spoken words. Only a man can do this who grew up in that part of the world and never lost touch, or who lived there for a long time. He should be able to understand what is said and to guess what must remain unsaid. The inhabitants of the Unfree World have learned to understand the meaning of silence.

In 1963, I spent several days in East Germany, one of the least accessible countries to American journalists. The sinister mixture of German thoroughness and Soviet suspiciousness makes the Deutsche Demokratische Republik a forbidding territory for inquisitive Westerners. Every foreign correspondent is automatically considered a spy and guilty, unless proved innocent. The East Germans are worse then the Soviets because they are more efficient.

When I tried to go there, I had no illusions of what I would be up against. Many people would try to hinder my work. Those willing to help, among the millions of people who still feel tied to the West, might be afraid to do so. Fear is widespread among the population of the

D.D.R. And there were "technical" difficulties. The D.D.R. authorities couldn't stamp a visa in my American passport because the United States has never recognized East Germany. So how can the East Germans officially recognize an American passport? If I went there, I would be a man without a passport, a man without identity. Such a man may be alive but doesn't exist officially.

I embarked upon the adventure at a time when the thaw, spreading from Moscow, had reached even the iciest wastes of East Germany. One day I crossed Checkpoint Charlie in Berlin and walked over to a nearby office which, I'd been told, had been set up for the convenience of foreign (meaning friendly foreign) journalists. Quite a few friendly foreigners from North Korea, Cuba, Ghana, were there. They had political priority. I was asked to wait. In America, I'd long been a second-class citizen because I was a foreigner, and now, because I was an American, I'd become a second-class foreigner in East Berlin. Under the circumstances, meekness might be misunderstood. The situation reminded me of the eminently practical advice of Dr. Spira, our rabbi and religion-teacher in my hometown. When we boys complained to him that we were discriminated against by non-Jewish boys, Dr. Spira, a man of Talmudic wisdom, said, "Since you remain Jews even if you won't be proud of it, you might as well be proud of being Jews."

Acting like a proud American, I was soon noticed and called in by two officials. (There are always two of them, for obvious reasons.) They were new-style Communists, young, intelligent, affable; they might even smile once in a while. Conceivably, you might argue with them, in an innocuous way, which might amuse them. But you couldn't have done it with the implacable, unsmiling Stalinists in the old days. There wasn't any point in arguing, though, since in the basic matters of Leninism-Marxism they were just as dogmatic as their predecessors. They were superbly trained dialecticians; they could easily prove to you that black was white, and red was blue. They always outargued me, and in the end I didn't even try.

Herr So-und-So indicated that I might be permitted to visit the country, but — there was a slight pause — I would have to be accompanied wherever I went, day and night. Really quite an advantage, he said, because my *Betreuer* (literally, "the man who takes care of you") would look after the boring details: hotel reservations, permits to visit factories, interviews to be arranged. He would be extremely helpful.

"And if I want to go alone?" I asked directly.

"You cannot go alone." He smiled, looking like a character in a James Bond novel. Only I wasn't Bond.

So that was that. I was asked to leave my personal data and my passport number. "Just write it down," Herr So-und-So said nonchalantly, refusing to take official notice of my passport. A surrealistic scene. We shook hands. I left. Weeks later, when I was in New York, I received a cable saying: JOURNEY PERMITTED STOP EXPECT YOU NEXT MONDAY MORNING CHARLOTTENSTRASSE 66.

I flew to West Berlin via Vienna, picking up some warm clothes (it was December) and buying a couple of bottles of Scotch at the airport that might be helpful in East Germany, which is strictly a vodka country. At West Berlin's Tempelhof Airport I rented an Opel Rekord, which would be less conspicuous in East Germany than my American Buick. The following morning I drove through Checkpoint Charlie and the opening in the Wall.

The East German Vopos became suddenly polite when I showed them the cable. I was ceremoniously taken to Charlottenstrasse 66, where I met Herr So-und-So. He smiled; we were great friends now. We shook hands. Both East and West Germans shake hands vigorously, and the Russians kiss you on the cheek, and so do the French — meaningless gestures, like being called "darling" after the briefest acquaintance, in Hollywood. Everything was fine, said Herr So-und-So. It hadn't been easy to get my visa. The Foreign Ministry had been rather displeased with my earlier *New Yorker* report from Dresden.

"I read it," my new friend said. "Well done, though not very flattering for us, I might say."

"You might," I said.

He laughed softly. We were still acting like characters in a cheap spy thriller.

"I'm afraid," he said, "we shall have to take *very* good care of you while you are our guest."

Now I laughed, not so softly. I said, "I've got a bottle of Scotch downstairs in my car. May I bring it up. To . . . celebrate?"

"Let's get the business over with first," he said, suddenly very matter-of-fact. "Here is your visa." He handed me a slip of paper which said, "Valid only in connection with Passport No. B483539." (It didn't say that it was an American passport.) "Issued under No. 3/8674. Entry and Exit Visa for Joseph Wechsberg. Two entries and exits, good for eleven days. Border control point: Berlin. Purpose: journey D.D.R."

"Nice, isn't it?" he said.

I nodded, putting the paper into my passport, and then I went down for the Scotch. Moral: even countries that don't recognize each other can easily avoid the difficulty of nonrecognition with a smile and a bottle of Scotch.

My escort was an East German journalist. He understood what I was trying to do, though he didn't approve of it. The third night, after a lot of Scotch (it was very cold, I should have brought a whole case), he told me that he'd been in the Hitler Youth, had served in the *Wehrmacht*, had seen terrible things, became a pacifist, and eventually arrived at Communism by way of pacifism: He was an honest man, an idealist. His father had been a locksmith and a Social-Democrat long before the Nazis came to power. After 1945, when the Social-Democrats had failed as an underground opposition against the Nazis during the war, he joined the Communist party. His father distrusted him, until one day, in 1944, the boy came into the living room just as the father was listening to B.B.C. London. The father looked frightened; people had been sent to prison for listening to the B.B.C. Then the boy said, "Don't be silly, Father, I listen to London myself," and from that day on they were friends.

I respected my escort for his honesty. Our problem was to communicate. We both spoke German, but our words had a different meaning. We couldn't even agree on such basic terms as "peace," "freedom," "democracy." "Your kind of freedom often means anarchy," he once said. "Think of Dallas." He admitted that the East German regime was not perfect, but it guaranteed "peace" while the West German militarists were thinking only of "war and revanchism." He used "revanchism" to describe the Ugly German, and "Wall Street" as a synonym for the Ugly American. He stuck to these clichés, even after the fourth Scotch.

We both agreed that I must get "the complete story," but couldn't agree on the meaning of "the complete story." My *Betreuer* thought it meant the official facts and figures, production quotas and work norms, questions asked and answers given, in his presence. To me this was not the complete story. I had already noticed a slight inflection in the voices of some people as they answered my questions, in his presence. Sometimes I noticed an imperceptible pause before they spoke. I sensed they were holding back something, though I wasn't sure what it was. Sometimes people would answer my questions, but while they spoke the expression in their eyes seemed to belie their words. Others — there were even party members among them — would suddenly grow silent when my *Betreuer* was around. Their voices recited a well-memorized lesson, but their eyes expressed doubts. They reminded me of my clients when I was a young lawyer in Prague. My clients had tried hard to convince me they were telling the truth.

I wondered whether I might be imagining things, until one day when I talked to a worker in the presence of my escort. He told me how satisfied he was with his job, with the regime, with his life. Somehow I managed to get him away for a couple of minutes. The moment we were alone, his manner changed abruptly.

"I told you the truth, but not the whole truth," he said, glancing nervously over his shoulder at my escort, who was talking to some people. He spoke fast; he knew there wasn't much time left. "Of course, I couldn't tell you in front of *him* that we are living under the dictatorship of the norms, that we feel observed while we are awake or asleep, that we are just cogs in a watchwork, no longer human beings. That gets you down. I am an old Socialist. How is it possible that the regime that pretends to do the most for us has such a dehumanizing effect on people. . . ."

He stopped. My escort joined us. Abruptly, the man discussed a technical aspect of his work, avoiding my eyes. We said good-bye to him. From that day on, I knew that silence can indeed be eloquent, that it wasn't only *what* the people told me, but *how* they said it. I learned to pay attention to ambiguous sentences, to certain words pronounced in a certain way. Sometimes an answer would be followed by a sudden silence, as though they were implying that the opposite was really true of what they'd told me.

A German proverb says, "Talk is silver, silence is golden." I learned the meaning of sudden pauses, unfinished sentences, eloquent silence. Later, as I recapitulated the conversations in my mind and reread my notes, the silence took on a definite meaning. Some insignificant contradictions and ambiguous answers fell into place. These people had learned the technique of telling you something by saying nothing. When in doubt, don't open your mouth; express your thoughts with your eyes. The eyes tell the story. Millions of people behind the Iron Curtain are masters of the silent technique. In my article for *The New Yorker*, I wrote:

I never had a similar experience in any country but then I've never traveled under similar conditions in a Communist country where my intimate knowledge of the language made me aware of subtle, hidden meanings. And so this will be a report on what I saw and heard, *and also on what sometimes remained unsaid.* [The italics are mine.]

The New Yorker bought the piece and sent me an edited proof. For once, I didn't agree with it. All references to "silence" had been removed. I complained to Shawn. He cabled me that he'd reluctantly decided not to run the East German piece. THE HEART OF THE PROBLEM IS YOUR THEME OF SILENCE WHICH WE THINK IS JOURNALISTICALLY UNSOUND. WE FEEL THAT IT IS IMPOSSIBLE FOR ANYONE REALLY TO REPORT OR INTERPRET SILENCE FROM A JOURNALISTIC POINT OF VIEW. . . .

It was a valid argument from the point of view of West Forty-third Street. *The New Yorker* released the material, and Little, Brown published it as a book, *Journey through the Land of Eloquent Silence.* I dedicated the book "To the Silent People Everywhere." A German translation was published by Ullstein in West Germany, and I was told that quite a few copies of *Land mit zwei Gesichtern* were smuggled into East Germany.

Months later, letters and messages from East Germans began to reach me, often by devious ways. Nearly all of them agreed with the conclusions of my report. Many admitted that I had correctly interpreted people's "silence" and "half silence," as one called it. Journalistically, silence might be unsound, but my story had not been shaken. Unorthodox situations demand unorthodox means.

I couldn't have done this story if I didn't speak German and know the mentality of the East Germans. There, and in Poland and Czechoslovakia, I hear both the things that are said to me as well as things not meant for my ears. One listens between the words as one reads between the lines. A man there called himself "one of the two-faced people":

> All of us have a convenient face, for outside use only, and a private face which we hide carefully. We are a schizophrenic nation. We've learned to switch faces consciously and subconsciously; we don't even know it any longer. . . . Duplicity has become our second nature. Everybody plays the game.

Quite a few Western reporters are not sufficiently trained to play the game. Their publications furnish them with generous expense accounts, but money will not buy exact information. Many don't speak the local language and depend on local stringers, translators, and hangers-on, who consider the correspondents a subsidiary source of income, cigarettes, whiskey. Some correspondents listen to the partisan army of Western-minded people behind the Iron Curtain who hope against hope that someday they will be liberated. The value of their information is doubtful. They may be honest, but they see the situation as they *want* to see it. The correspondents also depend on Communist party contacts — younger men who speak English, French, German, who lived in the West for some time and are well trained in the subtleties of friendly persuasion and psychological warfare. Their information is equally doubtful, for the opposite reason. The foreign correspondents are isolated from the local population.

I was in Prague just before the "Prague Spring" in Czechoslovakia ended with the invasion of the Soviet and Warsaw Pact troops on August 21, 1968. We didn't know that these were the last days of freedom and exhilaration, when anything went. For the first time in thirty years, the nation had found its true identity, its dignity, its self-respect. I remember a morning in the lobby of the Alkron Hotel, headquarters of many Western correspondents. My Czech friends called it "the snake pit," an allusion to the Western correspondents being surrounded by local snakes. The correspondents had occupied the strategic corners and recesses of the lobby, which they turned into journalistic pillboxes. The rumor mills were going full speed. One correspondent was having a late breakfast, listening to a Czech woman interpreter who read to him selected bits from the local morning papers. The selection of the items, and the emphasis, were left to her, since the correspondent didn't speak Czech or Slovak. Characters of doubtful credibility dropped in with bits of information, and were offered drinks. Once in a while, a correspondent was called over the loudspeaker to the telex or the telephone. To be called a dozen times during the morning gave a man status among his colleagues. Stringers came and were sent out again to check on something. Couriers and courtiers brought mysterious messages. A noted Czech journalist who was there with me said it reminded him of a ludicrous, updated version of *The Front Page*. He said it was rather depressing.

"They will write their stories, and in their homelands millions of people will read the stories in their papers and magazines, and believe they're extremely well informed," he said. The stories would certainly be interesting, but were they journalistically sound?

Where Anything Might Happen— and Did

MY FAVORITE HOTEL in the early postwar years was not one of the Ritzes or Palaces but that distinguished Balkan establishment known as the Hotel Moskva in Belgrade, haven of minor diplomats and major correspondents. Even the *New York Times* had (and still has) its local office there, in a cluttered-up room-and-shower on the second floor. It might have shocked some of the newspaper's eminent, foreign-office-type executives, had they ever come there.

Among Americans in the Balkans, many of whom served time at the Moskva, it was always good for another round of *slivovitz* (plum brandy) and nostalgic reminiscence. Like Titoism, the Hotel Moskva provoked either praise or criticism, but never indifference. Not many hotels can make that claim, though the Moskva is not mentioned in the best guidebooks. By conventional standards of luxury and comfort, it couldn't compete with the Ritzes or Palaces, but the Moskva's great asset was its total lack of convention. Its manager, Vladimir Tomasic, who called himself "a friend of every friend of the Moskva," was a dignified, silver-haired ex-*Rittmeister* (captain) of the former K. and K. (Imperial and Royal) Austrian Cavalry. Tomasic had the sad smile of a man whom nothing will surprise anymore. An enthusiastic Britisher of noble ancestry once said that Tomasic should run Claridge's in London.

Tomasic was flattered but not surprised. His powers of persuasion were legendary. He persuaded people that there was heat in cold radiators; that brownish, beetlelike spots on the floor were "marks in the wood"; that the Moskva was one of the world's great hotels. He did his persuading in Slovenian, Serbo-Croatian, German, Italian, French, and English, which he spoke fluently, and half a dozen other languages which he spoke well. His dignity was never impaired. At the end of World War Two, a guest noticed that Tomasic was walking around all day wearing a pair of old GI pants and a trenchcoat. The guest took this to be another Moskva eccentricity until he discovered, by accident, that Tomasic didn't own a jacket.

Tomasic loved to reminisce about his early army years in Wiener Neustadt, near Vienna, always remarking, as an aside, that a certain Josip Broz had been working in Wiener Neustadt at that time, long before he became President of Yugoslavia. One day, "the Old Gentleman," Emperor Franz Joseph I, had come out to Wiener Neustadt to review the young cadets. At that point, somebody would order more *slivovitz*, and Tomasic would add some unknown detail involving him and several young officers in some escapades to the Hotel Sacher in Vienna, "a nice place but no match for the Moskva." In their small way, he and his army friends had contributed to the collapse of the Habsburg monarchy. "My career has developed parallel with that of Marshal Tito," he would say. He was a Yugoslav patriot and admired Marshal Tito, but this didn't prevent him from having wistful feelings about his youthful days in the Habsburg monarchy. I understood exactly how he felt.

Tomasic hailed from Opatije, the former Austrian beach resort on the Adriatic known as Abbazia, where little boys worried their parents by falling off the cliffs. I was one of them, during the summer of 1912, when I was there with my parents. When I told Tomasic about my father, who had been his fellow officer in the Austrian army, he silently embraced me, and there were tears in his eyes. Ever since, I was *persona grata* at the Moskva, and always had one of the hotel's few rooms with private bath. This was a gesture of appreciation, since there was no hot water in the tub, and sometimes no water at all. Once the connection between the bathtub drain and the hole in the tiled floor was broken, and the water spilled all over the floor. A source of trouble, the bathroom was a powerful status symbol at the Moskva. One had to be with the *New York Times* or an ambassador to have one.

Habitués of the Waldorf Towers or the Beau Rivage in Ouchy might have found it difficult to adjust to the unpredictable behavior of heat, water, and power at the Moskva, the nonchalance of the service, and the local vermins' immunity to the strongest insecticides. Many guests had an electric plate in their room, on which they made their own Nescafé in the morning because they didn't like the hotel's Turkish-style coffee, sweet and thick, prepared in a metal container. Unfortunately, the electric system wasn't geared to several plates being turned on at the same time. There was a fuse in the corridor, equipped with a lever. If too many appliances were turned on, the lever would fall down, cutting off the current. Ingenious guests would place small wooden pegs under the lever to keep it from falling down. Presently, there would be a short circuit on the entire floor. Tomasic, operating on the principle of Help Yourself and God Will Help You, suggested that the guests communicate with each other by phone and coordinate their electric activities.

Another much discussed enigma was the whimsicality of the central heating system. During the terribly cold January of 1950, the rooms on the western side of the Moskva remained without heat. Tomasic explained that "this was not to be understood as an expression of the management's anti-Western leanings," and did nothing about the radiators. The following summer, on a sweltering day, the radiators in several rooms suddenly became hot, adding the hotel's insult to the climate's injury. I went down to complain to Tomasic.

Looking at me coolly, he said, "The sun shines on the hot-water tank and heats it." I was too angry to realize that the sun never shone in the cellar of the Moskva. Tomasic ended the conversation by politely reminding me that "to stay at the Moskva is an honor that carries certain obligations."

One of the obligations was to be insulted by the proud waiters who accepted tips only under protest against the bourgeois habit of tipping, or to be woken up at five-fifteen in the morning by a loud knock at the door. A waiter would come in, place a breakfast tray on my table, and walk out, impassively shrugging off my complaint that I hadn't ordered breakfast at dawn. Later that morning, I heard a guest downstairs complain to Tomasic that he'd missed his early plane because the waiter who was supposed to wake him at five-fifteen with his breakfast had never come. "Where was he?" shouted the guest. I could have told him.

Once the third-floor corridor was getting a new cement flooring. The outer doors of all the rooms were removed for a few days until the cement hardened under the doorsteps. Meanwhile, people would walk across wooden boards. The rooms were locked by their inner doors, that is, all but one, which never had a second door. During two nights and days the occupant, a melancholy foreign service acolyte working at the United States Embassy, was living in front of all the passersby. But such was the mentality at the Moskva that neither the junior statesman nor the passersby found anything strange about the arrangement. They knew that things could be much worse. An Old Balkan hand had been at the Moskva during the hectic days immediately after the war; his bed had no springs, and he had to steal two chairs and place them under his mattress. He discovered bullet holes in the closet door and bloodstains in the closet. Whoever had fired into the closet, must have fired first and looked afterwards to see whether the closet was occupied, perchance.

During one season, hot water was available only on Saturday night, and guests had the choice between a cocktail party and a hot bath. Many preferred the latter. One memorable morning, the warm water stopped running just after I'd lathered my face and wanted to shave. While I pondered what to do, there was a knock, and a waiter came in, carrying a hot plate and a small pot of water. He put the pot on the plate, plugged in the plate, and walked out. I considered this typical Moskva service by intuition, since I hadn't even rung the bell. Later the guest from room 402 raised hell in the lobby because he'd never got the hot plate which he'd asked for. Of course he hadn't, since it had been delivered to me, in 302. All the Moskva needed to make it perfect was the Marx Brothers.

Once a senior diplomat who had just been assigned to his embassy in Belgrade checked in with his wife. They left their passports with the concierge, which was the rule, and went out again. They came back after midnight. The night concierge, who also worked as part-time informer for the secret police, refused to let the gentleman go up with a lady he didn't know. The diplomat's assurance that the lady was his wife was not deemed satisfactory. "Anybody can say that," the night porter said. Tomasic had to be summoned, the hotel safe was opened, the passports were inspected, and at last the diplomat and his wife were permitted to go up together.

The next morning, Tomasic put on his semiformal attire, a third-hand cutaway that a British guest had once forgotten at the hotel, and went up to apologize to the diplomat.

"We only tried to protect you, sir," he said. "Suppose Madame had gone up with someone else?"

Tomasic later explained that he wanted "no Zagreb business" in this hotel. In Zagreb, Yugoslavia's second largest city, gentlemen guests at a large hotel had been shown by the night porter an album of alluring photographs of local ladies, some of them society, who might be persuaded to keep them company. The custom ended abruptly when a guest discovered among the photographs the picture of his wife.

There were strange customs in postwar Yugoslavia. Night driving was arduous. The courtesy-of-the-road rule demanded that you dim your headlights at the approach of another car, and shut them off completely when the car was about to meet yours. Two cars on a Yugoslav highway would pass each other in complete darkness, at a snail's pace, while the drivers said silent prayers, even if they happened to be Communist atheists. In the cities the rule was to sound the horn at an intersection once, if you wanted to go straight ahead; twice, for a right turn; three times, for a left turn; and six times — ta, ta-ta, ta-ta-ta — for a U-turn. I once had a large room (with bath) overlooking the corner of Terazije but gave it up when too many drivers made U-turns underneath my windows.

Habitués at the Moskva had to get used to the chambermaids' habit of bringing along their kids, who played in the guest rooms while Mama was cleaning up. A humorless Swiss diplomat once complained that the children had used his new toothbrush to clean their shoes. The chambermaid was insulted and told him not to bother with such trifles.

"I've lived with the partisans in the woods during the war," she said, "Where were *you*?" The Swiss apologized.

Lots of people invaded my room who had no business being there, but nothing was ever stolen. A Yugoslav might shoot into the closet but wouldn't steal your wallet. Once I was told, upon entering the lobby, that "the chambermaid lost your room key." Knowing my "obligations," I waited downstairs until the secret police had finished searching my room. The lobby was always filled with temporarily unemployed Balkan revolutionaries who kept their voices low and their hats on. They seemed to be plotting a new Sarajevo, but perhaps they were only talking about last week's soccer game. One night when I was there, a disheveled woman came down the stairway and wandered through the lobby, gesticulating and talking incoherently. No one paid any attention to her. After a while, two white-coated attendants arrived from the outside and took her back to the sanitarium where the poor woman was kept for schizophrenia, and from where she'd escaped, naturally, to the Moskva. Tomasic was not amused when I said I wasn't surprised.

The Moskva's manager has left the People's Republic of Yugoslavia for the Kingdom of Heaven. I no longer go to the Moskva. It isn't the same anymore. I now stay at the Metropol, a white-gleaming structure, early-Miami-Beach, that was originally built as the headquarters of the People's Youth Organization and was later turned into a hotel. The plumbing and central heating are working well, and there are neither beetlelike spots on the floor nor Balkan plotters in the hall. But I am often lonely for the old Moskva.

For a few months during those preposterous postwar years, my home was a castle — a thirteenth-century castle in Alsace, equipped with ancient history and modern appurtenances, four-hundred-year-old carved doors, and a ghost. A fine place for incurable romantics.

I was getting tired after moving around for years as a foreign correspondent for *The New Yorker*. The glamorous profession has its drawbacks. There is rarely a dull moment but too many exhausting ones, when one longs for the tranquil comfort of the bourgeois life. One does learn a great deal, though. I became a scholar in deciphering Continental railroad schedules, and an acrobat getting undressed in an upper berth of a wagon-lit sleeping car. I learned to leave the spoon in my demitasse in the dining car of the Orient Express, which kept the coffee from spilling over, and I knew all about illegal currency rates, the idiosyncrasies of certain customs officers, the secrets of how to get a visa for countries that don't like American correspondents. I learned that the only way of dealing with the secret police was to ignore them. If you are the sort of man who worries about anonymous characters trailing you or the hair you put into a certain spot in your luggage that isn't there anymore, you ought to look for another job. But the greatest problem is to use one's local sources without exposing them to danger. The foreign correspondent can always get out when things blow up, but what's going to happen to *them*?

In the spring of 1949, when I had spent much time in Berlin, Budapest, Prague, and other cold-war hot spots, I happened to be in Strasbourg, Alsace, visiting an American friend who was working in Europe for the United States government. Frank was an indefatigable missionary of the American Gospel, which he was trying to spread among the natives. I'd become skeptical about the natives' willingness to accept the Gospel. During the final phase of the last war, when we in Psychological Warfare had been trying, once more, to make Germany safe for democracy, I'd lost the hope that we would ever change them. The de-Nazification program of the United States Army was a tragic farce. Some high-ranking officers and officials who spent their days planning the program, spent their nights in the company of complaisant German women who only a while ago had kept company with high-ranking Nazis and *Wehrmacht* officers. Quite a few Germans with a doubtful political past were able to delude the gullible Allied investigators. The only people who would have been able to carry out the program — the small minority of decent Germans who had suffered during the Hitler regime — were ignored because *they* didn't try to ingratiate themselves with the occupiers.

Frank, an American idealist, still believed that much could be done. He was a restless, active man. Once he left Strasbourg on a Friday night, arrived in Marseilles on Saturday for an official lunch with local dignitaries, attended a "political" wedding and a reception, went to a dinner party with the mayor, got up at four A.M. on Sunday, caught a train for Monte Carlo, took a swim in the sea, lost eleven hundred francs gambling at the Casino, made a speech, sat up all night on the train because he couldn't get a sleeper, and was back at his office in Strasbourg on Monday morning, eager to get on with the job. He lived with his wife Jean in the wing of an old castle twelve miles west of

Strasbourg. He said he needed "complete solitude" after his strenuous work, and they'd given up their comfortable apartment in town. When I met him at his office, he invited my wife and me for dinner at the castle.

"We've got a wonderful dining room, called the *salle des chevaliers*. During the last session of the Council of Europe, we had a big party there. Sir Winston Churchill was the guest of honor. Did you ever live in a castle?"

I shook my head. The old castles in my native Moravia had been merely historical relics and picturesque landmarks. We boys used to play mysterious games in an uninhabited, romantic castle near Ostrava. The games stopped after two boys were hurt when a piece of castle fell down on them. Later, I visited the beautiful old castles near Merano. Few people lived in them. Sometimes the descendants of the former owner, unable to pay for expensive repairs, had moved to the small gatehouse, abandoning the castle, which slowly fell to pieces. Eventually it would be a noble ruin.

The castle where Frank and Jean lived was different. It was a beautiful structure in Rhine-castle style, with two circular towers ending in pointed, cone-shaped roofs, surrounded by an old park. The thick sandstone walls were crowned by battlements with loopholes between the embrasures, and there were turrets and jutting corners and dormer windows. There was a moat around it. A stone bridge that had replaced the former drawbridge led into a courtyard with an old well. It was a storybook castle, surrounded by the gently rolling, vine-covered hills, located in what optimists hope will once again be the heart of a united Europe. From the towers one could see both the French Vosges and the German Schwarzwald.

Frank had asked Madame S., the owner, for drinks. We visited the *salle des chevaliers*, a paneled dining room with church pews, a huge fireplace, a coat of arms, and a painting of the late Duke Eberhart, who had had his last meal in this room one day in 1390, before he went off to a tournament in Strasbourg where he was killed. Later the Swedes, and after them the English, had burned down some wings. In the First World War the French and the Germans had shelled it, and in the Second World War the Nazis had evicted Madame S. and used the castle as a storage for the paintings from the Strasbourg Museum. The walls were seven feet thick.

Madame S. showed us the wing where she lived. We walked through a dark corridor, past gilt-framed paintings of bearded knights. On the walls of a large hunting room, stenciled columns showed the number of partridge, quail, pheasant, venison, and wild boar killed every year since 1879. In 1893, they'd shot 3,891 pheasants. Frank said it had been a good year for Alsatian wines but not for the birds.

It was the first time I had dinner sitting in a church pew. An Alsatian peasant girl served the food. She was from the nearby village and got the equivalent of seventeen dollars a month. Jean told my wife there were lots of girls. That started it, I think, and Madame S.'s offer to rent us another wing, which had a library with stained-glass windows and a trapdoor underneath the writing desk, with a stairway leading into an underground passage. When the Swedes under General Mansfeld attacked the castle in 1440, the defenders ran out of food. The Swedes sent six emissaries to discuss the surrender terms. The defenders took a vote; six men preferred surrender to a long siege and death. The defenders arrested the Swedish emissaries, and forced the six men who had voted for surrender to put on Swedish uniforms. The "traitors" were hanged from the six windows overlooking the park. When the Swedish attackers outside saw that what they thought were their emissaries had been executed, they entered the castle through a gap in the outer wall. They found their own men alive. The defenders had escaped through the underground passage that started below the library desk. The Swedes got mad and burned down a couple of wings.

We went to look at the library.

"Wouldn't you like to work at that desk?" Frank asked temptingly.

We liked the paneled bedrooms and the beautiful view. The atmosphere was different from the hotel rooms in which we'd lived for years. Jean said she did most of her shopping in the village, where the vegetables came straight from the local gardens and the butcher made his own *charcuterie.* We walked back to the *salle des chevaliers,* and had more of the heady Alsatian wine. That's my only excuse. We moved in the next day. Too late it occurred to us that we hadn't even asked to see the bathroom. When you have a library with an underground passage and stained-glass windows, you mustn't be narrow-minded.

The circular bathroom was in one of the two round towers. Once it had been a dungeon. Madame S.'s grandfather, in 1899, after a cold winter, turned it into a bathroom. There was an ancient tub, with the enamel coming off, an iron stove, and a wooden box filled with firewood and briquettes. A typewritten sheet above the tub showed a drawing of the stove, in the colors of the French *tricolore,* with mysterious signs, letters, and abbreviations. Underneath it said: "Manner of Preparing Hot Bath and Avoiding Accidents." I translate:

Make sure when you open faucet (A), that the water is running. Close faucet (A) but not entirely so it will drip every three or four seconds. (This is necessary because the safety valve [B] doesn't function.) Put newspapers, small firewood and three large pieces of wood in lower opening (D 2). Open key (F) to valve (C 4) by turning it half left, and half close stove door. When the fire is burning, close door entirely and turn key (F) so that it almost closes. Place three briquettes on fire (if you wrap them in newspaper, they will last longer.) If you place another (fourth) briquette on top, you will have warm water all day long.

There was a second paragraph, typed in red letters, which said:

Never, never, never (*jamais, jamais, jamais*) place more than three briquettes into the stove at one time, if you propose to take only one bath. Place briquettes in front of the flames, near the opening. This will heat the water much faster.

Never, never open the cold-water faucet (D) above the tub while hot water comes out of faucet (A). If faucet (D) should stop running, immediately notify Désiré, the gardener. If Désiré and his mother are not in, fetch them at the village inn (La Couronne). Upon arrival Désiré will pump water into the cistern below the roof.

Never put in more briquettes before the cold-water (D) starts to run again. If, in spite of these precautions, the stove should blow up, notify Stoeber, the plumber, telephone 4–19.

After my experience as a night fireman in the American army, I should have known better than to play around in that bathroom, but boys will be boys when it comes to taking a bath. Suffice it to say that the stove almost blew up, and I decided to take a cold bath, but just as I was in the tub, covered with soap, the stopper fell out, there was a gurgling sound, and seconds later the tub was empty. I walked back through the corridor, cold and soapy. Later Lucille, our Alsatian servant, fixed a hot bath for me, but I didn't really enjoy it.

We met some interesting people in the nearby village. Monsieur Bickel, the mayor, lived in a half-timbered house where he kept his military decorations under glass in the salon. In the First World War, he'd been a *Gefreiter* in the Kaiser's army, and in the Second World War, he'd fought with the French against the Germans. He was quite philosophical about it; he said that Alsatians had become internationalists by force of habit.

"Consider the case of the mother of Désiré, who is your gardener at the castle. When she was born here in 1859, the village was French. In 1871, she became German. After 1918, she was French again until 1941, when the Nazis annexed Alsace and called it Gau Oberrhein. After the Liberation in 1945, she was once more French. Absurd, isn't it? In 1917, I was awarded a medal for bravery by the Germans, but they never sent it to me, and then the war was over. Later I complained to a friend in the French army. One day the French army, against which I'd fought, sent me *their* medal for valor. A colonel came from the War Ministry in Paris and gave me the accolade." M. Bickel touched both cheeks with his forefinger to indicate the honored spots. He said the village barber had had his right leg shot off in the Second World War when he'd fought on the side of the Germans against the British, and now the French were paying his pension, perhaps partly with American Marshall Plan money.

They had all kinds of fortifications around the village. Some had been built for the War of 1870, others for the First and the Second World Wars. The whole hillside was studded with subterranean galleries and tunnels, where the kids were now playing. The mayor said casually that at the start of an atomic war, they would all seek refuge there; he'd made his plans. He had no doubt that it would happen.

The northern side of the village was German and Protestant; the southern side was French and Catholic. People from both sides fell in love and out of love, got married or fought with each other, but on the whole got along. Mayor Bickel said that in a nearby village Catholics and Protestants used the same church at different times, and why not? Weren't they all praying to the same Lord? On Sunday, everybody met at the Couronne, the local bistro. The proprietress of the Couronne had successively been on friendly terms with German imperialists, French nationalists, Alsatian separatists, English tourists, Nazi storm troopers, French militiamen, German soldiers, and Gaullists. The mayor said she liked everybody who drank up and paid.

"Except her husband," he said. "She doesn't like him. He's the one behind the counter, washing the glasses. He washes five glasses and in between drinks two."

In the spring of 1945, the village had been liberated by a platoon of American soldiers under the command of a sergeant from Chicago. The Americans, like so many earlier conquerors, were soon captivated by the good Alsatian people and the good Alsatian wine. In no time, the sergeant from Chicago sat in Mayor Bickel's salon, where earlier the German *Oberleutnant* from Hannover sat, and later the French *capitaine* from Rouen. Eleven citizens had been killed during the war, and their names were added to the monument in the village square. Five were still missing. There was some trouble with the "radicals," whose leader was Jean-Baptiste, the man in charge of the tiny railroad station where a rarely frequented branch line went through. Jean-Baptiste was stationmaster, brakeman, ticketseller. He swept the station in the evening and let down the barrier across the street *if* he felt like it. Sometimes he stayed at the Couronne for hours, drinking *framboise*, raspberry brandy, which is said to go down like fire and to return, hauntingly, like raspberries.

When Jean-Baptiste was in a mean mood, he would let down the barrier, though no train was expected. He was an ardent Communist and carried on a running battle with Madame S., the owner of the castle, whom he considered an evil symbol of capitalism. Once he let the barrier down just as Madame S. was passing through in her small car; the car's left front fender was shaved off. No train was expected. Madame was suing the French National Railroads and Jean-Baptiste, but the suit might take years, and she didn't expect to be around when it was decided.

I met Jean-Baptiste at the Couronne. He offered me a *framboise* in a water glass. He said he opposed the political and social system of *les Etats Unis* but admired the diesel locomotives of *la Pennsylvanie*. In his bedroom he had pictures of Stalin, Thorez, and of a modern diesel locomotive. A second cousin in Pittsburgh sent him pictures of the new engines of the Pennsylvania Railroad. Some people at the Couronne said that Jean-Baptiste would give up Communism if *la Pennsylvanie* would offer him a job in America.

When Jean-Baptiste wasn't around, I had a drink with Désiré, our gardener and general handyman, who kept one eye closed most of the time, which gave him a cunning or amusing appearance, depending on how the light fell on him. Jean-Baptiste couldn't stand Désiré.

"His mental development ended with Feldmarschall Hindenburg. Here in the village we ask what is the difference between an accident and a tragedy. If Désiré should fall into the Rhine, it would be an accident, but if he should get out alive, it would be a tragedy."

At the Couronne I also met M. Sans-Prénom, the local *gendarme*, representing the executive branch of the French Republic in the village. He was a blond man with a spidery face, who labored under the handicap of having no first name. His parents couldn't agree on one, and decided to call him Sans-Prénom (Without First Name). He bothered me a lot, asked for references, wanted to know whether we had declared all foreign currency upon entering the country, and why we didn't have *cartes d'identité*. I was his new target of officialdom. For years he'd been kept busy by the undeclared state of war between the villagers and Madame S. at the castle. When Madame had returned after the Liberation, she discovered that her furniture, paintings, tapestries, books, had been given by the Germans to certain villagers. In return the villagers were expected to "cooperate." To preserve the fiction of legality, the Germans had held an auction, at which a Louis Sixteenth chair went for the equivalent of fifty cents, and a fine Aubusson rug for three dollars. A chair with a built-in chamber pot, which Madame's father had purchased especially for a hunting visit of King Edward VII of England in 1907, reached the highest price, the equivalent of seven dollars. The meticulous Germans made up a list with the names of all buyers and the articles purchased, which they deposited at the mayor's office. After her return, Madame S. found the list and made the villagers return the objets d'art, paying them exactly what they had paid. She was acting in accordance with French law, but the villagers claimed that possession was more than eleven points in the law, and hated to return her things, and ever since, the *gendarme* said, there had been trouble.

Many of the villagers had never been outside their village, but they were very much like people everywhere. They talked a lot, but rarely about matters closest to them. There were violent arguments about high prices and dirty politics, about the people in a neighboring village who had managed to get four Marshall Plan tractors with the help of their mayor, a politician and deputy of the party in power. In the summer they talked about the Tour de France, the world's toughest bicycle race, and later about the harvest. No one talked about the mother of Lucille, our servant girl, but everybody knew the old woman was dying of cancer. And it was only by accident that I heard about Désiré's brother, who had to be taken away to an asylum after his wife ran off with a commercial traveler from Strasbourg. I suppose it was just a typical Alsatian village.

It was at the Couronne that I was informed that our castle had a ghost. His name was Euloge Schneider, and he'd been the executioner in Strasbourg during the French Revolution and beheaded thousands of people. Jean-Baptiste lent me a leather-bound volume, a local chronicle with a chapter "How the Castle Fell into Ruins." Here are some excerpts:

At the beginning of the eighteenth century a young nobleman who had inherited the castle came to take possession. He was received by a severe-looking major-domo. An old gardener who had already known the young man's father implored him not to stay. "No one dares spend the night here. Go to the village where you will get good rooms and a hearty dinner. . . ."

The young man laughed carelessly and sent the gardener away. In the *salle des chevaliers* twelve torch bearers stood motionless. The major-domo entered, followed by servants carrying the dishes. The young nobleman noticed that the big table was set for seven people. He wanted to ask a question but suddenly a door was opened, and men with torches approached, followed by a pale-faced, bearded man in a black velvet dress. He sat down across from the young nobleman. Another door was opened. Four children came in and sat down next to the pale man, two on each side. Then a third door was opened, and a beautiful woman with black hair and bloodless lips walked in and sat down at the table.

The major-domo gave orders to serve the soup. The children started to eat hungrily, but after the first spoonful their heads fell back. They were dead. The woman uttered a piercing cry. The pale-faced man seized a knife and ran it through the major-domo's throat. Two servants threw his dead body on the table, next to the dead children. Two other servants tied the woman to her chair. . . .

The pale-faced man got up and bowed politely to the young nobleman. "You will now dine in peace, Monsieur," he said. "The saddle of venison looks delicious and there is the fruity Alsatian wine. I come here every night to punish my wife who betrayed me with the major-domo while I was away. She must suffer again and again for her crime. . . . Eat and drink, Monsieur, I beg you. You are very pale." He sat down and started to eat and drink, never looking at the woman. . . . The young nobleman felt the sweat break out on his forehead, and he fainted. At dawn, the old gardener found him lying under the table, unconscious. The young nobleman was sick for several months. After he recovered, he ordered the castle locked, and never returned there. And that is how the castle fell into ruins. . . .

I returned the chronicle to Jean-Baptiste and told him it must be an accident that I'd read a similar story in an English chronicle and also in an old German book. And where did Euloge Schneider, the Strasbourg executioner, come in?

Jean-Baptiste said these things were "matters of public knowledge." I asked the mayor, who neither confirmed nor denied the story. At last I went to Madame S.

"I could make money if I exploited the castle as a ghost haunt," she said. "Once an Englishman came here, a member of the Society of Psychical Research. He was affiliated with an outfit called something like Historic Homes and Tours. They collected Continental castles with documented ghosts. I turned him down."

I said that we'd sometimes been startled by the library door suddenly opening at night.

"When the temperature drops, the old wood contracts and some doors open," she said. "And you may have heard shuffling sounds in the attic?"

"Yes. We've heard them."

"Pay no attention to them. It isn't M. Schneider, the executioner, though I couldn't explain to you just what causes these sounds."

I thought Madame S. was a remarkably composed woman. She was angry only once, the last night we were there. Frank and Jean gave us a good-bye party in the *salle des chevaliers*, and there were about a dozen people. After a bright, sunny day it was cool, and Frank said he was going to build a fire in the big fireplace. He brought in pieces of wood, but they were damp and didn't burn well. Somebody suggested sprinkling the wood with the cheap brandy that they sold at the Couronne. Frank thought it was a great idea. He emptied half a bottle over the wood. The fire began to roar, and soon a pleasant warmth settled over the large hall.

Then the church bells began ringing and we heard shouts outside. We ran into the courtyard. Blue flames shot out of the chimney and sparks flew all over the roof, which was covered with dry, withered leaves. There was confusion, but everybody stood up to the emergency. The voluntary fire brigade arrived under the command of the mayor.

They had a primitive hand wagon with a pump and a long fire hose which got stuck. By the time they disentangled it, the water pressure proved insufficient. Jean-Baptiste and two other fellow Communists ran up and threw buckets of water on the capitalistic roof. Meanwhile, Frank and I, aided by M. Sans-Prénom, the *gendarme*, quenched the flames in the fireplace with buckets of sand. Afterwards everybody joined our party. In the early morning hours people were already talking about the Night the Castle Almost Burned Down. Everybody agreed it was the greatest local event since the Liberation.

The Ex-Expert

In the spring of 1965, I went to the Weizmann Institute in Rehovoth, Israel, one of the world's great institutions of fundamental research. I would try to write the report of a curious nonscientist walking through "the garden of science." I'd talked to scientists and was puzzled by the paradox of the modern scientist's getting closer to the mysteries of nature but also farther away from the heartbeat of humanity. Some of the great scientists were lonely men who had almost no one to talk to, and lived in self-created isolation. This, I thought, was my story. Shawn told me to go ahead.

In Rehovoth, a brilliant theoretical physicist said to me, "My constant fear is that someday I may not be able to talk to *anybody*. You gradually lose touch with the last few people on earth who understand you. In the end, I'm afraid, I may lose touch with myself."

The next day, Meyer W. Weisgal, the Weizmann Institute's guiding spirit and driving force, who is a nonscientist and administrator, reminisced about the laying of the cornerstone of the Nuclear Physics Institute, in 1953. Niels Bohr, who helped develop the quantum theory of atomic systems, delivered a lecture on the philosophy of physics before an audience of Nobel Prize winners and other star performers of science. Weisgal sat through the long lecture, unhappy and frustrated. He told me that he understood not a single sentence of what Bohr said.

Afterwards, Weisgal asked some of the scientists whether they had understood Bohr's lecture. One shrugged uncomfortably and said, "Oh, about twenty-five percent of it." Others said fifteen or thirty percent. One said, rather curtly, that he had understood "more than half," but he was not a great scientist, and Weisgal suspected that the man might have exaggerated.

The following day a symposium was held in an old hall, in the nearby town of Rehovoth. (There was no hall large enough then at the Weizmann Institute.) Weisgal left the symposium in midmorning to catch a breath of fresh air and get away from the bewildering mysteries of science. Outside, he saw Bohr. The great physicist was slowly walking up and down, in deep concentration.

Weisgal invited Bohr to come inside. Bohr didn't answer, just shook his head.

Weisgal insisted. "Professor Bohr, yesterday all these geniuses who came here from many corners of the world attended your lecture. I think you ought to be there today."

Bohr gave an unhappy shrug. He made Weisgal think of a little boy wrestling with an unexpected problem.

"I'll tell you the truth," Bohr said at last. "I have no idea what they are talking about. Although all of us speak English, each of us seems to use his own mysterious language that the others cannot understand."

Weisgal said that Bohr had comforted him a little, but not very much. Perhaps Weisgal was trying to comfort *me*. I had already experienced the usual frustrations of the visiting nonscientist, who stands outside the invisible walls of the garden and wonders whether he will ever be able to walk through for a brief glance. As time went on, some of the walls opened. I met some scientists in the twilight zone where nonscientists can just see faintly what happens. Some would helpfully take me by the hand and give me a conducted tour through their private labyrinths.

There was growing lack of communication between scientists and nonscientists, which worried many thoughtful men in Rehovoth. Some scientists felt that nonscientists mistrust science "because they don't understand it." The scientists resented it when they were told they were getting "computer-minded." Some were rather pleased when they met a nonscientist who was genuinely interested in them, and they became human and helpful. One showed me what Einstein had written:

> It is of great importance that the general public be given an opportunity to experience, consciously and intelligently, the efforts and results of scientific research. It is not sufficient that each result be taken up, elaborated and applied by a few specialists in the field. Restricting the body of knowledge to a small group deadens the philosophical spirit of people and leads to spiritual poverty.

Shawn regretfully turned down my long piece. He thought the approach had been right, but ultimately, only a scientist could write about an Institute of Advanced Thinking. I learned my lesson. I have no intention of going to the moon. That's the job for the space expert of *The New Yorker*.

The expert is a by-product of American twentieth-century civilization. In Washington there are experts (according to *Time*) who can "reel off facts and figures about complex problems without consulting a note." Something must be wrong, though, for the experts couldn't prevent blunders on a global scale, crises and complexities.

In prewar Europe, a man was respected for being a gifted dilettante, not an expert. We admired the universally interested amateur rather than the specialist. Experts were bores, talking only of their specialties and knowing little about the outside world. The dilettantes were much more amusing, interested in many things, unafraid to try some of them, though they knew they couldn't do them as well as the experts. There were notable precedents. Goethe had been a brilliant dilettante in zoology, botany, the natural sciences, deeply attracted by the mysteries of chemistry and alchemy, mathematics and statesmanship, medicine and mineralogy, philosophy and the science of colors. Even far below the Goethe and Leonardo da Vinci level, there is an army of dilettantes who do something out of love and fascination.

Nearly everything I did began as an exercise in dilettantism. I was a dilettante fiddler, a dilettante *claqueur*, a dilettante croupier, a dilettante salesman, a dilettante soldier, and certainly a dilettante writer. The writer is constantly experimenting. If the experiment succeeds and he turns out an "expert" piece of work, he is considered an expert in the writing game. In his heart the writer knows better; the next time he may fail again and will be thrown back to the ranks of the dilettantes.

Against my will, I became a political expert the day I arrived in America, in the fall of 1938. It was a few days after the Munich Agreement had been signed, which was the beginning of the end of Czechoslovakia's independence. I happened to be the only Czechoslovak journalist on the French Line boat on which we came to the United States. The shipboard reporters sought me out for my opinions on Czechoslovakia, Hitler, the future of Europe, and other world problems. My bewilderment at being suddenly elevated to a minor public figure did not improve my very basic English. The interview was a chain reaction of misunderstandings. Any similarity between what I'd tried to convey to the reporters and what they guessed and published was a coincidence, but my name and picture were in the papers. Suddenly I was an authority.

Several days later, at a pro-Czechoslovakia rally in Madison Square Garden, I was introduced as "the leading authority" on Czechoslovakia. Everybody applauded, and people came to shake hands with me. I had a slight feeling of guilt, wishing I were in my homeland, where I belonged. I was asked some important questions. No one understood my answers, but that was beside the point. Fortunately, Dr. Edvard Beneš, *the* authority, soon came to America, and people forgot about me.

In this blessed country, a man may become an expert by writing several articles or a book on a certain subject. One is reviewed and quoted, asked to appear at various breakfast programs, and one morning one wakes up and finds oneself an expert. There is little you can do about it. People write you, asking for advice. Sixteen years ago I wrote two articles about rare old Italian violins for *The New Yorker*, and I still get letters from people who discovered an old fiddle in their attic. There is a dusty Stradivarius label inside, and the people ask me hopefully whether they have a genuine sixty-thousand-dollar Strad, and where can they sell it? I tell them that in all probability they have a twenty-six-dollar factory fiddle, even though Grandpa had brought it from the Old Country forty-nine years ago. Practically all genuine Stradivari instruments are known to the trade, and there is an infinitesimal chance that one may be hidden in the attic of a house in South Dakota.

At this point, publishers ask you to write a book on violins. Minor colleges and obscure women's clubs invite you to talk on the subject. An anonymous caller threatens you over the telephone. A persistent women brings you a broken fiddle. Two reputable dealers told her it was worth nothing, but she is convinced that all dealers are crooks. She wants to hear the truth from *you*. You may begin to believe that you are an expert, and then you will *really* be in trouble.

Several articles on the pleasures of good food and good wine, and my book *Blue Trout and Black Truffles* established me as a full-fledged expert on gastronomy — a gourmet. A three-star general has to be confirmed by the United States Senate, but a three-star gourmet is confirmed by no one except his own conscience. Women said they would *love* to have me for dinner, "but I wouldn't dare cook for you." Men asked me for advice on Burgundy vintages. A woman columnist in Chicago asked me for my own recipe for coq au vin, as though I had one. A magazine asked me to write an article on "The Natural History of Goulash." Several restaurants asked me to be their guest, and one — in my favorite town of Merano, at that — barred me from the premises because I'd dared ask whether it was the chef's night out.

My promotion to gourmet coincided with my inability to eat a gourmet meal. Nowadays, my delicate stomach refuses to underwrite my palate's excursions into the realm of gastronomy. I no longer eat; I taste. I know many gourmets who eat little and wisely, but people won't believe it. They ask me, "How can you be a gourmet and keep your weight down?" The image of a fat gourmet hasn't changed since Brillat-Savarin, who was also a gourmand. He said that no man can be dignified with the title "gourmet" before he is forty. My first forty years were lean, financially and gastronomically. During the First World War and afterwards, there was hunger in Central Europe. A piece of buttered bread was a delicacy; usually it was bread with marmalade. To this day, I hate marmalade. As an impecunious student, I ate in cheap joints serving Wiener schnitzel that tasted like wrapping paper — exactly what it may have been. As a *claqueur* at the Vienna State Opera, my subsistence supper was a roll with raw bacon. During performances of interminable Wagnerian operas I had two rolls with bacon. I could afford a brandy if someone offered me one. I had my first whiskey and soda one hot afternoon in Singapore, in the house of a diplomat, at the age of twenty-three. I smoked opium in Saigon, but I don't remember much about it, and it wasn't habit-forming.

My education as a gourmet didn't improve when I worked as a

nightclub musician in Paris. I ate in a small *prix fixe* near the Place
Pigalle, where a small carafe of wine was included in the menu, and
bread was *à discrétion*, which meant not more than four pieces. The
menu was written in violet ink, but I don't think it was *grande cuisine*.
It was strictly *petite cuisine*, but the *petite filles* were pretty and charming, and that was more important. Everybody at the *prix fixe* was in
and out of love from one day to the next. Once I fell foolishly in love
with a girl from the Left Bank, which meant going there by the Nord-
Sud, at considerable expense and loss of time. She lived near the Quai
Grands-Augustins, and I often walked past Lapérouse, then and now a
famous restaurant. I would stop at the entrance to read the menu — a
single dish cost more than my whole menu at the *prix fixe* — and to
wait until the door was opened and I inhaled the fragrance of an incredibly delicate concoction drifting out. It almost made me faint. I closed
my eyes and tried to think of the *petite fille*. If I'd had a chance, I would
have betrayed her for a *gratin de langoustines Georgette*, though I
hadn't the faintest idea what that was.

Twenty years later, when I was less hungry but had more money,
I went to Lapérouse and had you-know-what, and I wistfully thought
it would be nice to have along the *petite fille*, whose name I'd forgotten.
Men will be men, I'm afraid. Lapérouse didn't disappoint me; the fragrance was still wonderful. The Duke and the Duchess of Windsor
were there, but the *gratin de langoustines Georgette* and the steak Lapérouse were better. France was making a fast gastronomical comeback
after the restrictions of the Second World War and the postwar years
of rationing and black market. I learned a few things about *la grande
cuisine* while eating. A gourmet needs enthusiasm, a fastidious palate,
and self-discipline. And lots of money. Like a music critic, he must be
strict toward himself as well as the performers.

My greatest teacher was Fernand Point, whom many bona fide gourmets in France call Escoffier's successor. Point *invented* new dishes, and

also was a wise and witty philosopher. In France alone, the philosophy of good eating is regarded as an abstract science and a major art. Point was aware of his responsibility as a guardian of French civilization when he made his restaurant, La Pyramide in Vienne, Isère, his country's greatest temple of *la grande cuisine*. When I met him, one day in 1949, we drank champagne and talked about people and the art of great cooking. I wrote an article for *The New Yorker* which I later incorporated in my book on gastronomy. Suddenly I was a gourmet, an authority, an expert.

For a while, I foolishly believed it. Lucius Beebe, reviewing my book in the *Saturday Review of Literature*, called me "the highest type of gourmet" and made me "an established expert in the field of literary gastronomy." Clifton Fadiman called me "an educator." My head reeled, though I'd had no champagne. Somebody else compared me to Brillat-Savarin, who also had been a student of law, had deserted the legal profession, loved to play the fiddle, and went to America as a refugee. Only one parallel was missing: I couldn't eat the gargantuan meals which Brillat-Savarin enjoyed. I would have dropped dead.

I saw Point often until his death in 1955, when he was only fifty-seven. I would make improbable detours to spend a day with him and his wife. Poppy was three when she ate her first meal at his round table, under the plane trees of the garden terrace, next to the running-water basin where they keep live trout. Three years ago, Poppy spent a whole summer in Madame Point's house. One can do that only at the age of sixteen, when one is always hungry; the right time to take a postgraduate course in applied gastronomy. 'Poppy may never eat that well again when she gets older, but she's learned a lot. I'm afraid she won't be fooled by the phony practitioners of "haute cuisine" who know nothing about classic French cooking.

After Point's death, his widow Marie-Louise ("Mado") took over, and made the most sensational comeback in the history of modern French gastronomy. My *New Yorker* profile on her — the first time in *New Yorker* history that husband and wife rated special articles —

perpetuated my standing as an expert. By that time, cuisine had become a fad in America. No one spoke of plain cooking; it was strictly cuisine. A wine cellar became a higher status symbol than a swimming pool. Restaurants were out; bistros were in. It became an honor to be insulted by the Italian headwaiters in the absurdly expensive French restaurants in Manhattan.

"Nothing is less suited to the joys of eating and drinking than a solemnity of approach," Beebe wrote about my book, and he liked "the sly and latent hooray that goes well with its content of truffled foie gras." Today there is little sly and latent hooray in the business. There are gourmet shops, gourmet supermarkets, gourmet canned foods, gourmet precooked sauces. The gourmet Establishment has gourmet cooks, gourmet writers, gourmet advisers, gourmet critics who teach the housewives shortcuts in "gastronomy." The critics have as much power in the restaurant world as the theater critics on Broadway. They can make or break a restaurant; they publish food guides; they award stars more liberally than the makers of American flags. The gourmet Establishment has cabinet-ranking officers and ambassadors of cuisine, courtiers and errand boys, intriguers and scandalmongers, prima donnas and star performers. It's like backstage at a great opera house, only much more sinister. There is a cookbook of the month, and a dish of the year. I missed the year of beef Wellington when I didn't feel well and preferred oatmeal. But there are still some sensible people left in America who know the difference between restaurant "cuisine" and fine home cooking, and keep away from the shortcuts to pseudo-gastronomy. I write occasionally for *Gourmet* and I get encouraging letters from the readers. All is not lost yet on the gastronomic front.

I have friends who serve me American things when I am in America and that's what I like best. I go out to the Reynoldses in Chappaqua for roast beef and a baked Idaho. Alfred Knopf respected my predilection for genuine hamburger, and Herman Elkon, a splurger, serves me wild rice. George Lang who has an encyclopaedic knowledge of the foods of the world, gives me fine crab meat and a striped bass. Simple but good.

I'll eat the gratin in France, the ravioli in Italy, and the mussels in Belgium.

My alleged standing as a gourmet eventually led to my safari into the jungle of group journalism, when Time-Life Books started the biggest cookbook project ever undertaken: sixteen volumes of the series *Foods of the World*. Truly a global project, with beautiful illustrations and large research teams. An experimental kitchen was set up in the labyrinth of the Time-Life Building in New York, where thousands of recipes from all over the world would be tried, analyzed, and spelled out in exact detail for the culinary erudition of America's homemakers, and later for the women of the world. We writers would be educators, performing a worldwide public service. M. F. K. Fisher and Emily Hahn of *The New Yorker* would write on French provincial cooking and Chinese cooking, and there were other experts of unquestionable standing.

I was asked to write *The Cooking of the Viennese Empire*, a nostalgic title. The empire has been dead and finished since 1918. The assignment was said to be a spectacular honor, and a contribution to Western civilization. Somebody from the Time-Life Building spoke of global significance. I went to work, doing my own research and starting to write.

Then the long arm of group journalism caught up with me, in the form of the memo. The memos from the Time-Life Building seemed to take a dim view of my individualistic approach. Some were queries of no consequence, and others were suggestions on how to do certain things. Though the memo writers pretended to know much about the subject, they were often ambiguous and sometimes downright enigmatic. Some suggestions seemed dated. Once I was directed to a restaurant that no longer existed. Another time I was queried about a custom in my native Moravia that has been extinct for two centuries. The memos didn't come from the people who would later edit my copy, but from other departments whose existence I hadn't known about. Once two memos arrived on the same day. The room numbers of the memo writers indicated that they were within walking distance on the same floor, but there had been no communication between them, because the memos canceled out each other.

I remembered gripes — often uttered after the fourth drink, by correspondents working for *Time*, the citadel of group journalism — that I'd often heard all over Europe in the past decades. The correspondents were able men, but they were driven toward Mother Alcohol by memos and cables telling them what and *how* to write it. Obviously, the only way to deal with group journalism was to ignore it. That turned out to be a mistake. The memos were followed by cables. Long, complicated recipes were cabled to me; and I was asked to verify a minor ingredient and cable back. The cables were far more expensive than the dishes which they described. For the accumulated cable expenses, we could have taken over Schönbrunn Palace for a night, and given a banquet featuring The Cooking of the Viennese Empire, perhaps with a member of the Habsburg family as guest of honor. I wanted to suggest it, but a friend who was better acquainted with group journalism advised me against it. The cables continued to arrive. A *Time* correspondent in Europe told me wistfully he would like to earn what he spent on cables, most of which were ignored.

After the cables came the long-distance calls. Jovial group journalism executives who happened to be between drinks in Rome, Madrid, or London called up Joe (me) in Vienna to inquire how I was getting along.

I'd never met them and didn't know what they meant. "Getting along with what?" I asked.

"What's that?" said the executive. "I can't hear you, Joe. Lousy connection."

"It's my phone. I've got an unlisted number. That's why you can't hear me well. The penalty of anonymity."

"How's that again? It sounds all garbled."

"The Russians," I said recklessly, and finished my third straight Scotch. Group journalism was driving me too toward Mother Alcohol. "The Russians live only a block away from our place." They really do.

"Well, glad the project is coming along fine," the faraway voice said. "We're all excited about it. I hear the *Viennese Empire* will be the best volume of all."

"You bet," I said. "There aren't many empires left. Why don't you come up here for a look at the empire?"

"Sorry, Joe. Got to go to Amsterdam tomorrow. Looking forward to seeing you in New York."

I was asked to send in the chapters after they were written. After a while, I heard from group-journalism correspondents and stringers in various European cities that they'd enjoyed the chapters. How did they know about them? They'd received mimeographed copies. Perhaps they were expected to advise and consent, or to check and balance. I never received mimeographed copies, but a stringer lent me hers.

Fred Lyon, the photographer of the *Viennese Empire*, arrived from America, and there was some trouble getting his cameras and films away from Austrian customs. George Lang, who runs the Four Seasons restaurant in New York and was adviser on the book project, also arrived, and led an expedition into his native Hungary, where he organized gypsy dances and folkloristic events that would look beautiful in color. Meanwhile, another group took over inns and other colorful places in Austria. Somebody asked me whether one couldn't tie Mayerling, and the immortal love story of Crown Prince Rudolf and Baroness Vetsera, into the cooking of the empire. The head of an aristocratic Viennese family called me to ask whether I had suggested that *verdammte* picnic? What picnic? They'd asked him and his family, including the eighty-six-year-old grandmother, to a picnic in the Vienna Woods, where the princes and princesses would be photographed, in color, eating Wiener schnitzel or something, under the very trees where Johann Strauss had been inspired to write *Tales from the Vienna Woods*. The owner of a popular restaurant invited me to the big schnitzel party the next day, when the pictures would be taken. I told him that I hadn't had Wiener schnitzel for the past thirty years. I envy people who eat schnitzel once a day in Vienna (I know some), but my gall bladder isn't schnitzel-minded. Nothing breaded. Yes, friends, the author of *The Cooking of the Viennese Empire* no longer knows what a Wiener schnitzel tastes like. There goes your expert.

The group-journalism people didn't take over the Vienna Opera for a night, as I'd hoped, during a *Don Giovanni* performance, to get color pictures of the Don's last supper before he goes to hell, but they invaded Demel's which has done for *patisserie* in Vienna what the Vienna Opera did for music. Fred Lyon took beautiful pictures of many genuine Demel *Torten* and cakes. (A *Torte* is a round cake, but not every cake is a *Torte*.) Months later, when I received a copy of the book, the cover showed the beautifully photographed *Spanische Windtorte* (Spanish wind cake) that had not been made at Demel's in Vienna but — where else? — in the experimental kitchen of the Time-Life Building on New York's Sixth Avenue. "Mastering Vienna's Pastry Magic," the description said, *not* written by me:

> Most beautiful of Vienna's round cakes, a baroque triumph in conception, design and execution, besides tasting of heaven, is the Spanische Windtorte. Austrians call many super-elegant things Spanish, and so the mixture of egg whites beaten with sugar, known as meringue in most places, is "Spanish wind" in Austria, and the basis of this fantastic cake. Folded into its sweetened whipped cream go many luscious things — strawberries, crushed macaroons, toasted hazelnuts, candies and shaved bitter choco-late. . . .

The recipe covered a whole page. Another page showed drawings of how to make spiral meringues that looked like a lunar orbit made of *Schlagobers* (whipped cream). The pastry cooks at Demel's had never seen anything like it, and were much impressed. And amused.

Earlier, when I was in New York, Richard L. Williams, the editor in charge of the project, had asked me to come up for a Conference, followed by Lunch, at the headquarters of group journalism. Dick almost audibly pronounced the capital letters. Two memos followed, with exact instructions, giving the names of the Other Guests. I was officially welcomed by the editor and his staff, who showed me complex graphs and colored charts relating to the project. They don't just publish books there; they launch them into space. I enjoyed the marvelous view from Dick Williams's office, but there was no time for idle contemplation. The Conference got under way. It wasn't clear to me what it was about, but it *was*.

Afterwards, we moved up for Lunch to one of the top floors. We changed elevators twice, the second time to a small, superexecutive elevator installed between the three uppermost floors. It was reserved for field marshals of group journalism, and possibly for the Almighty. Clearly, I was permitted a fleeting glance at the Olympus of group journalism.

The dining room on the forty-eighth floor was surrounded by fast-moving clouds in exciting patterns and colors that the late Wieland Wagner would have loved for *The Twilight of the Gods*. As guest of honor, I sat to the right of the top executive. The protocol was as strict as it had once been at Schönbrunn Palace, under the Habsburgs. It seemed a long way from the democratic dining room of the Algonquin Hotel, and for the first and only time, I felt a little homesick for its noise and semidarkness. The food, however, was much better up there amidst the Gods. We had a fine *chartreuse* of pheasant, thoughtfully ordered by Adviser Lang. I asked whether the dish had been prepared, perchance, in the experimental kitchen. Nobody laughed. Some speeches were made, with expressions of lasting mutual admiration. Two days later, at a cocktail party, the canapés *had* been made in the experimental kitchen, and they tasted that way too.

The wizards of group journalism made a beautiful-looking volume of *The Cooking of the Viennese Empire*, with spectacular photographs and a wealth of information, some of it even pertinent. Some of the names of Czech and Hungarian dishes were misspelled, in spite, or because, of multiple checking. Oddly, the photograph of boiled beef, *the* Viennese specialty, showed a cut not popular with Viennese cognoscenti. It had been made in New York. I didn't always recognize my text. It made me think of a child with a heavily painted face who goes to a ball during the Vienna *Fasching*, when the father isn't supposed to recognize his offspring, which would spoil the fun. Several Viennese housewives and experienced cooks asked me why the recipe for Wiener schnitzel in the book demanded that the veal escalopes be marinated for one hour in lemon juice. They said they'd never heard of such a thing. I explained they were really New York schnitzel. Group journalism is wonderful, especially when you are out of it.

Postscript

In my romantic moments, I dream of a dinner party I'm going to give. All my *New Yorker* profile subjects, dead and alive, will be there. And each of them will contribute something along his line.

It will be quite a party. The place will be the Bürgenstock, near Lucerne in Switzerland, the private mountain belonging to my friend (and former profile subject) Fritz Frey. Fernand Point and his friend Alexandre Dumaine, the two greatest practitioners of *la grande cuisine* in my time, will prepare the greatest dinner since Escoffier. Alexis Lichine will select the wines. Madame Point and Henri Soulé will supervise the service. Robert Bellet of the *Liberté* will create the happy atmosphere. Rudolf Bing of the Met will fight it out with the unions. (There are union demands, even in a dream.) Abe Feder will do the lighting.

The after-dinner entertainment will feature the Cleveland Orchestra under George Szell, playing partly on rare old Italian instruments provided by Emil Herrmann; the Budapest String Quartet, George London, Artur Rubinstein, Isaac Stern; Helmut Qualtinger will perform a Viennese parody of *The New Yorker*, or a *New Yorker* style parody of Vienna. There will be beautiful gifts; the men will get rare books published by Raffaele Mattioli, and for the ladies there will be Buccellati bracelets. I plan other attractions but would like to preserve the atmosphere of surprise.

The whole evening won't cost me a nickel. It will be generously financed by my profile subjects, the great merchant bankers Hambro, Baring, and Warburg. All my guests are nice people. Not one stuffed shirt among them. Truly a dream party.

As I leave the exuberance of my second youth behind, reluctantly, I seem to become more relaxed about the vicissitudes of my profession. My enthusiasm persists but has mellowed; and so has Shawn's, I presume. The adjectives that the editor uses in his cables — always a subtle and accurate reflection of his appreciation — become more meaningful. Some are the equivalent of a medal of honor, for achievements above and beyond the call of duty: "fascinating," "wonderful," "marvelous." Others are mere campaign ribbons: "good," "fine," "interesting." But his remarkable instinct for the deeper truth remains. After reading my profile of Prague, the beautiful, mystical city, that I'd wanted to write for twenty years, Shawn cabled: YOU HAVE CAUGHT THE CITY'S STRANGE AND ELUSIVE QUALITIES ONCE AND FOR ALL. I think he's right, though he's never been in Prague. Later, after I'd written my saddest Prague story — the short, glorious "Prague Spring" that ended after an even more glorious week of spiritual resistance — Shawn cabled: PRAGUE IS A WONDERFUL, WONDERFUL PIECE. YOUR TRIBUTE TO THE PEOPLE THERE MOVED ME DEEPLY AND I FELT PROUD OF WHAT YOU HAVE WRITTEN. When all is said and written, the stories that move us deeply remain the most important.

I keep Shawn's latest cable of acceptance on the shelf behind my desk. As Ross would have said, it encourages me to carry on. We writers feel so damn independent, but once in a while we need a little moral support. I also keep a few photographs on the shelf, one of Poppy's drawings, a Jewish menorah, a picture of Pope John XXIII during a Vatican audience that I attended, and a framed epigram, given to me by a very very dear friend:

> *Gewiss, der Fromme lebt gesünder —*
> *Schöner aber lebt der Sünder.*

That means, "Admittedly, the saint lives a healthier life, but the sinner lives better." In each of us, there is something of the saint and the sinner. Everything considered, things weren't so bad, though they might have been a little better. In fact, if I had to do it once more, I would do it all over again.